RXpert SERIES

# Industrial Pharmacy - I

*(as per Latest PCI Syllabus)*

RXpert SERIES

# Industrial Pharmacy - I

*(as per Latest PCI Syllabus)*

**Ajay Semalty**
*M.Pharm., MBA, Ph.D., PDF (Japan)*
*"Course Coordinator – Industrial Pharmacy - I (SWAYAM MOOC)"*
Assistant Professor,
Department of Pharmaceutical Sciences,
H.N.B. Garhwal University (A Central University)
Srinagar (Garhwal), Uttarakhand
Visiting Scientist
Faculty of Pharmacy, Meijo University Nagoya, Japan

Pharma Med PRESS
An Imprint of BSP Books Pvt. Ltd.

**PharmaMed Press**
*An imprint of BSP Books Pvt. Ltd.*
4-4-309/316, Giriraj Lane,
Sultan Bazar, Hyderabad - 500 095.

**Industrial Pharmacy - I**
***by Ajay Semalty***



***Disclaimer:*** The authors and the publishers have taken due care to provide the authentic, reliable and up to date information related to the subject. However, neither the authors nor the publisher shall be responsible for any liability for any damage caused as a result of use of this book. The respective user must check the accuracy from other sources too.

***Published by***

**PharmaMed Press**
*An imprint of BSP Books Pvt. Ltd.*
4-4-309/316, Giriraj Lane, Sultan Bazar, Hyderabad - 500 095.
Phone: 040-23445688; Fax: 91+40-23445611
E-mail: info@pharmamedpress.net
www.bspbooks.net/www.pharmamedpress.net

**ISBN: 978-93-91910-81-5**

Dedicated to my Mother.......
Late Mrs. Laxmi Semalty
(04 Nov. 1949- 21 Aug. 2019)

# Preface

The pharmaceutical industry is one of the fast-growing industry globally. The industry requires the skilled persons to meet the demand of fast growth. To meet the demand of the industry, the Pharmacy Council of India revised the pharmacy syllabi and came up with a uniform national syllabus in 2014. In the PCI syllabi 5 semester B. Pharm a paper "Industrial Pharmacy - I" is there to specifically cater this need and to fill the gap between industry and academia. Though the paper may be shifted to any other semester in a particular institute or University, the syllabi is uniform nationally. Moreover, in M. Pharm Industrial Pharmacy and Pharmaceutics many relevant topics of Industrial Pharmacy are there. The present book is an effort to present the Industrial Pharmacy - I subject in a very effective and unique way.

After the huge success of my previous book "Essentials of Pharmaceutical Technology", I am happy to present my new work to the B. Pharm/M. Pharm students, faculty members, researchers and industry personnel. The book is my latest endeavour after presenting India's first Pharmacy MOOC at Ministry of India's SWAYAM platform. In the online course the entire syllabi have been covered in 12 weeks, in 40 lectures of 30 minutes each. The course is available for credit transfer through SWAYAM MOOC for students. We got a huge response across the nation for our online course. More than 7500 learners are enrolled in the course across many countries. The course runs in every July - Dec semester. I welcome all the learners to join the free online course at SWAYAM platform (www.swayam.gov.in).

The book covers all the important aspects of Industrial Pharmacy including preformulation, tablets, capsules, liquid orals, parenteral, aerosols, ophthalmic, cosmetics and packaging. The content has been evaluated by the experts assigned by SWAYAM at national level for the quality. The content is power packed with easy to learn presentation for readers. The effective use of infographics, to the point presentation, quality content, reader friendliness and important links for further readings are USPs of the book.

I hope the book will be useful for all the stakeholders of pharmacy academia and industry. I welcome suggestions for improvement and feedback about the book.

***Dr Ajay Semalty***

# Acknowledgements

I would like to thank all the persons who helped in designing, planning and finishing this book. Firstly, I would like to thank my family members for their continued encouragement, support and assistance. Without them, it would not have been possible to complete the book.

As John Cotton Dana said "*Who dares to teach, must never cease to learn*", this is the teacher who is solely responsible for quality of teaching and learning process. In the process of teaching and learning, we also learned lot many things about the likes and dislikes of the students regarding the choice of books and reading habits. I have tried to focus my efforts on those points, to make the book student friendly. I am thankful to our students whose input again helped in designing and planning this book.

The learning is a never-ending process that will positively enhance our awareness and knowledge and will positively contribute to our abilities as teachers. So, I am also thankful to all the respected teachers who read, refer and recommend this book to their students.

I warmly acknowledge the contribution of Dr Mona Semalty, Assistant Professor, Department of Pharmaceutical Sciences, H.N.B. Garhwal University (A Central University) Srinagar (Garhwal) and Dr. Lokesh Adhikari, Senior Project Associate, UGC-DAE CSR project, Department of Pharmaceutical Sciences, H.N.B. Garhwal University (A Central University) Srinagar (Garhwal) for their vital contribution in many chapters of the book.

I humbly acknowledge Ministry of Education, Govt. of India, SWAYAM National Coordinator CEC, New Delhi, Prof. JB Nadda, Director-CEC, Er. Nageshwar Nath, Joint Director-CEC, Dr. Raj Kumar Bhardwaj, Director-EMRC Roorkee and the Team EMRC Roorkee for providing grant and vital support in development of Industrial Pharmacy online course.

I also thank Prof B. Suresh, President, Pharmacy Council of India, Prof. P.K. Sahoo, Director-Research, DPSR University New Delhi, Prof. S.H. Ansari, Faculty of Pharmacy, Hamdard University, New Delhi; Prof. Pawan Kumar Dubey, Director, Vivekananda College of Pharmacy, Indore; Prof Munish Ahuja, Department of Pharmaceutical Sciences, Guru Jambheshwar University of Science and Technology Hisar; Late Prof. Y. S. Tanwar, B. N. College of Pharmacy, B.N. University Udaipur (Raj.); Prof. Vandana Panda,

K.M. Kundanani College of Pharmacy, Mumbai; Prof. N.S. Hari Narayana Moorthy, Dean Pharmacy, Indira Gandhi National Tribal University, Amarkantak, and all the other well-wishers who always keep triggering me time to time for the work like this.

I am thankful to my project Associates (Mr Mukesh Pandey and Mr Himanshu Mishra) and all the staff members of Department of Pharmaceutical Sciences, H.N.B. Garhwal University, Srinagar Garhwal for their moral support. I also extend my gratitude to the entire University family of Garhwal University for their continuous support.

I humbly acknowledge Mr. Anil Shah, and his entire Publishing team of PharmaMed Press Hyderabad, India, with special thanks to Mr. Naresh Davergave and his entire production team for their efforts, guidance and timely support in preparation of this work.

I am always indebted to my Guru, Prof M.S.M. Rawat, Former Vice Chancellor and currently working as Advisor, Department of Higher Education Government of Uttarakhand and Prof. Annpurna Nautiyal, Hon'ble Vice-Chancellor, HNB Garhwal University for their continuous support and blessings.

Last but not the least, I thank my mother Late Mrs. Laxmi Semalty and God almighty for giving strength, patience and determination to complete this work on time in present form.

***Dr Ajay Semalty***

# Contents

**Preface** .......... **(vii)**

**Acknowledgments** .......... **(ix)**

1. Preformulation I (Physical form: Crystal and Amorphous) .......... 1
2. Preformulation I (Polymorphism, Particle Size/Shape) .......... 17
3. Preformulation I Solubility Profile (Solubility, pH and pKa) .......... 29
4. Preformulation I Partition Coefficient and Flow Properties .......... 41
5. Preformulation II Hydrolysis, Oxidation, Reduction .......... 49
6. Preformulation II Racemization .......... 59
7. Preformulation II Dissolution, Permeability and BCS .......... 71
8. Preformulation II Polymerization .......... 85
9. Tablets I Introduction .......... 93
10. Tablets II Manufacturing Tablets .......... 107
11. Tablets III Tablet Coating .......... 119
12. Tablets IV QC of Tablets .......... 133
13. Liquid Orals (Syrups and Elixirs) .......... 145
14. Emulsions I (Introduction Theories and Identification Tests) .......... 159
15. Emulsions II (Formulation of Emulsions) .......... 167
16. Suspension Dosage Form .......... 191
17. Parenterals I (Introduction: Preformulation of Parenterals) .......... 211
18. Parenterals I (Formulation of Parenterals) .......... 221
19. Parenterals I (Types of Parenteral Preparations) .......... 235

20. Parenterals I (Plant Layout for Parenterals) ........ 249
21. Parenterals II (Pyrogens and Pyrogenicity) ........ 259
22. Parenterals II (Sterility Test and Sterilization) ........ 271
23. Capsule I ........ 287
24. Capsule II ........ 297
25. Capsule III ........ 305
26. Capsule IV ........ 315
27. Pellets and Pelletization ........ 325
28. Ophthalmic Preparations: Introduction, Absorption through Eye, Formulation Considerations ........ 335
29. Ophthalmic Preparations: Dosage Form ........ 345
30. Ophthalmic Preparations: Evaluation ........ 353
31. Pharmaceutical Aerosols I (Introduction and Classification) ........ 361
32. Pharmaceutical Aerosols II (Components of Aerosols) ........ 371
33. Pharmaceutical Aerosols III (Components and Systems of Aerosols) ........ 381
34. Pharmaceutical Aerosols IV (Inhalers and Evaluation of Aerosols) ........ 393
35. Cosmetics I (Introduction) ........ 405
36. Cosmetics II (Sunscreen Preparations and Dentifrices) ........ 415
37. Cosmetics III (Shampoo, Hair Dye and Lipstick) ........ 425
38. Packaging Materials Science I Materials ........ 437
39. Packaging Materials Science II Official Requirements & Stability Aspects ........ 453
40. Packaging Materials Science III QC Tests of Packaging Materials ........ 469

## CHAPTER 1

# Preformulation I (Physical Form: Crystal and Amorphous)

**Dr Ajay Semalty**
Department of Pharmaceutical Sciences,
H.N.B Garhwal University (A Central University), Srinagar Garhwal-246174

### Learning Outcome

After completing this chapter, you will be able to understand the

- Basic concept of preformulation
- Need of preformulation in drug formulation development
- Various components of preformulation studies
- Effect of crystal and amorphous form on drug formulation
- Characterization of crystal form

### Lesson Plan

- Concept of Preformulation
- Need of Preformulation
- Introduction to Preformulation process
- Amorphous form
- Crystal form & habit
- Effect of crystallinity on drug delivery or formulation
- Characterization of crystal form

Dear students let us begin our discussion on preformulation with an example from the kitchen. Can you answer these questions?

Why do not you add turmeric in green vegetable?

Why don't you cook pumpkin in pressure cooker?

Why do you use oil for preparing dough for puris and not for chapatis?

What do we need to know before preparing a recipe in kitchen?

Of course, we should be familiar with the main ingredients, their nature, properties, quality, and effectiveness and about the desired characteristics of the product to be prepared. Then only we can go ahead. Or if we are preparing something for first time or developing a recipe, we follow some standard ways of establishing the method.

## Drug Formulation Development

In pharmaceutical sciences same holds true. We must have the knowledge of "Preformulation" before formulating a drug or active pharmaceutical in gradient (API) in to a dosage form.

API or drug is a chemical entity with affinity to the receptors and with positive or negative or nil intrinsic activity.

**Timing of Preformulation:** After the drug discovery cycle when preclinical and clinical trial confirm a medicinal effect of a drug, we plan to formulate it in a form that is called dosage form.

Or in case of developing a new dosage form of an existing API.

API is never administered in a raw chemical form. With the help of some excipients and additives a formulation is prepared to deliver the drug and it is called a dosage form. Like tablet, capsule, emulsion suspension etc.

The efforts are focused to have a dosage form with

- High degree of uniformity: in physical characteristics (weight. Content, hardness etc.) and drug release.
- Physiological availability, Bioavailability
- Therapeutic quality.

## Preformulation

All the activities of characterization of physicochemical properties of the drug under study which are important to develop a stable effective and safe dosage form.

So, please note these three words- **Stable, Effective and Safe**

All the Preformulation activities revolve around these three words. Anyone point is skipped, the formulation fails.

## Challenges

1. **Very small amount of API is available for the studies:** In initial stage of drug discovery, we have only a very tiny amount of API available sometimes in few mg. In natural products when you are synthesizing a drug or active ingredient from the natural product you have the yield in 0.1 mg, 0.2 or 0.5 mg sometimes. So, we have only a little amount (that to impure), this is the first challenge.
2. **Only preliminary data like melting point, spectral data and structure is available:** Now next question comes in mind. What kinds of properties we need to focus?

Let's move to these properties one by one.

(a) ***Physical properties:*** Physical form (crystal & amorphous), polymorphism, particle size, shape, flow properties, solubility profile (pKa, pH, partition coefficient),

(b) ***Chemical Properties:*** Hydrolysis, oxidation, reduction, racemization, polymerization

(c) ***Biopharmaceutical Classification System (BCS):*** dissolution & permeability

## Planning Preformulation

1. First identify the dosage form (solid/ semi solid/ liquid) to be selected for development and then focus the efforts accordingly. Got my point? It would not be suitable to expect a complete solubility in aqueous solution, if you are just planning for tablet preparation. But on the other hand, it is the utmost requirement in injectable.
2. Pick and study the relevant physicochemical properties (as per the desired dosage form) and take it in priority.

A poor Preformulation study may lead to the disasters.

- Unstable/ ineffective or less effective and unsafe dosage form
- Loss of development time (You have put your energy, time, money, all things will go in vain if preformulation fails)
- Increased expenditure on development

- Triggering repeated need for in vivo bioavailability/bioequivalence studies (if the preformulation fails)

The data and protocols of preformulation studies are passed on to the F&D department for further formulation work.

## Physical Properties

- Solid state properties
- Physical form
- Crystal & amorphous

Solid state is the most preferred state of API for developing any dosage form. Why?

- API can easily be crystallized
- Can easily be purified (by crystalizing)
- easy to handle than liquids
- better chemical stability than that of liquids

Solids may be of three types as per the internal structure (physical)

- Amorphous
- Liquid Crystal
- Crystal

**Then the crystals can be further classified as per this Figure 1.1.**

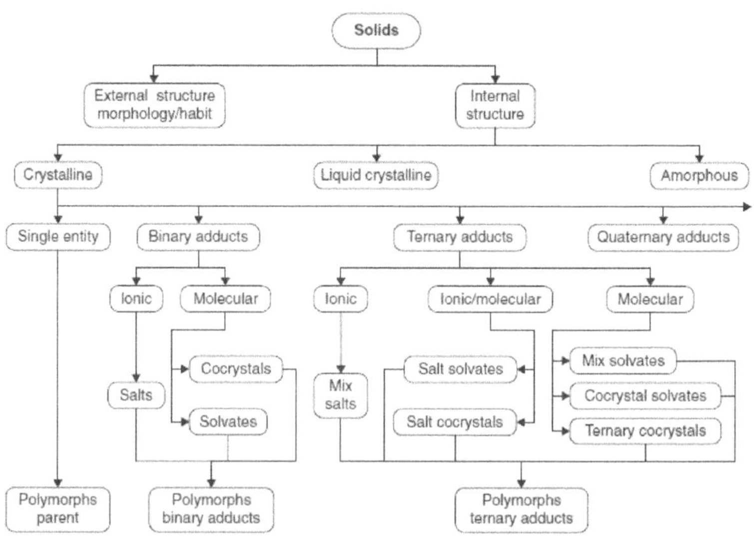


**Figure 1.1** Classification of solids.

## Amorphous

***"These are the solids which do not exhibit long-range order in any of the three physical dimensions."***

There may be the existence of short-range order for amorphous solids.

If you compare an amorphous phase with crystalline phase of a same drug, the amorphous phase always shows higher free energy, enthalpy, and entropy than the crystalline one. Let me clear you.

To be simple and straight, the amorphous form has the small particle size so more surface area and hence it is easily attacked by the solvent or the moisture. So, it is more hygroscopic. And more energy means less stability.

## Use of Amorphous Form

These phases are used in improving solubility and hence the oral bioavailability of the poor water-soluble drugs. But these are less stable as compared to their crystal phase. To be precise, there exists some amount of crystal form in amorphous forms also. And this two-state model is well documented in USP. ***"According to the USP, the degree of crystallinity depends on the fraction of crystalline material in the mixture"***

So, the challenge lies in overcoming its stability issues. Being thermodynamically unstable, they might change into crystalline form (specially in suspension or in some solid dosage forms) with the passage of time or are very hygroscopic or prone to hydrolytic degradation. In general, the complete amorphous drug is typical to be formulated. The matter of fact is that only few amorphous drugs containing dosage form are marketed (**Table 1.1**).

**Table 1.1** Drugs approved by FDA as amorphous drugs.

- Itraconazole,
- Nelfinavir mesylate
- Paroxetine
- Celecoxib
- Cefuroxime axetil
- Cefepodoxime proxetil
- Novobiocin

So, instead of complete amorphous phase many a times partial amorphization of a drug can be done using some techniques like solid dispersion, cyclodextrin-complexation etc. But the amorphous form should be avoided until the difference in solubility make a significant impact on bioavailability.

## Liquid Crystals

If the internal structure is having long-range order but only one or two dimensions, they are liquid crystalline materials. On the basis of number of components, these can be further classified as single, binary, and ternary LCs. But these are not of much use in pharmaceuticals.

## Crystal

A majority of APIs are crystalline in nature. These are the solids with the internal structure having long-range order in all three dimensions. The logical method of classification of crystal is based on the angle between the faces.

If three dimensions are given by a, b, and c, then these crystals may be of several types on the basis of length of the faces and angle between these faces.

If a = b = c and angle between all the faces is 90 degree it is called simple cubic crystal (three equal axes each at right angle). And in the same way tetragonal, orthorhombic etc. Several common crystal forms are shown in **Figure 1.2**.

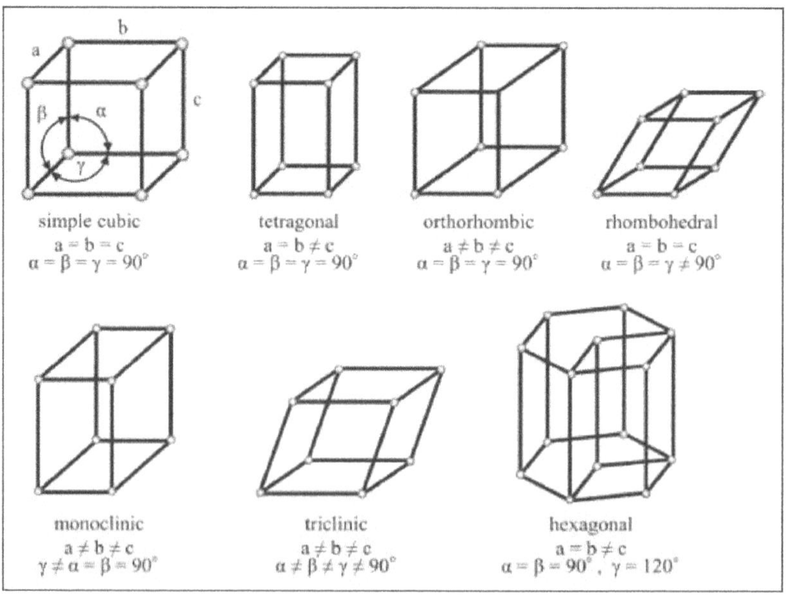


**Figure 1.2** Common crystal forms.

But in practical, the cubic crystal may be perfect symmetrical cube, plate, needle or an aggregate of the imperfect crystals. The angle between the faces is 90 degree to each other is the sole criteria for a cubic system and not the relative length of the faces. These are crystal form.

## Crystal Habit

We always talk about that "Habits die hard", actually it is our environment which makes our habit. By the form, we are unique. But our habits change, because we adapt with the environment or sometimes the environment forces us to adapt ourselves.

It is the relative development of different types of faces. Let's take the example of

NaCl in aqueous solution → Crystallizes into → Cubic face

NaCl in aqueous solution → Crystallizes in to → Octahedral (with small amount of Urea)

The crystals may have different habit depending on the process, impurities or conditions. (It refers to the types of faces developed and not the shape of the faces)

On the basis of number of components, they can be further classified as single entity, binary, and ternary adducts.

## Single Entity

"The ability of a substance to exist as two or more crystalline phases that have different arrangements and/or conformations of the molecules in a crystalline lattice is called polymorphism."

We will discuss this property and pseudo polymorphism exclusively in coming chapters because it is very important in pharmaceutical sciences and preformulation.

Further, if the drug forms a binary composite of crystalline lattice with another chemical it is called binary adduct. And so on like ternary.

On the basis of the ionization states of these species, the adducts may be ionic, molecular or ionic/molecular.

## Cocrystals

"Two or more molecules are hydrogen bonded to each other."

"Structurally homogeneous crystalline molecular adducts, made from components that are apparently neutral, that are by themselves solids at ambient conditions. The components are held together by interactions other than covalent or ionic bonds (hydrogen bonding, $\pi - \pi$, van der Waals, charge-transfer, halogen–halogen, etc.). "

The choice of cocrystal formation, depend on the need.

To control the hygroscopy of caffeine, its cocrystals with oxalic acid were prepared and showed the better stability even at high humidity also (Tarsk et al. 2005).

Carbamazepine-sachharin cocrystals showed better bioavailability, suspension stability and same stability as compared to its immediate release tablet (Hickey 2007)

## Importance of Crystallinity in Preformulation

1. Solubility of drug candidates can be altered by modifying the crystal form:
2. Solubility can be improved by partial amorphization through developing adducts or binary composites of drug.
3. Onset of action can be controlled by using the crystalline form. Using a crystalline form cane delay the onset of action and prolong the drug release. Amorphous acts quite early but duration of action is not longer one. But the crystalline form acts slowly but the duration of action is longer. So, if you mix both of the form you can have both the advantages with quicker onset of action (from amorphous form) and prolonged duration of action (from crystalline form). The classical example is: lente insulin, a physical mixture of 70% crystalline ultralente and 30% amorphous semilente insulin give quick action and prolonged release.

   So you can blend the both the forms.
4. The purity standards are laid down by the properties of a pure crystal.

   US FDA states

***"It is mandatory to establish whether or not the API being studied exist in more than one crystalline form. If yes, what are the properties of all different crystal forms. Like melting point, solubility, stability, safety and efficacy."***

## How Crystals affect Solubility

In general, when a crystalline molecule is to be dissolved, firstly it is to come out from the crystal lattice. The amorphous solute molecule are free to move in a solvent so easily dissolved. The enthalpy consideration delays the entry of drug molecule from crystalline lattice to solvent **Figure 1.3**.

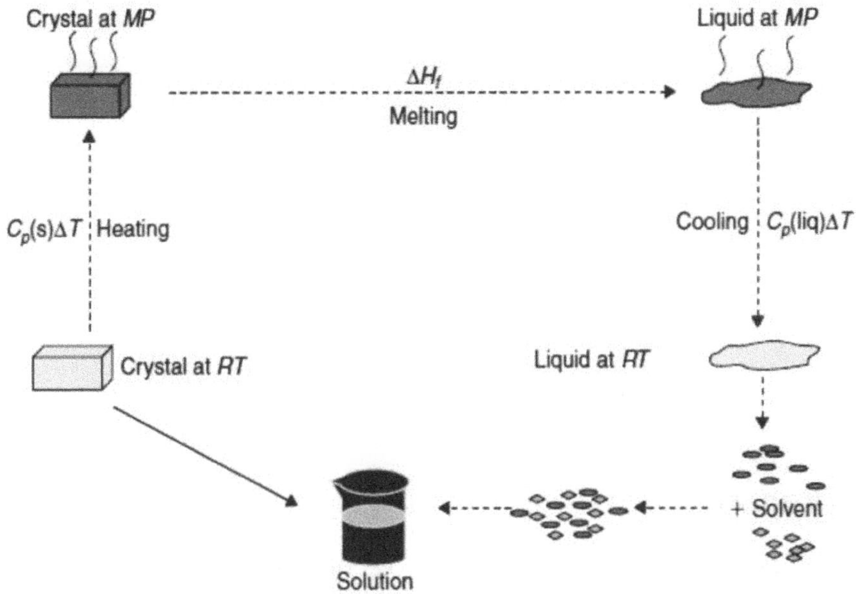


**Figure 1.3** Role of crystallinity in solubility.

## Characterization

**Melting point:** Melting point can indicate the type of crystal form. Melting point can be determined by

- **Capillary melting:** We observe the melting in acapillary tube in a heated metal block and note the melting range. (it is difficult to pinpoint the m.p. by this method)
- **Hot stage microscopy:** visual observation of melting under a microscope. The heating rate of sample is controlled and upto three transitions may be observed and recorded (onset of melting, half melt, completion)

### Thermal Analysis or Differential Scanning Calorimetry (DSC)

The standard thermal analysis technique is either done by DSC or DTA. DSC stands for Differential Scanning Calorimetry while the DTA stands for Differential Thermal Analysis. In DTA the difference of the temperature (between the sample and a reference) is measured as a function of temperature or time (**Figure 1.4**).

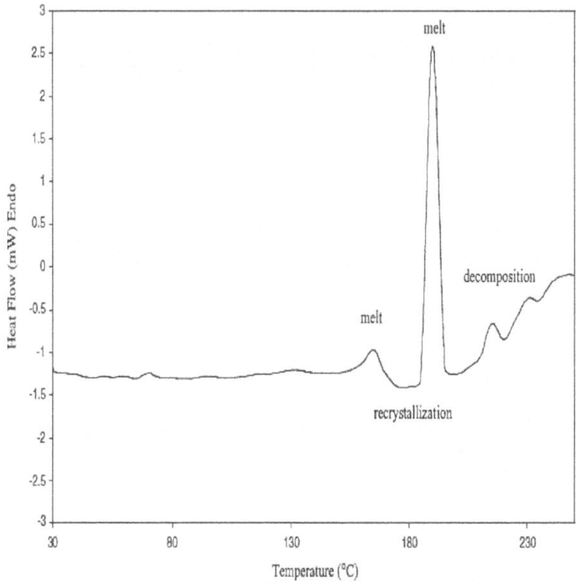


**Figure 1.4** Heat flow in DTA.

While in DSC, all things are same like DTA except additional measurement of enthalpy or energy required to keep the sample at same temperature as that of reference.

This is the most suited characterization method for preformulation because it requires only 2-5 mg of sample.

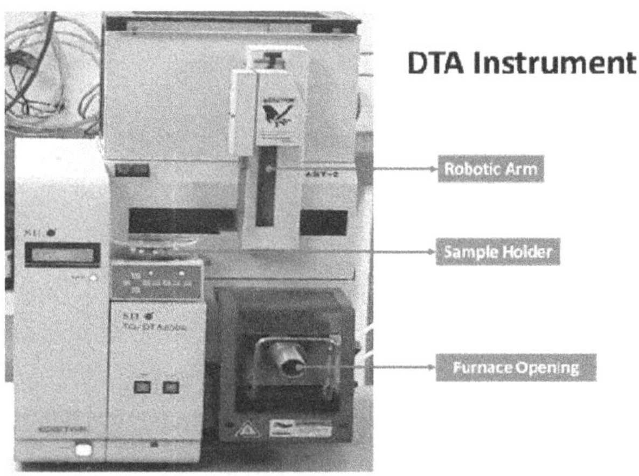


**Figure 1.5** Standard DTA instrument; Courtesy: Institute Instrumentation Centre, IIT Roorkee.

A standard thermal analysis instrument DTA is shown in Figure 1.5.

In the first step the sample is prepared for that sample is taken in the crucible or the sample holder. Now the robotic arm will do the rest of the work. It picks up the sample holder and places it in the furnace. In the furnace another reference sample holder is present. The comparison of heat flow between the sample and reference is the observable parameter for DTA. The sample and the reference, both are heated at a constant rate and difference of the temperature is measured as a function of temperature or time. In DSC, all things are same like DTA except additional measurement of enthalpy or energy required to keep the sample at same temperature as that of reference. As there is loss of heat or gain of heat by the sample when it changes the phase upon heating, exothermic or endothermic signals are registered and recorded. The crystalline fusion, transition, evaporation and sublimation stages can easily be visualized through these thermograms. Thermal analysis gives a lot more information than the m.p. In this particular example (Figure 1.6) the first thermogram is the DSC of drug which shows clear endothermic peak which was found shifted in case of its complex (the bottom one) with other carrier. It is visible that the complex was showing the unique peaks unlike the drug and the carrier. Now after completion of the analysis, the sample is removed by the robotic arm. Please be cautious while removing the sample holder and never use bare hands to touch the crucible just after analysis. During the analysis it gets very high temperature, and it might burn your skin.

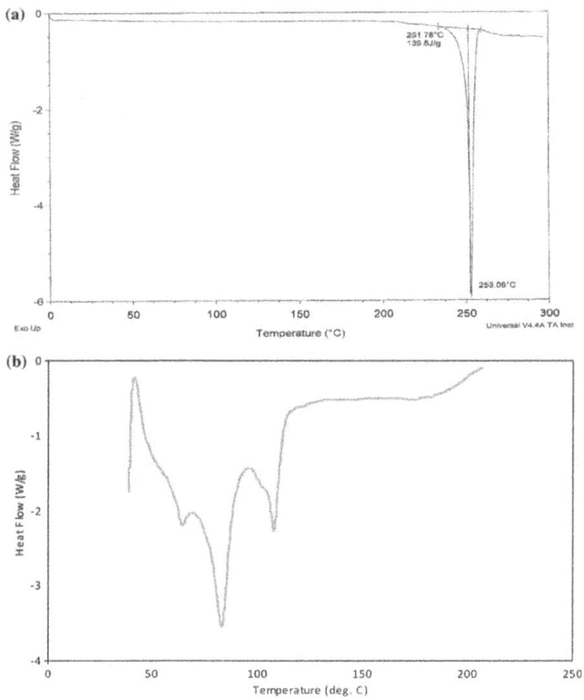

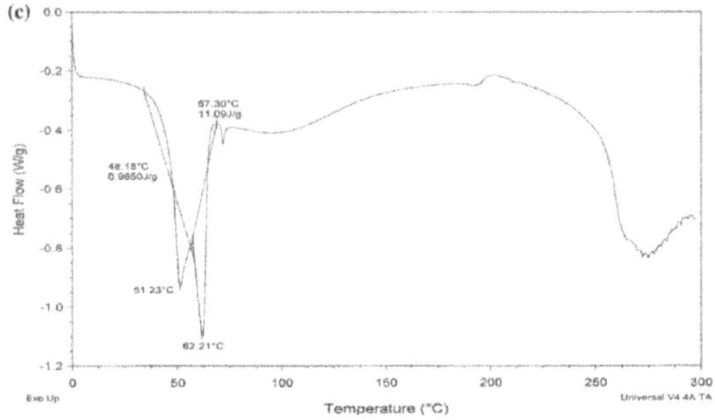


**Figure 1.6** DSC thermograms of (a) drug; (b) carrier and (c) its complex (Semalty et. al., Journal of Inclusion Phenomena and Macrocyclic Chemistry, 2010, 67, 253-60).

## X Ray Powder Diffraction (XRPD)

X rays are Electro Magnetic Radiations between UV and gamma rays. These are expressed in angstrom units.

When X rays are incident on crystalline solids, scattering of x rays takes place (Figure 1.7). This scattering is called diffraction. This diffraction is unique for a single pure crystal. And it is available in the repositories XRD data bank.

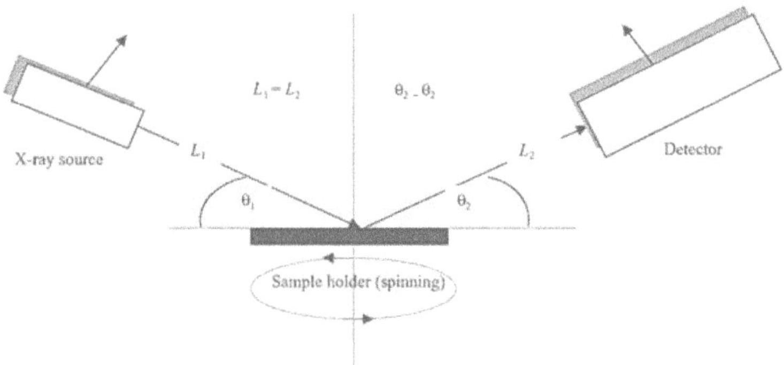


**Figure 1.7** Principle of X Ray diffraction.

Bragg's law define the diffraction

$$\mathbf{n\lambda = 2d\ Sin\ \theta}$$

Where $\lambda$ is wavelength of a perfectly and monochromatic X-ray beam

$\theta$ is the angle of incident beam on crystalline sample

n is the order of reflection (an integer, usually 1)

d is the distance between planes in crystal

As shown in (Figure 1.8), it is a huge instrument and generally housed in a cabinet with glass window. Sample preparation is a very crucial step in case of X-RPD analysis. The sample should be properly dried. First step of sample preparation is to clean the sampling wells properly. Then the sample is placed in the sample holder. The sample should fill the sample well properly which can be achieved be using small pressure over the sample holder. Now the prepared samples are placed on the sampling area of the instrument and rest of the work is automated. Using the software based controlling we can vary the parameter of the analysis as per our need and start the process.

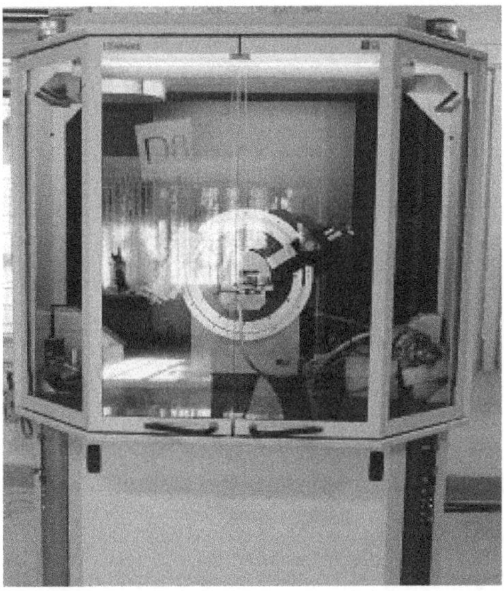

**Figure 1.8** Standard XR powder diffractometer; *Courtesy:* Institute Instrumentation Centre, IIT Roorkee.

Xray diffraction pattern gives the clear information about the crystallinity of the sample. Even the percent crystallinity can also be calculated using the X ray diffraction pattern. This is a non-destructive method. Sample can be recovered. But the sample size required is quite high, about 500 mg-1 g or more, depending on the instrument. The powder pattern consists of a series of peaks that have been collected at various scattering angles, which are related to d-spacings such that unit cell dimensions can be determined. In most cases, measurement of the d-spacings will suffice to positively identifying a crystalline material. The removal, shift and change in intensity of diffraction peaks give qualitative and quantitative information about the crystallinity of the sample in the crystal composite Figure 1.9. In the "Crystallographic Open Data Base" each drug molecule's unique XRD pattern is given for the reference. In this example, you can see that the sharp crystalline peak of drug is changed in XRD of its complex.

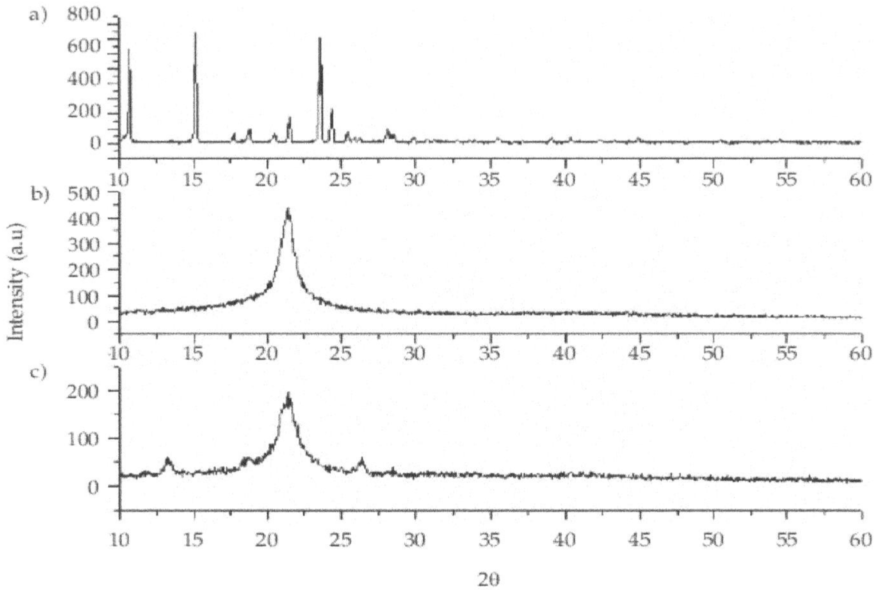


**Figure 1.9** XRD of (a) drug; (b) carrier and (c) its complex
*(Semalty et. al., Acta Pharmaceutica, 2009, 59, 335–344).*

After completion of analysis, the samples are removed from sampling area and the sample holders are cleaned properly, again.

## IR Spectroscopy

Infrared spectrum provides qualitative information about the solid under consideration. Different arrangement of atoms in solid state leads to a different molecular environment and subsequently leads to different stretching frequencies. This change can be used to distinguish a polymorphic form. Functional groups, change, and interactions may be detected with the help of IR.

IP and USP like official books possess a data bank of IR of standard drugs. This technique aids to XRD in confirming the purity of molecule.

### Scanning Electron Microscopy (SEM)

It is useful technique for surface morphology and particle size measurement. The crystal habit can be visualized with SEM (Figure 1.10).

**Figure 1.10** Scanning Electron Microscope (SEM);
*Courtesy:* Institute Instrumentation Centre, IIT Roorkee

First step in SEM is sampling preparation. The sample should be clean and free from moisture as the SEM instrument uses Vacuum in the process and presence of any moisture or dust can compromise the results as well as the analytical process. The sample preparation is done by coating the sample using gold thin film. The sample is stick to sampling disk and the disk is than placed in the sample preparation instrument. Vacuum is applied and flushing of instrument is done several times using argon gas. The sputtering is applied for required time while the vacuum of the sample preparation chamber is kept constant approximately 10-1 mbar. After sputtering stops, the sample disk is removed from the sample preparation chamber and placed in the SEM instrument. Now by using the software based controls, the parameters are set to the desired limits and imaging is started. Now the sample images are being shown in the computer screen. Freeze it, save and remove the sample. Precaution: Sampling area should not be kept open for a long time.

**Misc. Methods of Characterization:** Synchrotron radiation, solid state Raman spectroscopy, solid state NMR etc.

## Summary

- Preformulation is the heart of formulation development.

- Safety, stability and efficacy are the three desired key elements of preformulation.
- Amorphous form- unordered form, more soluble, high free energy, less stable
- Crystal form- defined shape, less soluble, more stable, less free energy
- Crystals can be characterized by XRPD, IR, DSC and SEM.

## Further Readings

- "Industrial Pharmacy-I" SWAYAM MOOC: www.swayam.gov.in
- Niazi SK, Handbook of Preformulation, Informa Health Care, 2007.
- Gibson M. (Ed), Pharmaceutical preformulation and formulation: a practical guide from candidate drug selection to commercial dosage form, II edn, Informa Healthcare, 60- 75.
- Qiu Y, Chang Y and Zhang GZ (Exe. Eds), Developing solid oral dosage forms: Pharmaceutical theory and practice, Elsevier, 2009, pp 25-35.
- https://jpharmsci.org/article/S0022-3549(15)00009-X/fulltext

## References


- Tarsk AV et al. Cryst Growth Des, 2005; 5:1-9.
- Hickey MB, Eur. J Pharm Biopharm, 2007; 67:112-19.
- Semalty et. al., Journal of Inclusion Phenomena and Macrocyclic Chemistry, 2010, 67, 253-60.
- Semalty et. al., Acta Pharmaceutica, 2009, 59, 335–344.)
- Niazi SK, Handbook of Preformulation, Informa Health Care, 2007, pp-197-206.

## CHAPTER 2

# Preformulation I (Polymorphism, Particle Size/Shape)

**Dr Ajay Semalty**
Department of Pharmaceutical Sciences,
H.N.B Garhwal University (A Central University), Srinagar Garhwal-246174

### Learning Outcome

After completing this chapter, you will be able to understand the

- Concept of Polymorphism
- Importance of polymorphism in Preformulation
- Concept of pseudopoly-morphism/ hydrates/solvates
- Importance of pseudopolymorphism in Preformulation
- Effect of particle size and shape on preformulation
- Characterization of particle size and shape

### Lesson Plan

- Polymorphism
- Importance of polymorphism in preformulation
- Origin of polymorphism
- Types of polymorphism
- Pseudopolymorphism
- Particle size and shape: Importance in preformulation
- Characterization of size and shape

In continuous to study of physical properties to be studied in preformulation, polymorphism will be discussed in this chapter.

Do you remember the definition of polymorphism which we discussed in the last chapter?

API or drug is a chemical entity with affinity to the receptors and with positive or negative or nil intrinsic activity.

***"The ability of a substance to exist as two or more crystalline phases that have different arrangements and/or conformations of the molecules in a crystalline lattice is called polymorphism."***

USFDA has the stringent guidelines regarding polymorphism. If drug shows polymorphism, every type should be completely reported.

## Importance of Polymorphism

Therefore, the polymorphic forms of drugs are very vital forms for drug developers because of their thermodynamic and physicochemical properties e.g. energy, melting point, density, stability, and in particular solubility. By using different polymorphs, these properties are modulated so as to improve the original form. By a factor of 2 the properties like solubility differ in any two polymorphs of a drug.

## Origin of Polymorphism

The differences in molecular packing and intermolecular interactions within the three-dimensional framework of the crystalline state leads to variation in crystal structure. The molecular structure governs the molecular packing and hence the different crystal forms with different stability, physical properties like density and the effectiveness also.

The polymorphism has been well exercised since decades. However, we understood quite later.

Let me tell you an interesting story. You now! Napoleon army soldiers used to wear the uniform with buttons made of tin. When Napoleon and a part of the Grande Army reached Moscow on 14 September 1812, at subzero temperatures of Moscow, the shinning and highly decorated buttons of soldiers turned into dirty grey. Soldiers believed that it is some wrath of God. There moral went so down that with the combined effect of cold, diseases and starvation they faced a pathetic defeat at the gate of Moscow. Actually, it was polymorphism. The metallic white tin underwent a polymorphic transition to the stable but nonmetallic grey tin, thus reducing the decorum of the mighty soldiers.

β-Tin or 'white' tin, stable above 18°C, Tetragonal, $I4_1$ /amd a = b = 5.832, c = 3.182 Å; Metallic. α-Tin or 'grey' tin, stable below 18° C, Cubic, Fd3m, a = b = c = 6.489Å, Non-metallic.

## Types of Polymorphism

(A) On the basis of mechanisms crystal lattice formation

1. Packing polymorphism
2. Conformational polymorphism.

"Packing polymorphism is the formation of different crystal lattices of conformationally rigid molecules that can be rearranged stably into different 3D structures through different intermolecular mechanisms."

For example estrone shows three polymorphic form (packing polymorphs) as shown in Figure 2.1.

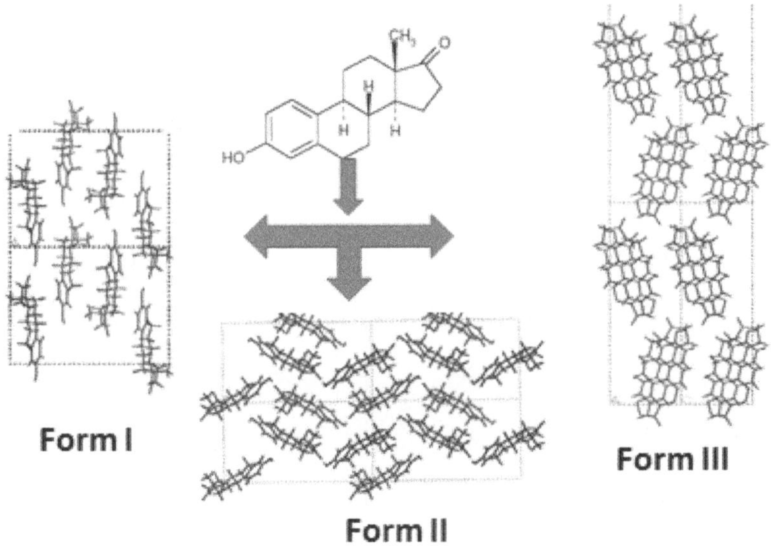


**Figure 2.1** Packing polymorphs of estrone.

"When a nonconformationally rigid molecule can be folded into alternative crystal structures, the polymorphism is categorized as conformational polymorphism."

These are broad classes of polymorphism.

**(B) Thermodynamic classification**

Depending upon whether or not one form can transform reversibly to another with respect to the change of temperatures and pressures, it can be classified into two forms

1. Monotropes
2. Enantiotropes

The temperature at which the two polymorphs have equal stability is defined as the transition temperature (*T*t).

If

Tt is located below the melting points of both polymorphs (**Figure 2.2**a) --- enantiotropic

Or

One polymorph can be reversibly changed into another one by varying the temperature or pressure. -- enantiotropic

Tt is located above the melting points of both polymorphs (Figure 2.2b) monotropic,

Or

The change between the two forms is irreversible- monotropic

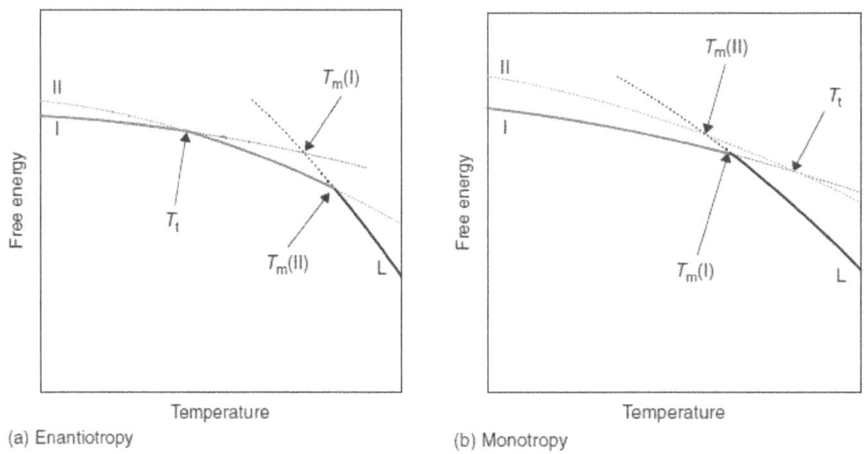


**Figure 2.2** Thermodynamic phase diagrams of polymorphs.

## Ritonavir Story

In March 1996, FDA approved Ritonavir (ABT-538). It was marketed as a semisolid formulation. In 1998, however, batches began to fail dissolution tests, and it was found that a more stable polymorph was precipitating from the formulation. As a result, Abbot had to withdraw the product from the market. It was a case of conformational polymorphism in which a stable enantiotrops (form II) was precipitated by formation of a degradation product of drug, later proved.

**(C) Pseudo polymorphs (on the basis of solvent or water incorporated in crystal)**

**"The phenomenon whereby solvent or water is incorporated in the crystal lattice or in interstitial voids, is termed as pseudopolymorphism."**

Solvates - (inclusion of the solvent of crystallization),

Hydrates (inclusion of water of crystallization)

[and amorphous forms (where no long-range order exists) may also exist.]

## Solvates

Residual solvents have been classified the ICH into three classes:

1. **Class I solvents:** Solvents to be avoided.

   **e**.g. Strongly suspected human carcinogens and environmental hazards, e.g., benzene, carbon tetrachloride and 1,2 dichloroethane.

2. **Class II solvents:** Solvents to be limited.

   e.g. These include non-genotoxic animal carcinogens or possible causative agents (e.g., acetonitrile, cyclohexane, toluene, methanol and N,N-dimethylacetamide) of irreversible toxicity such as neurotoxicity or teratogenicity. Also included are solvents suspected of other significant but reversible toxicities.

3. **Class III solvents:** Solvents with low toxic potential,

   e.g., acetic acid, acetone, ethanol, ethyl acetate and ethyl ether. Also included are solvents with low toxic potential to man are also included here; no health-based exposure limit is needed. Class III solvents have permissible daily exposures (PDEs) of 50 mg or more a day.

"Whilst the use of solvates is not a usual practice, because of toxicity, it is interesting to note that according to Glaxo's British patent 1,429,184, the crystal form of beclomethasone dipropionate used in the MDI is the trichlorofluoromethane solvate. By using the solvate, it was found that crystal growth due to solvation of the propellant chlorofluorocarbon (CFC) was prevented."

## Hydrates

When water molecule is present in crystal it is called hydrates. It is the most common case of solvation and it is almost always involved in hydrogen bonding.

The hydrogen bonding network contributes to the coherence of the crystal and hence hydrates usually show slower dissolution rates compared to the corresponding anhydrates.

Crystalline hydrates have been classified by structural aspects into three classes:

- Isolated lattice sites (water molecules reside in the crystal as isolate lattice),
- Lattice channels (water molecules fill the space but not in contact with each other in crystal), and

- Metal-ion coordinated water (metal coordinated water in salts of weak acids) e.g. nedocromil sodium trihydrate

Other examples of hydrates (with number of hydrates in brackets) as reported in USP are aminophylline (2), ampicillin (3), caffeine (1), dextrose (1), sodium acetate (3) etc.

Hydrates can also exist in various polymorphs, such as in the case of **amiloride hydrochloride**. "Amiloride hydrochloride dihydrate is present in two polymorphic forms. By milling or compressing both forms, it was shown that form A was more stable than form B. Moreover, it was shown that the anhydrate rapidly rehydrated to form A dihydrate on exposure to atmospheric RH." (Jozwiakowski et al., 1993).

During preformulation, polymorphs are selected on the basis of

- Physical and chemical stability
- Behavior to processing and formulation,
- Biopharmaceutical properties (predictive assessment of in vivo performance).

## Characterization Methods

As discussed in chapter 1, all the methods used for crystal characterization are used for polymorph form characterization. In characterization the complete profiling of all polymeric form are needed to be done.

Steps are as followed.

1. Characterize the forms: e.g. - X-ray Powder Diffraction, - DSC / Thermal analysis, Microscopy, Spectroscopy
2. If the forms have different properties? (solubility, stability, melting point) then move to next step other no further testing required
3. If drug product safety, performance or efficacy is affected, then move to step 4, otherwise no further testing is required.
4. Set acceptance criterion for polymorph content in drug substance with respect to control on the ratio of forms, dissolution and stability.

Now moving to next physical property to be studied in preformulation

# Particle Size and Shape

Particle size is one of the very basic parameter of preformulation and dosage form development.

- On the basis of dosage form to be developed the demand of particle size varies. E.g. the particle size should be in the range of 2-5 microns for inhalational therapy.
- Particle size directly affects the solubility and dissolution of the drug.
- Particle size ensure drug content uniformity and compressibility.
- Particle shape affects the flow property and binding in tablet manufacturing.
- Particle shape is also related to contact points and hence the solubility.

**Example:** flour needed for besan (gram flour) laddu (sweet)…. Coarse not fine…….

**As some basic rules are..**

**"Smaller means nearer or quicker to connect"**

**"Smaller means more reactive" e.g. sugar crystal v/s sugar powder**

**"Smaller means higher surface area."**

Let's see with the example (**Figure 2.3**)

- Take a dice (simple cube) of 1.7 cm side each
- Cut the cube 3 times (horizontal, vertical, and transversal)
- Divided similarly 24 times
- The resultant cubes will be 1 nanometer cubes and if spread in a single layer could cover a football field.

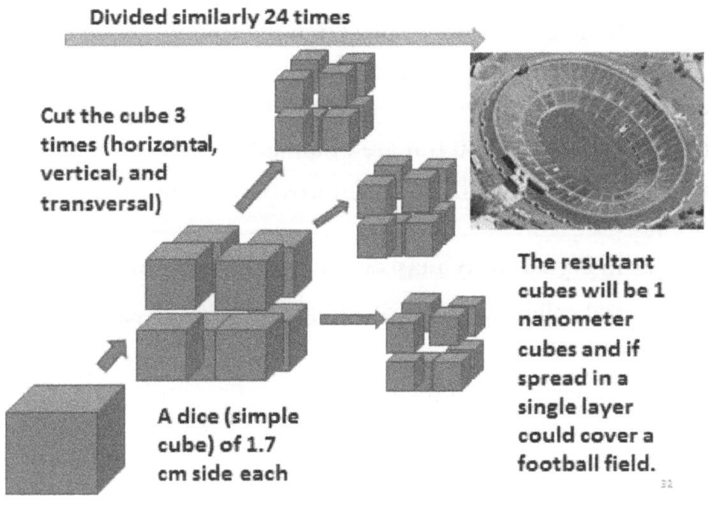


**Figure 2.3** Enormous surface area of nanoparticle.

But sometime decreasing the size may result in reduction of solubility e.g. aspirin. Aspirin is hydrophobic drug. And when we reduce its particle size, its surface area increases and being hydrophobic its hydrophobic surface area increases and hence the water solubility decreases more.

## Particle Size Reduction

- Mortar pestle:
  - for lab scale,
  - when material is less in quantity;
  - more suitable or feasible in preformulation stage
- Ball milling:
  - for batch process,
  - in relatively large scale,
  - when material is in large quantity;
  - through a combined process of compact and attrition
  - consist of a hollow cylinder (containing different sizes of balls), rotated for grinding
  - critical factors include speed, mill size, wet or dry milling and amount of sample
  - but continuous milling may be detrimental for stability and crystallinity of the compound
- Micronization
  - Routine method for large scale size reduction by air jet milling
  - It involves feeding the sample into a confined circular chamber and then exposed to high velocity stream of air
  - Particles of less than 10 µm are obtained.
  - Solubility and bioavailability improve with the micronized drug e.g. felodipine
  - Changes in crystallinity may occur e.g. salbutamol sulphate

There are several other methods of micronization. Please do refer from text given in further readings.

Now, moving to particle size distribution..

## Particle Size Distribution

The uniform distribution of particles is also an important property. The particle size analysis can be done by following methods.

- Microscopy: Optical microscopy, Electron Microscopy
- Mechanical: Sieving method
- Electronic: Coulter counter
- Laser light scattering (DLS)
- Miscellaneous techniques: Centrifugation, Air suspension, Sedimentation (Andreasen pipet, recording balance) etc.

  Each methods is responsible for yielding a particular size range (Table 2.1).

**Table 2.1** Particle size techniques and size range.

| Method | Size Range (μm) |
|---|---|
| Sieving (woven wire) | 20–125,000 |
| Sieving (electroformed) | 5–120 |
| Sieving (perforated plate) | 1,000–125,000 |
| Microscopy (optical) | 0.5–150 |
| Microscopy (electron) | 0.001–5 |
| Sedimentation (gravity) | 1–50 |
| Sedimentation (centrifugal) | 0.01–5 |
| Electrical Zone Sensing (e.g., Coulter) | 1–200 |
| Laser light scattering (Fraunhofer) | 1–1,000 |
| Laser light scattering (quasi-elastic) | 0.00–1 |

*Adapted from: Mullin JW, Anal. Proc. 1993; 30:455-456*

## Optical Microscopy

Using light microscope, the particles (Suspended in nondissolving fluid)) are observed through an ocular micrometer which is previous calibrated using a bench micrometer. The number of particles covered in one, two, three or more parts of ocular micrometer are noted and then particle distribution is plotted and the average particle size calculated.

## Electron Microscopy

We have discussed the technique in chapter 1. It is used for shape and size measurement of particles with very high resolution.

### Sieving Method

- Quantitative particle size distribution analysis.

- For size > 50 μm upward.
- Shape has strong influence on results.
- Nest of standard size sieves (coarsest on top and finest on bottom) is mounted on sieve shaker, certain weighed amount is charged on the top, sieve shaker shaken for 10-15 minutes, amount retained on each sieve is noted, weight size is calculated for each sieve set and then average is calculated (Table 2.2).

**Table 2.2** Average size calculation by sieving method.

| Sieve number (Passed/ Retained) | Arithmetic mean size of openings (micron) | Weight retained on smaller sieve (Gm) | Retained on smaller sieve | Weight size |
|---|---|---|---|---|
| (1) | (2) | (3) | (4) | (2) × (4) |
| 30/45 | 470 | 57.3 | 13.0 | 6100 |
| 45/60 | 300 | 181.0 | 41.2 | 12,380 |
| 60/80 | 213 | 110.0 | 25.0 | 5320 |
| 80/100 | 163 | 49.7 | 11.3 | 1840 |
| 100/140 | 127 | 20.0 | 4.5 | 572 |
| 140/200 | 90 | 22.0 | 5.0 | 450 |
| | | 440.0 | 100.0 | 26,662 |

$$d_{ave} = \frac{26{,}662}{100} = 267\nu$$

## Coulter Counter

Particles are forced to flow through an aperture or orifice situated between two electrodes (**Figure 2.4**).

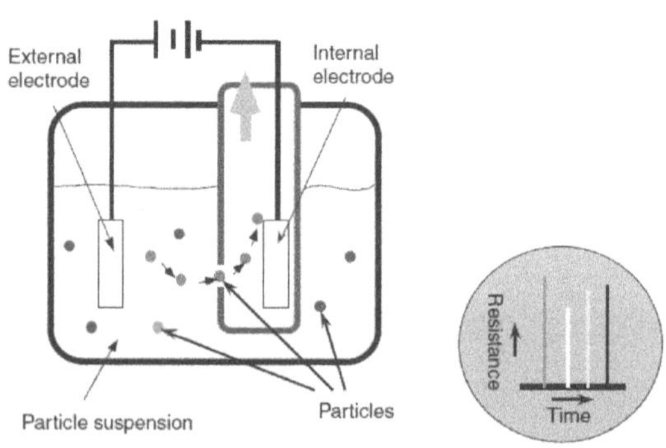


**Figure 2.4** Coulter counter method.

When the particle traverses the measurement zone, there is a change in voltage, current, resistance, and capacitance, all of which could be measured and used to count and size the particle.

## Laser Light Scattering (Dynamic Light Scattering or DLS)

- The most advanced technique used exclusively for the sub-100 nm region with wide range of 0.02 to 2000 μm
- The use of this technique is based on light scattered through various angles, which is directly related to the diameter of the particle. Thus, by measuring the angles and intensity of scattered light from the particles, a particle size distribution can be deduced.
- Rapid: single measurement in 0.001 seconds or quicker
- Compact instrument, tabletop
- But expensive

## Other Methods

Outdated and time consuming.

## Summary

- Polymorphism means one chemical can stay in two or more physical form;
- It may be of various types: packing, conformational, enantiotropic, monotropic, solvates and hydrates.
- Stable and effective polymorphic form must be identified.
- Particle size and shape influence solubility, dissolution, content uniformity and flow properties.

## Further Readings


- "Industrial Pharmacy-I" SWAYAM MOOC: www.swayam.gov.in
- Guidance for industry, ANDAs: Pharmaceutical Solid Polymorphism, https://www.fda.gov/downloads/drugs/guidances/ucm072866.pdf
- Censi R, Martino PD. Polymorph impact on the bioavailability and stability of poorly soluble drugs, Molecules 2015, 20, 18759-18776; doi:10.3390/molecules201018759
- Niazi SK, Handbook of Preformulation, Informa health care, 2007.

- Gibson M. (Ed), Pharmaceutical preformulation and formulation: a practical guide from candidate drug selection to commercial dosage form, II edn, Informa Healthcare, 60- 75.
- Qiu Y, Chang Y and Zhang GZ (Exe. Eds), Developing solid oral dosage forms: Pharmaceutical theory and practice, Elsevier, 2009, pp 25-35.
- https://mortada8.wordpress.com/tag/drug-polymorphism/
- http://www.scielo.br/scielo.php?script=sci_arttext&pid=S1984-82502014000100002
- Ballmill 3d speed demonstration, https://www.youtube.com/watch?v=gEWynTtguPo


## References


- Purohit R, Venugopalan P, Polymorphism: An Overview, Resonance, 2009, 882-893.
- Jozwiakowski MJ, Williams SO, Hathaway RD. Relative physical stability of the solid forms of amiloride, hydrochloride. Int J Pharm 1993; 91:195–207.
- Mullin JW, Anal. Proc. 1993; 30:455-456
- Censi R, Martino PD. Polymorph impact on the bioavailability and stability of poorly soluble drugs, Molecules 2015, 20, 18759-18776; doi:10.3390/molecules201018759
- Niazi SK, Handbook of Preformulation, Informa health care, 2007.
- Gibson M. (Ed), Pharmaceutical preformulation and formulation: a practical guide from candidate drug selection to commercial dosage form, II Edn, Informa Healthcare, 60- 75.
- Qiu Y, Chang Y and Zhang GZ (Exe. Eds), Developing solid oral dosage forms: Pharmaceutical theory and practice, Elsevier, 2009, pp 25-35.

# CHAPTER 3

# Preformulation I
# Solubility Profile (Solubility, pH and pKa)

**Dr Ajay Semalty**
Department of Pharmaceutical Sciences,
H.N.B Garhwal University (A Central University), Srinagar Garhwal-246174

## Learning Outcome

After completing this chapter, you will be able to understand the

- Concept of Solubility
- Importance of Solubility in Preformulation
- Concept of pH and pKa
- Interrelation of solubility, pH and pKa
- Methods of improving solubility
- Characterization of solubility

## Lesson Plan

- Concept of solubility
- Methods of improving solubility
- Characterization of solubility
- pH, pKa, concept and importance
- Determining/Characterization of pKa
- Importance, characterization and inter relation with respect to preformulation

After going through the crystallinity and polymorphism, let's learn some other physical properties like solubility, pH, pKa and partition coefficient with respect to preformulation.

Do you remember that in the last chapter we discussed about greater solubility of amorphous form or of the API in small particle size. Can you guess?

To enter in the systemic circulation, the API is needed to go into the solution (GIT fluid for oral route or in the solvent of formulation in case of injectable). And then it has to pass across the biological membranes to enter into the systemic circulation (vascular system). For passing across, it has to be partitioned into the non-aqueous or lipid phase present in lipid bilayer biomembranes. This partitioning is represented by the physical property partition coefficient or more precisely it is called permeability of the API.

Let's move to solubility first (Figure 3.1).

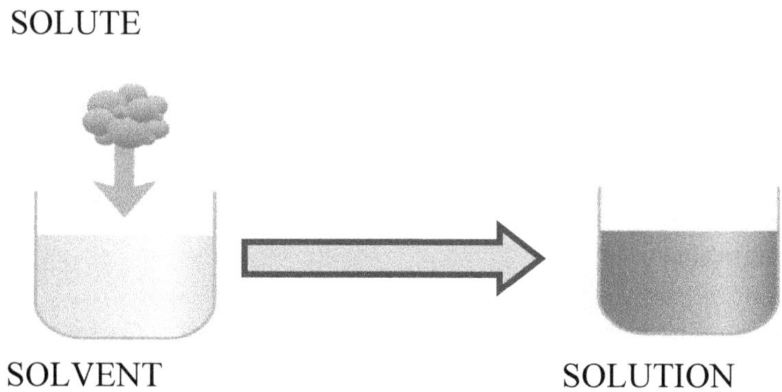


**Figure 3.1** The solubility concept.

"The extent of solute dissolved in a unit amount of solvent in certain conditions of temperature, and pH." - Solubility

Have you experienced dissolving sugar in normal water, chilled water and boiling water? With the increase in temperature you need more amount of solute to prepare a clear solution. So, solubility is dependent on temperature. It also depends on pH.

In preformulation, at the early stage of drug formulation development you may have only a very small quantity (about 50 mg) that to, not much in pure state. So, minimum requirement at that time is to determine solubility and pKa.

Solubility is required for dosage form development for oral route, injectables and other formulations.

The pKa determination allows using a particular pH to maintain solubility and to choose the suitable salt form for improved bioavailability, stability and powder properties.

## Minimum Expected Solubility

For formulation perspective, the drugs which have the water solubility less than the 10 mg/ml (over the pH range of 1 to 7 at 37 °C) show the potential bioavailability problems (Kaplan, 1972). Solubility and dissolution are well connected. Dissolution is the solubility with function of time in the suitable solvent (rate and extent of solute going in to the solution).

The lower limit (below this absorption and bioavailability problem occurs) of Intrinsic dissolution rate is 1mg/cm$^2$.min

While lower limit of dissolution rate is 0.1 mg/cm$^2$.min

So, in light of the above practically the lower limit of solubility is 1mg/ml.

If solubility < 1 mg/ml, then solubility improvement by use of suitable salt form is must. Rather it becomes necessary in the range of 1- 10 mg/ml.

If salt form is not possible by salt formation [like in case of neutral molecules – glycosides, steroids, alcohols or for API which have pKa < 3 (for a base) or > 10 (for an acid)] then liquid filling in soft or hard gelatin capsules remains the option.

`Depending on the nature of drug suitable salt can be selected for improving the solubility (Table 3.1).

**Table 3.1** Determining nature of drug and salt selection.

| Solubility in acid compared to aq. Solubility | Solubility in base compared to aq. Solubility | Nature of drug | Need of form |
|---|---|---|---|
| ⇑ | - | Weak Base | pKa can be measured; salt should be formed |
| - | ⇑ | Weak Acid | pKa can be measured; salt should be formed |
| ⇑ | ⇑ | Amphoteric or zwitterion | Two pKa, |
| - | - | Neutral Molecule | No measurable pKa; solubility manipulation by solvent or complexation |

## Salt Formation

For the salt formation strong acids or bases are avoided because they may be freely soluble but are too hygroscopic to be used in tablet or capsules. So it's better to prepare the salts of weak acid and bases. Salt forms are most commonly used for improving the solubility and dissolution. Sometime the less soluble salts are intentionally used for specific reasons masking the taste (chloramphenicol palmitate); protecting the parent drug from excessive degradation in the gut, e.g. erythromycin Propionate; sustained release (propranolol laurate) etc.

"In the case of propranolol, a drug subject to first-pass metabolism, the hydrophobic laurate counterion was selected to reduce the aqueous solubility and dissolution rate, thereby sustaining its release. When tested in dogs, the laurate salt resulted in improved bioavailability compared to the hydrochloride salt in immediate- and sustained-release formulations."

So, again stability, safety and efficacy may be the selection criterion of suitable salt form. However, the efficacy doesn't vary salt to salt of a parent drug until dosage is increased very highly. Biopharmaceutical properties like dissolution rate, onset of action, duration of action, concentration at particular site, Cmax, Tmax and stability vary with the salt selection.

In Pharma industry the hydrochloride, sulphate, maleate, potassium, sodium and calcium salts are used 43.0, 7.5, 3.0, 10.8, 62.0and 12.9 %, respectively.

We discussed in previous module that by selecting a suitable crystal form/ solvate/hydrate, the solubility can be modulated.

Other methods of improving or modulating solubility are

- Use of co-solvent
- Hydrotrophy method
- By addition of polar group
- Use of solid solution
- Solid dispersion
- Eutectic mixture
- Micronization
- Use of surfactants
- Alternation of pH of solvent
- Use of suitable crystal form or metastable polymorphs
- Solvates formation
- Selective absorption on insoluble carrier
- Cyclodextrin complexation
- Phospholipid complexation

Table 3.2 summarizes the various methods of improving solubility.

**Table 3.2** Methods of Improving/modulating solubility.

| Methods | Mechanism involved | Methodology | Examples |
|---|---|---|---|
| Use of suitable salt | Increase in dissolution | Salt formation with weak acid or base | Chlordiazepoxide maleate, diclofenac sodium |
| Use of co-solvent | Increase in solubility of drug | Addition of co-solvent ethanol, propylene, glycol, glycerin | Analgesic syrups of paracetamol |

**Table 3.2** ***Contd...***

| Methods | Mechanism involved | Methodology | Examples |
|---|---|---|---|
| Hydro-trophy method | Addition of large amounts of a second solute results in an increase in the aqueous solubility of another solute | Adding hydrotropic agents like urea, nicotinamide etc. | Paracetamol |
| By addition of polar group | Increasing water solubility by increasing hydrogen bonding and interaction with water | Addition of polar group in the structure of drug (carboxylic acid and amine) | -- |
| Use of solid solution | Improving solubility by preparing sol-gel form of the drug | Fusion, melting | Succinic acid |
| Solid dispersion | Decreasing the drug's particle size changes the microenvironment of the drug particle which increases the dissolution rate and absorption | Prepared by fusion, solvent evaporation, | Paracetamol-urea |
| Eutectic mixture | When exposed to water, the soluble carrier dissolves leaving the drug in micro crystalline state which solubilize rapidly | Fusion | Paracetamol-camphor |
| Micronization | Increasing the effective surface area of drug by decreasing particle size | By spray drying and by use of fluid energy mill | Griesiofulvin and several steroidal and sulpha drugs |
| Use of surfactants | By promoting wetting and penetration of dissolution fluid into the drug | Addition of suitable surfactants (polysorbate) | Spironolactone is a drug whose bioavailability is increased by this method |
| Alternation of pH of solvent | Changing the pH of drug in solution | Salt formation, addition of buffer | Buffered tablets of aspirin |
| Use of metastable poly-morphs | Metastable forms show better solubility than stable form | Converting the stable form to metastable form | Using B form of chlorom-phenicol than A and C forms |

**Table 3.2** ***Contd...***

| Methods | Mechanism involved | Methodology | Examples |
|---|---|---|---|
| Solvates formation | Powder of submicron size having increased surface area show the improved solubility | Freeze drying of solute with organic solvent | Benzene solvate |
| Selective absorption on insoluble carrier | Weak physical interaction between adsorbate and adsorbant through hydration and swelling of clay in aqueous media improves solubility | Use of highly active adsorbant, clay like bentonite | Indomethacin, Prednisone |
| Cyclo-dextrin comple-xation | Inclusion of hydrophobic groups of drug in the core of cyclodextrin cavity and thereby improving solubility | Formation of drug Complex with cyclodextrin (α, β, γ) or its derivatives | Meloxicam, phenytoin, |
| Phos-pholipid complex-ation | Drug-Lipid complexes improve amorphous nature of drug in the complexes and being amphiphilic in nature the complex show improved solubility and dissolution | The phospholipid complexes of drug without the presence of covalent bond are formed. | aceclofenac, aspirin, curcumin, silybin etc. |

**Adapted from Semalty et al. Essentials of Pharmaceutical Technology, II edn, Pharma med Press, Hyderabad, 2018.*

## Intrinsic Solubility ($S_o$)

Solubility of a pure weak acid in acid and pure weak basic in alkali is called Intrinsic solubility (So). It is the **fundamental solubility when completely unionized.**

The solubility should be measured at two temperatures- 4°C (for ensuring physical stability and extending short term storage and chemical stability) and 37 °C (for supporting biopharmaceutical properties at body temperature).

The solubility of the pure form is determined by phase solubility diagram.

In Phase Solubility study, the amount of drug to the amount of dissolving solvent is varied and solubility noted and recorded as in the **Figure 3.2.**

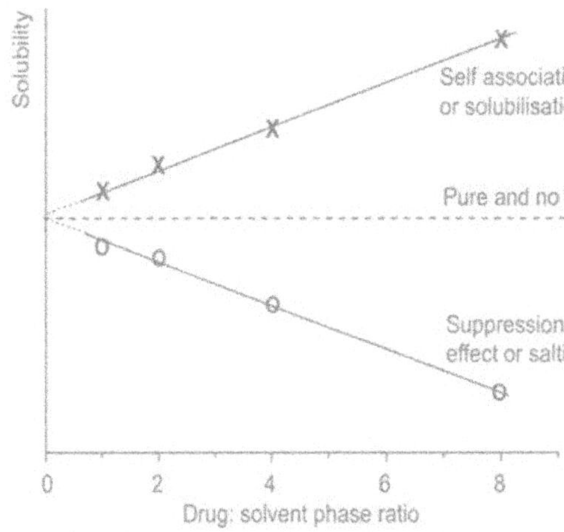


**Figure 3.2** Phase Solubility study.

Impurity either increases or decreases the solubility. Impure form gives a non-horizontal curve which intersects the y axis at a point which is actually the **intrinsic solubility.**

By this way, the solubility of the pure form of API can be determined from the impure form available at the time of preformulation stage (Table 3.3).

**Table 3.3** Solubility definition and classification (as per IP and USP).

| Description | Parts of solvent required for one part of solute |
|---|---|
| Very soluble | <1 |
| Freely soluble | 1-10 |
| Soluble | 10-30 |
| Sparingly soluble | 30-100 |
| Slightly soluble | 100-1000 |
| Very slightly soluble | 1000-10,000 |
| Insoluble | >10,000 |

## Measuring Solubility

Add excess amount of solute in a certain amount of solvent at specific temperature and pH. Allow the solution to be agitated/stirred overnight to establish equilibrium. After the overnight stirring, centrifuge or filter the sample and analyzed spectrophotometrically or by some other means for knowing the concentration. This will be the solubility at particular temperature and pH.

## pH

$pH = -\text{Log}[H^+]$

pH scales from 1 to 14

acid pH < 7

neutral = 7

alkali/basic= >7

## Importance of pH in Preformulation

1. Injections should be in range of pH 3-9 to prevent tissue damage and pain at injection site.
2. Oral syrups cannot be formulated too acidic for palatability reasons.
3. More alkali may attack the glass container.
4. If drug is susceptible to degradation in acidic pH, then its delayed release formulation is to be prepared.
5. The pH of formulation must not sensitize the site of application. e.g. pH for buccal application should in the range of 6.6 to 6.8.
6. GIT shows a variety of pH [pH 6.6 (buccal), pH 1.2 (stomach), pH 6.8 duodenum, pH 7-8 (small intestine)] throughout its length from oral cavity to colon. The dosage form should be stable at the pH of the intended or target site of absorption.

## Ionization Constant ($pK_a$)

Strong acids, e.g., HCl, are ionized at all pH values, whereas the ionization of weak acids is dependent on pH.

Why are we more concerned about weak acid or base? Because most of the drugs are either weak acid or base or its salt.

It is very important to know the extent to which the molecule is ionized at a certain pH, since properties such as solubility, stability, drug absorption and activity are affected by this parameter. The Ionization constant (pKa) provides this information.

## The relationship of pH and pKa

$$\mathbf{HA} \leftrightarrow \mathbf{H^+} + A^-$$

$$NaOH \leftrightarrow Na^+ + \mathbf{OH^-}$$

How strong an acid is determined by acid dissociation constant.

Smaller the acid/base dissociation constant weaker the acid or base.

$K_a = [H^+]\ [A^-]/ [HA]$ ..... for a weak acid

Bigger the Ka stronger the acid

$K_b = [Na^+]\ [OH^-]/ [NaOH]$ ........ for a weak base

Henderson Hasselbalch equation defines the ratio of the two species (unionized and ionized)

$pK_a = -\log K_a$ and; $pH = -\text{Log}\ [H^+]$

$pH = pK_a + \text{Log}\ [A^-]/ [HA]$ .....(3.1)

or $pH = pK_a + \text{Log}\ [\text{Base}]/ [\text{Acid}]$ .....(3.2)

for weak base

$pOH = pK_b + \text{Log}\ [BH^+]/ [B]$ .....(3.3)

or $pOH = pK_b + \text{Log}\ [\text{Acid}]/ [\text{Base}]$ .....(3.4)

**[It should also be noted that, usually, p*K*a values are preferred for bases instead of $pK_b$ values ($pKw = pK_a + pK_b$)]**

$pH = pK_a + \text{Log}\ [B]/ [BH^+]$ .....(3.5)

(for weak bases)

So, the HH Equation can be used

1. To determine $pK_a$ with the change in solubility
2. To predict solubility at a pH (If $C_o$ and $pK_a$ are known)
3. To select suitable salt and its properties like pH and solubility.

In the equation 1 when an acid is exactly half ionized, $[A^-] = [HA]$,hence $pK_a = pH$

So, the "$pK_a$ value is the pH at which acidic or basic groups attached to molecules exist as 50% ionized and 50% nonionized in aqueous solution."

"For acids, a pH below the $pK_a$ enhances absorption, while for bases; a pH above the $pK_a$ enhances absorption."

## Relating pH, pKa and Solubility

The relationship between pH and the solubility and $pK_a$ value of an acidic drug is given by modified Henderson Hasselbalch equation.

$pH = pK_a + \text{Log}\ (S - Su)/ Su$ ..... For weak acids

where S = Overall solubility

Su = Solubility of unionzed form (intrinsic solubility)

(S = Su + Si)

(The eq. provides the minimum pH that must be maintained to avoid precipitation of weak acids.)

In the same way..

**$pH = pK_a + Log\ Su/(S - Su)$ ..... For weak Bases**

**Determination of pKa**

$pK_a$ value may be determined by

- Potentiometric titration,
- UV spectotroscopy
- Solubility measurements
- HPLC techniques
- Capillary zone electrophoresis
- Foaming activity

## Importance of pKa

The $pK_a$ value provides valuable data

- on the interaction of an ionizable drug with charged biological membranes and receptor sites;
- information on where the drug may be absorbed in the GIT; The pH varies in GIT regions so the ionization and hence the absorption of drugs varies throughout the GIT
- to know how much to alter the pH to drive a compound to its fully ionized or nonionized form for analytical and other purposes, such as formulation, solubility, and stability.

## Summary

GIT shows a variety of pH (pH 6.6 (buccal), pH 1.2 (stomach), pH 6.8 duodenum, pH 7-8 (small intestine) throughout its length from oral cavity to colon. Depending on pKa, drug may be charged or uncharged in different regions and its absorption and hence the bioavailability may vary (pH partition hypothesis: Un-ionized drug is absorbed through membranes; Charged species don't get through easily; Ionization of drug molecule depends on pH of the site e.g. weakly acidic drugs are unionized at acidic pH of stomach and hence absorbed from the gastric region). For acids, a pH below the $pK_a$ enhances absorption, while for bases; a pH above the $pK_a$ enhances absorption.

## Further Readings

- "Industrial Pharmacy-I" SWAYAM MOOC: www.swayam.gov.in
- NDDS 11 Solubility AS, https://youtu.be/VMoK1vV30PY
- Semalty M, Solubility enhancement techniques, https://youtu.be/tQn6mCFFBzM
- pH, https://www.youtube.com/watch?v=LS67vS10O5Y
- Handerson Hasselbalch equation https://www.youtube.com/watch?v=LJmFbcaxDPE
- Acid/Base Dissociation Constant https://www.youtube.com/watch?v=7C_HsfB_6PQ&t=308s
- Distribution Coefficient (Partition Coefficient) https://www.youtube.com/watch?v=naUKY6y0Uu4
- Niazi SK, Handbook of Preformulation, Informa health care, 2007.
- Gibson M. (Ed), Pharmaceutical preformulation and formulation: a practical guide from candidate drug selection to commercial dosage form, II edn, Informa Healthcare, 60- 75.
- Qiu Y, Chang Y and Zhang GZ (Exe. Eds), Developing solid oral dosage forms: Pharmaceutical theory and practice, Elsevier, 2009, pp 25-35.

## References


- Niazi SK, Handbook of Preformulation, Informa health care, 2007.
- Gibson M. (Ed), Pharmaceutical preformulation and formulation: a practical guide from candidate drug selection to commercial dosage form, II edn, Informa Healthcare, 60- 75.
- Qiu Y, Chang Y and Zhang GZ (Exe. Eds), Developing solid oral dosage forms: Pharmaceutical theory and practice, Elsevier, 2009, pp 25-35.
- Semalty et al. Essential of Pharmaceutical Technology, Pharma Book Syndicate, Hyderabad.
- Aulton ME (Ed), Pharmaceutics, The science of dosage form design, II edn, Churchill Livingston, London, 2006, pp- 113-122.

CHAPTER 4

# Preformulation I
# Partition Coefficient and Flow Properties

**Dr Ajay Semalty**
Department of Pharmaceutical Sciences,
H.N.B Garhwal University (A Central University), Srinagar Garhwal-246174

## Learning Outcome

After completing this chapter, you will be able to understand the

- Concept and importance of partition coefficient
- Characterization of partition coefficient
- Importance of flow properties in preformulation
- Bulk density (Carr's Index, Hausner's ratio) and flow properties
- Determination of bulk density
- Concept of Angle of repose
- Determination of Angle of repose

## Lesson Plan

- Partition coefficient: Concept, Importance & Characterization
- Need to study flow properties
- Bulk density and (Carr's Index, Hausner's ratio)
- Method of determination of bulk density
- Angle of repose: Importance
- Determination of Angle of repose

Welcome again my dear learners, in preformulation we have studied the crystallinity, polymorphism, solubility, pH, pKa so far. Now let's learn two other important properties of solids that is partition coefficient and flow property.

## Distribution or Partition Coefficient

The intrinsic properties of atoms or functional groups within the molecule give rise to the properties like lipophilicity, $pK_a$, and aqueous solubility.

The lipophilicity of an organic compound is usually described in terms of a partition coefficient, log P, which can be defined as the ratio of the concentration of the unionized compound, at equilibrium, between organic and aqueous phases:

**Log P = [Unionized API]org / [unionized API]aq**

Being in a logarithmic scale, if API has a

log P = 0 → API is equally soluble in water and in the partitioning solvent

log P = 5, → API is 100,000 times more soluble in the partitioning solvent.

log P = 2 → API is 100 times more soluble in water, i.e., it is quite hydrophilic.

## Shake-Flask Method

It is the most common method for determining partition or distribution coefficients (**Figure 4.1**). In this technique, the API is dissolved in one phase and then shaken well for 30 minutes with other partition solvent like octanol in a separating funnel. The API is allowed to distribute itself between octanol and water layers. After allowing it to stand for 5 minutes, water layer is run off and centrifuged for 60 mints at 2000 rpm. From this an aliquot is taken and analyzed using UV absorption, HPLC, or titration. The UV absorbance of an aqueous solution is measured before ($\Sigma C$) and after ($C_w$) being shaken with a known volume of octanol.

$$Ko/w = (\Sigma C - C_w)/(C_w)$$

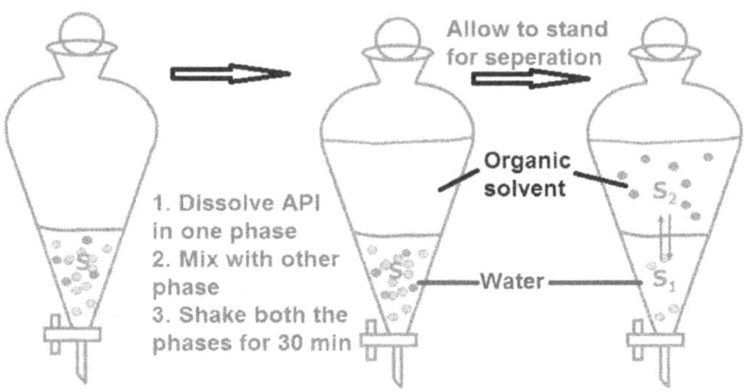


**Figure 4.1** Shake-flask method of partition coefficient.

Where the partition coefficient is high, it is the practice to increase water phase from 1:1 to 1:4 or 1:9; so that aqueous concentration ($C_w$) may be increased to a measurable level.

The shake-flask method is the oldest and the most tedious wayof measuring log P values.

Despite its disadvantages, this remains the only method that can be used in cases of very low log P values.

## Partitioning Solvents

Many solvents are used for determining log P values. In practical it is not possible to determine log P in a realistic biological medium. So, the octanol-water system has been widely adopted as a model of the lipid phase.

The Partitioning of solute may be differ on the basis of organic solvent selected for the study.

On the basis of relative polarity to octanol the partitioning solvents may be of two types (Figure 4.2).

**Hypodiscriminating solvents**: Solvents more polar than octanol. E.g. butanol, pentanol; reflect more the lipophilicity of buccal region

**Hyperdiscriminating solvents:** Solvents less polar than octanol. E.g. oleyl alcohol, nitrobenzene, chloroform, Carbon tetra chloride, cyclohexane etc.; reflect more the lipophilicity of blood brain barrier

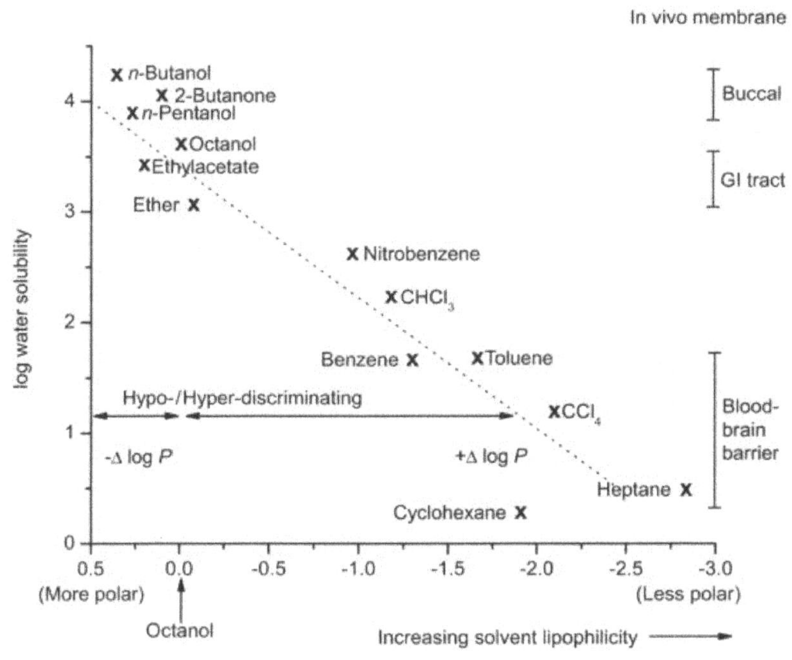


**Figure 4.2** Selection of Partitioning Solvents.

## Flow Properties

Why and how flow property is important in preformulation. Let me take an example. Sugar……. What kind of sugar you like…… that flows or that is wet?

Or same in case of salt….. we prefer a free-flowing product. We all take it as a sign of good quality. Isn't it?

### Preformulation and Flow Property

In preformulation stage the drug is available in small quantity so flow property is determined by bulk density and angle of repose.

**Importance of flow property in Pharmaceutical Industry**

- For easy handling of drug powder in storage
- For easy handling in processing like flow through the hopper of tablet punching machine etc.
- For ensuring good mixing
- For ensuring content uniformity
- For ensuring the particle size uniformity and stability.
- Increase in crystal size or more uniform size leads to smaller angle of repose and smaller Carr's index

## Bulk Density

First poured density and tapped densities are calculated and compared (Ralph L. Carr in 1965).

Carr's /Compressibility index (%) = [(Tapped density – poured density) / Tapped density] × 100

With small quantities these can be determined. On the basis of Carr's index type of flow can be predicted as followed (Table 4.1).

**Table 4.1** Carr's index and type of flow.

| Carr's index (%) | Type of flow |
|---|---|
| 5-15 | Excellent |
| 12-16 | Good |
| **18-21** | **Fair** |
| **23-35** | **Poor** |
| 33-38 | Very Poor |
| >40 | Extremely Poor |

***The fair and poor flow may be promoted using glidant like aerosil (0.2%).***

***Another scientist Hausner defined a new index:***

Hausner Ratio = (tapped density/poured density) × 100

Hausner ratio < 1.25 → Good flow (= 20 % Carr)

Hausner ratio > 1.25 → Poor flow (= 33 % Carr)

Glidant should be used between Hausner ratio of 1.25 to 1.5 to improve flow.

USP provide the standard relation between these (**Table 4.2**).

**Table 4.2** Relation between Carr's Index and Hausner Ratio (USP).

| Carr's Index (%) | Flow property | Hausner ratio |
|---|---|---|
| **≤ 10** | Excellent | **1-1.11** |
| **11-15** | Good | **1.12-1.18** |
| **16-20** | **Fair- aid not needed** | **1.19-1.25** |
| **21-25** | **Passable- may hang up** | **1.26-1.34** |
| **26-31** | **Poor- must agitate / vibrate** | **1.35-145** |
| **32-37** | Very Poor | **1.46-1.59** |
| **> 38** | Very, very Poor | **>1.60** |

## Angle of Repose

"The angle of repose, or critical angle of repose, of a granular material is the steepest angle of descent or dip relative to the horizontal plane to which a material can be piled without slumping. At this angle, the material on the slope face is on the verge of sliding."

The angle of repose can range from 0° to 90°.

**Angle of repose** is the angle of height to base of the heap or cone of powder funneled through a hopper/funnel from a fixed height (the area on which sample is poured may be fixed in some automatic instruments) (**Figure 4.3**).

**Figure 4.3** Angle of repose concept.

**Fixed Funnel Method:** The flow property of the API is determined by the angle of repose, using fixed funnel method. The sample of API is passed through the funnel (fitted at a fixed height) and the conical heap is formed on a graph paper. The formed heap on paper is encircled. From the radius of the circle and height of the conical heap, angle of repose was calculated.

Specialized automatic equipment are also available which provide more precise angle of repose.

**The angle of repose depends o**n the particle shape, density, surface area, coefficient of friction, high moisture, high mechanical interlocking and, electrostatic charges of the sample under study (refer further reading)e.g. Smooth, rounded particles cannot be piled as steeply as can rough, interlocking particles. The angle of repose can also be affected by additions of solvents; if a small amount of water is able to bridge the gaps between particles, electrostatic attraction of the water to particle surfaces may increase the angle of repose.

Angle of repose is a good indicator of flow property (**Table 4.3**).

**Table 4.3** Angle of repose and flow property (USP).

| Angle of repose (Degrees) | Type of flow |
|---|---|
| 25-30 | Excellent |
| 31-35 | Good |
| **36-40** | **Fair- aid not needed** |
| **41-45** | **Passable- may hang up** |
| **46-55** | **Poor- must agitate / vibrate** |
| 56-65 | Very Poor |
| >66 | Very, very Poor |

If Angle of Repose in degrees is <20 then flow is excellent; 20-30 then Good; 30-34 Fair/passable; >40 then very poor

Relationship between AR, Carr's index and type of flow is shown in Table 4.4 & Figure 4.4.

**Table 4.4** Relationship between AR, Carr's index and type of flow.

| Flow | Angle of repose | Carr's index (%) |
|---|---|---|
| Excellent | <25 | 5–15 |
| Good | 25-30 | 12-16 |
| Fair to passable | 30-40 | 18-21 |
| Poor | >40 | 23-35 |
| Very Poor | | 33-38 |
| Extremely Poor | | >40 |

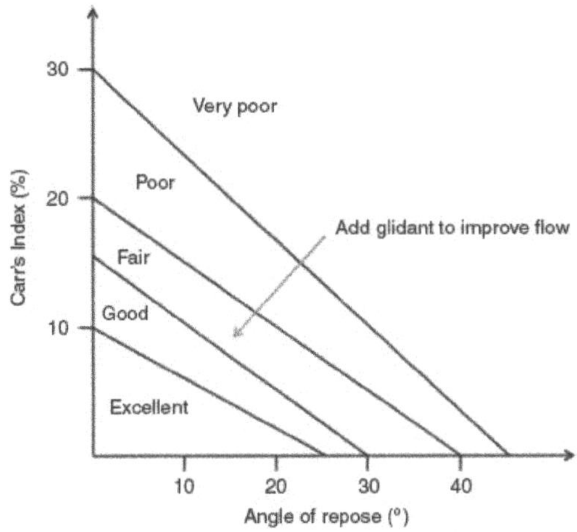


**Figure 4.4** Relationship between AR, Carr's index and type of flow.

## Summary

- Partition coefficient mimics the permeability across the biological membranes. Like the dissolution is important partitioning is also important. The selection of solvent to measure the partition coefficient is crucial.
- Flow property is a simple but very effective and affective property.
- Flow property is dependent on particle shape, density, surface area, moisture, mechanical interlocking, electrostatic charges
- Bulk density, Carr's index and angle of repose can easily predict the flow.
- Use of glidant may promote the flow property.

## Further Readings

- "Industrial Pharmacy-I" SWAYAM MOOC: www.swayam.gov.in
- Bulk density testing, https://www.youtube.com/watch?v=baFHheiG3Hc
- Classifying Flow Properties of Solid https://youtu.be/05NjG_LhgwQ
- Angle of Repose, Fall & Spatula Testing with the Micron Powder Characteristics Tester PT-X, https://www.youtube.com/watch?v=GcuDLv_wDFQ
- Mechanisms that Contribute to Powder Flow, https://www.youtube.com/watch?v=rohSKhvvByw
- http://www.pharmacopeia.cn/v29240/usp29nf24s0_c1174.html

- Gibson M. (Ed), Pharmaceutical preformulation and formulation: a practical guide from candidate drug selection to commercial dosage form, II edn, Informa Healthcare, 60- 75.
- Qiu Y, Chang Y and Zhang GZ (Exe. Eds), Developing solid oral dosage forms: Pharmaceutical theory and practice, Elsevier, 2009, pp 25-35.

## References


- http://www.pharmacopeia.cn/v29240/usp29nf24s0_c1174.html
- USP. <1174> Powder flow. USP30 NF 25 (2007).
- USP. <616> Bulk density and tapped density. USP30 NF 25 (2007).
- Carr R. L. Evaluating flow properties of solids. Chem. Eng. 1965;72:69–72.
- Hausner H. H. Friction conditions in a mass of metal powder. Int. J. Powder Metall. 1967;3:7–13.
- https://en.wikipedia.org/wiki/Angle_of_repose
- Niazi SK, Handbook of Preformulation, Informa health care, 2007.
- Gibson M. (Ed), Pharmaceutical preformulation and formulation: a practical guide from candidate drug selection to commercial dosage form, II edn, Informa Healthcare, 60- 75.
- Qiu Y, Chang Y and Zhang GZ (Exe. Eds), Developing solid oral dosage forms: Pharmaceutical theory and practice, Elsevier, 2009, pp 25-35.
- Aulton ME (Ed), Pharmaceutics, The science of dosage form design, II edn, Churchill Livingston, London, 2006, pp- 113-122.

## CHAPTER 5

# Preformulation II
# Hydrolysis, Oxidation, Reduction

**Dr Ajay Semalty**
Department of Pharmaceutical Sciences,
H.N.B Garhwal University (A Central University), Srinagar Garhwal-246174

**Learning Outcome**

After completing this chapter, you will be able to understand the

- Distinguish between major chemical reactions
- Learn the effect of chemical reactions in preformulation

**Lesson Plan**

- Types of major chemical reactions
- Hydrolysis
- Oxidation
- Reduction
- Effect of temperature
- Effect of humidity
- Photolysis

## Preformulation and Chemical Reactions

In preformulation the stability is one of the three most important issues. Remember three key words.

"Safety, efficacy, stability."

Any API is likely to undergo changes due to many chemical reactions with the passage of time during storage, processing and its shelf life. The degradation through various chemical reactions is triggered by the factors like temperature, pH, Humidity, light etc.

The preformulation aims to ensure the stability of API during storage, processing and throughout its shelf life. Let's see the major chemical reactions one by one.

## Hydrolysis

It is the most common degradation reaction of any API. As water is a universal solvent, the hydrolysis is almost always associated with any formulation development directly or indirectly. Basically, for a drug in a solution, it is a nucleophilic attack of labile bonds by water.

"Hydrolysis is a two-stage process, where a nucleophile, such as water or the hydroxyl ion adds to, for example, an acyl carbon, to form an intermediate from which the leaving group breaks away in the second stage."

The structure of the compound affects the hydrolysis rate; the stronger the conjugate acid that leaves, the faster the reaction.

Some functional groups are more vulnerable to hydrolysis.

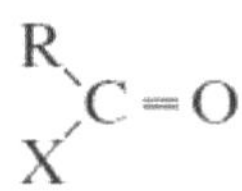


Where in Type I hydrolysis X may be ester or amide

While in type II hydrolysis X may be a halogen or any other good leaving group

Type I hydrolysis reactions are catalyzed by acid or bases and hence they can be well controlled by pH modulation.

Can you remember some examples for acid or base catalyzed reactions? Get back to us with chemical reactions in discussion forum with examples...

These example of hydrolytic prone compounds are

ester example aspirin

thiol ester example spironolactone

amide example chloramphenicol

sulfonamide example sulfapyrazine

imide example phenobarbital

lactam example methicillin

lactone example spironolactone

halogenated aliphatic example chlorambucil

**The classic example of hydrolysis of atropine**

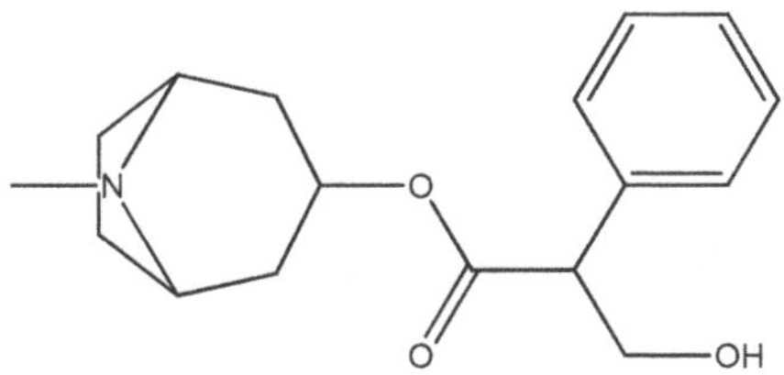


## Atropine

- Undergoes hydrolysis at pH values higher than four;
- Higher the pH, lower the stability;
- Soda lime glass avoided as container;
- aqueous atropine solutions buffered at around pH 3.5–4

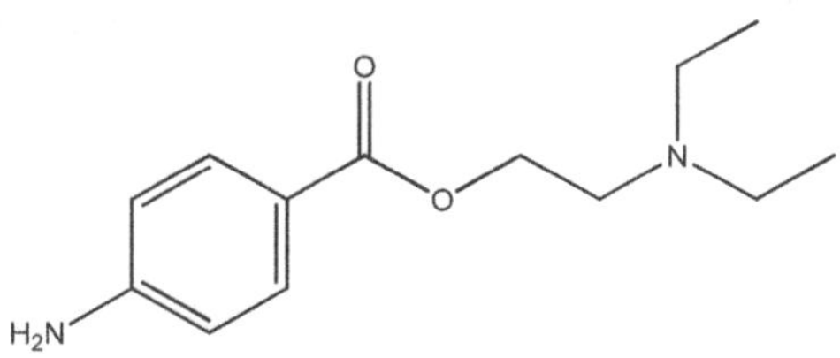


## Procaine (anesthetic agent)

- Undergoes acid-catalyzed hydrolysis < pH 2.5;
- Base-catalyzed hydrolysis > pH 5.5
- Maximum stability at pH 3.5;
- Hydrolysis protection is done by increasing solubility in a nonaqueous solvent and;
- By micellization of the drug using surfactant for shielding the drug hydrolysis

## Factors affecting hydrolysis:

- Solution pH,
- buffer salts,
- ionic strength
- Use of nonaquoeus solvents
- presence of co-solvents,
- presence of complexing agent
- presence of surfactant
- temperature
- humidity

**pH, Buffer, ionic strength:** We have studied the relation of pH, ionic strength, solubility already in the earlier modules.

**Solvents:** For the intramuscular and subcutaneous routes, the use of nonaqueous vehicles may be considered as a method of avoiding hydrolysis. Same we studied for procaine. On the other hand, the use of a cosolvent (a water-miscible solvent) in the formulation may increase stability by

- suppressing ionization
- reducing the extreme of pH required to achieve solubility.
- reducing water activity by reducing the polarity of the solvent, e.g. 20% propylene glycol in chlordiazepoxide HCl injection.

**Complexation/micellization/solubilization:** The effect of complexation and micellization is also well practiced for protection of drugs from hydrolysis. Complexation with various agents like EDTA, lipids etc. may shield the prone groups of the drug and can protect it from hydrolysis. The micellization with surfactants and other molecules also shield the molecule from hydrolytic attack. Solubilization (either by cosolvent, complexation or micellization) shows a modifying effect on the rate of hydrolysis of drugs. The location of nonpolar and polar compound in the micelles governs their level of protection from hydrolysis (**Figure 5.1**).

## Location of Drug in Solubilization

The non-polar compounds which are solubilized deep in the hydrocarbon core of a micelle are generally better protected than that of polar compounds located closer to the micellar surface.

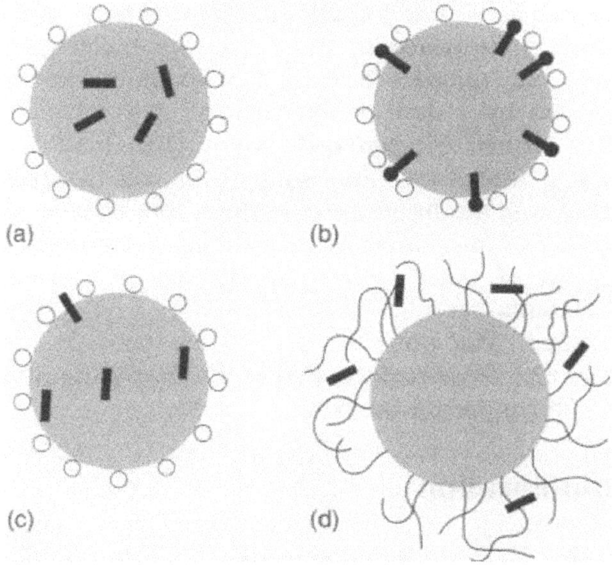


**Figure 5.1** Location of drug in solubilisation.

## Temperature and Humidity

The higher temperatures may reduce the moisture content of the product, thus slowing hydrolysis. High humidity may trigger hydrolytic degradation.
TRY TO LEARN MORE EXAMPLES…

## Oxidation

After hydrolysis the oxidation is the most common chemical reaction pathway of degradation. Oxygen being the most common element present in the molecules, the **sensitivity to oxidation is also common for many molecules.**

**The oxidation is**

- LEO: Loss of Electron is Oxidation
- Removal of hydrogen atoms from a carbon atom or addition of an oxygen atom to a carbon atom.
- The most difficult reactions to understand,
- Difficult to prevent.
- Accelerated by the presence of trace metals

- Should be understood for the molecule under study and the formulation should contain suitable and compatible antioxidant or blend of antioxidants to prevent the same.
- Prevented by using antioxidants
  - **Type 1: water-soluble**: sodium bisulfate/sulfite/metabisulfite /thiosulfate, sodium formaldehydesulfoxylate, L- and D-ascorbic acid, cysteine, acetylcysteine, thiolactic acid, thioglycollic acid, thioglycerol, thiourea, dithithreitol;
  - **Type 2: Oil-soluble:** propylgallate, butylated hydroxyanisole, butylated hydroxytoluene, ascorbyl palmitate, nordihydroguaiaretic acid, and a-tocopherol.

The oxidation problem is very common with vitamins and iron supplements. In that case, a little amount (as allowed by regulatory bodies like FIP) is added extra into the formulation to achieve the desired shelf life. This is called overages.

*Always use suitable antioxidants. Also see the effect of antioxidant on other reactions. E.g. the most common antioxidant- metabisulfite catalyze hydrolysis reactions.*

## Reduction

Reduction is the third most important chemical reaction after hydrolysis and oxidation.

Basically, reduction is indispensable with oxidation reaction. If one thing is oxidized the other reactant is reduced.

- GER: Gain of Electron is Reduction
- Removal of an oxygen atom from a carbon atom or addition of hydrogen atoms to a carbon atom is called reduction.
- Unlike oxidation which involves an increase in the oxidation number of an atom, the reduction involves decrease in oxidation number.
- An alkene upon reduction forms the corresponding alkane (by reacting with hydrogen).
- All the factors, which affect oxidation, also affect reduction.
- If oxidation is being prevented the same time, we are preventing the reduction.

Dear learners can we have some **classic examples of reduction**? I will wait in discussion forum. Pease do share the examples. You can use free software like "chemdoodle" and "xdrawchem" for drawing structures. If you are uncomfortable in using chemical structure drawing software, please do write the equations from your hand, put your name and the enrollment number on the sheet, scan it and post it onto the discussion forum.

## Effect of Temperature

Process of degradation generally increases with the increase in temperature. As per a well experienced fact, the rate of a chemical reaction increases by a factor of between to three-fold for every 10 °C rise in temperature. This may be understood by that fact that the reaction rates are proportional to the number of collisions per unit time. And the frequency of collisions increases with the increase of temperature.

Arrhenius studied the effect of temperature on the reaction rate constant (k) and expressed their relationship by the following equation (Arrhenius equation).

$$K = A\, e^{-Ea/RT}$$

Where A = a constant which is termed as the frequency factor

or $$\log K = \log A - \left(\frac{Ea}{2.303RT}\right)$$

Integrating the above equation between limits $k_1$ and $k_2$; and $T_1$ and $T_2$ the following equation is obtained.

$$\log\frac{K_2}{K_1} = -E_a / 2.303R.\left(\frac{1}{T_2} - \frac{1}{T_1}\right)$$

or $$\log\frac{K_2}{K_1} = \frac{-E_a\left(T_2 - T_1\right)}{2.303R.T_1T_2}$$

Where $k_1$ and $k_2$ are the reaction rate constant at temperature $T_1$ and $T_2$; Ea is the energy of activation (cal/mole): representing the minimum energy required by reacting molecule to undergo reaction; R is gas constant 1.987 (cal/mole. degree); T is absolute temperature (t °C + 273). Therefore, the common logarithms of the reaction rate constant at the various temperatures, plotted against the reciprocals of the absolute temperatures (1/T) will yield a straight line whose slope (negative) will be Ea/2.303R (Figure 5.2).

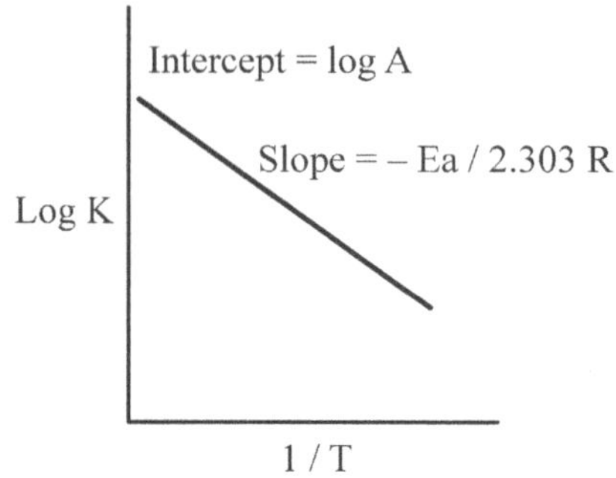


**Figure 5.2** Arrhenius plot.

**Limitations of Arrhenius Equation**

- Arrhenius equation was based on the assumption that the reaction mechanism does not change as a function of temperature, i.e., *Ea* is independent of *T*, but this is not true practically for every case. Therefore, it may not be valid for some reactions, especially the complex reactions.
- Higher temperature may evaporate solvents thus producing unequal moisture content at different temperatures.
- At elevated temperatures, there is less relative humidity and oxygen solubility, which makes it difficult to predict the stability of drugs (which are sensitive to the presence of moisture and oxygen) at room temperature.
- The viscosity of disperse systems is decreased at high temperatures, and thereby altering the physical characteristics.

## Relative Humidity (RH)

Have you experienced to visit coastal area or if you live in the area like Mumbai, Goa Vishakhapattnam, you better know what the humidity is exactly.

You might have seen that the biscuits, snacks, chips and sugar crystals absorb moisture in rainy season, if remained open at room temperature.

**"Water vapor carrying capacity of air is called humidity."**

The water vapor present in the air should be controlled in the pharma plant and storage. The vapor present in the air (moisture) when adsorbed onto the drug or excipients may trigger the degradation reaction like hydrolysis, oxidation, reduction and microbial degradation. These adsorbed films of moisture are saturated with drug compared to the dilute solutions as in injectables.

When a piece of air of certain temperature and pressure is saturated with water vapors, then the humidity of that air is called saturation humidity or 100 % RH. In comparison to this the humidity is expressed in % RH. Actually, at a particular temperature and pressure air can carry a certain amount of water vapor only. After that the vapor gets condensed and this is called dew point. This thing you might have experienced when you add chilled water in a glass. The outer surface shows the dew formation.

This is the difference of partial vapor pressure of the surface and the free vapor pressure of environment which leads either to evaporation or condensation. Higher the RH higher will be the water absorption onto the drugs or the excipients. And other associated degradation reactions.

The drug in crystal form may be damp if exposed to higher RH environment.

Therefore, to ensure the stability, a critical humidity must be maintained so as to make the drugs or excipients dry.

ICH guidelines on stability gives the specific range of RH along with temperature for performing the stability studies.

## Photolysis

Various drugs are sensitive to sunlight and upon exposure to the light these are degraded. For example, indomethacin, amphotericin B, riboflavin, tetracycline etc.

The energy associated with the light radiation increases from UV light to IR but it is independent of temperature. Out of the natural sunlight EMR range 280-790 nm, the UV range of 280-320 nm is the one which causes the photodegradation. The photons are absorbed at a particular wavelength by molecules. And then depending on the nature of drug it may cause degradation, energy or heat emission, or emission of light at a new wavelength (phosphorescence, fluorescence).

### Avoiding Photolysis

Work in dark/ cover the apparatus by dark paper/film using

- amber glass bottles,
- cardboard outers
- aluminium foil overwraps
- blisters

## Summary

- Hydrolysis, oxidation and reduction are the major chemical degradation reactions.
- In preformulation the sensitivity of the drug and excipient must be studied and the protection of drug and excipients against these reactions must be ensured.
- Effect of temperature, relative humidity and Photolysis should also be studied thoroughly and vulnerability against these must be minimized.

## Further Readings

- Introduction to Oxidation Reduction (Redox) Reactions https://www.youtube.com/watch?v=5rtJdjas-mY
- Gibson M. (Ed), Pharmaceutical preformulation and formulation: a practical guide from candidate drug selection to commercial dosage form, II edn, Informa Healthcare.
- Qiu Y, Chang Y and Zhang GZ (Exe. Eds), Developing solid oral dosage forms: Pharmaceutical theory and practice, Elsevier, 2009.

## References

- Niazi SK, Handbook of Preformulation, Informa health care, 2007.
- Gibson M. (Ed), Pharmaceutical preformulation and formulation: a practical guide from candidate drug selection to commercial dosage form, II edn, Informa Healthcare, 60- 75.
- Qiu Y, Chang Y and Zhang GZ (Exe. Eds), Developing solid oral dosage forms: Pharmaceutical theory and practice, Elsevier, 2009, pp 25-35.
- Aulton ME (Ed), Pharmaceutics, The science of dosage form design, II edn, Churchill Livingston, London, 2006, pp- 113-122.
- Semalty A, Semalty M, Rawat MSM, Essentials of Pharmaceutical Technology II edn, Pharma Med press, Hyderabad India.

CHAPTER 6

# Preformulation II Racemization

**Dr Ajay Semalty**
Department of Pharmaceutical Sciences,
H.N.B Garhwal University (A Central University), Srinagar Garhwal-246174

### Learning Outcome

After completing this chapter, you will be able to understand the

- Distinguish between isomerism, sterioisomerism and racemization
- Apply the concept in preformulation or formulation development

### Lesson Plan

- Stereochemistry and isomerism
- Chirality/Racemization: basic concept
- Examples
- Application

## Stereochemistry and Isomerism

The chemicals are 3D structures. The bonding, type of bonding, plane of that particular bonding etc. may change the chemical.

E.g. starch and cellulose

Starch and cellulose they are the isomers. What is the difference?

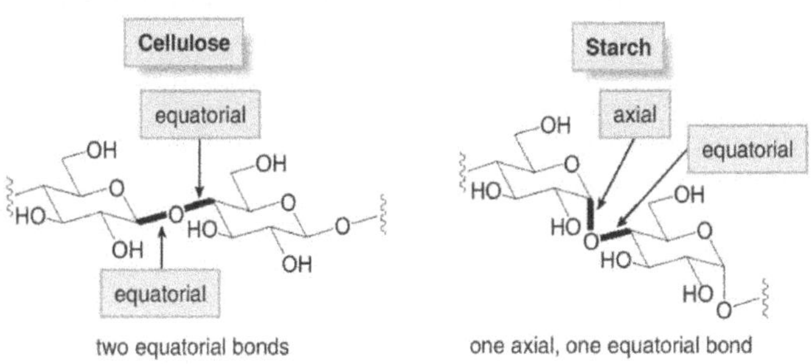


**Figure 6.1** Isomerism: cellulose and starch.

The two are different with respect to the nature of bonds, two bonds which is connecting two cycles. When they both are equatorial in nature, it is cellulose, when one is axial and one is equatorial then the starch. You know, same formula just that change in plane, changes the chemical itself. This is called isomerism (Figure 6.1).

## Isomerism

Now we can classify the isomerism, isomerism is different compound with same chemical formula (**Figure 6.2**).

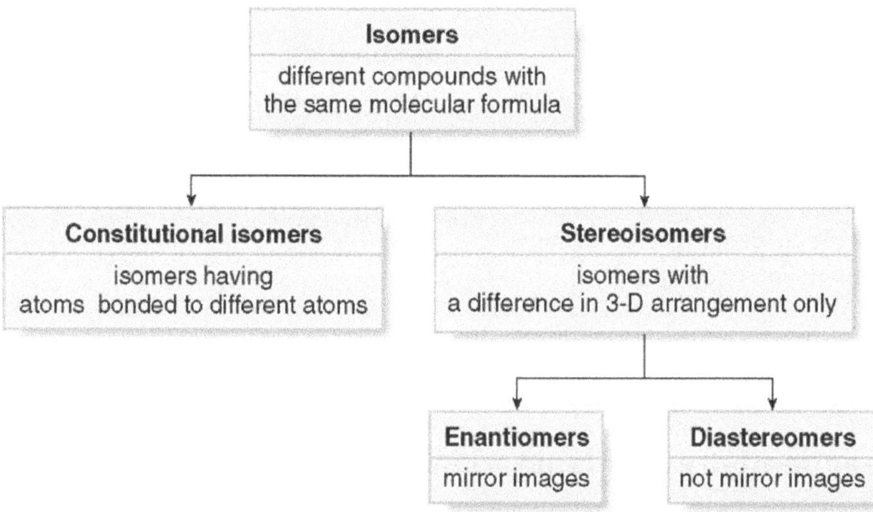


**Figure 6.2** Types of isomerism

These isomers may be constitutional isomers or stereoisomers. Constitutional isomers are isomers having atoms bonded to different atoms, while the stereoisomers are isomers with different 3D arrangements. They can be further classified into enantiomers and diastereomers. Enantiomers are mirror images, diastereomers are not mirror images. This is the key difference.

Now let me give the clarity about the mirror image and superimposabilty concepts in defining the enantiomers and diastereomers.

## Mirror Image/Superimposability

Two mirror images may or may not be superimposable. Like enantiomers first type of stereoisomerism that these **Enantiomers:** non superimposable mirror images **(all chiral)** while in case of **diastereomers** they are not mirror images (may or may not be chiral). This is the difference between the enantiomers and diastereomers.

## Chirality

As far as the chirality is concerned, all dear learners please raise your hands like this in this plane left hand, right hand and in this orientation, you can imagine a mirror in between the both the hands. You can see that one hand is the mirror image of another hand, in this plane they are mirror images but in one plane they are not superimposable. So, they are mirror images but not superimposable. That's why they are chiral in nature. We can say that our hands are chiral. In the same manner chemicals the 3D structure may have the orientation in the space in such a manner that one molecule which is D-form and second L- form both the forms are mirror images but they are not superimposable (**Figure 6.3**).

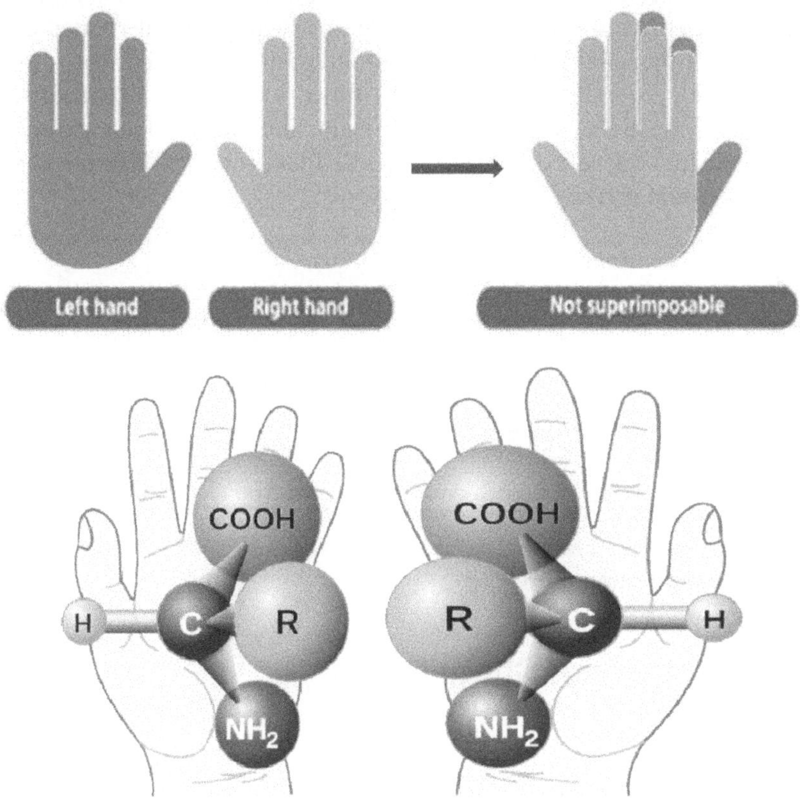


**Figure 6.3** Concept of chirality.

You can see in this example chemically they are same, but the arrangement is like that they are mirror images, but they are different. They differ but they are not superimposable that's why it is called chirality and the two forms are called enantiomer.

Defining Racemization

- "**Racemization** is a process that occurs when a compound undergoes a reaction in which the transformation produces an equal mixture of both possible enantiomers. When two compounds are classified as enantiomers of one another, it means they are **non-superimposable mirror images**."
- "the conversion of an **optically active** substance into an optically inactive mixture of equal amounts of the dextrorotatory and levorotatory."

**What is dextrorotatory and what is levorotatory, we have mentioned in this example?**

Let me clarify you about this thing please recall your 10+2 level knowledge in the physics you might have studied. That optical activity when plane polarized light is passed through chiral sample or a sample say for example a drug because it is having chirality, the molecule has beauty that it rotates the plane polarized light either into the clockwise direction or into the counter-clockwise, respectively they are called D-form and L-form, so they are dextrorotatory and levorotatory. If the light is rotated in the right direction, it is dextrorotatory if light is rotated into the left direction it is called levorotatory (**Figure 6.4**). So, it is called the optical activity of chiral drugs.

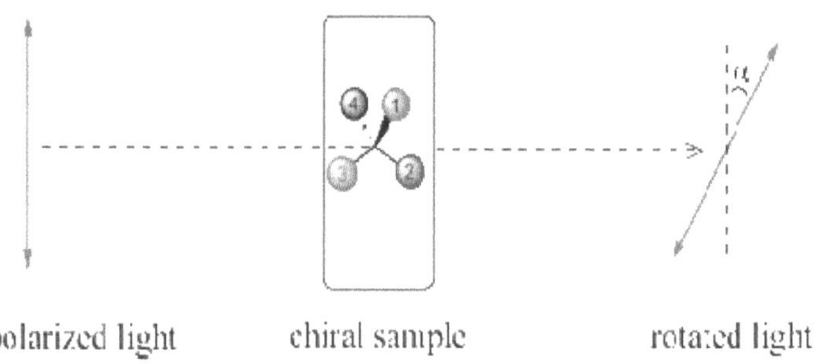


**Figure 6.4** Optical rotation of light.

## Optically Activity of Chiral Drugs

**Chirality: It is in nature**

- Axis/ plane/ shape wise chirality may be there in nature
- Proteins

- Myoglobin
- Enzymes
- Structural elements of membranes
- Receptors

These are the examples of protein which shown the chirality in nature

- Carbohydrates
- Nucleic acids
- Chiral “building blocks” of L-amino acids and D-carbohydrates. All these show the chirality. It’s there in nature.

## Isomers

First, we will see the isomers with respect to preformulation. Let us see some examples.

MDA (3,4- Methylene dioxy amphetamine), it is ecstasy drug and phenacetin it is analgesic, they both are isomers but are showing the different therapeutic activity (Figure 6.5).

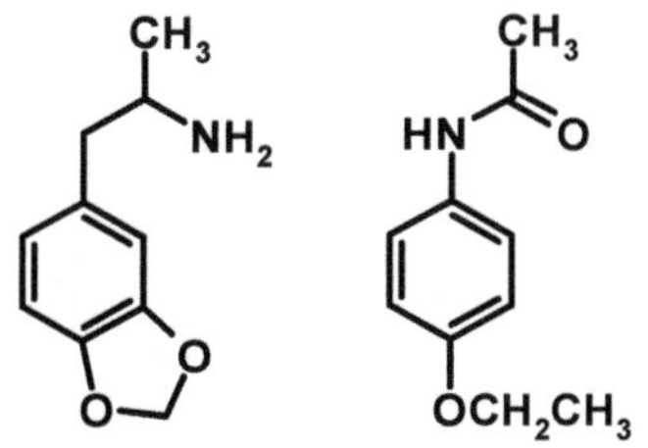


**3,4-MDA** (Ecstasy) **phenacetin** (analgesic)

**Figure 6.5** Isomerism in 3,4-Methylene dioxy amphetamine.

Another example is of mepiridine, one isomer is analgesic and other one is not analgesic (Figure 6.6). So, depending on the type of isomerism we can have different therapeutic use of that particular drug.

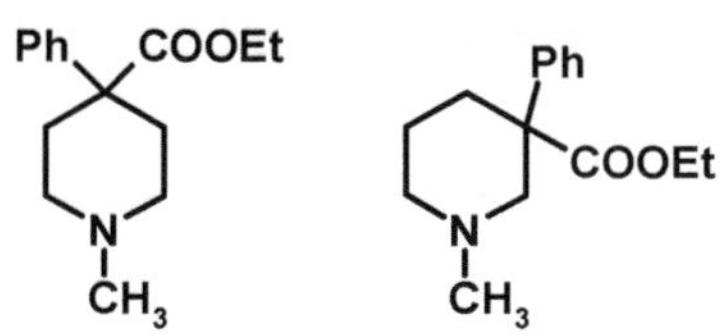


**Mepiridine** (Analgesic) (not analgesic)

**Figure 6.6** Isomerism in mepiridine.

**Cisplatin and transplatin:** These are the examples of stereoisomers they are different from isomers. They are having specialty in having the chirality; mirror images which are not superimposable, that's why they are chiral molecules. They are isomers but they also show stereoisomers (Figure 6.7).

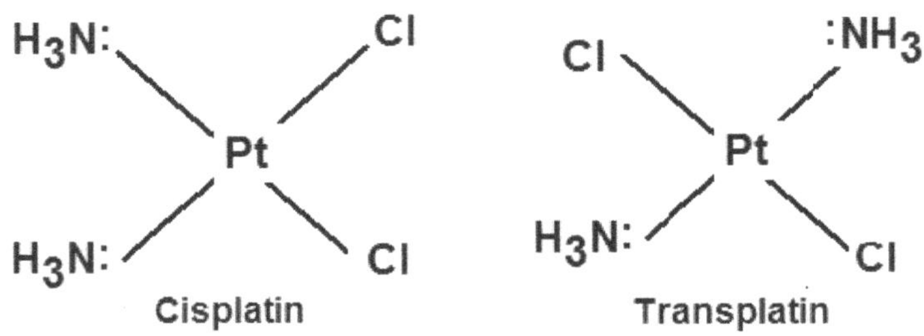


**Figure 6.7** Stereoisomerism: Cisplatin and Transplatin.

The cisplatin, cis form is anticancer while trans form is not anticancer. So these chiral molecules may have different activity.

Another classic example is vitamin-A. Vitamin-A as you can see its structure double bonds you are saying. All double bonds are in E-form and there is no Z form (Figure 6.8). Even a single chain may destroy its integrity and it wouldn't be vitamin A.

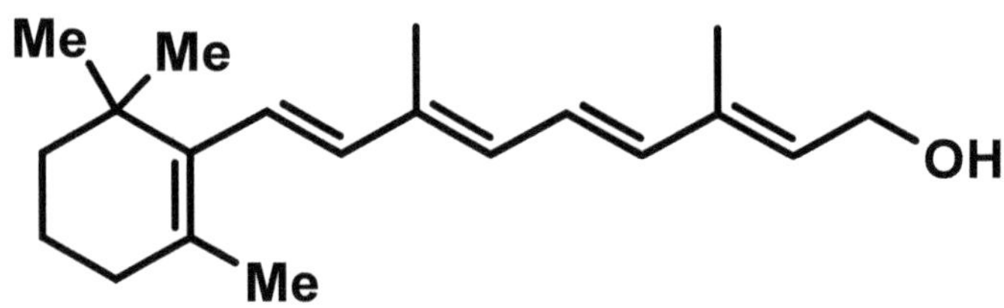


**Figure 6.8** Geometrical isomerism: Vitamin A.

## Enantiomers

- Optical isomers: They differ in interaction with plane polarized light. They are optically active compounds.
- Two optical isomers show almost same properties with respect to the
  - Solubility
  - M.P.
  - B.P.
  - Color

- Chemical reactivity (with achiral molecules)

- Because they differ in chemical reactivity with another chiral reactant.

**The effect**

The drug–receptor interactions.

- It is highly stereospecific, it means each and every receptor has got that unique stereochemistry that's why the interaction is unique
- Stereoselectivity often leads to complete change in
  - Selectivity
  - ADME (Absorption, Distribution, Metabolism and Excretion)/PK (Pharmacokinetics)
  - Toxicity and
  - Potency

**Stereoselectivity in history**

- ***Piutti*** (1886) - (+)-asparagine has a sweet taste while the natural (-)-enantiomer is insipid.
- ***Pasteur*** (1886) - "--- this difference due to the presence of an optically active substance in the nervous mechanism of taste --"
- (-)-Hyoscyamine almost exactly twice as active as atropine [(±)-hysocyamine] (1904).
- (-)-Adrenaline twice the potency of (±)-adrenaline as a vasoconstrictor (1908)

This is the beauty that one form has unique property as compared to another form while there is almost always difference in taste and odour.

Enantiomers may show the difference in the taste due to the stereoselectivity (**Table 6.1**).

**Table 6.1** Difference of Taste due to chirality.

| Enantiomers | Taste | |
|---|---|---|
| | D Form | L Form |
| Asparagine | Sweet | Tasteless |
| Leucine | Sweet | Bitter |

***(Please search the example of difference of Odor due to chirality.)***

Chiral molecules behave differently.

- Classic example of thalidomide disaster. It was generally prescribed in morning sickness for preventing the morning sickness to the pregnant women. It was found that they cause the phocomelia.
- Thalidomide (for morning sickness) was found to cause the teratogenic effect (phocomelia).
- Banned worldwide by WHO (World Health Organization) in 1962.

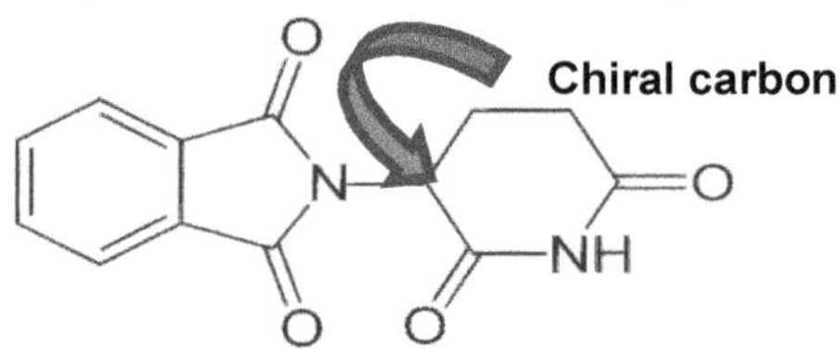


**Figure 6.9** Thalidomide: Chiral molecule.

**Thalidomide:** There is a chiral carbon in the molecule of thalidomide (**Figure 6.9**).This is responsible for its unique stereochemistry or enantiomeric activity. Actually, it is having the two enantiomers now what are these, these two enantiomers R-form and S-form. You can see that these two structures are mirror images of each other R-form is basically showing the tranquilizing effect while the S-form is teratogenic one (**Figure 6.10**).

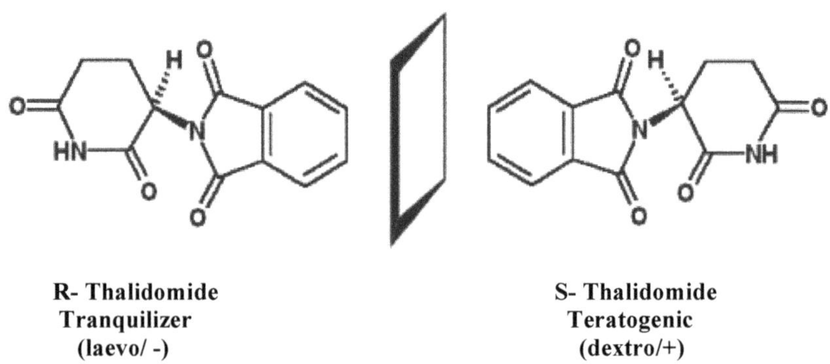


**Figure 6.10** Enantiomers of Thalidomide.

You might be confusing, or you might not clear-cut thing like, *What does the R mean in this thing?*

R means laevo form and we can also denote with (-) and S means dextro (+) form. R form can be used

- To treat some symptoms of Hansen's disease (Leprosy).
- To treat some types of cancer (trials going on)

- In the treatment of Erythema Nodosum Leprosum (ENL), a painful inflammatory dermatologic reaction of leprosy

## (US FDA Granted Approval for Thalidomide in May 2006)

*"But still problem is there: Once thalidomide is present in the human body, it undergoes a process called racemization."*

*You can use it invitro for some type of activity but when any one enantiomer goes into the human body, the racemization happens and another form is there in the mixture which may be teratogenic so it is a challenge there.*

**Set of enantiomers**

- One active other inactive
- More Potent Enantiomer
- One beneficial other with adverse effect
- Enantiomers have Entirely Different Therapeutic Possibilities
- One beneficial other antagonist
- Both Enantiomers with Equal Therapeutic potency/effect

***These are set of enantiomers.*** Learn the examples of each class. You will get the examples of each class. Some examples are as follows.

Uses of enantiomers...

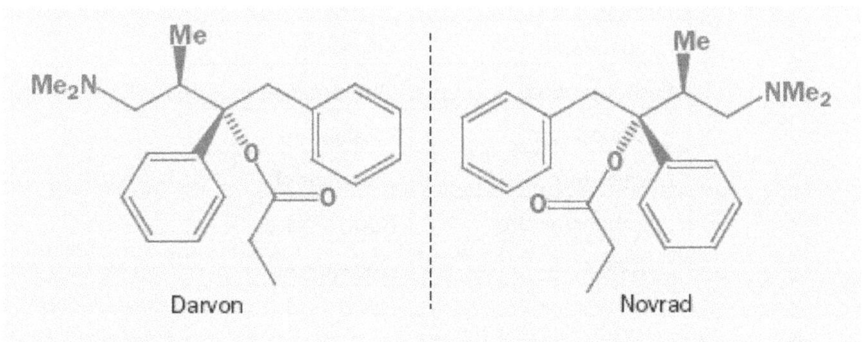


**Figure 6.11** Enantiomers with different activity; Darvon is analgesic; Novrad is antitussive.

**Darvon and Novrad:** It is easy to learn. See the spelling, you reverse it, the other form will be there, and this is the key to learn the enantiomers with analgesic and antitussive activity (**Figure 6.11**).

## Advantages of using Single Isomeric Products

When you use a single product single isomeric product you are having a mixture of these two things you are using only one isomer what are the advantage

- Improved therapeutic index will be there
- There will be Reduced drug interactions
- Less complex and more selective pharmacological profile will be there
- Less complex pharmacokinetic profile will be there

**As far as the FDA concern FDA say that;**

**"the use of single enantiomers may be advantageous by permitting better patient control, simplifying dose-response relationships." - FDA**

So, FDA also admits its role. And that's why FDA says that whenever there is some case please study it whether the stereochemistry is being shown by that molecule or not.The single isomers have been very good blockbusters in the market (**Table 6.2**). So single enantiomers are very effectively used

**Table 6.2** Single isomer drugs.

| Single-enantiomer | Racemic mixture |
|---|---|
| Levocetrizine | Cetrizine |
| Levofloxacin | Ofloxacin |
| Esomeprazole | Omeprazole |
| Escitalopram | Citalopram |
| Levalbuterol | Salbutamol |
| Levobupivacaine | Bupivacaine |
| L-dopa | Dopamine |

## Single Enantiomers as Blockbusters

- Pfizer's "Lipitor" (atorvastatin) and "Zoloft" (sertraline),
- Amgen's "Epogen" (epoetin alfa),
- Johnson & Johnson's "Procrit" (epoetin alfa), and
- Merck & Co.'s "Zocor" (simvastatin)

**"Chiral drugs make up 40-50% of the market today."**

## Racemization: Importance in Preformulation

- Therefore, in Preformulation racemization must be studied exhaustively. You might have got the essence why
- If the molecule is chiral, check the enantiomers for properties/activity difference.
- Check for potency, selectivity, ADME, PK and toxicity of enantiomers. These things must be kept in mind and after that
- Chose the best suited enantiomers for the formulation.

## Summary

We studied, what is stereoisomerism, "mirror images, not superimposable are called enantiomers".

Chiral molecules are the hot topics and the blockbusters in the industry. We use one particular isomeric form rather than using the racemic mixture. This is the best suited strategy. So depending upon the racemic form, the activity may change, that's why we focus on to a particular optically active form of the drug of that chiral drug.

- Chiral molecules are the hot topics and the blockbusters in industry
- Polymers and their polymerization properties may be used to develop suitable dosage form with improved biopharmaceutical and pharmacokinetic properties.
- Onset, duration, release and targeting can be modified by using suitable polymers.

## Further Readings


- "Industrial Pharmacy-I" SWAYAM MOOC: www.swayam.gov.in
- Racemic Mixtures, https://youtu.be/g0qZ6BDRsZIWhat are Enantiomers?, https://youtu.be/q3pw-keMQGY
- Introduction to chirality, https://youtu.be/tk-SNvCPLCE
- Gibson M. (Ed), Pharmaceutical preformulation and formulation: a practical guide from candidate drug selection to commercial dosage form, II edn, Informa Healthcare.
- Qiu Y, Chang Y and Zhang GZ (Exe. Eds), Developing solid oral dosage forms: Pharmaceutical theory and practice, Elsevier, 2009.

## References


- Niazi SK, Handbook of Preformulation, Informa health care, 2007.
- Gibson M. (Ed), Pharmaceutical preformulation and formulation: a practical guide from candidate drug selection to commercial dosage form, II edn, Informa Healthcare, 60- 75.
- Qiu Y, Chang Y and Zhang GZ (Exe. Eds), Developing solid oral dosage forms: Pharmaceutical theory and practice, Elsevier, 2009, pp 25-35.
- Aulton ME (Ed), Pharmaceutics, The science of dosage form design, II edn, Churchill Livingston, London, 2006, pp- 113-122.

CHAPTER 7

# Preformulation II
# Dissolution, Permeability and BCS

**Dr Ajay Semalty**
Department of Pharmaceutical Sciences,
H.N.B Garhwal University (A Central University), Srinagar Garhwal-246174

**Learning Outcome**

After completing this chapter, you will be able to understand the

- Define dissolution and distinguish between the dissolution theories
- Learn the factors affecting dissolution
- Perform the permeability study
- Apply the Biopharmaceutical Classification System (BCS) for preformulation and drug delivery

**Lesson Plan**

- Dissolution: Goals, basic concept and theories
- Dissolution apparatus
- Factors affecting dissolution
- Permeability; Concept
- Determining Permeability: Diffusion Cells
- BCS: Concept
- Class of drugs and examples
- Application of BCS

## Dissolution

*"Dissolution is defined as the process by which a known amount of drug substance goes into solution per unit of time under standardized conditions."* It is used for characterizing the bio-pharmaceutical quality of a product at different stages in its lifecycle. It is used for choosing between different alternative formulations for further development. Dissolution testing is an official test recommended by all pharmacopoeias (viz. official books) for evaluating drug release of solid and semisolid dosage forms.

## Dissolution: Goals

Dissolution aims for the prediction of *in vivo* performance, actually we can have some ideas how the drug is going to behave in the actual biological system, we can use it for assessing the lot-to-lot quality of a drug product or batch to batch consistency. For example; we have to produce a lot of 50000 tablets and then second lot is also there of 50000 tablets, how will you come to know that the both the batches are similar in performance with the help of dissolution we can predict that they are same in quality. Dissolution is a quality control test basically, it is used to guide development of the new formulation, to ascertain the need for *in vivo* comparative bioavailability and bioequivalence studies, it is mandatory requirement for regulatory approval, it is used to assess quality (stability/expiration dates) and optimization of the products.

## Dissolution

Dissolution is drug going into the solution (media of GIT).

**Dissolution:** Concept

**It is a two steps process**

Step 1- Molecules are released from dosage form to media creating a saturated layer/stagnant layer, adjacent to the solid surface.

Step 2- Drug is diffused as per concentration gradient from higher concentration to lower concentration.

**And it can be expressed with the help of Modified Noyes-Whitney's equation**

$$\frac{dx}{dt} = \frac{A.D.K}{h} Cs - \frac{xd}{V}$$

- dx/dt is the dissolution rate,
- A is the surface area of the particle available for dissolution,
- D is the diffusion rate constant,
- K is the oil water partition coefficient,
- h is the thickness of the stagnant layer surrounding the particle,
- Cs is the saturation solubility of the drug,
- Xd is the amount dissolved of drug at time t and
- V is the volume of the dissolution media.

As far as the other parameters are concerned the surface area of drug, it is governed by particle size or the wettability (Table 7.1).

Surface area we are talking about the active surface area which is involved in that process of diffusion or dissolution. As far as the physiological conditions/properties are concerned which are governing this factor are surfactants in gastric juice and bile.

**Table 7.1** Dissolution: Factors.

| Factor | Physicochemical properties | Physiological properties |
|---|---|---|
| Surface area of drug (A) | Particle size, Wettability | Surfactants in gastric juice and bile |
| Diffusion coefficient of the drug (D) | Molecular size | Viscosity of luminal contents |
| Stagnant layer thickness (h) | | Motility patterns and flow rate |
| Solubility (Cs) | Hydrophilicity, crystal structure, solubilization | pH, buffer capacity, bile and food composition |
| Amount of drug already dissolved (Xd) | | Permeability |
| Volume of solvent available (V) | | Secretion, co-administered Fluids |

## Dissolution: Theories

Dissolution can be explained with the help of some theories/ models. There are three major theories;

- Diffusion layer Model (Film Theory)
- Penetration or Surface Renewal Theory (Danckwerts' Model)
- Interfacial Barrier Model (Double Barrier Mechanism or Limited Solvation Theory)

## Diffusion Layer Theory

It has two step process

- I - formation of a saturated stagnant layer around the drug particle in solution (Rapid step)

- II- Drug is slowly diffused from high to low concentration (Slow/ rate limiting step)

In the diffusion model, the diffusion is the rate limiting step (Figure 7.1).

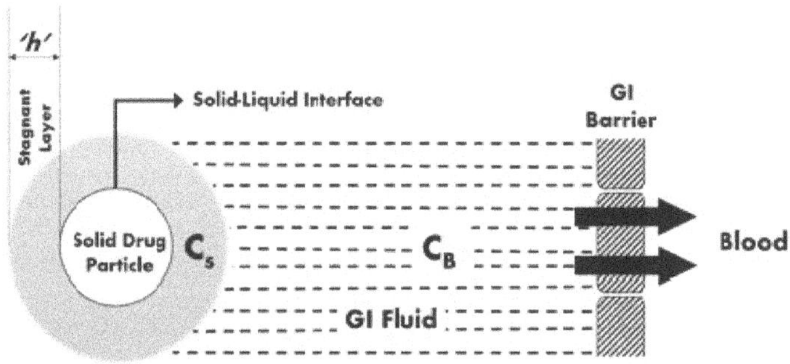


**Figure 7.1** Diffusion Layer Model.

(Adapted from Semalty et al. Essentials of Pharmaceutical Technology, II edn, 2018, Pharma med Press, Hyderabad)

## Surface Renewal Model

In this drug particle is continually exposed to fresh dissolution medium, numerous eddies or packets are there in the agitating medium. The solute diffuses in to the packets and is carried to the bulk medium. Unlike previous theory, no stagnant film layer is there due to turbulance/ constant surface renewal and that's why it is called surface renewal model (Figure 7.2).

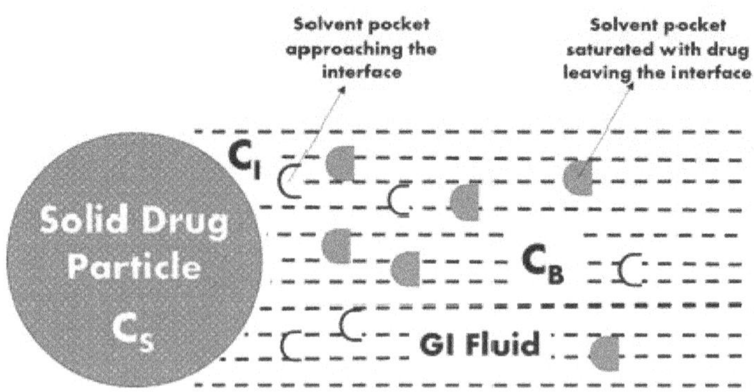


**Figure 7.2** Surface Renewal Model.

(Adapted from Semalty et al. Essentials of Pharmaceutical Technology, II edn, 2018, Pharma med Press, Hyderabad)

## Interfacial Barrier Model

In this model, it is also called limited solvation theory. A crystal undergoes dissolution through an interfacial process in the dissolving medium. The true surface area of the crystal must be considered. Each surface provides a different contribution to the dissolution process (Figure 7.3).

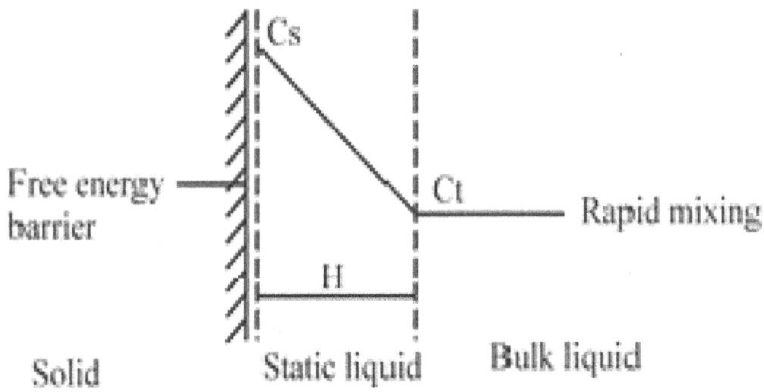


**Figure 7.3** Interfacial Barrier Model.
(Adapted from Semalty et al. Essentials of Pharmaceutical Technology, II edn, 2018, Pharma med Press, Hyderabad)

And by this way the dissolution can be understood with the help of these three theories. And you can also learn the equation which express these theories or models. So, what we got here that dissolution is a process which is used for various aspects of drug delivery can be explained with the help of three major theories which must be understood with respect to the drug development.

## Dissolution Apparatus

These apparatuses are designed in such a way that we try to mimicking/simulate the environment of gastrointestinal tract or the physiological conditions. It contains ajar, jar is of hemispherical bottom (bottom is hemispherical because intestine is hemispherical nature) to mimic that physiology. Volume we maintain to 900-1000 mL (viz. volume in the gastric environment) and that is simulated in this apparatus with keep that media in the range of 900-1000 mL. Temperature we maintain at just like as the body temperature around 37±1°C with the help of heaters in that apparatus. We provide the agitation with the help of motor guided paddle or basket to mimic the gastric motility. What is gastric motility? With the help of gastric motility, the food content and the oral content move to the lower intestine and ultimately to the cecum or rectum. To mimic that motility, we give that agitation and that is helpful for the drug dissolution or permeation. And these apparatuses may be single station or multi station (6, 8 or more assemblies are put together in dissolution apparatus)

## Official Dissolution Test App. IP

These dissolution apparatuses are standard, standard means each and every specification is final say for example in IP there are two types of official dissolution test apparatus (1) Paddle type apparatus is called type I apparatus and basket type apparatus is called type II apparatus (**Figure 7.4**). In both apparatus each specification is unique, you have to learn. Dear learners do remember each specification of length and diameter of each parts of dissolution test apparatus. It is important with respect to your viva-voce preparation. It is important with respect to your GPAT examination.

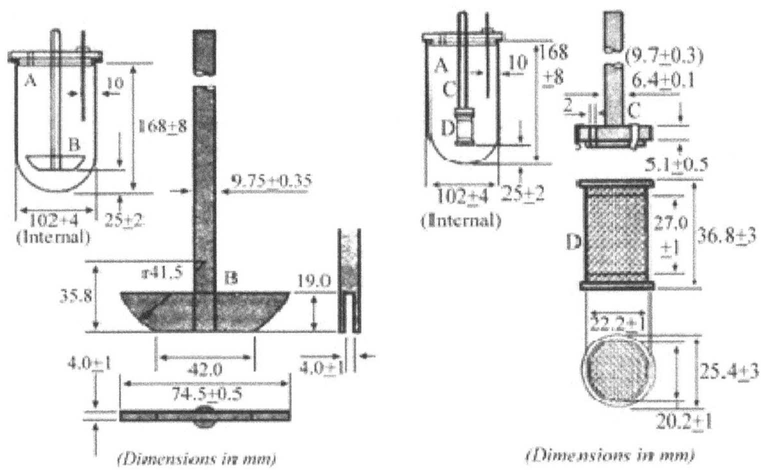


**Paddle type (Type I)** **Basket Type (Type II)**

**Figure 7.4** Dissolution Test Apparatus IP.

## Official Dissolution Test Apparatus USP

As far as the USP apparatus is concerned, USP prescribes seven dissolution test apparatus first two are the same but here type I is rotating basket remember this thing always.

It is always asked, it is tricky question in some examination that in USP type I apparatus is rotating basket while IP type I apparatus is rotating paddle and in the type II USP apparatus it is rotating paddle and rest of the equipment are used only when these two first basket or paddle fails to perform this thing with respect to the requirement of the oral immediate release or modified release products, we can use these seven types of dissolution test apparatus, and you can go through the further links for getting more information about each and every dissolution test apparatus prescribed by the USP (**Table 7.2**).

**Table 7.2** Dissolution Test Apparatus USP.

| App. No. | Description | General Application |
|---|---|---|
| 1 | Rotating Basket | Oral IR and MR |
| 2 | Rotating Paddle | Oral IR and MR |
| 3 | Reciprocating Cylinder | Oral MR |
| 4 | Flow Through Cell | Oral MR |
| 5 | Paddle over disk | Transdermal DS |
| 6 | Cylinder | Transdermal DS |
| 7 | Reciprocating Holder | Transdermal DS or non-disintegrating oral MR |

*IR = Immediate release, MR = Modified Release, DS= Delivery System

So, we perform dissolution in dissolution test apparatus which are official and every component and aspect is standard. The size, shape, length, diameter of every part of the dissolution test apparatus is standard either in IP or USP. You must learn these things, and this is helpful in having an idea about the drug release. So, dissolution test apparatus is very important with respect to study of drug release.

Now let me enter the domain of the factors related to dissolution apparatus, we have discussed factors related to dissolution. Now we are discussing the factors of dissolution apparatus.

## Dissolution Apparatus Factors

- Type of apparatus
- Dissolution Medium
- Agitation
- Temperature

## Type of Apparatus

We have discussed there are so many types of apparatus depending upon choice we can have things; we can select the apparatus.

## Dissolution Medium

As far as the medium is concerned, as we have discussed that we try to mimic or simulate the environment, simulate the physiological conditions with respect to the Volume and pH or may be the presence or absence of some enzymes. We need try to have SIF (Simulated Intestinal Fluid) we will keep the pH 6.8, SGF (Simulated Gastric Fluid) we keep the pH 1.2, we use the phosphate buffer pH 6.8 and pH 1.2 acidic buffer in case of in case of SGF. We may add cosolvent or surfactant depending upon the requirement, it is not mandatory that we always try to mimic the nature of media sometimes we have entirely different type of media just to have a similar kind of dissolution profile as that of the standard drug when you are performing the bioequivalence studies. You will study it when you will be studying somewhere what is the bioequivalence, how is the bioequivalence is performed. We try to have that similar dissolution profile for that we select a suitable kind of media it may be completely different from the natural media presence in biological system.

### FIP Recommended Dissolution Media

FIP recommends four major media

- 0.1N hydrochloric acid
- Buffer solution pH 4.5
- SIF without pancreatin pH 7.5
- 0.05M phosphate buffer solution of pH 5.8 to 8.0

## Dissolution: rapid dissolving?

An IR drug product is characterized as a rapid dissolving when no less than 85% of the labeled amount of the drug substance dissolves within 30 minutes using USP Apparatus I at 100 rpm or USP Apparatus II at 50 rpm in a volume of 900 mL or less of each of the recommended media.

**(FIP recommends 4 dissolution media)**

## Agitation

We want to mimic gastric motility, our gastrointestinal tract motility starts from the GIT like this movement this kind of motility is there, to mimic this motility mild agitation conditions should be maintained during dissolution testing to allow maximum discriminating power. Agitation is done to detect products with poor in vivo performance, generally the agitation is kept at 50-75- 100 rpm and in general it is mentioned in each monograph in pharmacopoeias for particular kind of dissolution test apparatus for a particular API.

## Temperature

Obviously, it should be at the body temperature (37±1 ˚C). Temperature of apparatus must be maintained before the beginning of test, you cannot do like that when you are starting it putting your tablet into the dissolution test apparatus and then you are starting you dissolution test apparatus. No, it is not like that, when you prepare the cake in your microwave you preheat it, you have to maintain the temperature before beginning the process. So, before starting the test you have to maintain the temperature at 37 ˚C first and attain the temperature then allow the apparatus to maintain that tempearatre. Guess, what would be the problem if we are unable maintain the temperature? Increase or decrease in temperature may affect the solubility. It may increase or decrease the solubility as well as the dissolution. So, overall dissolution test may get affected if there is increase or decrease in temperature.

So, it can be concluded that dissolution test apparatus is affected by the design, type of apparatus, kind of media, kind of agitation or temperature. These are the major factors which are associated with the dissolution test apparatus.

Now let us enter into the domain of the permeability.

## Permeability

Drug slowly dissolves, goes into the solution and there after it passes across the biological membrane, this is called permeability; then only it gets absorbed. If a drug is found potent and active but if it is not permeated, it wouldn't be absorbed. So, permeability is very vital. It is very critical and without the permeability, no absorption occurs.

## Permeability

Permeability can be predicted by partition coefficient which we have explained in our one of the modules which we discussed in the first week that with the help of partition coefficient we can predict the permeability it depends on chemical nature, molecular weight and micro-environment of the drug. A drug substance is considered *highly permeable* (when the extent of intestinal absorption is determined to be 85 % or higher it is called highly permeable). Permeability is assessed by the in vitro diffusion cells or in vitro permeation apparatus.

## *In vitro* Diffusion Cells

Let us discuss *in vitro* diffusion cell (**Figure 7.5**). This is the *in vitro* diffusion cell, this is very small instrument which is made up of glass as you can see it contains two compartments one is receptor compartment which is bigger as compared to the donor compartment.

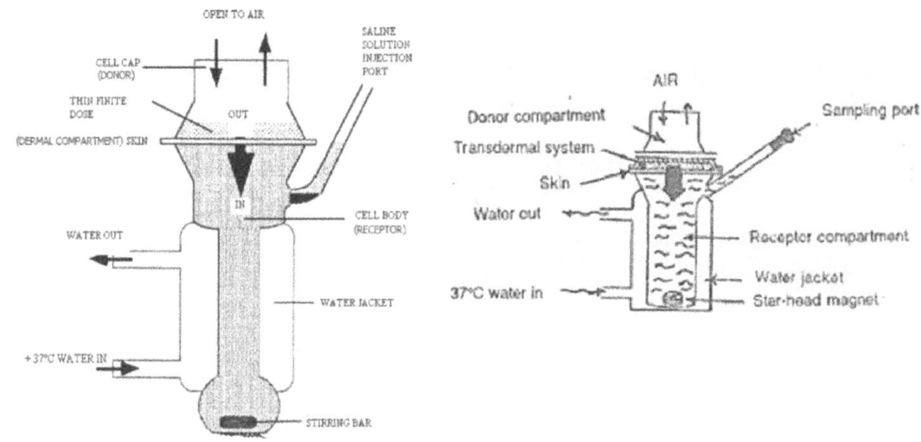


(a) Franz Diffusion cell (b) Keshary-Chein (KC) cell

**Figure 7.5** Vertical Diffusion Cells.

Donor compartment is placed on the receptor compartment and it is clamped with the help of these two clamps, see these are the clamp holders, with the help of them we can put them tightly closed what happens that in between these two compartments we can place a semi permeable membrane which may be natural intestine, natural skin or the artificial membrane which may be made of cellophane as you can see inside this receptor compartment is a internal compartment which is actually the receptor compartment which filled with pH 7.4 phosphate buffer as the receptor media. Generally the volume may be 3.5, 5 or may be 12.5 depending upon the requirement. And you can see the outer jacket it is there to water inlet, water outlet for maintaining the temperature of this whole assembly at the body temperature.

We put the drug into the donor compartment, pre-wet drug is loaded here and we put this donor compartment on the receptor compartment in between that membrane is mounted and then the prefilled receptor compartment which is always on touch with this cellophane membrane what happens that drug starts diffusing from donor compartment slowly to the receptor compartment and for mimicking the agitation, we put small bead inside this receptor compartment and put it upon the magnetic stirrer, the agitation is given there with the help of magnetic stirrer that bead moves inside the receptor compartment and give the required agitation and with the passage of time this is the sampling port, we take out the sample 1mL or 0.5 mL or lesser amount and replace the same amount of pre-warmed media into this receptor compartment and by this way, by analyzing the samples, we can have the idea that with respect to time how much amount of drug is permeated across this membrane. So, this is the purpose of in vitro diffusion cell.

So, you have seen that it is a very small apparatus made up of glass and remember, it is unofficial, it is not official in any pharmacopoeia design and fabrication differs from one model to another model depending upon the requirement or by the inventions made by some scientist like say for example there are two cells Franz diffusion cell and Keshary-Chein cell, you can see and learn the design of the these cells. These are called vertical diffusion cells. There are some horizontal cells also, please search the name of the horizontal diffusion cells.

So, we have learnt that diffusion cells are required for the permeation studies. The permeation studies provide the information of drug permeation across the biological membrane. as . In vitro diffusion cell, gives the permeation profile just like the way the dissolution apparatus/ study give the drug release profile.

## Biopharmaceutical Classification System (BCS)

BCS is Biopharmaceutical Classification System (BCS). It is a drug development tool Proposed by Amidon et al. in 1995based on aqueous solubility and intestinal permeability the drugs are classified into four major classes.

**The rate and extent of drug absorption from solid oral dosage forms depend on three things**

- dissolution,
- solubility and
- Intestinal permeability

## Biopharmaceutical Classification System (BCS)

Depending upon solubility and permeability Amidon 4 box model, it is classified into four classes (Table 7.3 & Table 7.4);

**Table 7.3** Biopharmaceutical Classification System (BCS).

| Class | Solubility | Permeability |
|---|---|---|
| I | High | High |
| II | Low | High |
| III | High | Low |
| IV | Low | Low |

**Table 7.4** Four Box Amidon Model.

| | |
|---|---|
| **1**<br>**High Solubility**<br>**High Permeability** | **2**<br>**Low Solubility**<br>**High Permeability** |
| **3**<br>**High Solubility**<br>**Low Permeability** | **4**<br>**Low Solubility**<br>**Low Permeability** |

## Greater Prevalence of LS

In US, if you go through the top 200 marketed drugs, BCS class I and class II are predominant, and if you see further new chemical entities the prevalence of low solubility drugs is as much as 70 %. BCS class II drugs are 70 %, so this shows the importance of BCS classification (Figure 7.6). That we can have some idea that we can develop the drugs which are having good biopharmaceutical properties with respect to solubility and the permeability.

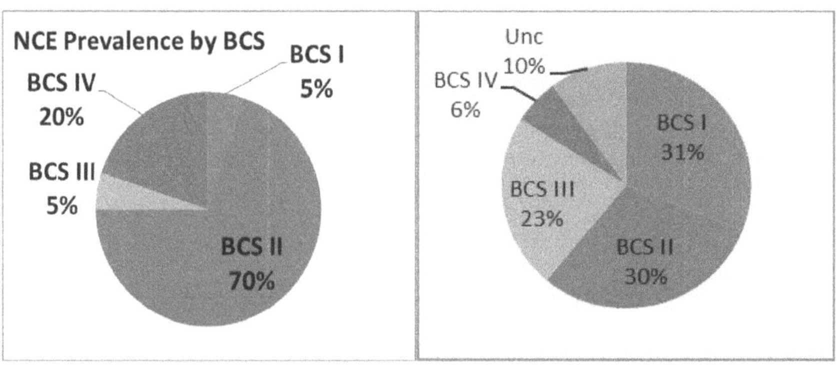


**Figure 7.6** Top 200 marketed drug USA by BCS.
(Source: Takagi et al 2006, Mol. Pharm., 2006; 3(6):631-43)

## Solubility

As far as the solubility is concerned, in the BCS solubility is based on the highest dose strength in an Immediate Release product.

"A drug substance is considered *highly soluble* when the highest strength is soluble in 250 mL or less of aqueous media over the pH range of 1.0-6.8."

Remember it was the limit of pH 1-7.5 earlier, it has been reduced to pH 6.8 in the recent guidelines.

## Permeability

Based directly on the extent of intestinal absorption *in vivo* in humanor indirectly on the *in vivo* drug transfer across the human intestinal membrane as we performed in the diffusion cell .

**"A drug substance is considered *highly permeable* when the extent of intestinal absorption is determined to be 85% or higher."**

## BCS

All the drugs can be classified into these four classes. Say for examples **(Table 7.5)**

**Table 7.5** BCS Class and examples of drugs.

| Class | Examples of the class |
|---|---|
| I | Rofecoxib, Paracetamol, Propranolol, Metoprolol, |
| II | Nimesulide, Nifedipine, Phenytoin, Digoxin |
| III | Acyclovir, atenolol, ranitidine, diphenhydramine |
| IV | Cyclosporin A, Furosemide |

You can learn more of the examples of each of the class. Come back to us in discussion forum we can discuss the things also in the forum.

## BCS: Application

- For correlating the *in vitro* dissolution profiles with *in vivo* bioavailability of drugs
- For developing the *in vitro* dissolution specification
- For developing a strategy for improving the bioavailability of new chemical entities
- For predicting drug bioavailability: solubility or permeability limited.

This is the beauty of BCS that each and every aspect of drug development is need to know about the BCS class of particular drug

## Summary


- Dissolution, a QC test helps to predict the drug release, batch to batch consistency, in vivo performance, bioequivalence and is a regulatory requirement.
- Solubility, Dissolution and permeability govern the absorption of drug after oral ingestion.
- BCS is a drug development tool based on aqueous solubility and intestinal permeability of drugs.
- BCS classifies drugs in four classes (4 Box model).


## Further Readings

- "Industrial Pharmacy-I" SWAYAM MOOC: www.swayam.gov.in
- Semalty A, Dissolution and Biopharmaceutical Classification System, https://youtu.be/UnoV7oO0s3M
- IP/USP
- Abdou HM, Theory of dissolution and Theoretical concepts for the release of a drug from a dosage form. In *Dissolution, Bioavailability and Bioequivalence*, Gennaro A., Migdalof B., Hassert G. L., Medwick T., Eds.; Mack Publishing Company: Easton, PA, 1989
- Dressman JB, Karmer J, *Pharmaceutical Dissolution Testing,* 2005, Taylor and Francis, New York.
- Bayliss et al. 2016, Drug disc. Today, 2016;21(10):1719-27

## References


- Semalty et al. Essentials of Pharmaceutical Technology, II edn, 2018/2019, Pharma med Press, Hyderabad
- Takagi et al 2006, Mol. Pharm., 2006; 3(6):631-43
- WHO Expert Committee on Specifications for Pharmaceutical Preparations, 40th Report, 2006.
- Amidon GL, Lennernas H, Shah VP, Crison JR, *Pharm Res.*1995, 12:413-420.

CHAPTER 8

# Preformulation II Polymerization

**Dr Ajay Semalty**
Department of Pharmaceutical Sciences,
H.N.B Garhwal University (A Central University), Srinagar Garhwal-246174

## Learning Outcome

After completing this chapter, you will be able to understand the **Polymerization** with respect to

- Observe concept of polymerization
- Learn the Importance of polymers
- Use the most suitable polymer in preformulation or formulation development

## Lesson Plan

- Polymerization: basic concept
- Examples
- Application

What is polymerization? First question comes in our mind. Single monomer joined together multiple time to form a polymer.

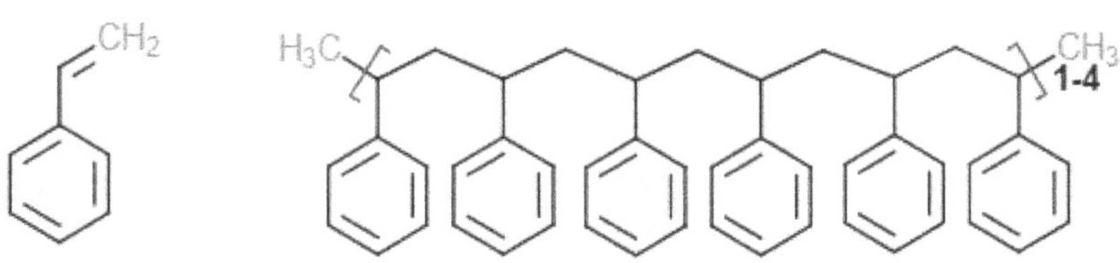


**Figure 8.1** Polystyrene: Polymer of styrene monomer units.

## Styrene Polystyrene

Styrene is a one monomer. We joined it multiple times. It gives polystyrene (Figure 8.1). Polymers are the key to success in formulation development specifically modified dosage forms. For conventional dosage forms also they are useful in binding, disintegrating, coating and other purposes.

## Classification of Polymers

We can classify in many ways. A common classification is on the basis of origin of these polymers.

- Natural: Cellulose, guargum, xanthan gum, chitosan, alginate etc.
- Semisynthetic: Hydroxy ethyl cellulose, HPMC
- Synthetic: SCMC, CA, CAP, MC, EC, PVA, PVP etc.

They may be natural. Depending upon the natural sources, they may be obtained from the plant, animals or marine sources. Depending on that like Cellulose, guargum, xanthan gum, chitosan, alginate. These are natural polymers. Now Semisynthetic which are slightly modified natural polymers. That's why they are called semisynthetic like Hydroxy ethyl cellulose, hydroxyl propyl methyl cellulose (HPMC) etc. Synthetic polymers which are purely synthesized in laboratory like sodium carboxy methyl cellulose (SCMC),cellulose acetate (CA), cellulose acetate phthalate (CAP), methyl cellulose (MC), ethyl cellulose (EC), polyvinyl alcohol (PVA),polyvinyl pyrrolidone (PVP) .

***Search the classification based on the***

- ***Structure of the Monomer Chain***
- ***Polymerization***
- ***Monomers***
- ***Molecular Forces***
- ***Biodegradability***

**Role of polymers in formulation development**

They are used in tablet as binder, disintegrating agent or release modifier etc. They are used in capsule shell manufacturing. They are used in preparation of emulsions, suspensions, gels, modified release tablets, creams, hydrogels etc. In preparation of various noble drug delivery systems (NDDS) like transdermal films, other films microcapsules, microspheres, nanoparticles, liposomes etc. in every NDDS you need a polymer. In modifying the drug release, their kinetics and bioavailability of drugs, polymers are required for targeting of drugs to specific organ, region, or tissue. Polymers are the key to success.

***Let me give you some examples of Matrix-forming agents for hydrophilic matrices.***

Examples include (HPMC) Hydroxypropyl methylcellulose (HV grade). What does HV means? High viscosity grades, PVP (Polyvinyl pyrrolidone), SCMC (Sodium carboxymethyl cellulose), alginates, Xanthan gum, Xanthan gum/locust bean gum combinations and Carbopol. These are matrix forming polymers.

**How do they work actually?**

These kinds of Polymer when react with the water, they forma swollen network (they are formed in the presence of a crosslinking agent). They swell in water but cannot dissolve because of stable crosslinking and are used for formulation of floating tablet/implants etc. So, these matrices help in prolonging the release of drugs.

## Now Other Types of Uses

### Enteric Coating

Cellulose acetate phthalate, hydroxypropyl methylcellulose phthalate, the copolymers of methacrylic acid and their esters and polyvinyl acetate phthalate. These phthalates are used for enteric coating but what they do? How do they show their action? These materials do not dissolve over the gastric pH range but dissolve rapidly at the less acid pH (about 5) or more basic pH associated with the small intestine. Why we need it. You might have seen that enteric coated aspirin is used for avoiding the gastric irritation. This is the enteric coated aspirin. It does not dissolve in gastric environment. It dissolves only when it reaches to the small intestine at the basic pH. So, the polymer used in the way that it does not dissolve in the gastric region because it is the pH sensitive one. Now in the same are colonic delivery systems we can plan. With the help of pH-sensitive polymers like combinations of Eudragit 100-55 (pH 5.5) with Eudragit S (pH 7.0). These polymers can be used for colonic delivery systems. They are used to coat the drug/delivery system with a polymer that is sensitive to bacteria in the colon. Degradation of the polymer permits release of the active drug only in the colonic environment. The polymers used include glassy amylase (which is mixed with ethylcellulose), azo polymers (a group of polymer which is cleaved only by the colonic bacteria), guargum (in the same way colonic bacteria cleave that gum), xanthan gum, Cellulose acetate and Cellulose acetate phthalates. These are the classic examples of polymers which are used for colonic targeting or colonic delivery systems.

### Drug Targeting

It is the hot topic. What is drug targeting?

**Drug targeting is the ability of the drug to accumulate in the target organ or tissue selectively and quantitatively, independent of the site and methods of its administration.**

It is the beauty that with the help of polymers, we can target drug to the site of action.

With the use of polymers in conventional dosage form, the release can be modified and Modified release dosage forms can be developed (**Figure 8.2** & **Figure 8.3**).

**USP defines *"Modified release dosage forms'* as "one for which the drug release characteristics of time course and/or location are chosen to accomplish therapeutic objectives not offered by the conventional dosage forms." Please remember this definition because it is the official definition and cannot be changed.**

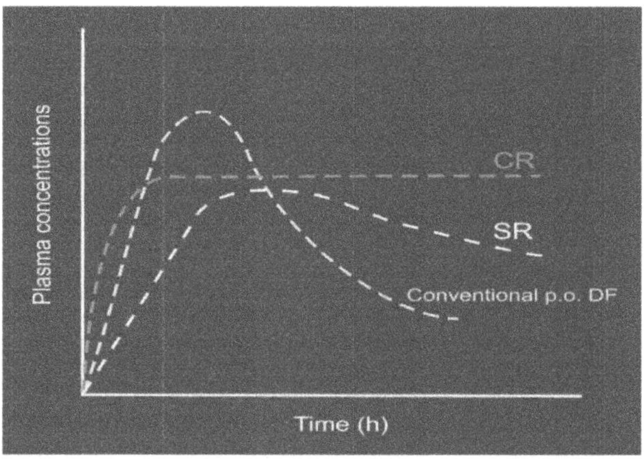


**Figure 8.2** Plasma concentration time profile curve: Conventional and Modified release dosage forms.

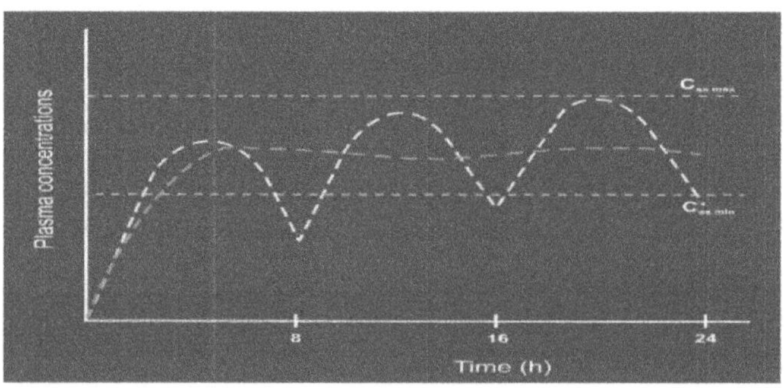


**Figure 8.3** Plasma concentration time profile curve: Conventional and Modified release dosage forms.

Now what are the advantages of Drug targeting. By using drug targeting protocols, we can simplify the drug administration protocols. Drug dosages are greatly reduced, and drug therapy cost is also reduced. Say for example that the drug concentration in the target site is increased without undesirable effects on non-target sites.

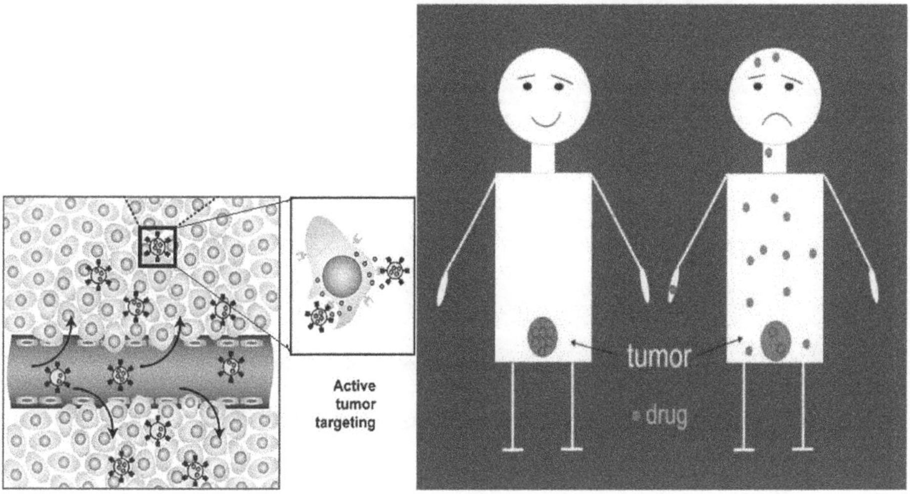


**Figure 8.4** Effect of drug targeting on patient compliance.

You can see that the patient who got the drug distributed across the entire body is suffering while one who is having targeted drug delivery is happier because of better patient compliance, better safety and better effectiveness (**Figure 8.4**). Another example we can take. We can make the smart drug delivery systems. Recently, in Europe market and US market smart insulin drug delivery systems are there (**Figure 8.5**). They are available in market that depending upon pH change in pH of drug, the insulin is released. What happens when pH is 7.4 (normal pH) the system is intact. When glucose level increases, glucose is converted into glucuronic acid and the pH is reduced. In the lower pH, when pH reaches to 4.5 or in between 4-5, that polymer is sensitive to that pH change. In that acidic pH it starts releasing the insulin because at this time it is required and whenever insulin is there the glucose is absorbed more rapidly and again homeostasis like condition is achieved again pH is 7.4. Whenever pH will reach 7.4again that polymer will be intact. Insulin will no more release. So, it is released only when it is required. So, it is a smart polymeric insulin delivery. It is the beauty of polymer that we can give the effectiveness, safety and magical effects to dosage forms or drug delivery systems.

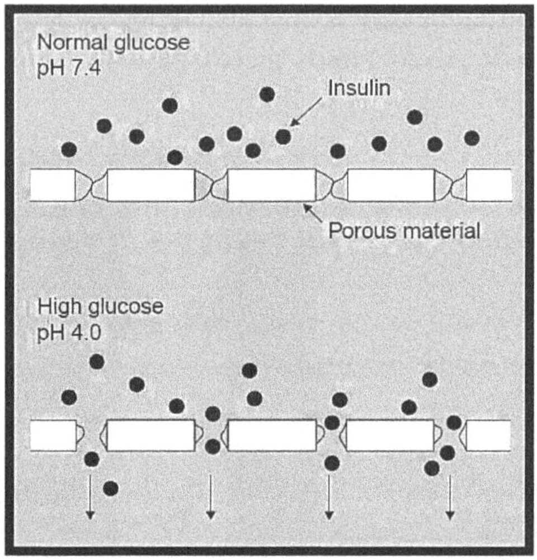


**Figure 8.5** pH Sensitive smart polymeric Insulin delivery.

*Sodium carboxymethylcellulose (SCMC)*

- AVAILABLE IN 2 GRADES Low and high viscosity grades
- Produces clear solutions in both hot and cold water, which are stable over a pH range of about 5-10.
- It is anionic, so it is incompatible with polyvalent cations and the acid will be precipitated at low pH.
- Heat sterilization reduces its viscosity,
- Widely used up to 1 % in topical, oral and parenteral products.

*Microcrystalline cellulose*

- crystals of colloidal dimensions which disperse readily in water (but are not soluble) to produce thixotropic gels.
- It is a widely used suspending agent and the rheological properties of its dispersions can often be improved by the incorporation of additional hydrocolloid like in particular CMC, MC, HPMC
- These stabilize the product against the flocculating effects of added electrolyte.

So, you have to learn about the polymers in the way we listed above. Enlist and classify the polymers in your notebook on these major topics: Chemical nature, Physical properties, Its Solubility, Grades, Response to change in pH, temperature on any other specific property and Major applications. Chalk out the above points for the common polymers which you are seeing in the laboratories and also which you are observing in the text in which you are seeing the major applications with respect to the drug targeting and other examples of drug delivery or modified release dosage forms.

## Summary

Polymers and their polymerization properties may be used to develop suitable dosage form with improved biopharmaceutical and pharmacokinetic properties. Onset, duration, release and targeting can be modified by using suitable polymers.

## Further Readings

- "Industrial Pharmacy-I" SWAYAM MOOC: www.swayam.gov.in
- Semalty A, Novel Drug Delivery Systems, https://youtu.be/QS4_rH08V-E
- Semalty A, Polymers in NDDS, https://youtu.be/NecSxqI0akI
- Semalty A, Targeted Drug Delivery-I, https://youtu.be/8PfYDxpu6YA
- Semalty A, Targeted Drug Delivery-II, https://youtu.be/Uo-CaS8gUaM
- IP/ USP
- Gibson M. (Ed), Pharmaceutical preformulation and formulation: a practical guide from candidate drug selection to commercial dosage form, II edn, Informa Healthcare.
- Qiu Y, Chang Y and Zhang GZ (Exe. Eds), Developing solid oral dosage forms: Pharmaceutical theory and practice, Elsevier, 2009
- Handbook of Pharmaceutical Excipients, CRC Press
- Niazi SK, Handbook of Preformulation, Informa health care, 2007.

## References


- Semalty et al. Essentials of Pharmaceutical Technology, II edn, 2018, Pharma med Press, Hyderabad
- Targeted drug delivery, *ACS Nano 2009, DOI: 10.1021/nn900002m*
- Synthetic Polymers, https://www.youtube.com/watch?v=LWxoDV-Ll8k

CHAPTER 9

# Tablets I Introduction

**Dr Ajay Semalty**
Department of Pharmaceutical Sciences,
H.N.B Garhwal University (A Central University), Srinagar Garhwal-246174

## Learning Outcome

After completing this chapter, you will be able to understand the

- Define tablet and enumerate its advantages and disadvantages
- Classify tablets.
- Practice tablet granulation for tablet manufacturing

## Lesson Plan

- Definition and ideal properties
- Advantages, Disadvantages, and Classification of tablets.
- Types and classification of excipients
- Basic steps of Formulation of tablets,
- Granulation methods: process, factors and equipment
  - Wet Granulation (WG)
  - Dry Granulation (DG)

## Tablets

Tablets are the most common and convenient dosage form. About 70% of the total medicines are in Tablet form.

**"Tablets are solid, flat or biconvex dishes, unit dosage form, prepared by compressing a drug or a mixture of drugs, with or without diluents."**

Do you know what unit dosage form is? The dosage form which deliver one single unit of dosage of the drug. Tablet is a unit dosage form. Can you tell any other example of unit dosage form? And multi-unit dosage form?

## Ideal Characteristics of Tablets

A tablet should have the following ideal properties.

- Elegant product identity
- Free of defects like chips, cracks, discoloration, and contamination
- Sufficient strength (to withstand mechanical shock and agitation during its production, packaging, shipping, and dispensing.
- Chemical stability: shelf life
- Physical stability: color, physical integrity like shape etc.
- Release the drug in desired and reproducible manner.

## Advantages of Tablet Dosage Forms

Tablet has a number of advantages, one of the major advantages over capsule, is that tablet is an essentially tamperproof doses form. Other potential advantages of tablets are as followed:

- These are the unit dosage forms which offer the greatest flexibility (with respect to doses) of all oral doses forms.
- Its cost is lowest of all oral dosage forms.
- These are the lightest and most compact of all oral doses forms.
- These are in general the easiest and cheapest to package and ship of all oral dosage forms.
- Product identification is simplest and cheapest, requiring no additional processing steps.
- These may provide the greatest ease of swallowing with least tendency for "hang-up' above stomach, especially when coated, provided that tablet disintegration is not excessively rapid.
- These are better suited to large scale production than other unit oral forms.
- These have best combined properties of chemical, mechanical, and microbiological stability of all the oral forms.
- Objectionable odor and bitter taste can be masked by coating technique.
- Generally, more stable than liquids with longer expiration dates.
- Release rate of the drug from tablet can be tailored to meet pharmacological requirements.

## Disadvantages of Tablet Dosage Form

- Drugs which are destroyed in stomach cannot be prepared in tablets e.g proteins/peptides etc.
- Drugs with bitter taste or odour cannot be formulated in tablets without modification (capsules may be tried)
- Peak and valley effect in plasma time concentration curve for IR dosage forms
- The drug with too short half-life can not be formulated.

## Classification of Tablets (USP)

**I. Immediate-release tablet**

- Disintegrating tablet (conventional tablet)
- Chewable tablets
- Effervescent tablets
- Sublingual and Buccal tablets
- Lozenges

**II. Modified-release tablet**

- Extended-release
- Delayed-release

**I. Immediate-release tablet**

***Conventional/Disintegrating tablet***

It is the most common type of tablets. It is released rapidly after administration. It is intended to be swallowed and undergo disintegration and dissolution in the GIT. The commonly required excipients in these are filler (with low dose drug), disintegrant, binder, glidant, lubricant and antiadherent.

***Chewable tablets***

These tablets are designed for children and elderly people and can be taken without water. The tablet is to be chewed and thus mechanically disintegrated in the mouth, so that no disintegrant is included in its composition. Its important excipients are Flavoring, sweetening and coloring agents. e.g. Chewable Antacid tablets

***Effervescent tablets***

The effervescent tablet is dropped into a glass of water before administration during which Carbon di oxide ($CO_2$) is liberated. It can be taken without water.

It facilitates rapid tablet disintegration and drug dissolution. The special packaging is needed to avoid exposure of these tablets to moisture. It is used to obtain rapid drug action e.g Effervescent antacid tablets. The important excipients of these tablets are acid with alkali effervescing compound, flavoring, and coloring agents

## Sublingual and Buccal tablets

They are used for drug release in mouth for systemic delivery by avoiding first pass metabolism. Here the drug diffuses into the blood, directly through tissues under the tongue in case of sublingual tablets and through oral mucosa in case of buccal tablets. It facilitates rapid tablet disintegration and drug dissolution. For example, Nitroglycerin sublingual tablet exerts its action within two minutes for rapid relief of "Angina pectoris" attack, because the sublingual area is rich in blood supply. Nitroglycerine suffers from first-pass metabolism if taken orally.

***Lozenges***

These are the tablets which dissolve slowly in the mouth. These are used for local medications in the mouth or throat, e.g. local anesthetics, antiseptics and antibiotics and for systemic drug uptake. In the lozenges no disintegrant is included. Other additives (binder and filler) must have pleasant taste.

**II. Modified-Release Tablets**

According to the USP/NF the term 'modified release dosage forms' is defined as **"one for which the drug release characteristics of time course and/or location are chosen to accomplish therapeutic objectives not offered by the conventional dosage forms."**

***Classification***

Modified release dosage forms may be classified into two types (Figure 9.1).

- Extended-release
- Delayed release

***Extended-release Tablets***

It is defined as the one that allows at least a twofold reduction in the dosing frequency as compared to that of conventional (immediate release) dosage form. For example: controlled release or sustained release tablets

***Delayed release Tablets***

"the dosage form that releases a discrete portion or portions of drug at a time (or times) other than promptly after administration." -USP

Enteric coated tablets are the example of delayed release dosage forms

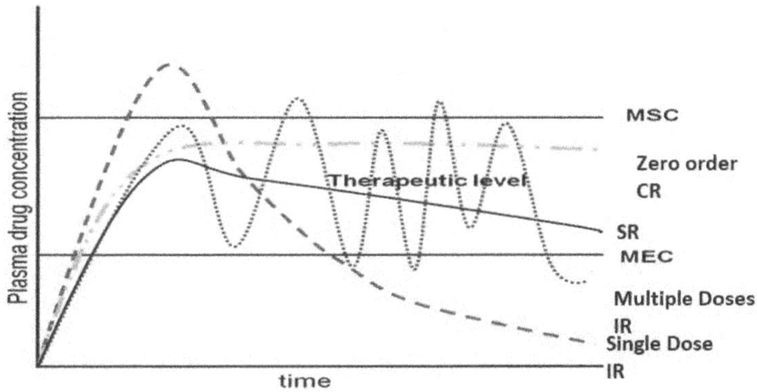


**Figure 9.1** Plasma Concentration Time profile Curve for Immediate release and Modified Release dosage form.

## Excipients

"An excipient is an inactive substance used as a carrier for the active ingredients of a medication".

The excipients are selected on the basis nature of drug, nature of other excipients, compatibility with drug and other excipients and the desired release or performance characteristics of tablet.

### Classification of Excipients

A. **Primary Excipients:** The primary excipients impart satisfactory compression characteristics to the formulation. E.g. diluents, binders, glidants and lubricants

B. **Secondary Excipients:** The secondary excipients give additional desirable physical characteristics to the finished tablet. e.g. disintegrants, coloring, flavoring and sweetening agents.

### Filler / Diluent

Filler or diluents add bulk to the tablet for compression and easy handling. Diluents weigh 10 to 20 fold of the dosage of API. E.g. Glucose, Sodium chloride, Sucrose, Mannitol (chewable tablet, freely soluble in water, cool taste), Microcrystaline Cellulose (excellent compression property, highly stable and disintegrating property).

## Binder

Do you remember why we need cement to build a house? Binder is added for cohesive strength after compression. e.g. Acacia mucilage, Gelatin, providone (PVP), Starch mucilage

## Disintegrant

Tablet is needed to be dissolved in GI fluid for getting absorbed and for getting dissolved it is needed to be disintegrate in smaller particles **(Figure 9.2 & 9.3)**.

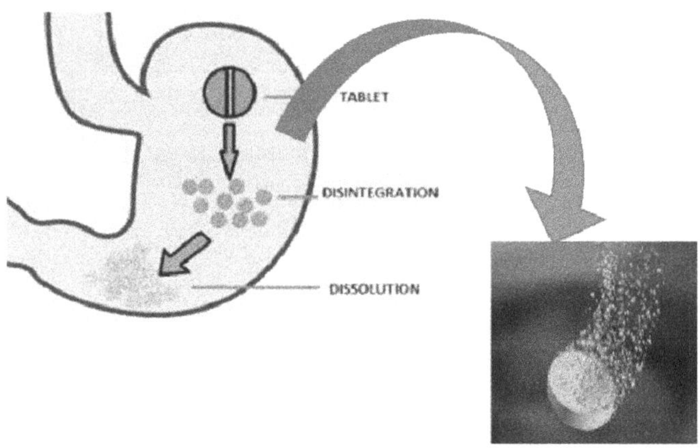


**Figure 9.2** The disintegration process.

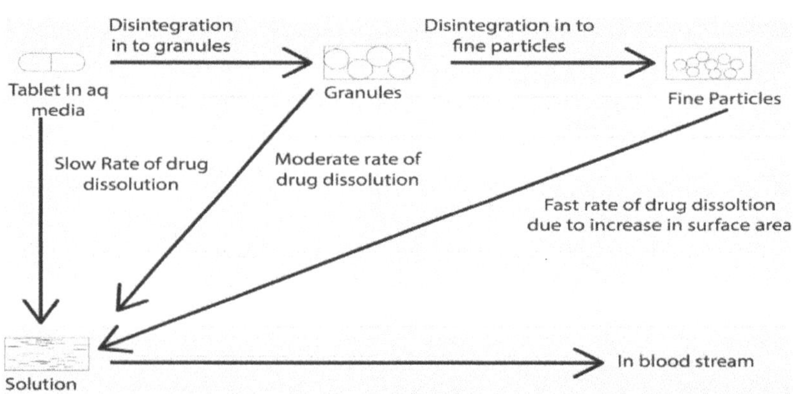


**Figure 9.3** Importance of disintegration.

The disintegrants make the tablet to break down in smaller particles after oral ingestion.

E.g. crospovidone, croscarmellose sodium, sodium starch glycolate etc.

## Glidant

Glidants are used for reducing the friction between particles. Glidants improve the flow properties of tablet granules and powders during processing (mixing, moving for compression etc). e.g. Corn starch, Talc, Colloids silicates.

## Lubricant

Lubricants ensure that tablet possess a smooth surface. Lubricants act by reducing the friction between tablet wall and die walls. e.g. Talc, stearic acid, silicates.

## Antiadherent

The antiadherents stop the powder from sticking to the equipment as the tablet is being made. Exp- Talc, Magnesium stearate, Starch derivatives.

## Miscellaneous

Colors, flavors etc.

## Manufacturing Tablet

Tablet is the most complex Dosage form. The tablet manufacturing is an art as well as a science. It consists of the two important steps:

Step1: Blending of drug with excipients (mixing and granulating) and;

Step 2: Compression (by punches onto die cavity)

Direct compression (skipping granulation) may be practiced for drug and excipients with good compatibility and low stickiness (but not always feasible)

## Mixing and Granulation

"Granulation is the process of combining particles together by creating bonds between them"

The definition is looking typical? Let me make it simpler for you

Have you seen preparation of besan (gram flour) laddu (sweet)?

Coarse besan or fine besan?

Why the coarse besan is needed? Because it has the good binding.

### Objectives of granulation

Conversion Powder to granules is granulation and it is performed with the following objectives.

- To assure an even distribution of the active compound in the final tablet
- To ensure content uniformity due to narrow size range
- To increase the density for easy storage and shipment
- To improve flow and compaction

There are several different methods of granulation. The most popular, which is used by over 70% of formulation in tablet manufacture is wet granulation. Dry granulation is another method used to form granules.

### Mechanism of Granulation

The granulation occurs due to following events.

- Wetting
- Nucleation
- Coalescence/ growth
- Consolidation
- Attrition/ breakage
- By solid bridges/ chemical reaction/ sintering/ crystallization/ deposition of particles/ adhesive and cohesive forces of High viscous binders

### Wet Granulation

Imagine preparing dough for chapati

What do you need for that?

Yes...water in optimum amount

"using a liquid binder (in optimum amount) to lightly agglomerate the powder mixture"

Wet granulation is a process of using a liquid binder to lightly agglomerate the powder mixture (**Figure 9.4**). The amount of liquid must be properly controlled, as over-wetting will cause the granules to be too hard and under-wetting will cause them to be too soft and friable. Aqueous solutions have the advantage of being safer to deal with than solvent based systems.

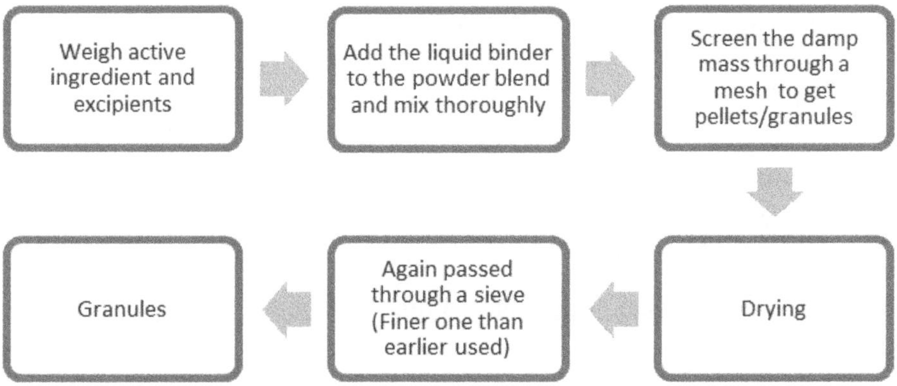


**Figure 9.4** The wet Granulation Process.

**Figure 9.5** Fluidized bed granulator.

## Fluidized Bed Granulation (FBG)

FBG is a multiple step wet granulation process. It is All in one process: pre-heat, granulate, and dry the powders. It allows close control of the granulation process.

It's a huge equipment and it is used in mixing/granulation, drying and film coating (**Figure 9.5**). The lower part contains a perforated basket of SS which contains the mixture to be granulated. The air enters from the bottom of the perforated basket. The particles are uplifted with the stream of air. The fountain like movement of particles is called Wurster process. The granulating fluid is sprayed (Top/bottom or tangential spray). At a stage the bed of solid become fluidized and behaves like fluid. Hence it is called FBG or FBD.

**Factors affecting granulation**

- Blend factors: Particle size of the drug and excipients
- Binder factor: Type, Volume and concentration of binder
- Granulation process factor: granulation time, equipment and drying rate

## Dry Granulation

Dry granulation (DG) is done for moisture and heat sensitive products and the products which are not compressed well after WG. It is done without the use of liquid binder. It is simpler than wet granulation and is a low-cost technique. The DG involves creating granules by light compaction of the powder blend under low pressures. The prepared slugs are broken into granules (Figure 9.6).

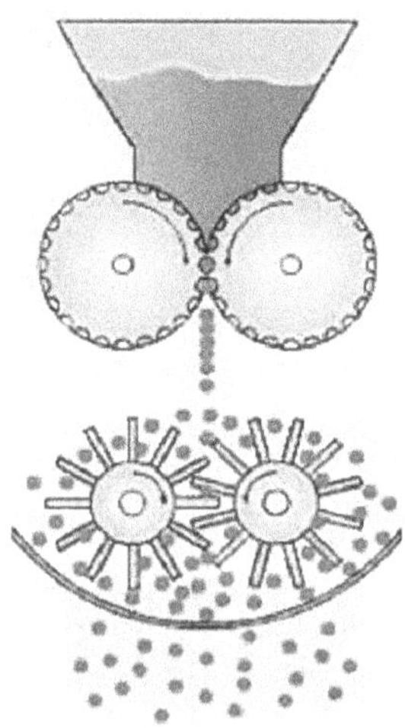

**Figure 9.6** Dry granulator (general diagram).

## Process of DG

- Milling (Cutter Mill)
- Mixing (Sigma Blade Mixer)
- Slugging
- Screening (Oscillating Granulator)
- Mixing with Disintegrant and Lubricant
- Compression

## Equipment for granulation

The granulation may be done by any of the following equipment. The choice of the equipment depends on various factors like nature of drug, type of product desired etc.

- Roller compaction, extrusion spheronization, spray drying equipment
- Low shear/ High shear granulators
- Fluidized Bed Dryer (FBD)
- Continuous spouted bed
- High shear granulator (with the help of counter current operating blades) e.g. RMG (Rapid Mixer Granulator).

## New Advanced Techniques

There are many advanced techniques which have made the granulation easier than the conventional granulators. These techniques and their salient features as followed (**Table 9.1**).

- Steam Granulation,
- Melt Granulation,
- Moisture Activated Dry Granulation (MADG),
- Moist Granulation Technique (MGT),
- Thermal Adhesion Granulation Process (TAGP),
- Extrusion-spheronization (ES),
- Continuous twin screw wet granulation (cTSWG)

**Table 9.1** The advanced techniques in Granulation.

| Technique | Description |
|---|---|
| Steam Granulation | Modification of wet granulation; steam is used as a binder in place of water |
| Melt Granulation / Thermoplastic Granulation | Granulation is done by addition of meltable binder (binder is in solid state at room temperature but melts in the temperature range of 50 – 80°C). |
| Moisture Activated Dry Granulation (MADG) | Minimal moisture addition, distribution and agglomeration. No drying step is required. Water distribution is via high shear mixer, or low-shear mixer with highly atomized water spray |
| Moist Granulation Technique (MGT) | Works on the principle of MADG. A small amount granulating fluid is added to activate dry binder and to facilitate agglomeration. Then a moisture absorbing material like Microcrystalline Cellulose (MCC) is added to absorb any excess moisture. |
| Thermal Adhesion Granulation Process (TAGP) | Used for preparing direct tableting; performed under low moisture content or low content of pharmaceutically acceptable solvent by subjecting a mixture containing excipients to heating at a temperature in the range from about 30°C to 130°C in a closed system under mixing by tumble rotation until the formation of granules. |
| Foam Granulation | Liquid binders are added as aqueous foam. |
| Extrusion-spheronization (ES) | Extrusion (forming a raw material into a product of uniform shape and density by forming it through an orifice or die under controlled conditions) followed by spheronization (a rapid and flexible process where wet extruded mass is converted to small spheres) through multi step processing |
| Continuous twin screw wet granulation (cTSWG) | Advanced technique of ES; Preblend of crystalline poorly soluble API and amorphous polymer is charged into Twin screw granulator |

## Summary

- Tablets are unit dosage forms which are the most common, cost effective, and convenient dosage forms
- Tablets may be of different types: IR or modified release.
- Various excipients with different functions are needed

- Mixing, granulation and compression are three important steps in manufacturing of tablets.
- Wet and dry granulation are two methods of granulation

## Further Readings

- "Industrial Pharmacy-I" SWAYAM MOOC: www.swayam.gov.in
- Semalty A, Spray Drying, https://youtu.be/DQYKq1DWYPc

- Aulton ME (ED), Pharmaceutics: The science of Dosage form design, II edn, Churchill Livingstone, London, 2002.
- Semalty et al., Essentials of Pharmaceutical Technology, II Edn, 2018, Pharma Med press, Hyderabad, India
- Qiu Y, Chang Y and Zhang GZ (Exe. Eds), Developing solid oral dosage forms: Pharmaceutical theory and practice, Elsevier, 2009.

## References/ Credits


- USP-40
- Semalty et al., Essentials of Pharmaceutical Technology, II Edn, 2018, Pharma Med press, Hyderabad, India

## CHAPTER 10

# Tablets II
# Manufacturing Tablets

**Dr Ajay Semalty**
Department of Pharmaceutical Sciences,
H.N.B Garhwal University (A Central University), Srinagar Garhwal-246174

### Learning Outcome

After completing this chapter, you will be able to

- Identify various factors of Tablet punching and the process
- Identify the steps of compression
- Enumerate and identify tablet defects

### Lesson Plan

- Basic preparation method of Tablet
- Tablet punching (equipment & process)
- Concept of compression
- Processing problems/ Tablet defects

## Tablets Manufacturing

Tablet manufacturing is all about MGC.

- Mixing (drug and excipients)
- Granulation
- **Compression (Tablet punching)**

  We have discussed mixing and granulation, now let's discuss compression.

## Tablet Punching Machine

A standard tablet compression machines consist of following components.

- **Hopper:** for temporary storing the material for compressing.
- **Feed frame:** for distributing the materials into the dies.

- **Dies:** for controlling the size and the shape of the tablet.
- **Punches**: for compressing the materials within the dies.

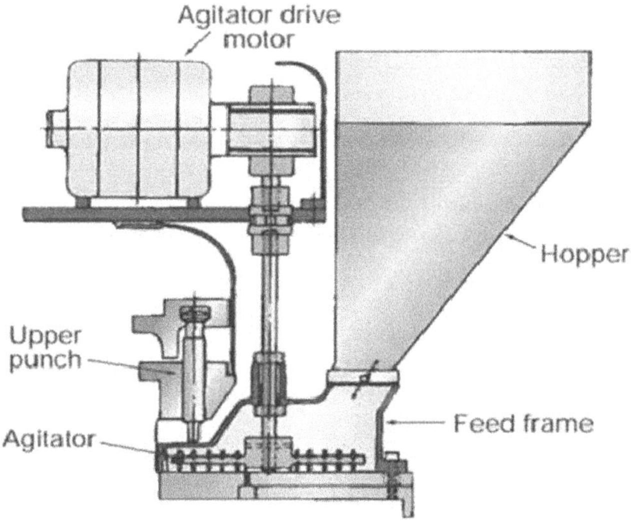


**Figure 10.1** Hopper.
*Courtesy:* Induced die feeder, Ansel's Pharmaceutical Dosage Forms and Drug Delivery Systems. Philadelphia: Lipincott Williams and Wilkins.

## Hopper

Have you seen wheat flour mill? The upper funnel like part is hopper and it is more or less same in tablet punching machine (Figure 10.1). Flow properties govern the movement of blend through hopper.

## Feed Frame

This part govern the movement of powder to die fill (Figure 10.1). The powder/ granules moving to die fill are guided by feed frame.

## Die Fill

Die is filled with blend through hopper (Figure 10.2). Fill weight is adjusted to govern the final weight of tablets.

**Figure 10.2** Die.

## Punches

Compaction is done by punches. Upper punch moves with pressure onto the die filled with blend. Compression force governs the hardness and friability of tablets.

### Tablet Punching Machines

A tablet compression machine compresses a powder in the dies and ejects them in the form of tablets. The basic steps in compaction cycle are mentioned in the following Figure 10.3.

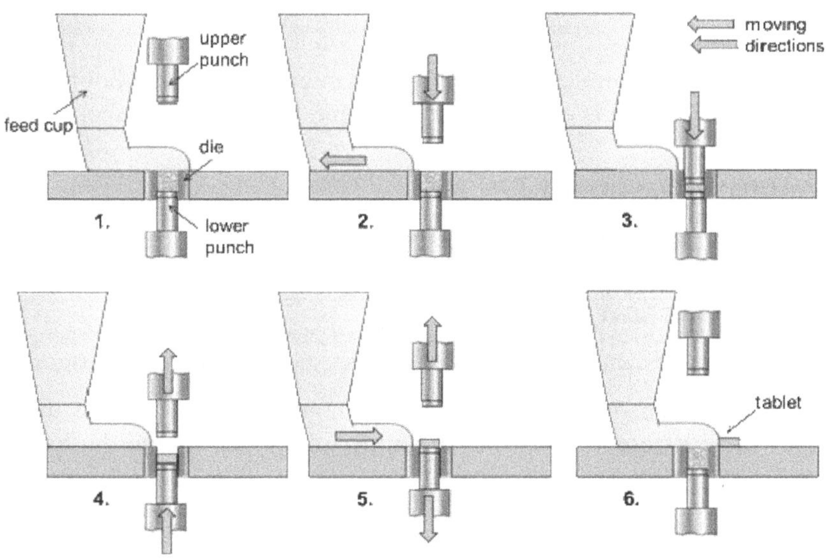


**Figure 10.3** The basic steps in compaction cycle.
*https://www.saintyco.com*

## The Compaction Cycle

A typical complete tablet manufacturing cycle consists of the four steps **(Figure 10.3 & Figure 10.4)**:

(i) Die filling,
(ii) fill weight adjustment,
(iii) Tablet compaction and
(iv) Tablet ejection (from the die).

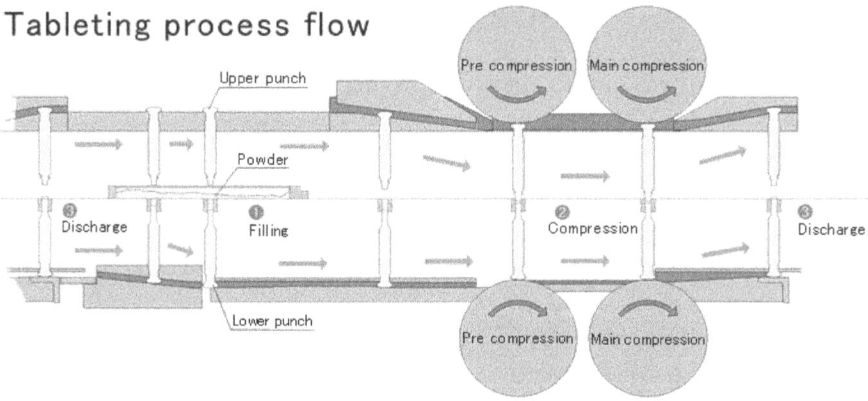


**Figure 10.4** Process flow in tablet punching.

## Die Filling

Flow of powder (or granules) of the drug and excipients from a hopper into the die fills the die. The die is closed at its lower end by the lower punch.

### Fill Weight Adjustment

Using vibration fill weight adjustment

### Tablet Compaction

The upper punch descends powder is compressed until a tablet is formed.

The lower punch may be stationary or moving upward in the die. After maximum applied force is reached, the upper punch leaves the die by moving upward.

### Tablet Ejection

The lower punch rises up until its tip reaches the die top. The tablet is subsequently removed by a pushing device.

## Types of Tablet Press

The tablet presses may be of various types.

- Single punch: One pair of punch and a die
- Rotary punching machine (16 station, 49 station)

Process flow of tableting in rotary tablet press can be seen as animated working model or GIF in https://en.wikipedia.org/wiki/Tablet_press (Figure 10.5).

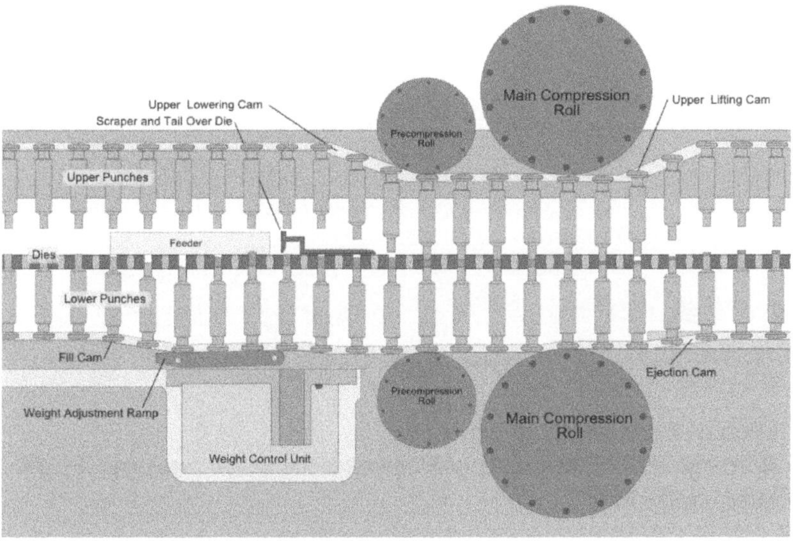


**Figure 10.5** Process flow of tableting in Rotary Tablet Press.

## Compression and Consolidation in Tablet Manufacturing

Tablet formation is one of the most complex process which involves the volume reduction of a blend of particles/granules (compression) followed by consolidation (into a defined solid dosage form/ tablet). So, tablet manufacturing or the tablet compaction consists of two steps

**Step I:** Compression (volume reduction)

**Step II:** Consolidation (shaping in tablet)

**Step I: Compression (volume reduction)**

For volume reduction granules/powder is placed in a die and then a set of punches reduce the volume by pressing the powder.

**Step II: Consolidation (shaping in tablet)**

The process of compaction can be described by a set of events or phases (Figure 10.6 & Figure 10.7). The initial volume reduction of particles leads to their rearrangement which in turn results into a closer packing structure. After a threshold rearrangement point , further reduction beyond the point in compact volume results in the elastic (reversible), viscoelastic and plastic (irreversible) deformation of the particles along with the particle fragmentation. These processes finally lead to the formation of interparticulate bonds which may later break thereby facilitating further compression or compaction.

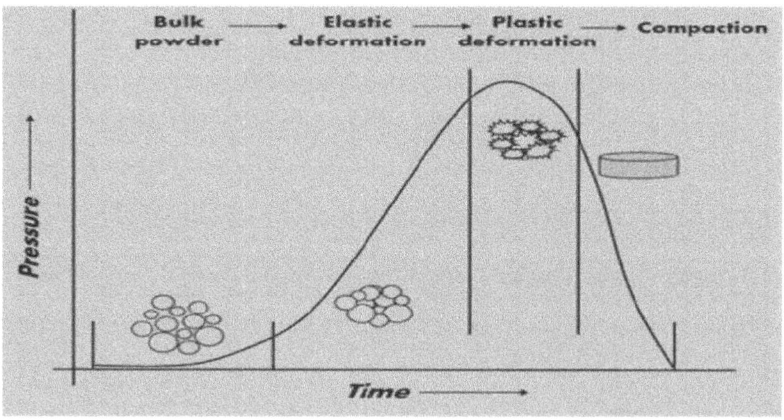


**Figure 10.6** Punch and die stress vs. time.
*(adapted from Semalty et al., Essentials of Pharmaceutical Technology, II Edn Pharma Med Press, Hyderabad)*

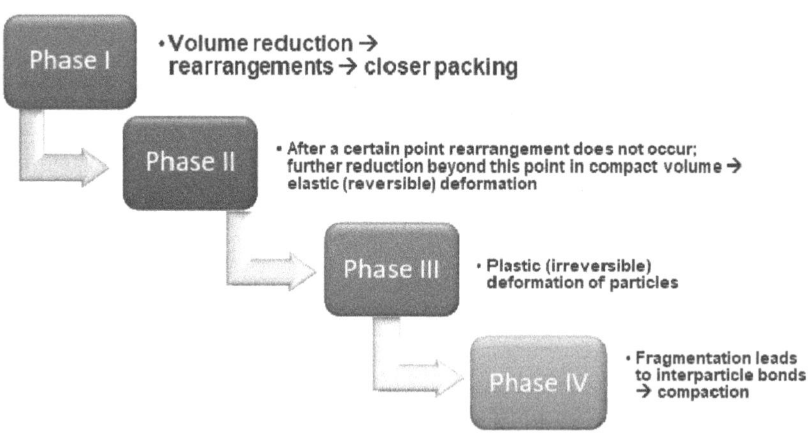


**Figure 10.7** Compression and consolidation in tablet manufacturing.

Therefore, the process of compaction of a powder include following steps:

1. Particle rearrangement
2. Elastic, viscoelastic and plastic deformation of particles
3. Fragmentation of particles
4. Formation of interparticulate bonds

The type of bonds during tablet formation may be of following types:

1. Mechanical interlocking (between irregularly shaped particles)
2. Interparticulate attraction force s (e.g., intermolecular force s, such as Van der Waal forces. electrostatic forces. and hydrogen bonding)
3. Solid bridges (due to melting)

## Volume reduction mechanism during compression

The Heckel equation is among the most popular methods used in pharmaceutical research to determine the volume reduction mechanism during compression. According to the relationship, the degree of compact densification with increasing compression pressure is directly proportional to the porosity.

Heckel plots are helpful to identify the predominant deformation behavior of the material between substances that consolidate by fragmentation and those which consolidate by plastic deformation.

Empirical evidence shows that materials with low mean yield pressures undergo plastic deformation, whereas, tableting materials with high mean yield pressure tend to be brittle and consolidate via fragmentation. Based on Heckel plots and the compaction behavior of materials can be classified into three types, A (MCC, corn starch, maize starch), B (lactose and di calcium phosphate), and C **(Figure 10.8)**.

Inspite of several criticism Heckel relationship is still the most common method of studying the compression behavior of pharmaceutical powders/granules in R&D and F&D of pharmaceutical solids. Other compaction analyses include Kawakita equation, mechanical analysis, 3D viscoelastic analysis, Hiestand tableting indices etc.

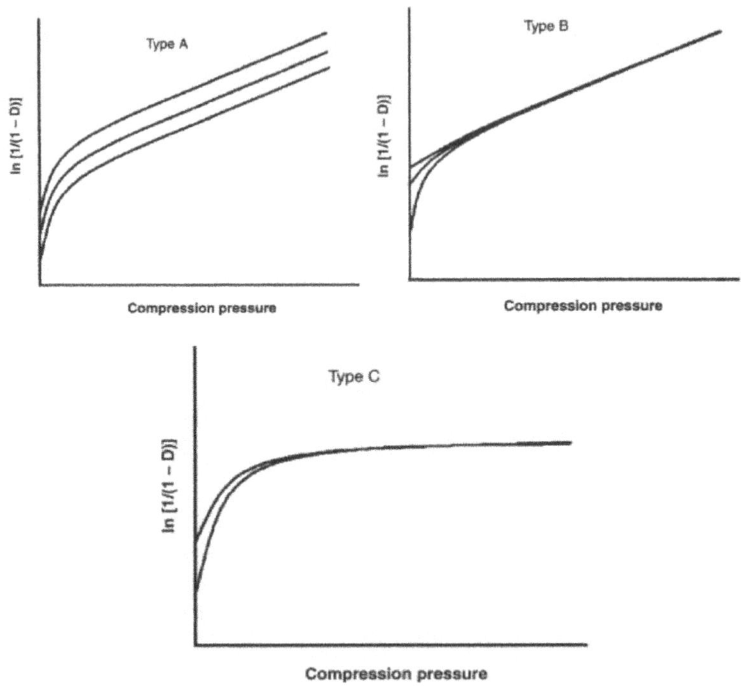


**Figure 10.8** Three phases of particle deformation shown by a typical Heckel plot. (adapted from Augsburger LL, Hoag SW (Eds), Pharmaceutical Dosage Forms: Tablets, Volume 1, III Edn, Informa healthcare, 2008)

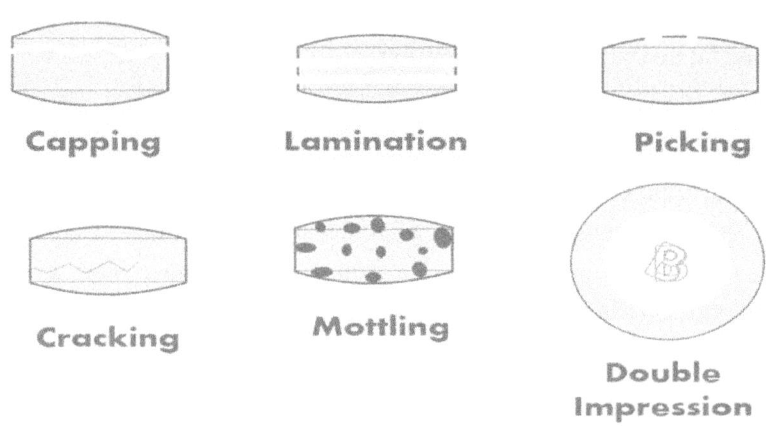


**Figure 10.9** Tablet Defects.
(adapted from Semalty et al., Essentials of Pharmaceutical Technology, II Edn Pharma Med Press, Hyderabad)

## Tablet Defects

The tablet manufacturing is a multivariable complex process. Mixing, drying, spraying, moisture, sieving, use of suitable nature and amount of excipients, process and equipment are some of the many factors which govern the tablet manufacturing process. Therefore, there are chances of many defects, if a single factor is not managed properly. The common tablet defects, their causes and remedies are as followed **(Figure 10.9 & Table 10.1)**.

**Table 10.1** Causes and Remedies of Tablet Defects.

| Tablet Defect | Causes | Remedy |
|---|---|---|
| **Capping**<br>Partial or complete separation of top or bottom crowns of a tablet from the main body of tablet<br>**Lamination**<br>Separation of tablet in two or more distinct layers | • Air entrapment in the granules<br>• Rapid decompression<br>• Deep concave punches<br>• Use of too dry granulation tends to cap or laminate for lack of cohesion<br>• Incorrect setup at the press | • **Precompression**- Slowing the rate of tableting or reducing the final compression pressure.<br>• Use of flat punches<br>• Maintenance of optimum moisture in the processing of granulation<br>• Use of special durable dies with tungsten carbide insert |
| **Picking**<br>Surface materials from a tablet that is sticking to the punch and being removed from the tablet surface is *picking.*<br>**Sticking**<br>It refers to tablet materials adhering to the die wall. | • Adhesion of materials to the punch faces<br>• Over-wetting the tablets, by under-drying, or by poor tablet quality.<br>• Tablet material sticking to the punch tips with engraving or embossing | • Use of large lettering on punches with small diameter<br>• Reformulation of tablets to large size<br>• Plating of the punch faces with chromium<br>• Addition of colloidal silica to the granules as polishing agents<br>• Use of more or new binder to increase cohesiveness of tablets<br>• Addition of more high melting point lubricants/ reduction of low m.p. lubricants |

**Table 10.1** ***Contd...***

| Tablet Defect | Causes | Remedy |
|---|---|---|
| **Mottling**<br>It is an unequal distribution of colors on a tablet with light and dark areas on tablet surface. | • Use of a drug whose color differs from tablet excipients<br>• Use of a drug whose dehydration products are colored<br>• Migration of dyes to the surface of a granulation during drying | • Changing the Solvent system<br>• Reduction of drying temperature<br>• Dispersing a dry color additive during powder binding steps. |
| **Weight Variation**<br>Variation of tablet weight beyond the acceptable limits | • Non uniform granule size and size distribution<br>• Poor Flow through the feed frame<br>• Punch variation<br>• Poor design of the granulation hopper<br>• Poor mixing | • Addition or increase of a glidant like talcum, colloidal silica.<br>• Use of vibrators attached to the hopper<br>• Use of well-designed hopper |
| **Double Impression**<br>Faulty engraving by punches with monogram or engraving | • Slight rotation of punch after precompression | • using non-rotating cam track |

(Adapted from Semalty et al., Essentials of Pharmaceutical Technology, II Edn Pharma Med Press, Hyderabad)

## Summary

- Tablet manufacturing involves Mixing, Granulation and Compaction (MGC).
- We discussed tablet punching tools and the process
- After M & G Tablet compaction cycle involves Die filling, fill weight adjustment and Tablet compaction
- Compression and consolidation are two basic stages of compaction.
- Compaction is mediated by Particle rearrangement, Elastic, viscoelastic and plastic deformation of particles, Fragmentation of particles, and Formation of interparticulate bonds
- Capping, lamination, picking sticking, mottling, weight variation and double impression are the major tablet defects.

## Further Readings


- "Industrial Pharmacy-I" SWAYAM MOOC: www.swayam.gov.in
- Semalty A, Spray Drying, https://youtu.be/DQYKq1DWYPc
- Banker GS, Rhodes CT, Modern Pharmaceutics, CRC Press.
- Aulton ME (ED), Pharmaceutics: The science of Dosage form design, II edn, Churchill Livingstone, London, 2002.
- Semalty et al., Essentials of Pharmaceutical Technology, II Edn, 2018, Pharma Med press, Hyderabad, India
- Qiu Y, Chang Y and Zhang GZ (Exe. Eds), Developing solid oral dosage forms: Pharmaceutical theory and practice, Elsevier, 2009.


## References


- USP-40
- Ansel's Pharmaceutical Dosage Forms and Drug Delivery Systems. Philadelphia: Lipincott Williams and Wilkins.
- https://en.wikipedia.org/wiki/Tablet_press
- Augsburger LL, Hoag SW (Eds), Pharmaceutical Dosage Forms: Tablets, Volume 1, III Edn, Informa healthcare, 2008
- Semalty et al., Essentials of Pharmaceutical Technology, II Edn, 2018, Pharma Med press, Hyderabad, India
- https://www.saintyco.com

CHAPTER 11

# Tablets III
# Tablet Coating

**Dr Ajay Semalty**
Department of Pharmaceutical Sciences,
H.N.B Garhwal University (A Central University), Srinagar Garhwal-246174

### Learning Outcome

After completing this chapter, you will be able to

- Identify and distinguish between different methods of tablet coating
- Learn the basics of coating equipment
- Identify the tablet coating defects and take the steps to avoid / remove defects.

### Lesson Plan

- Tablet coating: Types Coating materials, formulation of coating composition,
- Methods of coating,
- Equipment employed and
- Defects in coating: Definitions, causes and remedies

## Tablet Coating

Tablets may be coated or uncoated. Various tablet coatings are done for various purposes. The main purposes of coating are given as below.

***We can learn the same with (PMMAIS)***

- Protection of the drug from the surrounding (environment) (air, light and moisture) and thus improve stability.
- Modifying drug release, as in enteric coating and extended-release formulation.
- Masking unpleasant taste or odour of the drug & batch differences in the appearance of raw materials
- Appearance: Improving product appearance

- Identification: Facilitating rapid identification by the manufacturer, the pharmacist and the patient (mostly colored).
- Strength: Increasing the mechanical strength of the product.

## Types of Tablet Coating Processes

Tablet coating may be of three major types.

- **Sugar coating**
- **Film coating**
- **Compression coating**

### Sugar coating

The sugar coating comprises of successive application of sucrose-based coating solution to tablet cores in suitable equipment. In principle, in the sugar coating, water evaporates from the syrup leaving a thick sugar layer around each tablet. Sugar coated tablets are shiny and highly colored.

In the sugar coating, the tablets are taken in a rotating coating pan for uniform application of coating solutions which is gently poured or sprayed, portion wise onto the tablets with warm air blown to hasten drying (**Figure 11.1**). In the process, the second coat is given after drying of previous one.

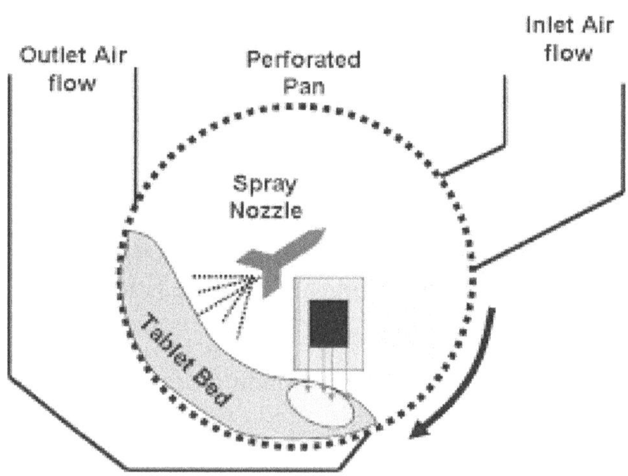


**Figure 11.1** Sugar Coating in coating pan.

***Steps for sugar-coating process***

- Sealing/waterproofing (of the tablet cores)
- Subcoating
- Smoothing

- Coloring
- Polishing
- Printing

***Sealing/waterproofing***

Sealing or waterproofing involves application of one or more coats of a waterproofing substance on to the tablet surface. These waterproofing substances (**Table 11.1**) may be Alcoholic spray, Shellac or Synthetic polymers e.g. Cellulose Acetate phthalate (CAP).

**Table 11.1** Constituents of coating solutions used for sugar coating.

| Seal coating | Sub coating | Syrup coating | Polishing solution |
|---|---|---|---|
| PEG 4000 | Gelatin | Colorant | Bees wax (white) |
| Zein/Shellac | Acacia | Sub coating powder | Naphtha |
| Propylene glycol | Sugar cane powder | Cal. Carbonate | Carnauba wax(yellow) |
| Oleic acid | Syrup | Cane sugar powder | Paraffin wax |
| Alcohol | Corn syrup | Syrup | |
| Methylene chloride | Distilled water | Corn starch | |

This step involves application of many coats of partially or completely water-insoluble polymers. Sugar-coatings are aqueous layers which allow water to penetrate directly into the tablet core and thus potentially affecting product stability and possibly causing premature tablet disintegration. This step involves application of many coats of partially or completely water-insoluble polymers enables sugar-coated product to exhibit modified-release pattern (extended release or delayed "enteric"- release characteristics).

***Subcoating***

Large quantities of sugar-coatings are applied to the tablet core (50- 100 % weight increase) for rounding off the tablet edge in the subcoating stage. Much of this material build-up occurs during this stage and is achieved by adding a bulking agent such as Calcium carbonate, to the sucrose solution.

Antiadherents e.g. Talc may be added after partial drying to prevent sticking of the tablets together.

***Smoothing***

The subcoating stage results in tablets with rough surfaces. To facilitate the color application (which requires a smooth surface), subcoated tablets are smoothed out by a thick sucrose syrup coating.

***Coloring***

Color coatings usually consist of thin sucrose syrup containing the requisite coloring materials. (Water-soluble dyes or water-insoluble pigments may be used).

***Polishing***

After the coloring step, the tablet surfaces tend to be smooth but somewhat dull in appearance. To achieve glossy finish, final stage involving application of waxes (beeswax or carnauba wax) is employed in polishing pan (**Figure 11.2**).

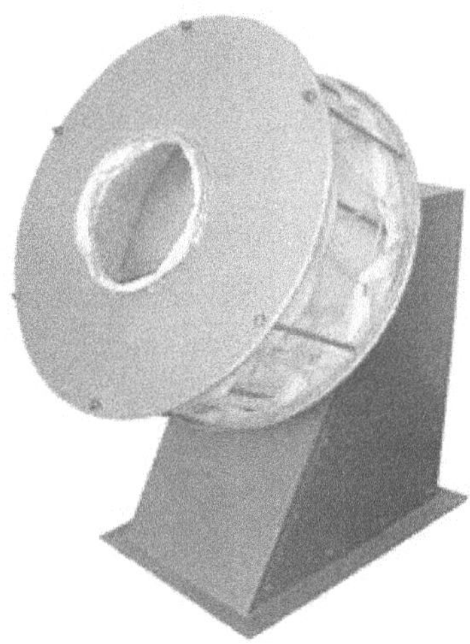

**Figure 11.2** Polishing Pan.

***Printing***

Different tablets could be identified by manufacturer' logo, product name, dosage strength or other appropriate code. For sugar-coated tablets, such identification could be only achieved by printing process using special edible inks.

**Film Coating**

Let us discuss film coating. In layman term, it is just like spray painting.....

**"It involves the deposition, usually by spraying method, of a thin uniform film of a polymer formulation surrounding a tablet."**

Film coating provides an alternative means of masking the taste of the medicament and providing protection against adverse climatic conditions without significantly altering the tablet weight or size.

***Major types***

Film coatings are a mixture of solids and liquids. For many years, the liquid component of coatings was a volatile solvent, such as alcohol or other quick-drying substances like methylene chloride. While solvent-based coatings performed well in many respects, they presented problems in handling, operator safety, recovery, and odor. Solvent-based coatings are still used in some applications, but water based, or aqueous, coatings have largely replaced them.

***Types of Film Coating***

1. *Immediate-release (non-functional) film coating*: They do not affect the biopharmaceutical properties of the tablet. They are readily soluble in water.
2. *Modified-release (functional) film coating*: They allow the drug to be delivered in a specific manner; i.e. they affect drug release behavior. Modified release film coatings are sub-classified into;
    - *Delayed-release coating (enteric coating)*:Only soluble in water at pH ≥ 5-6. Intended to protect the drug from gastric acidic pH (for acid labile drugs). Used for colonic drug delivery systems.
    - *Extended-release coating*: Mostly water-insoluble. Designed to ensure consistent drug release manner over a long period of time (6-12 hr) and thus decreasing dosing regimen and improving patient compliance.

**Composition of Film Coating Agents**

Film coating formulation/ materials are composed of

- Polymer,
- Plasticizer,
- Colorants,
- Solvent (vehicle)

***Polymer:*** A film former capable of producing smooth thin films reproducible under the prescribed coating conditions films e.g. cellulose, vinyl derivatives, carbomers, methacrylate etc.

***Plasticizer:*** Affords flexibility and elasticity to the coat and thus provide durability. Examples: Polyethylene glycol (PEG), Polypropylene glycol and coconut oil.

***Colorants:*** Provides an elegant appearance. Ex. Iron oxide pigment, Titanium dioxide and Aluminum lakes.

***Solvent (vehicle):*** Volatile organic solvents may be used to allow good spreadability of the coat components over the tablet and allowing rapid evaporation, but they are expensive and show environmental hazards and solvent residue in the formulation must be investigated (certain limit). Aqueous vehicles are safer, but they show slower evaporation and may affect drug stability.

## Coating Equipment and Process

### Film Coating Equipment

The conventional "coating-pan" and "fluid-bed coating equipment" are both used for coating.

Basic procedure involves spraying of the coating liquid (solution or suspension) onto the rotating tablets (in the coating-pan), or tablets held in suspension by column of air (in the fluid-bed coating equipment), followed by drying to remove the solvent, leaving a thin film around each tablet core.

### Coating-pan

Tablet coating system combines several components:

- a coating pan,
- a spraying system,
- an air handling unit,
- a dust collector, and
- the controls.

**Figure 11.3** Conventional coating Pan.

The tablet coating pan is used for both film coating as well as sugar coating. The coating pan is a perforated drum that rotates within a cabinet (Figure 11.3).

The cabinet enables to control airflow, air temperature, air pressure, and the coating application. The spraying system consists of several spray guns mounted on a manifold, a solution pump, a supply tank and mixer, and an air supply. The pump delivers the coating solution to the guns, where it combines with atomizing air to create a fine mist that is directed at the bed of tablets in the coating pan (**Figure 11.4** & **Figure 11.5**). The air handling unit heats and filters the air used to dry the coating on the tablets. Depending on the circumstances, it may include a humidifier or dehumidifier. The dust collector extracts air from the coating pan and keeps a slightly negative pressure within the cabinet. The controls enable to modulate the operation of all the components to achieve the desired results.

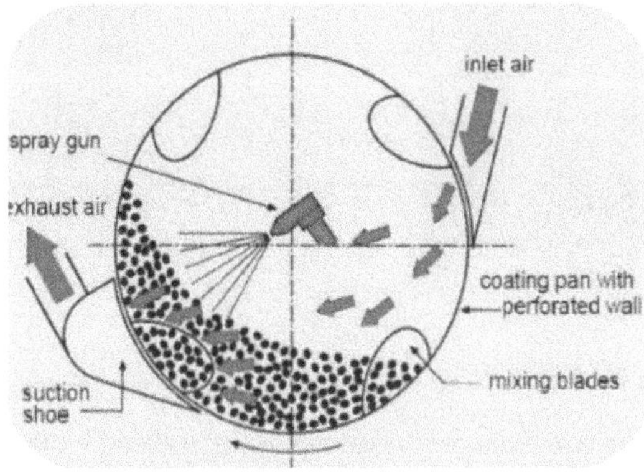


**Figure 11.4** Schematic diagram of working of conventional coating pan.

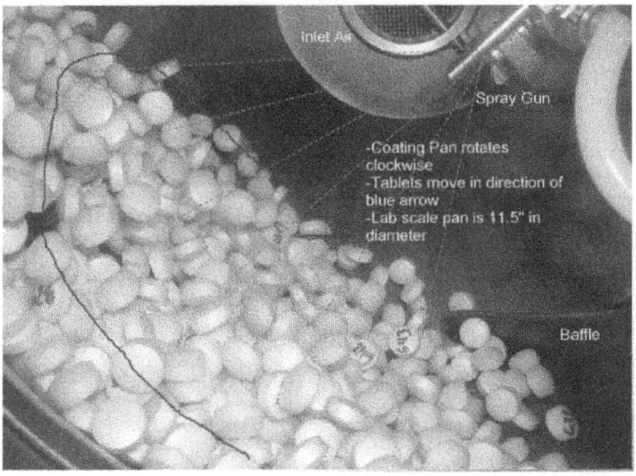


**Figure 11.5** Actual Picture of working of conventional coating pan. (Courtesy:http://newmaeweb.ucsd.edu/groups/lasheras/papers/Pfpres.pdf )

## Fluidized Bed Coating

Fluidized Bed Dryers (FBDs) are used in granulation, drying and coating. (studied in granulation). Wurster (1959) first described the application of sugar or film coatings to tablets suspended in an air stream (**Figure 11.6**).

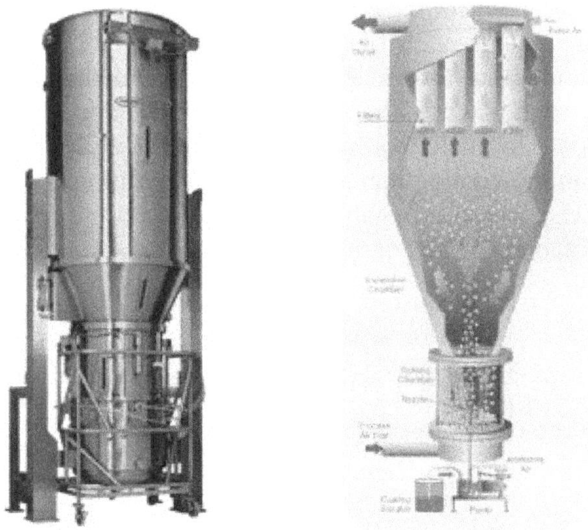

**Figure 11.6** Fluidized Bed Coating.

In that equipment the coating solution is introduced into the fluidizing air stream at the base (or top or tangential) of a tall vertical tube in which tablets circulate as they are coated (**Figure 11.7**).

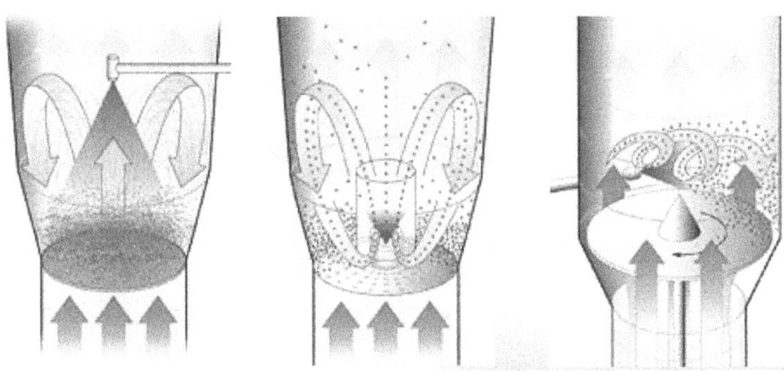

**(a) Top Spray** **(b) Bottom Spray** **(c) Tangential Spray**

**Figure 11.7** Types of spray in Fluidized Bed Coating.

*(Source: http://newmaeweb.ucsd.edu/groups/lasheras/papers/Pfpres.pdf)*

Evaporated solvent and air are removed at the top of the chamber. As the tablets circulate in the air stream, they are subjected to considerable abrasive action and for this reason they are compressed with extra firmness on punches which give a well-rounded profile.

## Compression-coating of Tablets

Although less popular, it gained increased interest in the recent years for creating modified-released products.

It involves the compaction of granular materials around a preformed tablet core using specially designed tableting equipment.

Compression coating is a dry process. Mechanically, it is a complex process, as the tablet may be tilted when transferred to the second die cavity (**Figure 11.8**).

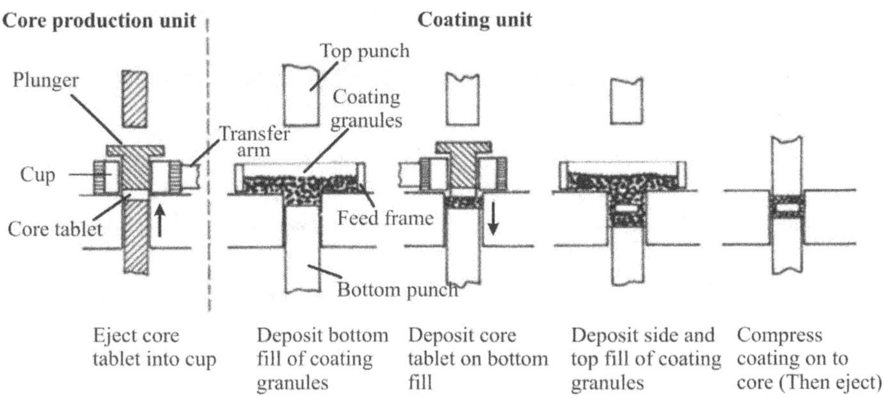


**Figure 11.8** Compression coating of tablet.

(Adapted from Semalty et al., Essentials of Pharmaceutical Technology, Pharma Med Press, Hyderabad, with permission)

# Tablet Coating Defects

Like the tablet manufacturing tablet coating is also associated with chances of occurrence of some defects. Mixing of colors, rate of spraying, application of colors, presence of moisture, process and equipment are some of the many factors which govern the tablet coating process. The coating adds another group of variables to the tableting which is itself a multivariable complex process. The common tablet coating defects are:

- Twinning
- Cracking
- Blistering
- Chipping
- Cratering
- Picking
- Pitting
- Blooming
- Blushing
- Color Variation
- Infilling
- Orange peel.

The Table 11.2 summarizes the coating defects, causes and remedies.

**Table 11.2** Causes and Remedies of Tablet Coating Defects.

| Tablet Defect | Causes | Remedy |
|---|---|---|
| **Twinning**<br>Two tablets stick together;<br>Most common in capsule shaped tablets | • Coating suspension can not be evaporated<br> | • Reducing spray rate<br>• Increasing pan speed |
| **Cracking**<br>Small, fine cracks observed on the upper, lower or side surface of tablets | • Use of higher M. Wt. polymers or polymeric blends<br>• Higher internal stresses in the film ( more than tensile strength of the film )<br>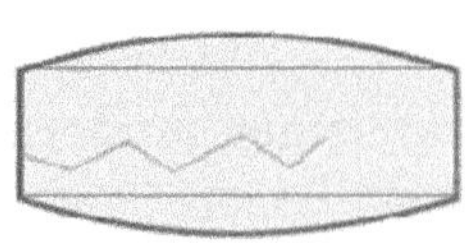 | • Use low molecular weight polymer<br>• Adjust the plasticizer & pigment types and concentration to minimize internal stresses |

**Table 11.2** ***Contd...***

| Tablet Defect | Causes | Remedy |
|---|---|---|
| **Blistering**<br>It is local detachment of film from the substrate forming a blister (due to compromised elasticity or adhesive properties. | • Overheating during the spraying and drying process<br> | • Use mild drying conditions, and<br>• ensure moderate temperatures at other stages of the coating process |
| **Chipping**<br>occurs when the film becomes dented and chipped (mostly on the edges of the tablet.) | • Decrease in the rotation speed in the machinery during the coating process.<br>• Poor polymer or coating solution (incorrect amount of plasticizer is used in the coating solution).<br>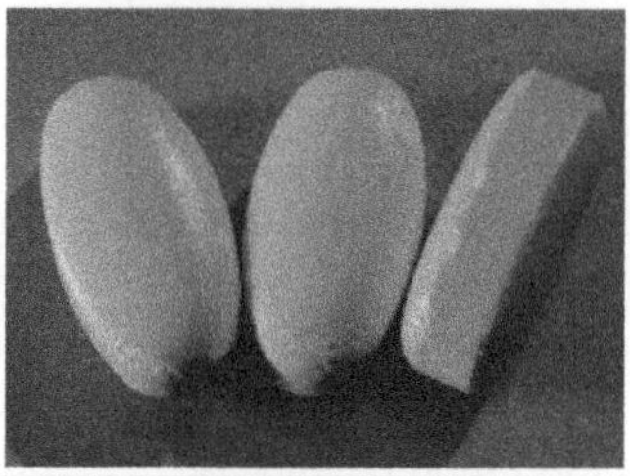 | • Increase the hardness of the film by adjusting the proportion of plasticizer in the coating solution<br>• Selecting a polymer with a higher molecular weight. |
| **Cratering**<br>Volcanic-like craters appears exposing the tablet surface | • Insufficient drying time to seal the film or<br>• Use of a high volume of coating solution.<br>• Penetration of the excess coating solution into the surface of the tablet.<br>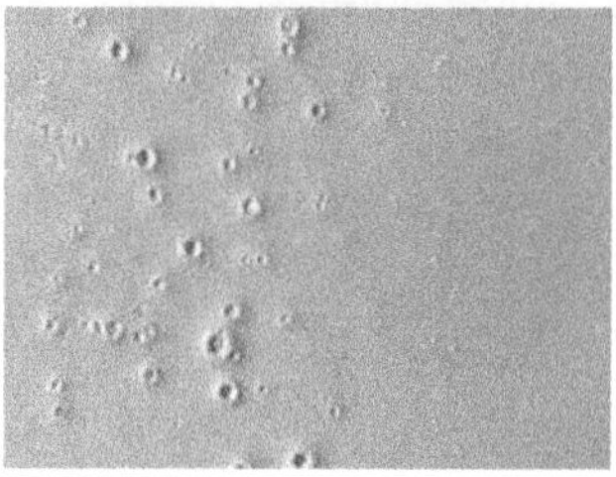 | • Check the efficiency of the drying process, decrease spray application rate and optimise drying conditions |

Table 11.2 *Contd...*

| Tablet Defect | Causes | Remedy |
|---|---|---|
| **Picking**<br>"part of the film sticks to the pan resulting to some of the tablet pieces being detached from the core." | • Over wetting of tablets by the polymer solution,<br>• Insufficient/rapid drying<br>• Higher rate of application of coating solution<br>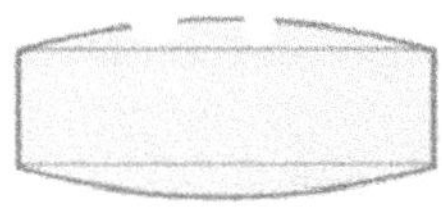 | • Increasing the efficiency of the drying process e.g, by increasing the air inlet temperature.<br>• Decreasing the rate of applying coating solution<br>• Increasing the solution viscosity. |
| **Pitting**<br>Deformation of the core of the tablet without any visible signs of disruption of the film coating. | • Increase of the tablet core temperature than the melting point of the materials used in its preparation<br>• Nonuniform spreading of film.<br>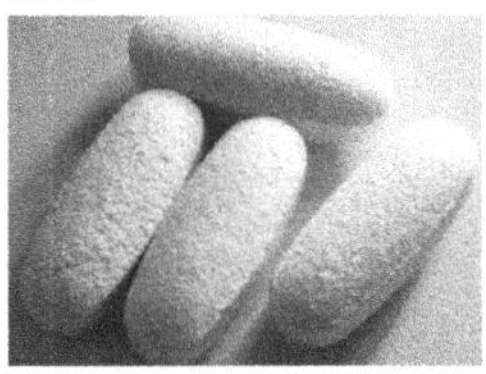 | • Control drying temperature |
| **Blooming**<br>"the fading or dulling of a tablet colour after a prolonged period of storage at a high temperature." | • Changes in the composition of the surface film.<br>• Using too much plasticizer or<br>• using a plasticizer with a low molecular weight.<br> | • Decrease the concentration of the plasticizer in the polymer.<br>• Using high molecular weight plasticizer |
| **Blushing**<br>A haziness or appearance of white specks (particles of polymer that has precipitated in the film) in the film | • Use of excessively high coating temperature.<br>• Gelation of the polymer<br> | • Decrease the drying temperature<br>• Avoid the use of sorbitol with polymers such as hydroxy propyl cellulose, hydroxy methyl cellulose, methyl cellulose and cellulose ethers |

**Table 11.2** ***Contd...***

| Tablet Defect | Causes | Remedy |
|---|---|---|
| **Mottling**<br>Variation in the colour of tablets within a batch. | • Poor mixing,<br>• Uneven spray patterns of the machinery,<br>• Insufficient coating, migration of soluble dyes-plasticizers and other additives during drying.<br>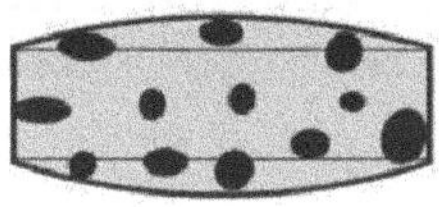 | • Use lake dyes (free from dye migration problem)<br>• Aim for even geometric mixing,<br>• reformulate with different plasticizers and additives and/or use mild drying conditions. |
| **Infilling**<br>The monogram or bisect is filled and become narrow | • Uneven spreading of coating solution and film<br>• High amount and rate of application of coating solution<br>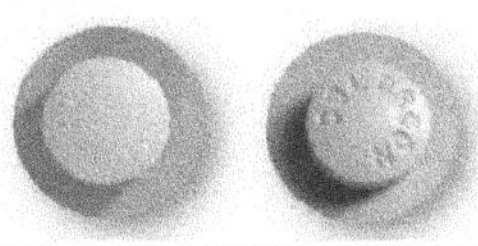 | • Add alcohol to the polymer solution to improve dispersion,<br>• Use a spray nozzle capable of finer atomization. |
| **Orange Peel (Roughness)**<br>a rough surface like orange peel | • Rapid drying<br>• Poor tablet composition causing it to become soft.<br>• Too high a spray pressure combined with a fast spray rate<br>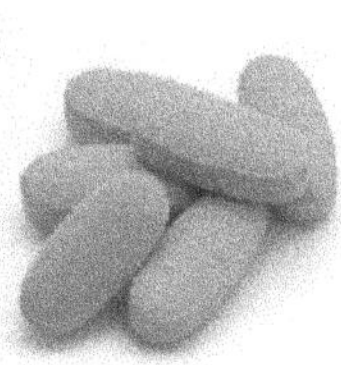 | • Use mild drying conditions<br>• Use additional solvents to decrease the viscosity of the polymer solution so that spraying rate can be reduced. |

## Summary

- Film Coating: Thin polymeric layer application
- Coating pan and FBD/FBG are used.
- Compression coating: Dry coating, tablet inside tablet
- Tablet coating defects: major 12, twinning, cracking blistering, chipping, blooming, blushing etc.

## Further Readings

- "Industrial Pharmacy-I" SWAYAM MOOC: www.swayam.gov.in
- Semalty A, Spray Drying, https://youtu.be/DQYKq1DWYPc
- Banker GS, Rhodes CT, Modern Pharmaceutics, CRC Press.
- Aulton ME (ED), Pharmaceutics: The science of Dosage form design, II edn, Churchill Livingstone, London, 2002.
- Qiu Y, Chang Y and Zhang GZ (Exe. Eds), Developing solid oral dosage forms: Pharmaceutical theory and practice, Elsevier, 2009.

## References


- Ansel's Pharmaceutical Dosage Forms and Drug Delivery Systems. Philadelphia: Lipincott Williams and Wilkins.
- https://en.wikipedia.org/wiki/Tablet_press
- Augsburger LL, Hoag SW (Eds), Pharmaceutical Dosage Forms: Tablets, Volume 1, III Edn, Informa healthcare, 2008
- Semalty et al., Essentials of Pharmaceutical Technology, II Edn, 2018, Pharma Med press, Hyderabad, India
- http://newmaeweb.ucsd.edu/groups/lasheras/papers/Pfpres.pdf
- Semalty et al., Essentials of Pharmaceutical Technology, II Edn, 2018, Pharma Med press, Hyderabad, India

CHAPTER 12

# Tablets IV
# QC of Tablets

**Dr Ajay Semalty**
Department of Pharmaceutical Sciences,
H.N.B Garhwal University (A Central University), Srinagar Garhwal-246174.

## Learning Outcome

After completing this chapter, you will be able to

- Perform the Quality Control (QC) Tests of tablets
- Execute Evaluation process and presentation

## Lesson Plan

- QC of tablets:
  - Apparatus,
  - Official and unofficial Methods
- Graphical presentations of Evaluation study

## Tablet

In the tablets we discussed about

- Drug
- Excipients
- Mixing/ granulation
- Compaction
- Coating

Now, the evaluation/ QC is to be addressed. Quality control test ensure that the dosage form is stable, safe and effective throughout its shelf life. Various official and unofficial evaluation test are there for tablets.

- **Official test**
  - Dissolution
  - Content uniformity (weight variation)
  - Disintegration

- **Unofficial test**
  - Mechanical strength
  - Tensile strength
  - Friability Test for Tablets
  - Tablet size and shape
  - Thickness
  - Average weight

## Dissolution

"Dissolution is defined as the process by which a known amount of drug substance goes into solution per unit of time under standardized conditions."

The test is performed

- For characterizing the bio-pharmaceutical quality of a product at different stages in its lifecycle.
- For choosing between different alternative formulations for further development

**"Dissolution testing is an official test recommended by all pharmacopoeias for evaluating drug release of solid and semisolid dosage forms."**

### Need of Dissolution Testing

- To help assure lot-to-lot uniformity USP requirement applies even if there is no correlation with *in vivo* data because it is a very discriminating and useful control over manufacturing variables.
- To guide formulation development
- To help establish stability/expiration dates

To demonstrate to FDA that products after scaleup and post-approval changes are bioequivalent to the originally approved product.

- When correlated with *in vivo* data, dissolution may be used instead of human biostudies.
- Used without *in vivo* correlation for minor changes.

## Dissolution

It is a two steps process

**Step 1:** Molecules released from dosage form to media creating a saturated layer/stagnant layer, adjacent to the solid surface.

**Step 2:** Drug diffusion as per concentration gradient

## Dissolution Test

### Official Dissolution Test Apparatus

In *U.S. Pharmacopeia* (USP), seven dissolution test apparatus are mentioned, while Indian Pharmacopoeia (IP) provides only two apparatus (Figure 12.1 & Figure 12.2).

Various dissolution test apparatus official in USP are given in Table 12.1 USP Official Dissolution Test Apparatus (Table 12.1). The most commonly employed dissolution test methods are (1) the basket method (Apparatus 1) and (2) the paddle method (Apparatus 2). The basket and the paddle methods are simple, robust, well standardized, and used worldwide. These methods are flexible enough to allow dissolution testing for a variety of drug products.

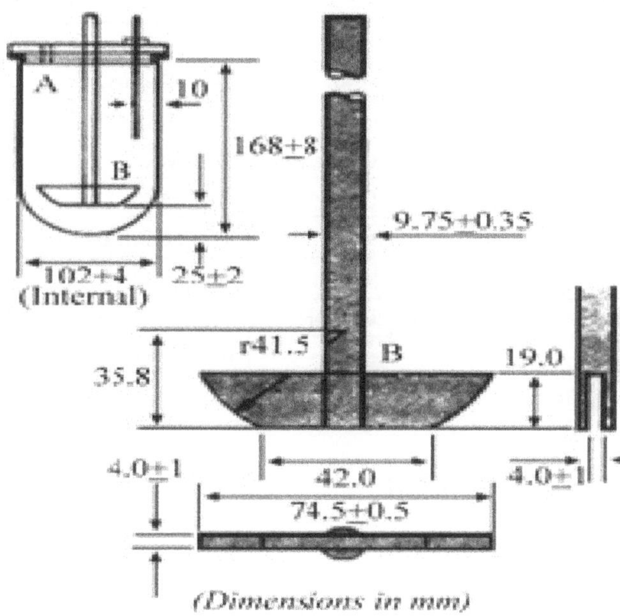


**Figure 12.1** Dissolution Test apparatus (IP), Paddle type (Type I).

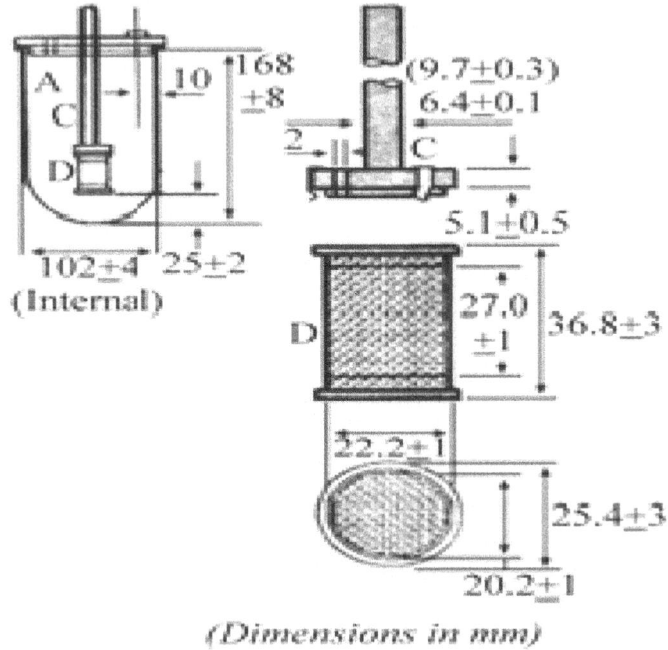


**Figure 12.2** Dissolution Test apparatus (IP); Basket Type (Type II).

**Table 12.1** USP Official Dissolution Test Apparatus.

| Apparatus No. | Description | General Application |
|---|---|---|
| 1 | Rotating Basket | Oral IR and MR |
| 2 | Rotating Paddle | Oral IR and MR |
| 3 | Reciprocating Cylinder | Oral MR |
| 4 | Flow Through Cell | Oral MR |
| 5 | Paddle over disk | Transdermal DS |
| 6 | Cylinder | Transdermal DS |
| 7 | Reciprocating Holder | Transdermal DS or non-disintegrating oral MR |

*IR = Immediate release, MR = Modified Release, DS= Delivery System

## Dissolution Test (U.S.P.)

For dissolution test Pharmacopoeias specify dissolution test medium and volume,

- type of apparatus to be used,

- rpm of the shaft,
- time limit of the test and
- assay procedure

**Practical approach: What to do?**

- Prepare the calibration curve of pure API.
- Determine the calibration curve equation.
- Refer monograph in pharmacopeia and chose apparatus, media, volume, rpm and study time.
- Preheat the apparatus and media, set rpm.
- Put one tablet in the dissolution media in jar.
- Withdraw the sample at set time as per monograph or requirement of the study.
- Replace the prewarmed same volume of media in the jar for longer studies.
- Filter, dilute the sample and analyze.
- Determine the drug release and check with acceptance criteria.

**Three stage acceptance criteria (USP)**

**The USP** prescribes the following three stage criteria of acceptance of dissolution data (**Table 12.2**).

**Table 12.2** Three stage acceptance criteria (USP).

| Stage | Number Tested | Acceptance Criteria |
|---|---|---|
| $S_1$ | 6 | Each unit is not less than Q + 5% |
| $S_2$ | 6 | Average of 12 units ($S_1$ + $S_2$) is equal to or greater than Q, and no unit is less than Q – 15% |
| $S_3$ | 12 | Average of 24 units ($S_1$ + $S_2$ + $S_3$) is equal to or greater than Q, no more than 2 units are less than Q – 15%, and no unit is less than Q – 25%. |

Q, is the amount of dissolved active ingredient.

## Graphical Presentation

Most common graphical presentation of dissolution data involves

- %CDR V/S Time
- Log % Drug remaining V/S Time
- % CDR V/S square root of time (Higuchi plot)
- Log %CDR V/S Log Time (Korsmeyer-Peppas)

Alternatively, t25, t50 etc. may also be calculated or shown. This is the time taken to release the said percent of the labelled drug amount (Figure 12.3).

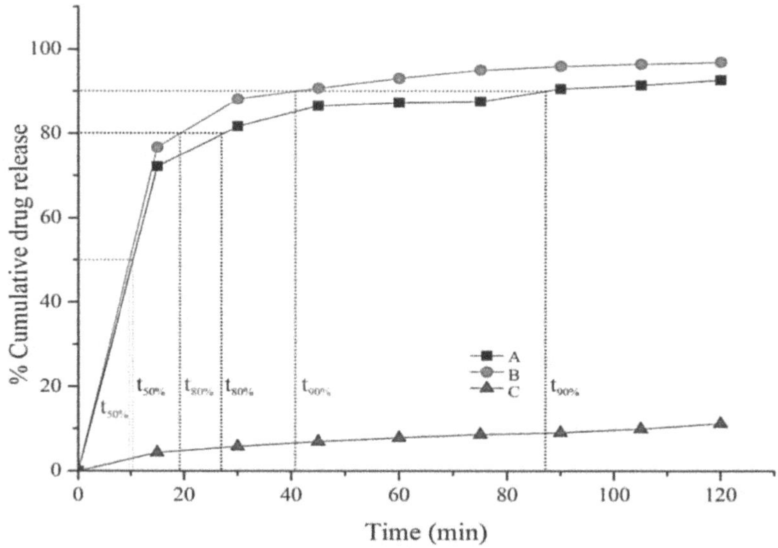


**Figure 12.3** Graphical presentation of dissolution data.

## Weight Variation (USP/IP)

This test is used for assessing batch to batch uniformity. It is applicable when the tablet contains 50 mg or more of the drug.

Weigh individually 20 units selected at random and calculate the average weight. Not more than two of the individual weights deviates from the average weight by more than the prescribed percentage and none deviates by more than twice that percentage (**Table 12.3**).

**Table 12.3** Acceptance Criteria of weight variation (IP/BP/USP).

| Average weight of tablet (According to IP/BP) | Limit | Average weight of tablet (According to USP) |
|---|---|---|
| 80 mg or less | ±10% | 130 mg or less |
| More than 80 mg or less than 250 mg | ± 7.5% | 130 mg to 324 mg |
| 250 mg or more | ± 5% | More than 324 mg |

## Content Uniformity

The test is performed for all coated and uncoated tablets and all capsules intended for oral administration with the size range of the dosage form 50 mg or smaller sizes. This is to note that the tablet monographs with a content uniformity requirement do not have weight variation requirements.

## Acceptance criteria (IP/USP)

30 tablets are selected and 10 are assayed individually. At least 9 must assay within ±15% of the declared potency and none may exceed ± 25%.

If two or three of the individual values are outside the limits ±15% of the average value and none is outside the limits ± 25%, repeat the test using another 20 tablets. The tablets comply with the test if in the total sample of 30 tablets not more than three of the individual values are outside the limits 85 to 115% and none is outside the limits 75 to 125% of the average value.

## Tablet Disintegration Test

The break-up of the tablet or disintegration is must for its subsequent dissolution and bioavailability (Figure 12.4).

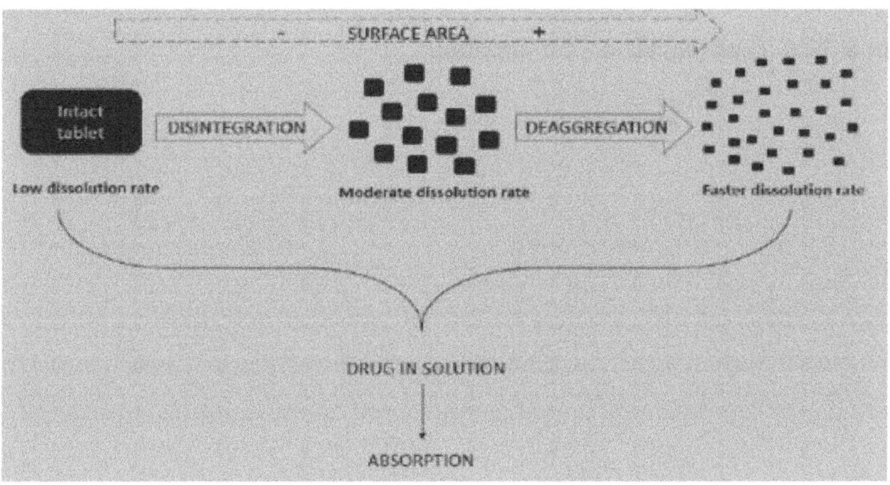


**Figure 12.4** Importance of disintegration.

"The disintegration test is a measure of the time required under a given set of conditions for a group of tablets to disintegrate into particles which will pass through a 10-mesh screen."

It is useful as a quality assurance tool for conventional dosage forms.

The disintegration test is carried out using the disintegration tester (type A and B) which consists of a basket rack holding 6 plastic tubes (vary in Inner diameter in type A and B), open at the top and bottom, the bottom of the tube is covered by a 10-mesh screen; disk (diameter vary) on the tablet top (Figure 12.5). The apparatus' specifications are mentioned in pharmacopeia and any apparats must comply with the same (Figure 12.6).

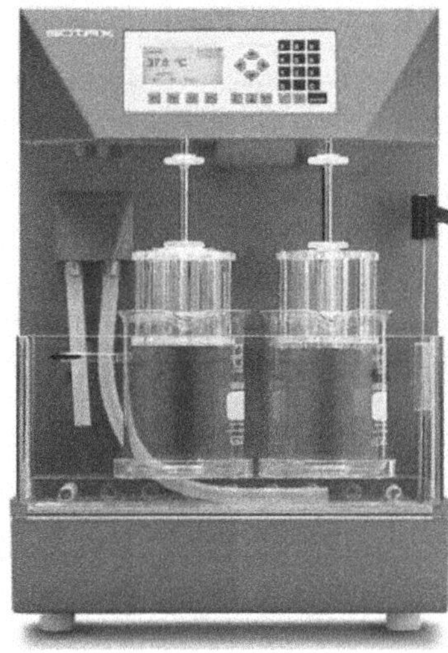

**Figure 12.5** Disintegration Test apparatus.

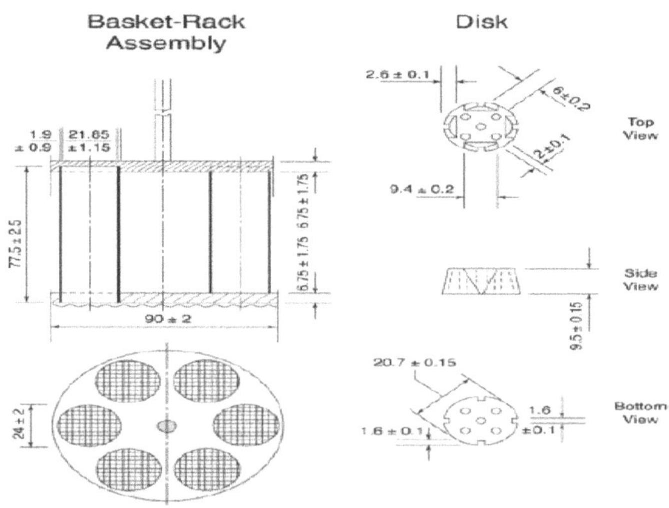


**Figure 12.6** Official Specifications of Disintegration Test Apparatus.

The working of disintegration test is shown in (Figure 12.7). The basket is immersed in a bath of suitable liquid held at 37 ° C, preferably in a 1 L beaker (water or simulated gastric fluid is used).

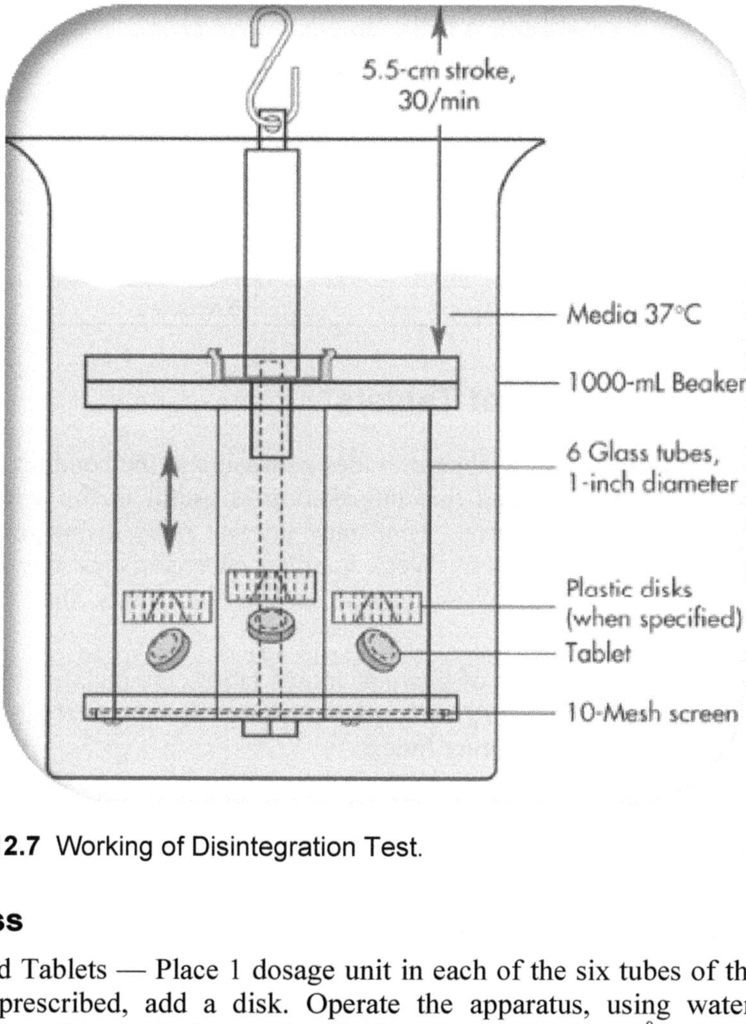


**Figure 12.7** Working of Disintegration Test.

## Process

Uncoated Tablets — Place 1 dosage unit in each of the six tubes of the basket and, if prescribed, add a disk. Operate the apparatus, using water or the specified medium as the immersion fluid, maintained at 37 ± 2$^0$C. At the end of the time limit specified in the monograph, lift the basket from the fluid, and observe the tablets: all of the tablets have disintegrated completely. If 1 or 2 tablets fail to disintegrate completely, repeat the test on 12 additional tablets. The requirement is met if not fewer than 16 of the total of 18 tablets tested are disintegrated. For uncoated tablets the disintegration time should be about 15 mint (Table 12.4).

**Table 12.4** Disintegration Test Acceptance criteria (IP) / as per Monograph.

| Type of capsule | | Disintegration time |
|---|---|---|
| Uncoated Tablets | | 15 minutes |
| Coated Tablets | film coated | 30 minutes |
| | Other coated tablets | 60 minutes |
| Enteric-coated tablets | 0.1 M hydrochloric acid | Should not disintegrate in 120 minutes |
| | Mixed phosphate buffer pH 6.8. | 60 minutes |
| Dispersible and Soluble Tablets | | Within 3 minutes |
| Effervescent Tablets | | 5 minutes |

## Mechanical Strength of Tablets

The mechanical strength of a tablet provides a measure of the bonding potential of the material concerned and this information is useful in the selection of excipients. An excessively strong bond may prevent rapid disintegration and subsequent dissolution of a drug. Weak bonding characteristics may limit the selection and/or proportion of excipients, such as lubricants, that would be added to the formulation.

The mechanical properties of pharmaceutical tablets are quantifiable by the friability, hardness or crushing strength, crushing strength-friability values, tensile strength and brittle fracture Index.

## Tensile strength/ hardness

It is a non-compendial method. "This is the force required to break a tablet in a diametric compression test." (Crushing strength).

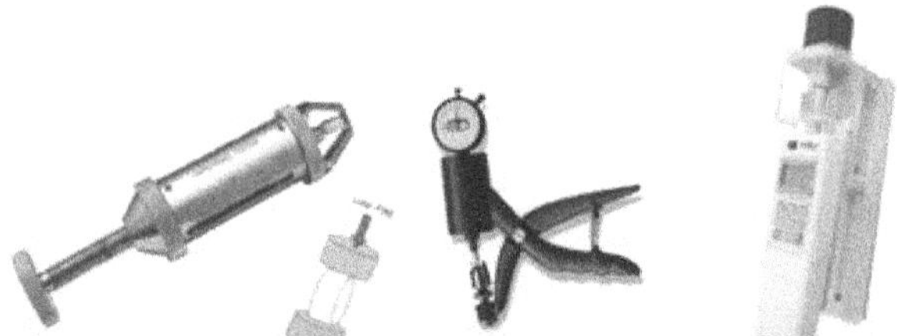

(a) Monsanto (b) Pfizer (c) Digital

**Figure 12.8** Manual and digital hardness tester.

The hardness tester may be of various types for measuring radial/axial tensile strength hardness. The tester may be Manual (Monsanto, Pfizer) or digital (Figure 12.8)**Figure 12.**. The tablet hardness generally ranges 5-8 Kg.

## Friability Test

The test has been included in IP 2014. So, now it has become official test.

"The test is designed to evaluate the ability of the tablet to withstand abrasion in packaging, handling and shipping."

Tablets are weighed and placed in the Roche friabilator (Figure 12.9) which is then rotated 4 minutes @ 25 rpm. Tablets are fallen from 6 inch height in the apparatus, weighed again and % loss reported (not more than 1 % loss).

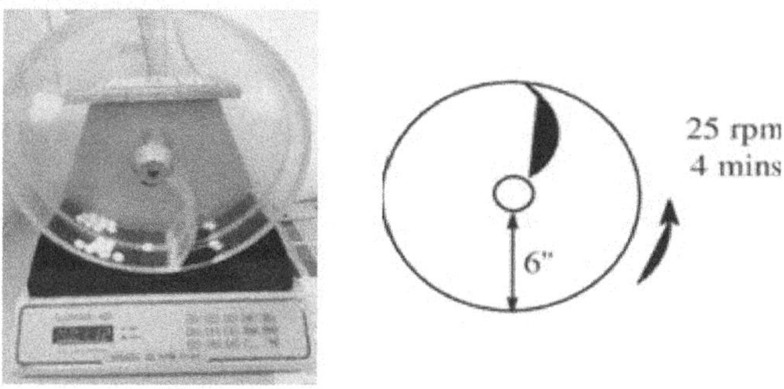


**Figure 12.9** Roche Friabilator Apparatus.

## Tablets Size and Shape

The thickness of individual tablets may be measured with a micrometer.

Tablet thickness should be controlled within a ±5% variation of a standard value.

## Take Away Message

- Tablet QC test ensure the quality.
- Types: Official/ unofficial
- Dissolution, disintegration, weight variation and content uniformity, friability, are official/ compendial test
- Hardness, thickness, shape, and size are unofficial test.

## Further Readings


- "Industrial Pharmacy-I" SWAYAM MOOC: www.swayam.gov.in
- USP/ IP
- Banker GS, Rhodes CT, Modern Pharmaceutics, CRC Press.
- Aulton ME (ED), Pharmaceutics: The science of Dosage form design, II edn, Churchill Livingstone, London, 2002.
- Semalty et al., Essentials of Pharmaceutical Technology, II Edn, 2018, Pharma Med press, Hyderabad, India
- Qiu Y, Chang Y and Zhang GZ (Exe. Eds), Developing solid oral dosage forms: Pharmaceutical theory and practice, Elsevier, 2009.


## References/ Credits


- USP/ IP
- Ansel's Pharmaceutical Dosage Forms and Drug Delivery Systems. Philadelphia: Lipincott Williams and Wilkins.
- Augsburger LL, Hoag SW (Eds), Pharmaceutical Dosage Forms: Tablets, Volume 1, III Edn, Informa healthcare, 2008
- Semalty et al., Essentials of Pharmaceutical Technology, II Edn, 2018, Pharma Med press, Hyderabad, India.

CHAPTER 13

# Liquid Orals (Syrups and Elixirs)

**Dr Mona Semalty and Dr Ajay Semalty**
Department of Pharmaceutical Sciences,
H.N.B Garhwal University (A Central University), Srinagar Garhwal-246174.

### Learning Outcome

After completing this chapter, you will be able to learn about

- Different types of liquid orals
- Solutions and its types
- Solubility/ methods of enhancement and stability of solutions
- Syrups, components of syrups, methods of preparation and packaging
- Elixirs, components of elixirs/ methods of preparation and packaging

### Lesson Plan

- Introduction to liquid orals/ Classification of liquid orals /definitions
- Solutions /merits demerits/ Different types /
- Solubility (methods to enhance)
- Methods of preparation of solution/stability of solutions
- Syrups, components of syrups, method of preparations of syrups
- Elixir, components of elixir, method of preparation of elixirs
- Packaging and storage

## Introduction to Liquid Orals

Liquid orals are the pharmaceutical dosage form in liquid form to be administered orally either in the form of solution, suspension, emulsions, elixir and many more.

### Classification of Liquid Orals

Liquid orals may be of various types (Figure 13.1).

- Monophasic liquids
  - Solution Elixir
  - Syrup
  - Liquid drops etc.

- Biphasic liquids
  - Suspensions
  - Emulsions

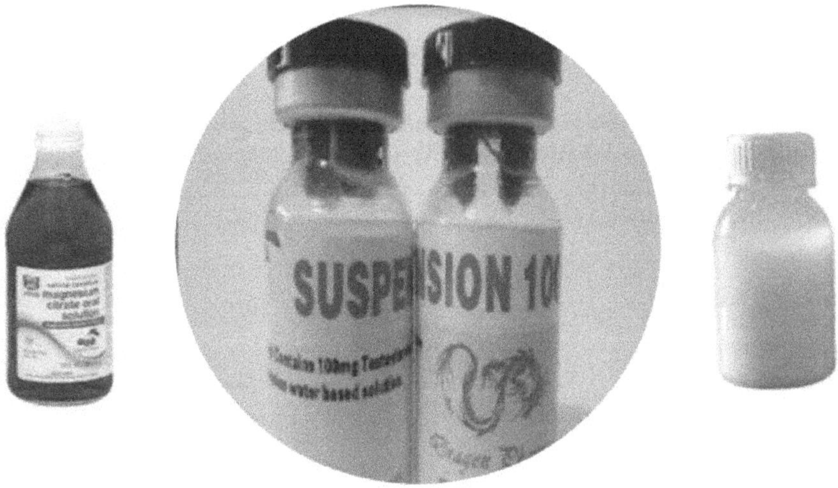

**Figure 13.1** Different liquid oral dosage forms.

## Introduction

### Syrup

"In medical terminology, medicinal syrups are nearly saturated solutions of 85% of sugar in water in which medicinal substances or drugs are dissolved".

### Elixirs

"Elixir are clear, flavored Oral Liquids containing one or more active ingredients dissolved in a vehicle that usually contains a high proportion of sucrose or a suitable polyhydric alcohol or alcohols and may also contain Ethanol (95 %) or diluted Ethanol".

### Suspensions

"Suspensions are Liquids containing one or more active ingredients suspended in a suitable vehicle. Suspended solids may slowly separate on keeping but are easily redispersed".

## Emulsions

"Emulsions are Liquids containing one or more active ingredients and are stabilized oil-in-water or water-in-oil dispersions, either or both phases of which may contain dissolved solids".

**Classification of solutions based on for the purpose it is to be used**

- Oral
  - Syrups
  - Elixirs
  - Spirits
  - Linctuses
  - Drops
- In mouth & throat
  - Mouth washes
  - Gargles
  - Throat paint
  - Throat sprays
- On Body Surfaces
  - Collodions
  - Lotions
  - Liniments
- In Body Cavities
  - Douches
  - Enemas
  - Ear drops,
  - Nasal sprays

## Solutions

In pharmaceutical terms, solutions are "liquid preparations that contain one or more chemical substances dissolved in a suitable solvent or mixture of mutually miscible solvents". It may be classified as oral, ophthalmic, or topical and parenterals.

**Advantages**

- Easier to swallow
- Onset of action is quick
- Homogenous uniform dose
- Any route of administration
- Flexible dosing
- Diluted irritant action of some drugs (aspirin, Kl, KBr)
- Minimize adverse effects in the GIT

**Disadvantages**

- Bulky preparations
- Unpleasant taste or odors are difficult to mask.
- Accuracy in dose measurement needed
- Some drugs poorly soluble difficult to formulate
- Less stable than solid dosage forms.

## Classification of Solutions

As per the type of Vehicle is used:

(a) Aqueous solutions

(b) Non-aqueous solutions

Aqueous solutions are homogeneous preparations that are prepared by dissolving a solid, liquid or gas in an aqueous medium (vehicle).

Aqueous vehicle

- Water
- Aromatic water
- Extracts.

**Non- Aqueous Solutions**

- Alcoholic/hydroalcoholic – Example solutions, elixirs and spirits,
- Ethereal solutions –Example collodions
- Glycerin solutions -Glycerites
- Oleaginous solutions-Liniments, medicated oils, oleo- vitamins, sprays, and toothache drops.

## Solubility

"Solubility is defined as number of parts of solvent (by volume) that will dissolve one part of solute (by weight of a solid or liquid). Solubility is the amount of a solute that passes into solution (per ml). Solute and solvent of same polarity get dissolves good" (**Figure 13.2**).

**Figure 13.2** Concept of solubility.

The solubility is defined specifically by USP as mentioned in **Table 13.1**. It defines or classify solubility in 7 classes on the basis of parts of solvent required for one part of solute.

**Table 13.1** Solubility definitions (USP).

| Description | Parts of solvent required for one part of solute |
|---|---|
| Very soluble | <1 |
| Freely soluble | 1-10 |
| Soluble | 10-30 |
| Sparingly soluble | 30-100 |
| Slightly soluble | 100-1000 |
| Very slightly soluble | 1000-10,000 |
| Insoluble | >10,000 |

## Selection Criteria for Solvents

Solvents are selected based on following properties.

- Solubility
- Clarity
- Low toxicity
- Viscosity
- Compatibility with other ingredients

- Chemical inertness
- Palatability
- Odor, color
- Economy

## Selection Criteria of a Solute

- Particle size – Size must allow maximum contact with solvent.
- Agitation – Agitation allow effective and uniform contact of solvent with solute
- Temperature-- Increasing the frequency which solvent molecules collide with the surface of the dissolving mixture
- Exothermic reaction – Solute gives off heat during the process of solution; solubility is decreased with an increase in temperature.
- pH-weak acids or weak bases their aqueous solubility depend upon the pH of the solvent.

**Methods to enhance/optimize the solubility of therapeutic agents depends on**

- Appropriate selection of drug salt
- Optimization of the pH of the formulation
- Use of co-solvents
- **Appropriate selection of salt of drug e.g.**

  Salt of salicylic acid acetyl salicylic acid

  Salt of diltiazem to form diltiazem hydrochloride
- **Optimization of the pH of the formulation**

  Solubility of an ionized therapeutic agent is a function of both the pKa of the compound and the pH of the formulation. Oral administration accepts pH from 5 to 8.
- **Use of co-solvents**

  Co-solvents are primarily liquid components that are incorporated into a formulation to enhance the solubility of poorly soluble drugs to the required level. Commonly employed co-solvents include glycerol, propylene glycol, ethanol and poly (ethylene glycol).

## Preparation of Solution

- Preformulation of solution
- Formula setup
- Selection of method of preparation
- Evaluation of the product

## Method of Preparation of Solution

- Simple solution: Prepared simply by dissolving solute in the solvent.
- Solution by chemical reaction: It is prepared by mixing two or more solutes with each other in a suitable solvent.

**Solution by Extraction:** Plant or animal products are prepared by suitable extraction process. Preparations of this type may be classified as solutions but more often, are classified as extractives.

## Stability of Solutions

A solution must be stable physically and chemically. It includes a solution must retain its clarity, color, odor, taste and viscosity over its shelf life. There should be no chemical interactions in the components of a solution that may alter the product's stability and potency. Esters of p-hydroxybenzoic acid (methyl-, ethyl-, propyl-and butylparabens), frequently used preservatives in oral preparations, have a tendency to partition into certain flavoring oils. This partitioning effect could reduce the effective concentration of the preservatives in the aqueous medium of a pharmaceutical product below the level needed for preservative action.

## Syrup

Syrups are concentrated aqueous preparations of a sugar or sugar substitute with or without flavoring agents and medicinal substances.

**Concentration of Syrup**

According to B.P: 67.7% W/W

According to USP: 85% W/V

## Classification of Syrups

### Medicated–Contains Therapeutic Agents in it

Analgesics-meperidine HCI

Anticholinergic-Dicylomine HCI

Anticonvulsant-Sodium valproate

Antiviral –amantadine HCI

**Non medicated "Syrups** containing flavoring agents, but not medicinal substances are called non-medicated or flavored syrups"

Cocoa syrup

Orange syrup

Raspberry syrup

**Advantages of syrup**

- Appropriate for any age group patient,
- Easiest route of administration
- Economical and safe to the patient
- No nursing is required, which means the patient can take it with no help
- The liquid dosage form is expected for certain types of products like cough medicines

**Disadvantages**

- Delayed onset of action because absorption takes time
- Not suitable in emergency and for unconscious patients
- Not convenient for a patient with a gastrointestinal disorder such as diarrhea,
- Constipation, ulceration, and hyperacidity in stomach
- Can't avoid first pass metabolism

## Components of Syrup

In addition to the purified water, syrup conatins

**Sweetening Agent**-the sugar, usually sucrose, or sugar substitute used to provide sweetness and

**Antimicrobial Preservatives:** Benzoic acid (0.1 to 0.2%), Sodium benzoate (0.1 to 0.2%), Methyl-, propyl-, and butylparabens (0.1%), Alcohol (15 to 20%) [if alcohol soluble components are present in syrup]

## Flavorings Agents

1. Naturally occurring materials: Volatile oils i.e. Orange oil.
2. Synthetic flavorings agents: Vanillin and others.

## Colorants

To enhance the appeal of the syrup, a coloring agent that correlate with the flavoring agent is used (green with mint and chocolate with brown)
Methods of preparation of syrups

There are four methods.

Based on the physical and chemical properties on the ingredients, the choice of the method is selected

- Solution with heat
- Agitation without heat
- Addition of sucrose to liquid medicament
- Percolation method

### Solution with Heat

Temperature of purified water is increased to 80 to 85 C and it is taken off from the heat source.

Sucrose is added and shaken thoroughly. Add heat sensitive and volatile agents are added after the solutions attain the room temperature. During heating, the sucrose gets hydrolyzed, results in the formation of dextrose and fructose these two sugars together called as invert sugar and the process is known as inversion. This inversion leads to darkening of the solution.

### Agitation without Heat

IN this method stainless steel Vessel or glass vessel is used. The vessel should be larger than the desired volume of syrup required Then the ingredients according to the formulation are added to water and mixed It is better to dissolve solid ingredients in the water first and then to add them to syrup. This result in easy mixing as sugar solution generally retards mixing.

### Addition of Sucrose to Liquid Medicament

This method is generally used for fluid extracts. But those substances which are soluble in alcohol will precipitate out as soon as the addition of water. An alternation is to first dissolve all the ingredients in water. Now after some time all the precipitates formed are filtered out. Now add sucrose but this method is of no use if the precipitates formed has active ingredients.

## Percolation

The principle of percolation is used

A sucrose bed is prepared and then water or vehicle containing therapeutic agent is passed.

Here the sucrose bed should be coarse, and shape of percolator must be cylindrical or cone shaped.

## Packaging

Syrup requires safe, secure and tamper-proof handling while packaging. Syrups need to ensure complete protection from contamination and microbial growth. Our inevitable packaging support assures the safe and secure packaging of syrups to ensure their extended shelf life.

**The general process:** Filling › Sealing › Capping › Coding & labeling › Wrapping

## Process Involved in Syrup Packaging

Empty Bottles are rinsed though Air jet cleaning. Bottles are tested & transferred ahead for filling.

- Filling machines with their automatic piston fills the bottles with accurate volume of syrup. Capping is done on bottle through capping machines. Plastic or aluminum capsules are bound over the neck of the bottle for secure sealing.
- Important details regarding packaging date & expiry date are printed on bottles.

## Storage and Labeling

All the products dispense extemporaneously require some form of additional storage instructions to be detailed on the label. This information can be the addition of just a product expiry date through to a number of important additional label Labeling. Every pharmaceutical preparation requires a label to be produced before the product can be dispensed or sold to patient. The accuracy of the label is very important as it conveys essential information to the patient on the use of preparation.

## Elixirs

Elixir is clear, sweetened hydro-alcoholic solution. Alcoholic content vary from 10% to 12% and up to 40% Intended for oral use usually flavored to enhance palatability. Usually less sweet than syrups and less viscous.

**They are classified into two classes,**

Medicated /Non-Medicated

Medicated elixir is used for therapeutic effects. Examples of medicated elixirs are-

- Antihistamine Elixir: Diphenhydramine HCl
- Analgesic Elixir: acetaminophen
- Cardio tonic Elixir: digoxin
- Antispasmodic Elixir: hyoscyamine sulfate
- Sedative Elixir: phenobarbital

## Non Medicated Elixirs

Do not contain any therapeutic agent can be used for dilution of an existing medicated elixir. These only contain Water, alcohol, sweetening agent and coloring agent

Most common non medicated elixir is following-

- Aromatic elixir perfumes
- Compound benzaldehyde elixir
- Isoalcoholic elixir

**Advantages of Elixirs**

- Better able to maintain both water-soluble and alcohol-soluble components in solution.
- Has a stable characteristic.
- Easily prepared by simple solution.

**Disadvantages**

- Less effective than syrups in masking taste of medicated substances.
- Contains alcohol, accentuates saline taste of bromides

## Components of an Elixir

Purified water and alcohol are the main component of the elixir. This is employed as a co-solvent to ensure solubility of all ingredients. As highlighted above, the concentration of alcohol varies depending on the formulation. Generally, the concentration of alcohol is greater than 10% v/v; however, in some preparations, the concentration of alcohol may be greater than 40% v/v.

## Polyol Co-solvents

Polyol co-solvents, e.g. propylene glycol, glycerol, may be employed to enhance the solubility of the therapeutic agent and associated excipients.

Sweetening agents. Less concentration is required as compared to syrups

## Flavors and Colors

All pharmaceutical elixirs contain flavors and colors to increase the palatability and enhance the aesthetic qualities of the formulation.

## Preservatives

Elixirs containing more than 10 to 12% of alcohol are usually self-preserving and do not require the addition of an antimicrobial agent. Otherwise Parabens and Benzoates.

**Method of preparation:**

- Dissolve the water-soluble ingredients in part of the water,
- Dissolve the sucrose in it.
- Dissolve the other ingredients in the alcohol (5-40%)
- The aqueous solution is then added to the alcoholic solution with constant stirring and make up the volume with the solvent or vehicle specified in the formulation.
- Sucrose increases viscosity but decreases the solubility properties of water so in addition of viscosity-enhancing agents, e.g. hydrophilic polymers, may be required to optimize the rheological properties of elixirs.
- Elixirs should be brilliantly clear and therefore strained or filtered, if necessary, subjected to clarifying action of purified talc or siliceous earth.

## Packaging of Elixirs

Elixir should be packed in glass or plastic containers as selected based on the requirements. Due to the volatile nature of some of the components of elixirs, elixirs should be packaged in tight containers and not stored at high temperatures.

## Further Readings

- "Industrial Pharmacy-I" SWAYAM MOOC: www.swayam.gov.in
- https://www.youtube.com/watch?v=pLBFUEKgu6Q
- https://www.youtube.com/watch?v=2P57NU1pmjM
- https://www.youtube.com/watch?v=KgKskhek13s
- https://www.youtube.com/watch?v=exNJCDPLRgc

## References


- http://sbmu.ac.ir/uploads/Remington_Essentials_of_Pharmaceutics_-_Felton,_Linda.pdf
- https://www.slideshare.net/MohammadZainIdrees/pharmaceutical-elixirs
- https://www.researchgate.net/publication/318380297_Vehicles_for_Liquid_Preparations
- https://www.slideshare.net/MMK_Shahid/syrups-elixirs-introduction
- https://www.pharmpress.com/files/docs/ft_pharm_dosage_sample.pdf

CHAPTER 14

# Emulsions I (Introduction Theories and Identification Tests)

**Dr Mona Semalty, Dr Ajay Semalty**
Department of Pharmaceutical Sciences,
H.N.B Garhwal University (A Central University), Srinagar Garhwal-246174

### Learning Outcome

After completing this chapter, you will be able to understand about

- Introduction of emulsion
- Its types and uses
- Theory of emulsification
- Different test for identification

### Lesson Plan

- Introduction, definitions as per IP, USP
- Classification
- Advantages & Disadvantages
- Uses (oral/systemic/local and other routes)
- Test for identification
- Different theories of emulsification

## Introduction

Emulsions are thermodynamically unstable biphasic liquid dosage form, and it contains two immiscible phases i.e. oil and water (Also called as Heterogeneous preparations). Emulsions are formulated with the use of emulsifiers and one phase is dispersed in to the other phase.

## Definition

An emulsion is a colloidal dispersion of one liquid (disperse phase) in another (continuous phase) one. The particle size of the dispersed phase commonly ranges from 0.1 to 100 µm. In an emulsion, however, oil and water can be forced to mix. Instead of forming two separate layers with a clear boundary between them, small droplets of one liquid (dispersed phase) are spread throughout the other liquid (continuous phase).

Hence, an emulsion can be defined as **a thermodynamically unstable system consisting of at least two immiscible liquid phases, one of which is dispersed as globule (dispersed phase) in the other liquid phase (continuous phase), stabilized by the presence of an emulsifying agent** (**Figure 14.1**). Typical examples of emulsion include such everyday products as milk, butter, mayonnaise, and cosmetic creams.

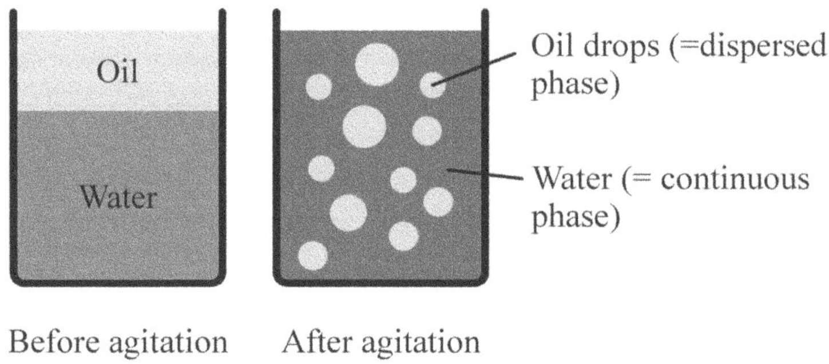


**Figure 14.1** Formation of an emulsion.

Oral Emulsions are **Oral Liquids containing one or more active ingredients and are stabilized oil-in-water dispersions, either or both phases of which may contain dissolved solids.** Solids may also be suspended in Oral Emulsions. Emulsions may exhibit phase separation but are easily reformed on shaking. **-Indian Pharmacopoeia**

**Emulsions are two-phase systems in which one liquid is dispersed throughout another liquid in the form of small droplets. If oil is the dispersed phase and an aqueous solution is the continuous phase, the system is designated as oil-in-water emulsion. If water or an aqueous solution is the dispersed phase and oil or oleaginous material is the continuous phase, the system is designated as a water-in-oil emulsion.**

**-USP**

Emulsions are stabilized by emulsifying agents that prevent coalescence, the merging of small droplets into larger droplets and, ultimately, into a single separated phase. Emulsifying agents (surfactants) are used to stabilize emulsions by providing a physical barrier around the particle to coalescence. Surfactants also reduce the interfacial tension between the phases, thus increasing the ease of emulsification upon mixing.

## Theories of emulsification

Droplets can be stabilized by five methods:

- By reducing interfacial tension

- By preventing the coalescence of droplets.
    - By formation of rigid interfacial film
    - By forming electrical double layer.
- Film theory or adsorption theory.
- Viscosity theory.
- Wedge theory

## Film Theory (or) Adsorption Theory

As per this theory, the added emulsifying agent forms a mechanical film by adsorption at the interface of the liquid and offers stability to the emulsion. However, this theory could not explain the formation of type of emulsion.

## Viscosity Theory

As per this theory, an increase in viscosity of an emulsion will lead to an increase in stability. This theory failed to explain about the milk which shows considerable stability even though its viscosity is less.

## Wedge Theory

According to this theory, monovalent soap like sodium stearate give o/w type emulsion and divalent soap like calcium stearate give w/o type emulsion. This was explained by successful accommodation of the soap molecules to give the type of emulsion.

### Types of Emulsions

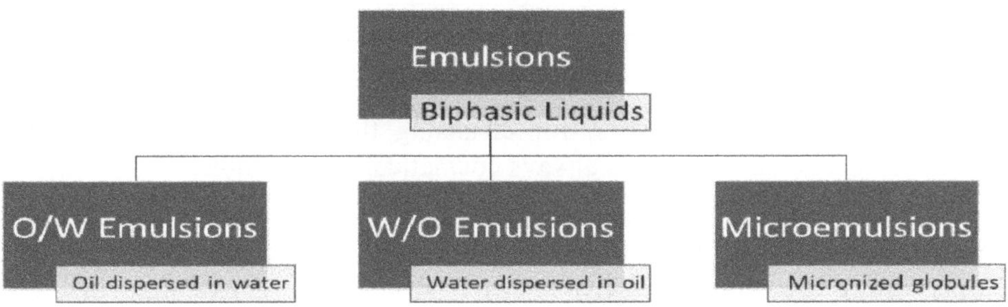


**Figure 14.2** Classes of emulsions.

The emulsions can be of various types: Two phase, three phase, micro emulsions. Among the two-phase systems O/W, W/O are the major types, while the three phase systems may be O/W/O and W/O/W (**Figure 14.2** & **Figure 14.3**). Micro and nano emulsions are other major types.

## Oil in Water Emulsion

The oil droplets are dispersed throughout the aqueous phase. Fats or oils for oral administration, either as medicaments or as vehicles for oil soluble drugs, are always formulated as oil in water (O/W) emulsions. They are non-greasy and are easily removable from the skin surface and they are used externally to provide cooling effect and internally to also mask the bitter taste of oil.

Water soluble drugs are more quickly released from O/W emulsion. O/W emulsion give a positive conductivity test as water, the external phase is a good conductor of electricity.

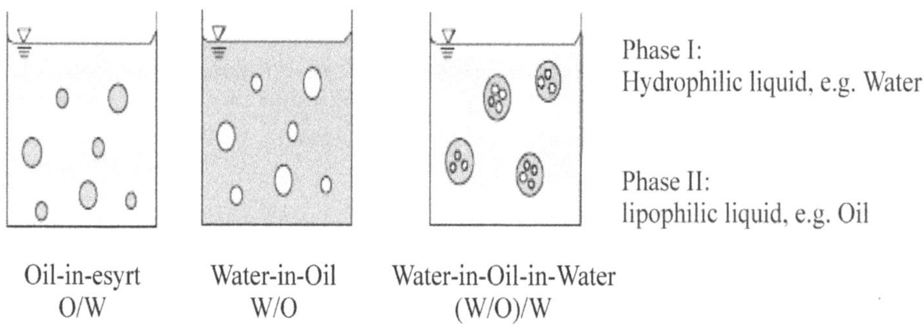


**Figure 14.3** Types of emulsions: Two and Three phase systems.

## Water in Oil Emulsion

A system in which the water is dispersed as globules in the oil continuous phase is termed water-in-oil emulsion (W/O).

Water-in-oil emulsions will have an occlusive effect by hydrating the stratum corneum.

W/O emulsion is also useful for cleansing the skin of oil soluble dirt, although its greasy texture is not always cosmetically acceptable.

They are greasy and not water washable and are used externally to prevent evaporation of the moisture from the surface of skin e.g. cold cream. Oil soluble drugs are more quickly released from W/O emulsion. They are preferred for formulation meant for external use like cream.

## Microemulsions

Microemulsions are systems consisting of water, oil and surfactant which constitute a single optically isotropic and thermodynamically stable liquid solution. There are two types of microemulsions:

- O/W microemulsion.
- W/O microemulsion.

To this emulsion, an aqueous solution of high Hydrophilic Lipophilic Balance (HLB) number surfactant is added while stirring at a certain amount of addition, a 'gel' phase is produced and further addition of surfactant solution, an inversion into O/W emulsion take place.

For W/O microemulsion, one start with O/W emulsion stabilized with an ionic or nonionic surfactant. This emulsion is titrated with a co-surfactant and the emulsion passes through a gel phase, after which further addition of co-surfactant result in the production of W/O microemulsion.

## Uses of Pharmaceutical Emulsions

The Pharmaceutical Emulsions may be used for systemic as well as topical uses.

**A. Systemic**

**Oral**

- For Nutrition- triglycerides (e.g. vegetable oils)
- For masking unpleasant flavour

**Parenteral**

- For nutrition - triglycerides
- For delivery of drugs poorly soluble in water
- For site-directed delivery of drugs
- For the small droplet size,
- For comparable to chylomicrons
- For delayed-release drug release (e.g. i.m.)

**Topical**

- These may be o/w or w/o. These can be applied or rubbed (Viscous in nature).
- For emollient effect, greasiness (enhancing acceptability).

## Radiopaque Emulsions

These emulsions are used as contrast media in conventional X-ray examinations and are being used since decades.

## Emulsions as Drug Delivery Systems

The Emulsions can also be sed as drug delivery systems in many ways.

- Diazepam: Emulsion eliminates pain due to crystallization of a solubilized drug following dilution in the bloodstream
- Vegetable oils: Delivery of substrates high in metabolic energy
- Propofol: Liquid anesthetic dissolved in emulsified oil
- Fluorocarbons: Artificial blood substitutes

### Advantages of Emulsion

- Unpalatable oils can be administered in palatable form.
- Unpalatable oil-soluble drugs can be administered in palatable form.
- The aqueous phase is easily flavored.
- The oily sensation is easily removed.
- The rate of absorption is increased.
- It is possible to include two incompatible ingredients, one in each phase of the emulsion.

### Disadvantages of Emulsion

- Formulation needs to be shaken well before use.
- A measuring device is needed for administration.
- Certain degree of technical accuracy is needed to measure a dose.
- Stability is affected by the storage conditions.
- Bulky, difficult to transport and prone to container breakages.
- Prone to microbial contamination which can lead to cracking.

### Identification Tests

Since emulsion (o/w or w/o) looks the same in appearance with naked eyes, therefore certain tests have been developed to differentiate between them.

At least two tests should be done to reach a conclusive decision about the identity of the emulsion (**Table 14.1**).

- **Dilution test**
- **Dye Test**
- **Cobalt Chloride Test**

- **Fluorescence Test**
- **Conductivity Test**

**Dilution test**

Here, the emulsion is diluted either with oil or water. O/W emulsion remains stable when diluted with water because the water is the dispersion medium in O/W emulsion. But if it is diluted with oil, the emulsion will break as oil and water are not miscible with each other.

O/W emulsion can easily be diluted with an aqueous solvent whereas W/O emulsion can be diluted with an oily liquid.

**Table 14.1** Methods of Determination of Emulsion Type.

| Test | Observation | Comments |
|---|---|---|
| Dilution | Emulsion can be diluted only with external phase | Useful for liquid emulsions only. |
| Dye test | Water soluble solid dye tints only o/w emulsions and reverse. (Microscopic observation) | May fail if ionic emulsifiers are present. |
| $CoCl_2$/ filter paper | Filter paper impregnated with $CoCl_2$ and dried (blue) changes to pink when o/w emulsion is added. | May fail if emulsion is unstable or breaks in presence of electrolyte. |
| Fluorescence | Since oils fluoresce under UV light, o/w emulsions exhibit dot pattern, w/o emulsions fluoresce throughout. | Not always applicable |
| Conductivity | Electric current is conducted by o/w emulsions, owing to presence of ionic species in water | Fails in nonionic o/w emulsions. |

**Dye Test**

In this test, when an emulsion is mixed with a water-soluble dye such as amaranth and observed under the microscope.

If the continuous phase appears red, then it means that the emulsion is o/w type as water is the external phase and the dye will dissolve in it to give color. But if the scattered globules appear red and continuous phase colorless, then it is w/o type. Similarly, if an oil soluble dye such as Scarlet red C or Sudan III is added to an emulsion and the continuous phase appears red, then it is w/o emulsion.

**Cobalt Chloride Test**

A filter paper soaked in cobalt chloride solution is added to an emulsion and dried. If it turns from blue to pink, indicating that the emulsion is O/W type. If there is no color change, it indicates that the emulsion is W/O type. This identification test may fail if emulsion is unstable or breaks in presence of electrolyte.

**Fluorescence Test**

If an emulsion on exposure to ultra-violet radiations shows continuous florescence under microscope, then it is W/O type.

On the other hand, if it shows only spotty fluorescence, it is O/W type. This test can be only used when the oil has property of fluorescence.

**Conductivity Test**

This test is based on the basic principle that water is a good conductor of electricity. Therefore, in case of O/W emulsion, this test will be positive as water is the external phase. In this test, an assembly consisting of a pair of electrodes connected to a lamp is dipped into an emulsion. If the emulsion is O/W type, the lamp glows; if the emulsion is W/O emulsion type, there is no glowing of lamp.

## Further Readings

- "Industrial Pharmacy-I" SWAYAM MOOC: www.swayam.gov.in
- https://www.tandfonline.com/doi/abs/10.3109/03639048609048050
- https://www.researchgate.net/publication/306939950_Formulation_of_Emulsions

## References


- Attwood D. In: Aulton ME (Editor), Pharmaceutics: The science of dosage form design. 2nd Edn., 2002, Churchil Livingstone, New York, pp. 70-99.
- Semalty et al., Essentials of Pharmaceutical Technology, II Edn, 2018, Pharma Med press, Hyderabad, India, ISBN 9789386819994.
- Becher P. Emulsions, Theory and Practice (2nd Ed.) 1965, Reinhold, New York, pp.2-149.
- Becher Paul. Encyclopedia of Emulsion Technology. Volume 4. Marcel Dekker, Inc.New York: 1996.
- Billany M. In: Aulton ME (Editor), Pharmaceutics: The science of dosage form design. 2nd Edn., 2002, Churchil Livingstone, New York, pp. 334-58
- Comelles F, Pascual A. Microemulsion-based media as novel drug delivery system. Adv.Drug Del.Rev. 1996; 45:89-121.

## CHAPTER 15

# Emulsions II (Formulation of Emulsions)

**Dr Mona Semalty, Dr Ajay Semalty**
Department of Pharmaceutical Sciences,
H.N.B Garhwal University (A Central University), Srinagar Garhwal-246174

### Learning Outcome

After completing this chapter, you will be able to understand about

- Formulation of emulsions
- Stability of emulsions
- Added excipients
- Methods of preparation of emulsions
- Evaluation of emulsions
- Packaging and labelling of emulsions

### Lesson Plan

- Formulation of emulsions
- Stability of emulsions
    - Sedimentation and creaming.
    - Thermodynamic instability (coalescence or cracking).
    - Phase inversion
- Additives for formulation of emulsions
- Methods of preparation and Evaluation of emulsions
- Packaging and labeling of emulsions

## Formulation of Emulsions

**There are two phases in an emulsion**

**Oil phase & Aqueous phase**

## Oil Phase

Selection of oil phase is important as it requires analysis of toxicity of the oil its consistency and possible chemical incompatibilities. Example includes Mineral oils and Edible vegetable oils.

Aqueous phase is water, and the internal phase concentration of water will be determined by the dosage requirement and Consistency desired.

The other additives used are-

- Emulsifying agents
- Auxiliary emulsifiers.
- Antimicrobial preservatives
- Antioxidants

## Stability Problems of Emulsions

The stability problems may occur due to change in physical attributes of emulsion such as increase in particle size or coalescence of droplets or phase inversion (**Figure 15.1**).

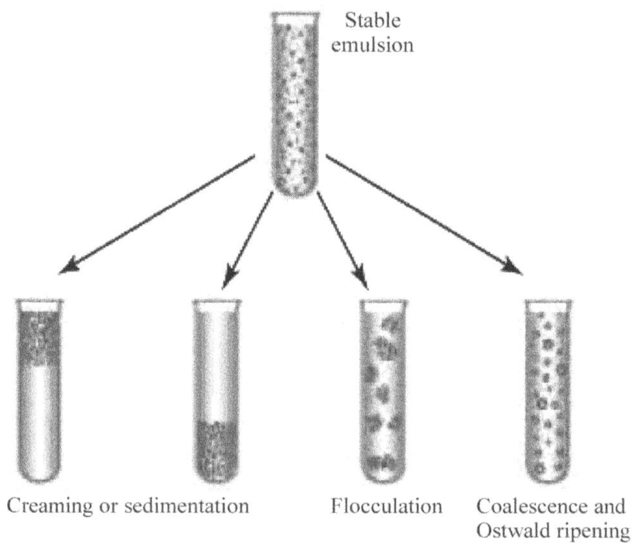


**Figure 15.1** Principal mechanisms of physical instability of emulsions.

The stability problems of emulsions may be of following types.

- Flocculation
- Cracking or coalescence
- Creaming and sedimentation
- Phase inversion
- Ostwald ripening

## Flocculation

It is reversible aggregation of droplet of internal phase in the form of three-dimensional clusters.

Flocculation of emulsion droplet can occur only when the mechanical and electrical barrier is sufficient to prevent droplet coalescence. Flocculation differs from coalescence by the fact that the interfacial films and individual droplet remains intact.

Redispersible association of particle within an emulsion to form large aggregates is called flocculation.

## Cracking or Coalescence

The oily and watery phase is completely separated due to merging droplets to form large drops.

"Coalescence is the fusion of two or more droplets of the disperse phase forming one droplet".

The Emulsions are thermodynamically unstable systems and there is positive interfacial free energy (IFE) between the two phases: IFE = Interfacial tension × surface area. To enhance their stability, the dispersed droplets come closer to each other and fuse to decrease the exposed surface area.

Unlike flocculation, Coalescence is irreversible. And redispersion cannot be achieved by shaking case in this.

An increase in the surfactant concentration or a replacement of the emulsifier being used can often improve the resistance of emulsions to coalescence.

Since coalescence is a function of droplet collisions with a subsequent merger of interfacial membranes, layers with strong repulsive interactions are better suited to stabilize emulsion droplets. A strong repulsive force may prevent collisions between droplets in the first place. Repulsive interactions can be altered by modifying the charge at the droplet surface or by using a surfactant that has a different thickness of the interfacial layer. Emulsions with sufficiently small droplets, which are prevented from aggregating or coalescing by the use of suitable emulsifiers, exhibit great physical stability.

Cracking or coalescence can be prevented by

- Monitoring globules size
- Viscosity of the continuous phase

- Selection of emulsifying agents
- Storage temperature

Smaller the particle slower is the creaming or sedimentation. Stable emulsions require a greater number of small size globules. A homogenizer is used to reduce droplet size by forcing the emulsion through a small aperture to reduce the size of the globules.

**Creaming and sedimentation:** When gravitational force is applied in dispersed droplet it moves upward or downward. When it moves upward it is called creaming and when it moves downward it is called sedimentation.

Creaming usually happens in o/w emulsions. Sedimentation usually happens in w/o emulsion.

Stoke's law expresses the rate of sedimentation or creaming by.

$$v = \frac{2r^2(\sigma - \rho)g}{9\eta}$$

Where $v$ = velocity of sedimentation or creaming of a dispersed particle of radius r, and density $\sigma$, in a liquid of density $\rho$, and viscosity $\eta$, and where g is the acceleration due to gravity.

**Viscosity of the continuous phase:** Increase in viscosity of the continuous phase will decrease the chances of creaming and coalescence as it reduces the movement of globules. Viscosity can be enhanced by -

- Using viscosity enhancers.
- Higher percentages of oil phase (o/w).
- Higher percent of solid fats in the oily phase
- Using emulsifying agents
- Forming interfacial film mechanical barrier
- Using surfactants
- Hydrocolloids enhance the viscosity of the medium.

Storage temperature: Increase in temperature can lead to an emulsion cracking as increased temperature decreases the viscosity of the continuous phase and disrupts the integrity of the interfacial film. An increasing number of collisions between droplets will also occur, leading to increased creaming and cracking.

## Phase Inversion

Phase inversion is a phenomenon of changes in the emulsion type i.e., the emulsion may spontaneously revert from oil-in-water to a water-in-oil emulsion or vice versa (Figure 15.2).

An approximate estimation may be obtained visually. Accelerating the separation by centrifugation followed by appropriate analysis of the specimen may be useful to quantitatively determine the phase separation.

The most stable range of disperse phase concentration is 30-60%. If the amount of disperse phase approaches or exceeds a theoretical maximum of 74% of the total volume, then phase inversion may occur. Addition of substances (which alter the solubility of an emulsifying agent) may also cause phase inversion. This process is irreversible.

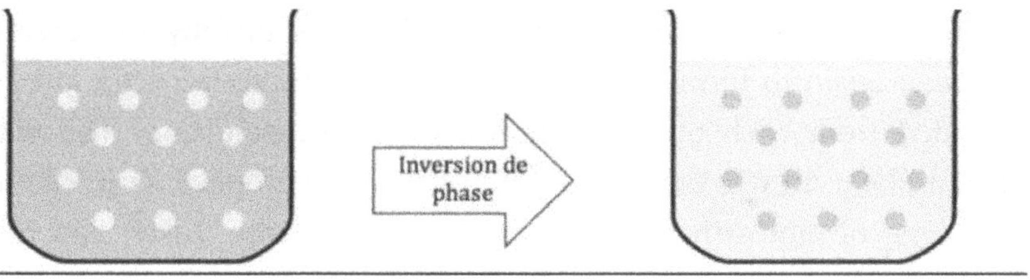


**Figure 15.2** Phase inversion.

**Ostwald ripening:** Ostwald ripening is the process whereby larger droplets grow at the expense of smaller ones, because of the transport of dispersed phase molecules from smaller to larger droplets through the intervening continuous phase (Figure 15.3).

Ostwald ripening is a function of the solubility of the dispersed phase, the addition of a second nonpolar lipid with a substantially lower solubility to the high-solubility dispersed phase can strongly reduce the growth of droplets. Another approach of minimizing the Ostwald ripening is to produce droplets as equal in size as possible (uniform size), so as to reduce the differences in capillary pressures.

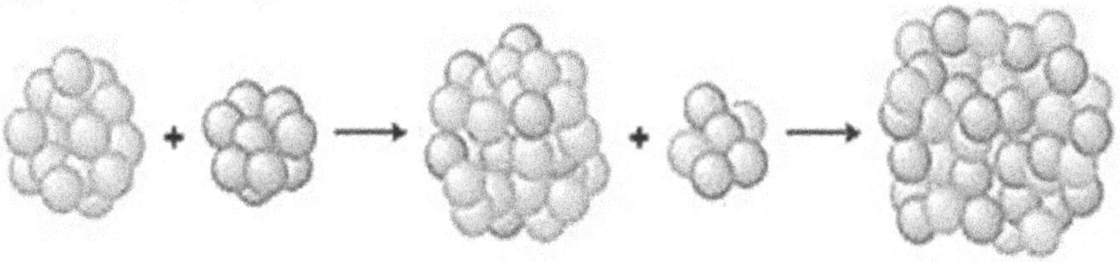

**Figure 15.3** Basic concept of Ostwald ripening.

**Additives for formulation of emulsions**

- Emulsifying agents
- Auxiliary emulsifiers.
- Antimicrobial preservatives
- Antioxidants

## Emulsifying Agents

Emulsifiers are compounds able to stabilize the dispersed droplets in the continuous phase (i.e. Prevention of coalescence and reducing creaming). Emulsifiers are molecules consisting of a water loving (hydrophilic) part and water-hating but oil-loving (lipophilic) part. With their lipophilic part emulsifiers wrap around and incorporate oil drops thereby preventing them from reunite again to form a separate oily phase. In this way, the oil particles are shielded from each other resulting in a stable emulsion. The choice of emulgent to be used will depend on Shelf life of the product; Type of emulsion desired; Cost of emulsifier; Compatibility; Nontoxicity; Taste; and Chemical stability.

**Properties of ideal emulsifying agents**

- Should reduce the interfacial tension between the two immiscible liquids.
- Physically and chemically stable, inert and compatible with the other ingredients of the formulation. Completely nonirritant and non-toxic in the concentrations used.
- Organoleptically inert i.e. should not impart any colour, odour or taste to the preparation.
- Should form a coherent film around the globules of the dispersed phase and should prevent the coalescence of the droplets of the dispersed phase.
- Should Produce and maintain the required viscosity of the preparation.

**Types of Emulsifying agents**

- Hydrocolloids.
- Surface active agents (SAA) (surfactants).
- Finely divided solids.
- Auxiliary emulsifiers

# Emulsifying Agents

## Hydrocolloids

Most of the emulsifiers form hydrated lyophilic colloids (called hydrocolloids) that form multimolecular layers around emulsion droplets. Hydrocolloid type emulsifiers (**Table 15.1**) have little or no effect on interfacial tension, but exert a protective colloid effect, reducing the potential for coalescence by:

- providing a protective sheath around the droplets
- imparting a charge to the dispersed droplets (so that they repel each other)
- swelling to increase the viscosity of the system (so that droplets are less likely to merge)

**Table 15.1** Organic hydrocolloids used in emulsion formulation.

| Source | Name | Comment |
|---|---|---|
| Tree exudate | Gum Arabic (acacia)<br>Gum Ghatti<br>Karaya<br>Tragacanth | Essentially neutral polysaccharide (ENP)<br><br>ENP<br>ENP |
| Sea weeds | Agar, carrageenan<br>alginates | Sulfated polysaccharides<br>Acidic polysaccharides |
| Seed extracts | Locust bean<br>Guar<br>Quince seed | ENP<br>ENP |
| Synthetics cellulose | Carboxy methyl-ether | Anionic polysaccharides |
| Collagen synthetic | Gelatin<br>Carboxyvinyl polymer<br>Polyoxethylene poly. | Amphoteric protein<br>Neutral<br>Anionic |

## Classification of Hydrophilic Colloids

- Natural-Plant origin and Animal origin
- Semisynthetic

## Natural Emulsifying agents from Plant Origin

These consist of agents which are carbohydrates and include gums and mucilaginous substances. Since these substances are of variable chemical composition, these exhibit considerable variation in emulsifying properties.

They are anionic in nature and produce o/w emulsions. They act as primary emulsifying agents as well as secondary emulsifying agents (emulsion stabilizers). Since carbohydrates acts a good medium for the growth of microorganism, therefore emulsions prepared using these emulsifying agents have to be suitably preserved in order to prevent microbial contamination. E.g. tragacanth, acacia, agar, chondrus (Irish Moss), pectin and starch.

## Natural Emulsifying agents from Animal Origin

The examples include gelatin, egg yolk and wool fat (anhydrous lanolin). Type A gelatin (Cationic) is generally used for preparing o/w emulsion while type B gelatin is used for o/w emulsions of pH 8 and above. Lecithin and cholesterol present in egg yolk also act as emulsifying agent. They show surface activity and are used for formulating o/w emulsions. However they are used only for extemporaneous preparation and not for commercial preparation as it darken and degrade rapidly in unpreserved systems. Wool fat is mainly used in w/o emulsions meant for external use. They absorb large quantities of water and form stable w/o emulsions with other oils and fats. Animal derivatives are more likely to cause allergic reactions and are subject to microbial growth and rancidity. Their advantage is their ability to support formation of w/o creams.

### Semi-synthetic hydrocolloids

This class includes mainly cellulose derivatives like sodium carboxy methyl cellulose, hydroxyl propyl cellulose and methyl cellulose. They are used for formulating o/w type of emulsions. They are nontoxic, and are less subject to microbial growth. They primarily act by increasing the viscosity of the system. Examples include low-viscosity grades of

- Methylcellulose (MC)
- Carboxymethylcellulose (CMC)
- Hydroxypropylmethylcellulose (HPMC)

### Synthetic hydrocolloids

Among the synthetic hydrocolloids Carbopol, Polyvinyl alcohol (PVA), Polyvinyl pyrolidone (PVP) etc. are there.

### Surface Active Agents (SAA) (surfactants)

Surface active agents (surfactants), also known as emulsifiers or emulsifying agents, are needed to provide the stability required over time. The stability of the emulsion determines its appropriate use. Surfactants are chemical compounds with a surface activity which, when dissolved in a liquid, especially water, lowers its interfacial or surface tension by preferential adsorption at the vapor/liquid surface or other interfaces. Surfactant molecules have two opposite affinities, one part is made up of a polar group yielding hydrophilic (water-loving) properties and one part is made up of a non polar radical giving it lipophilic (oil-loving) properties. There are numerous natural compounds that act as surfactants, but more commonly chemical compounds are synthesized to produce the desired characteristics. Surfactants can be grouped according to the type emulsions they yield.

**Anionic surfactants:** The long anion chain on dissociation imparts surface activity, while the cation is inactive. These agents are primarily used for external preparations and not for internal use as they have an unpleasant bitter taste and irritant action on the intestinal mucosa. e.g., alkali soaps (sodium stearate and potassium oleate; o/w), amine and ammonium soaps (triethanolamine oleate; o/w)., metallic soaps, alkyl sulphates (such as sodium lauryl sulphate (SLS); (o/w).) and phosphates and alkyl sulphonates., Soaps of divalent and trivalent metals (calcium oleate; w/o).

**Cationic surfactants**: The positive charge cations produced on dissociation are responsible for emulsifying properties. These are mainly used in external preparations such as lotions and creams. Quaternary ammonium compounds such as cetrimide, benzalkonium chloride and benzethonium chloride are examples of important cationic surfactants. These compounds besides having good antibacterial activity are also used in combination with secondary emulsifying agents to produce o/w emulsions for external application.

**Non-ionic surfactants:** These are the class of surfactants widely used as emulsifying agents. These are extensively used to produce both oil in water and water in oil emulsions for internal as well as for external use. The emulsions prepared using these surfactants remain stable over a wide range of pH changes and are not affected by the addition of acids and electrolytes. These surfactants also show low irritancy as compared to other surfactants. The examples of these surfactants include glycerol esters such as glyceryl monostearate, propylene glycol monostearate, macrogol esters such as polyoxyl stearates and polyoxyl-castor oil derivatives, sorbitan fatty acid esters such as spans and their polyoxyethylene derivatives such as tweens (polysorbates).

## Finely Divided Solids

Finely divided solids can be adsorbed at the oil water interface forming a coherent film that physically prevents coalescence of the dispersed phase. This group consists of finely divided solids having balanced hydrophilic lipophillic properties. They accumulate at the oil/water interface and form a coherent interfacial film around the droplets of dispersed phase globules and prevent coalescence. If the solid particles are preferentially wetted by oil, a w/o emulsion is formed; while o/w emulsion is formed when wetting is done by water. The emulsions formed using finely divided solids are stable and less prone to microbial contamination.

Examples:

- Natural clays as bentonite and aluminium magnesium silicate.
- Synthetic materials as colloidal silicon dioxide (Aerosil®).
- Colloidal aluminium and magnesium hydroxides are used for internal preparations.

**The Hydrophilic lipophilic balance system (HLB)**

An HLB number (1-20) represents the relative proportions of the lipophilic and hydrophilic parts of the molecule. High numbers (8-18) indicate a hydrophilic molecule and produce an o/w emulsion. Low numbers (3-6) indicate a lipophilic molecule and produce a w/o emulsion. Oils and waxy materials have a 'required HLB number' which helps in the selection of appropriate emulsifying agents when formulating emulsions. Liquid paraffin, for example, has a required HLB value of 4 to obtain a w/o emulsion and 12 for an o/w emulsion.

**Auxiliary emulsifying agents (Sterol-containing substances)**

These agents act as water-in-oil emulsifying agents. Examples include beeswax, wool fat and wool alcohols.

## Other Formulation Additives

**Buffers:** The inclusion of buffer may be necessary to maintain chemical stability, control tonicity or ensure physiological compatibility.

**Density Modifiers:** From Stoke's law, it can be seen that if the dispersed and continuous phase both have the same density then the sedimentation and creaming will not occur. Minor modification to the aqueous phase of a emulsion by incorporation of sucrose, dextrose glycerol or propylene glycol can be achieved.

**Consistency Builder:** It is possible to manipulate consistency of an emulsion system to an appreciable extent by changes in surfactant concentration, phase volume ratio etc. If adjustment in these components do not serve the purpose fully hydrocolloids may be added to aqueous phase or long chain waxes to the oil phases.

**Humectants:** They are added to emulsion in order to reduce the evaporation of water, either from packed product when the closure is removed or from the surface of skin after application e.g. Glycerol, Polyethylene glycol and Propylene glycol.

**Antioxidants:** Oxidation of emulsion component leads to rancidity of oil component with resultant bad odor and bad appearance. Oxidative tendency can be countered by inclusion of 0.001% to 0.1% of antioxidants like butylated hydroxytoulene, a-tocopherol etc. Combinations of antioxidants leads to synergistic effect. Other common antioxidants are propyl, octyl and dodecyl ester of gallic acid recommended for use at concentration up to 0.001% for fixed oils and up to 0.1% for essential oils. Efficiency of antioxidants depends upon its compatibility with other ingredients, its oil/water partition coefficient, the extent of its solubilization within molecule of the emulgent and its sorption on to the container and its closure. These antioxidants are liable to discoloration by light and hence emulsions should be packed in amber color or blue color bottles.

**Viscosity Enhancers:** It may be difficult for aqueous based topical solution to remains in place on the skin or in the eyes for any significant time because of their low viscosity. To counteract this effect low concentration of gelling agents can be used to increase the apparent viscosity of the product. Examples include Povidone, Hydroxyethyl cellulose and Carbomer.

**Preservative:** When choosing a suitable preservative it must be insured that adsorption of the preservative onto the container from the product does not occur and its efficiency is not impaired by the pH of the solution or by interactions with other ingredients. The effect of the partition coefficient is also important: A preservative with a low oil/water partition coefficient will have a higher concentration in the aqueous phase and hence better antimicrobial activity. A combination of preservatives may give the best preservative cover for an emulsion system. Some typical preservative used in pharmaceutical and cosmetics emulsions are given in **Table 15.2**.

Some preservatives in use are listed below:

- Benzoic acid: effective at a concentration of 0.1% at a pH below 5
- Esters of parahydroxybenzoic acid such as methyl paraben (0.01-0.3%)
- Chloroform, as chloroform water (0.25% v/v)
- Chlorocresol (0.05--0.2%)
- Phenoxyethanol (0.5-1.0%)
- Benzyl alcohol (0.1-3%)
- Quaternary ammonium compounds, e.g. cetrimide, (can be used as a primary emulsifying agent and also as a preservative)
- Organic mercurial compounds such as phenyl mercuric nitrate and acetate (0.001--0.002%).

**Table 15.2** Preservative used in emulsions.

| Type | Example | Characteristic and utility |
|---|---|---|
| Acids and acids derivatives | Benzoic acid sorbic acid and salt | Antifungal |
| Alcohol | Chlorobutanol<br>Phenoxy-2-ethanol | Eye preparation<br>Synergist |
| Aldehyde | Formaldehyde<br>Glutaraldehyde | Broad spectrum |
| Formaldehyde Donors | Mono-(and-)methylodimethyl hydantoin | Broad spectrum |
| Phenolic | Phenol, cresol,<br>Chlorothymol,<br>*o*-phenltphenol<br>*p*-Chlorometaxylenol | Broad spectrum |
| Quaternaries | Chlorhexidine and salt ,<br>Benzethonium chloride | Broad spectrum |
| Mercurials | Phenylmercuric acetate | Broad spectrum |

**Sweetening Agents:** Low molecular weight carbohydrates and in particular sucrose, are traditionally the most widely used sweetening agents. Sucrose has the advantage of being colorless, very soluble in water, stable over a pH range of about 4 to 8 and increasing the viscosity of fluid preparation. Artificial sweeteners can be used in conjugation with sugars and alcohol to enhance the degree of sweetness, in formulations for patients who must restrict their sugar intake. They are hundred and even thousands of times sweets than sucrose and are therefore rarely required a concentration greater than about 0.2%. Polyhydric alcohols such as sorbitol, mannitol and glycerin can also be used.

**Flavor and Perfumes:** The simple use of sweating agents may not be sufficient to render palatable a product containing drugs with particularly unpleasant taste. In many cases, therefore, a flavoring agent can be included (**Table 15.3**).

**Table 15.3** Suitable masking flavors for various product tastes.

| Type of products | Suitable Masking Flavors |
|---|---|
| Salty | Apricot, butterscotch, peach liquorice, vanilla |
| Bitter | Anise, chocolate,mint wild cherry. |
| Sweet | Vanilla. Fruits, berries |
| Sour | Citrous fruit, liquorice, raspberry. |

**Colours:** The overall appearance of liquid product depends on their color and clarity. Color selection is usually made to be consistent with flavor. Green or blue for mint and Red for berry.

## Theory of Emulsification

Emulsions are formed when the two phases are stabilized with the help of emulgents. The droplets can be stabilized by the following methods

A. By reducing interfacial tension

B. By preventing the coalescence of droplets.

- By formation of rigid interfacial film
- By forming electrical double layer.

## Interfacial Tension

The force causing each liquid to resist breaking up into smaller particle is called interfacial tension. Surfactants promote the lowering of this resistance.

## Interfacial Film

When water and oil are mixed in the presence of an emulsifier an interfacial film is formed at the oil water interface.

Amphiphilic molecules align themselves at a water-oil interface in the most favorable position - oleophilic portion in the oil phase and hydrophilic portion in aqueous phase. It is also well established that the surface active agents tend to concentrate at interface and that emulsifier are adsorbed at oil-water interfaces as monomolecular films. If the concentration of the emulsifier is high enough, it forms a rigid film between the immiscible phases, which acts as a mechanical barrier to both adhesion and coalescence of the emulsion droplets.

An interfacial film alters the rate of coalescence of droplets by acting as barriers. The similar film can produce repulsive electrical forces between approaching droplets. Such repulsion is due to an electrical double layer, which may arise from electrically charged groups oriented on the surface of emulsified globules. The potential produced by the double layer creates a repulsive effect between the oil droplets and thus hiders coalescence.

# Manufacturing of Emulsions

These are several physical and chemical parameters are selected which favors emulsion formation. The application of energy in the form of mechanical agitation, ultrasonic vibration or electricity is required to reduce the internal phase into small droplet. The amount of worked input depends on the length of time during which energy is supplied thus timing becomes another important physical parameter. Similarly chemical parameters like chemical stability, safety, choice of lipid phase and phase ratio is important to be considered for the formulation. As also discussed in theory of emulsion, emulsification techniques involve breakup of the internal phase and stabilization and coalescence.

## Techniques of Emulsification

Techniques of Emulsification can be classified in following way.

**A. Laboratory scale preparation techniques**

- Continental or dry gum method
- Wet gum method
- Bottle or Forbes bottle method
- Auxiliary method
- In situ soap method

**B. Large scale preparation techniques**

- Emulsification by vaporization
- Emulsification by phase inversion
- Low energy emulsification

# Laboratory Scale Preparation Techniques

## Continental or Dry Gum Method

The continental method is used to prepare the initial or primary emulsion from oil, water and a hydrocolloid or "gum" type emulsifier (usually acacia). The primary emulsion or emulsion nucleus is formed from 4 parts of oil, 2 parts of water and one part of gum. The 4 parts of oil and 1 part of gum represent their total amount for the final emulsion. In a mortar the 1 part of gum (acacia) is levigated with 4 parts of oil until the powder is thoroughly wetted; then the 2 parts water is added all at once and the mixture is vigorously and continuously triturated until the primary emulsion formed is creamy white (**Table 15.4**).

**Table 15.4** Ratio of oil: gum: water in primary emulsion.

| Type of Oil | Ratio of oil: gum: water |
|---|---|
| Fixed oil | 4:1:2 |
| Mineral oil | 3:1:2 |
| Volatile oil | 2:1:2 |
| Oleo gum resin | 1:1:2 |

Additional water or aqueous solutions may be incorporated after the primary emulsion is formed. Slid substances (e.g. active ingredients, preservatives, color, flavors) are generally dissolved and added as a solution to the primary emulsion; oil soluble substances in small amounts may be incorporated directly into the primary emulsion. Any substance which might reduce the physical stability of the emulsion, such as alcohol (which may precipitate the gum) should be added as near to the end of the process as possible to avoid breaking the emulsion. When all agents have been incorporated, the emulsion should be transferred to a calibrated vessel, brought to final volume with water, then homogenized or blended to ensure uniform distribution of ingredients.

## Wet Gum Method

The proportion of oil and water and emulsifier (gum) are the same as in dry gum method, but the order and technique of mixing are different. The gum is triturated with water to form mucilage; then oil is slowly added in portions, while triturating. After all the oil is added, the mixture is triturated for several minutes to form the primary emulsion. Then other ingredients are added as in continental method. Generally speaking, this method is more difficult to perform successfully, especially with more viscous oils, but may result in more stable emulsions.

## Bottle Method

Bottle method is used to prepare emulsions of volatile oils, or oleaginous substances of very low viscosities. Acacia (or other gum) is placed in a dry bottle and oil is added, the bottle is capped and thoroughly shaken. To this the required volume of water is added all at once and the mixture is shaken thoroughly until the primary emulsion is formed. It is important to minimize the initial amount of time the gum and oil are mixed. The gum will tend to imbibe the oil and will become water proof.

## Auxiliary Method

An emulsion prepared by other methods can also be improved by passing it through a hand homogenizer, which forces the emulsion through a very small orifice, reducing the dispersed droplet size to about 5 microns or less.

## In situ soap Method

This method involves the use of soaps as an emulsifier/surfactants e.g. calcium soaps. Water in oil emulsions contains oils such as oleic acid, in combination with lime water (calcium hydroxide solution, USP). Emulsion is prepared by mixing equal volumes of oil and lime water.

## Large Scale Preparation Techniques

### Emulsification by Vaporization

Heat is important factor to be considered because vaporization is an effective way of breaking almost all the bonds between the molecules of liquids. An increase in temperature decreases the internal tension as well as viscosity. When emulsion is stored at elevated temperature for a longer period of time the kinetic energy of droplets is raised thereby facilitates their coalescence.

Changes in temperature alter the distribution coefficients of emulsifiers between the two phases and cause emulsifier migration. The distribution of the emulsifier as a function of temperature cannot be correlated directly with either emulsion formation or stability.

## Emulsification by Phase Inversion

The temperature at which the inversion occurs depends upon emulsifier concentration and is called phase inversion temperature (PIT). This type of inversion can occur during emulsion formulation because they are generally prepared at high temperature and then allowed top cool at room temperature. Emulsions formed by a phase inversion technique are generally considered quite stable and are believed to contain finally dispersed internal phase. So the emulsions must have a PIT as high more possible as, always higher than the storage temperature. The phase inversion temperature is considered to be the temperature at which the hydrophilic and lipophilic properties of the emulsifier are in balance and is therefore also called the HLB temperature.

## Low Energy Emulsification

The classic process of emulsification described requires considerable expenditure of energy during both the cooling and the heating cycles of emulsion formation. In this process all of internal phase, but only a portion of external phase is heated. After emulsification of heated portions, the remainder of external phase is added to the emulsion concentrate, or the preformed concentrate is blended into the continuous phase. In those emulsion in which a phase inversion temperature exists, the emulsion concentrate is preferable prepared above the phase inversion temperature, which results in emulsions having extremely small droplet size.

## Equipment for Emulsification

The most important factor involved in the formation of emulsion is degree of share and turbulence required to produce a given dispersion a liquid droplets. The amount of agitation required depends on total volume of liquid to be mixed, the viscosity of the system, Interfacial tension at oil/water interface. Emulsion can be formulated using the following equipment.

- Mechanical stirrers
- Ultrasonifier
- Homogenizers
- Colloid mills

**[Please refer "Semalty et al., Essentials of Pharmaceutical Technology II Edn, pharma Med Press, 2019" for the details of the equipment.]**

## Quality control tests for Emulsions

Stability of emulsions can be done keeping the following points in focus.

Final evaluation should be done in final container as:

- The ingredients may interact with the container.
- Some material may leach out from the container.
- Loss of water and volatile ingredients may occur through the container or closures.

Further to study emulsion stability following parameters are generally studied under stress condition (accelerated stability studies; refer Chapter 12, ***"Semalty et al., Essentials of Pharmaceutical Technology II Edn, pharma Med Press, 2019"***) for:

- Thermal stress
- Aging and temperature
- Phase inversion temperature
- Gravitational stress
- Agitation

## Physical Parameters of Evaluation

- **Phase separation:** Phase separation is a phenomenon of changes in the emulsion type i.e., the emulsion may spontaneously revert from oil-in-water to a water-in-oil emulsion or vice versa. An approximate estimation may be obtained visually. Accelerating the separation by centrifugation followed by appropriate analysis of the specimen may be useful to quantitatively determine the phase separation.
- **Viscosity:** Cone and plate viscometers are suitable for emulsions but instruments using coaxial cylinders are easy to use. Penetrometres can be used when the preparation is too viscous. Use of heliapath attachment with Brookfield viscometer helps in detection of creaming tendency and hence it is advisable to study rheological properties over extended period of time which can help in prediction of long-term behavior.
- **Globule size:** The globule size in emulsions is measured by microscopic methods or by electronic devices such as coulter counter. In either of these two techniques the original product has to be suitably diluted before estimation. The dilution may introduce errors because of incomplete deflocculation or new pattern of flocculation. Hence while making judgment about the stability of the emulsions this aspect should be kept in mind. Globule size also determines the appearance of emulsion (Table 15.5). Therefore, the appearance of an emulsion may also indicate the globule size in an emulsion.

**Table 15.5** Globule size and appearance of emulsions.

| Globule size(mm) | Appearance |
|---|---|
| >1 | White |
| 0.1-1.0 | Blue-white |
| 0.05-0.1 | Opalescent, semitransparent |
| <0.5 | Transparent |

- **Electrical Conductivity:** It is determined by using Platinum electrodes (diameter 0.4 mm, distance 4 mm) microamperometrically to produce a current of 15 to 50 mA. Measurements are made on emulsions stored at room temperature or at $37^0$ C for short time. Stable o/w emulsions offer less resistance, but droplet aggregation increases resistance. A stable w/o emulsion doesn't conduct electricity, but with droplet coagulation conductivity increases.
- **Electrophoretic Properties:** Zeta potential (See Chapter 5; Suspension) of emulsion can be measured with the aid of moving boundary method or more quickly and directly, by observing the movement of particles under the influence of electric current. The Zeta potential is essentially useful for assessing the flocculation since electrical changes on particles influences the rate of flocculation.

## Stability Testing

Stability testing of emulsions involves determining stability at long term storage conditions, accelerated storage conditions, freezing and thawing conditions. Stress conditions are applied in order to speed up the stability testing. The stress conditions used for speeding up instability of emulsions include: Centrifugal force, Agitational force, Aging and temperature

The following physical parameters are evaluated to assess the effect of any of the above stress conditions:

- Phase separation
- Viscosity
- Electrophoretic properties
- Particle size and particle count

1. **Gravitational stress:** Centrifugation at 3750 rpm in a 10 cm radius centrifuge for a period of 5 hrs is equivalent to the effect of gravity for about one year:

**2. Thermal stress**

- Aging and temperature
- Phase inversion temperature

PIT is more, rate of coalescence will be less. So the emulsions must have a PIT as high as possible as – always higher as the storage temp.

## Packaging of Emulsions

Depending on the use, emulsions should be packed in suitable containers. Emulsions meant for oral use are usually packed in well filled bottles having an air tight closure. Light sensitive products are packed in amber color bottles. For more viscous emulsions, wide mouth bottles should be used.

## Labeling of Emulsions

The label on the emulsion should mention that these products have to be shaken thoroughly before use.

External use products should clearly mention on their label that they are meant for external use only.

## Storage of Emulsions

The production rate of emulsion plants is generally greater than demand; therefore, storage facilities make it possible to have longer production runs, thus improving plant productivity. Present day emulsions may be stored for up to several months without major changes in physical properties. It is advisable to use small diameter vertical storage tanks with a minimum horizontal cross section with a dip tube filling pipe which reaches to or near the bottom of the storage tank. Emulsions of different ionic types should never be mixed and tanks should be thoroughly cleaned before refilling with a different ionic type. Provisions should also be made to ensure proper agitation of stored emulsion to prevent settling, decantation or creaming. Emulsions are sensitive to frost which can cause irreversible breaking; therefore, provisions should also be made to prevent stored emulsion from freezing.

## Microemulsions

Microemulsions are recently developed advanced type of emulsions. Microemulsions can be defined as isotropic, thermodynamically stable solutions in which substantial amounts of two immiscible liquids (i.e., water and oil) are brought into a single phase by means of an appropriate surfactant or surfactant mixture. The majority of microemulsions are produced in the presence of co-surfactants of which the most commonly used are low molecular weight alcohols. Microemulsions can be sterilized by filtration and their production is relatively simple and inexpensive. Because of these properties, they have attracted a great interest as drug delivery vehicles. Some more advanced emulsions with extremely smaller globule size have also been investigated by various scientists (Table 15.6).

## Major advantages of Microemulsions

- Ease of preparation, clarity, stability
- Ability to be filtered
- Ability to encapsulate drugs of different HLB in the same system because the microemulsions can solubilize oil soluble, water soluble and interface soluble drugs
- Low viscosity

## Preparation of Microemulsions

Microemulsions can be prepared by blending oil, water, surfactant and cosurfactants with mild agitation or mild heat. For preparing o/w microemulsions, w/o emulsion containing a lipophilic surface-active agent may be used as a base. In this process, hydrophilic surface-active agent is added by stirring which initially forms cubic structure but on further addition of hydrophilic surface-active agent forms microemulsions.

## Characterization of Microemulsions

The internal structure elucidation of microemulsions can be done by Small angle X-ray scattering (SAXS), small angle neutron scattering (SANS), dynamic (or laser) light scattering (DLS), transmission electron microscopy, nuclear magnetic resonance, and time resolved fluorescence quenching methods have also been used. Other physicochemical parameters of evaluation include conductance, viscosity, dielectric permittivity, ultrasonic interferometry, ultrasonic absorption, thermal conductivity and infrared spectroscopy.

## Applications of Microemulsions

Microemulsions can be applied as liquid membrane carriers to transport lipophilic substances through an aqueous medium or to carry hydrophilic substances across lipoidal medium Microemulsions have been used mainly for peroral delivery of peptides and have also been reported as drug carriers for topical, dermal, transdermal and pulmonary administrations of drugs. Microemulsions have also great potential as i.v. vehicles for sparingly soluble substances by virtue of their high solubilization capacity.

**Table 15.6** Comparative features of emulsions, nanoemulsion and microemulsion.

| | Name | Diameter | T/D Stability | Appearance | Surfactant: Oil |
|---|---|---|---|---|---|
| $R_1$ | Emulsion | 0.1 -100μm | No | Opaque | <1:10 |
| $R_2$ | Microemulsion | 10-100nm | No | Clear Cloudy | ≈1:1 |
| $R_3$ | Nanoemulsion | 5-50nm | Yes | Clear cloudy | >1:1 |

## Further Readings

- "Industrial Pharmacy-I" SWAYAM MOOC: www.swayam.gov.in
- https://www.tandfonline.com/doi/abs/10.3109/03639048609048050
- https://www.researchgate.net/publication/306939950_Formulation_of_Emulsions

## References


- Semalty et al., Essentials of Pharmaceutical Technology, II Edn, 2019, Pharma Med press, Hyderabad, India, ISBN 9789386819994.
- Attwood D. In: Aulton ME (Editor), Pharmaceutics: The science of dosage form design. 2nd Edn., 2002, Churchil Livingstone, New York, pp. 70-99.
- Becher P. Emulsions, Theory and Practice (2nd Ed.) 1965, Reinhold, New York, pp.2-149.
- Becher Paul. Encyclopedia of Emulsion Technology. Volume 4. Marcel Dekker, Inc.New York: 1996.
- Billany M. In: Aulton ME (Editor), Pharmaceutics: The science of dosage form design. 2nd Edn., 2002, Churchil Livingstone, New York, pp. 334-58
- Comelles F, Pascual A. Microemulsion-based media as novel drug delivery system. Adv. Drug Del.Rev. 1996; 45:89-121
- Corswant C., Thoren P., Engstrom S. Triglyceride- based microemulsion for intravenous administration of sparingly soluble substances. J.Pharm.Sci. 1998; 87:200-208
- Dickinson E. 1992. An Introduction to Food Colloids. Oxford University Press, Oxford.
- Emsap W, Paeratakul O, Siepmann J, In; Banker GS, Rhodes CT (Eds). Modern Pharmaceutics. 2005 (Vol. 121) Marcel Dekker, Inc. New York, Basel, US, pp 237-85.

- Florence AT and Whitehill D. Multiple Emulsions, Formulation and stability. Int. J. Pharmaceutics, 1982;11:277-278
- Florence AT and Whitehill D. The formulation and stability of multiple emulsions. J. Pharm.Pharmacol. 1982; 34: 687.
- Herbert, W. J. Multiple emulsions, a new form of mineral-oil antigen adjuvant. Lancet 1965;2: 771.
- Iliescu, Cristina-Alina. Investigation on the thermal stability of technical and cosmetic emulsions 2005; 30; 21-22.
- IUPAC, Brownian motion. IUPAC Compendium of Chemical Terminology 1990, 62, 2177.
- Laetitia O, Monique S, Lev B, Madelein B, Thi-Nhat

# CHAPTER 16

# Suspension Dosage Form

**Dr Mona Semalty, Dr Ajay Semalty**
Department of Pharmaceutical Sciences,
H.N.B Garhwal University (A Central University), Srinagar Garhwal-246174

### Learning Outcome

- What are suspensions?
- What are advantages / disadvantages of suspensions?
- What are theories of suspensions?
- Flocculated and deflocculated suspensions, their properties
- Formulation evaluation packing and storage of pharmaceutical suspensions

### Lesson Plan

- Introduction of suspension, merits and demerits
- Classification
- Ideal properties of suspensions
- Theories of suspension
- Flocculated and deflocculated suspensions
- Formulation aspect of suspensions
- Evaluation, stability/packaging storage

## Suspension

Suspension is heterogeneous system consisting of two phases. This biphasic dosage form is a coarse dispersion in which insoluble solid particles are dispersed in a liquid medium. The particles have diameters for the most part greater than 0.1 µm. The disperse phase is distributed in particulate form throughout another (the continuous phase).

"Suspension is a dispersion of finely divided insoluble solid particles (disperse phase) in a fluid (dispersion medium). Dispersion medium is mostly aqueous or may be oily liquid, while dispersed phase comprises insoluble solids."

### Advantages of Suspension

- Suspension can improve chemical stability of certain drugs.

  e.g. Procaine penicillin G

- Drug in suspension exhibits higher rate of bioavailability than other dosage forms.
- Duration and onset of action can be controlled.
  e.g. Protamine Zinc-Insulin suspension
- Suspension can mask the unpleasant/ bitter taste of drug.
  e.g. Chloramphenicol.

## Disadvantages

- Physical stability, sedimentation and compaction can cause problems.
- It is bulky, sufficient care must be taken during handling and transport.
- It is difficult to formulate.
- Uniform and accurate dose cannot be achieved unless suspension are packed in unit dosage form.

Most pharmaceutical suspension consists of aqueous dispersion medium but in some instances it may be an oily liquid. The particles have diameter for the most part greater than 0.1 μm and some particle and some particles are observed under the microscope to exhibit Brownian movement if the dispersion has low viscosity. Pharmaceutical suspension may be classified into three groups on the basis of routes of administration, particle size, electrokinetic nature of particles, and proportion of solid particles (**Table 16.1**).

**Table 16.1** Classification of Pharmaceutical suspensions.

| Based on Routes of Administration | Based on Size of Solid Particles | Based on Electrokinetic Nature of Solid Particles | Based on Proportion of Solid Particles |
|---|---|---|---|
| • Oral suspension<br>• Externally applied suspension<br>• Parenteral suspension | • Colloidal suspension (< 1 μ)<br>• Coarse suspension (>1 μ) | • Flocculated suspension<br>• Defloc-culated suspension | • Dilute suspension (2 to10%w/v solid)<br>• Concentrated suspension (50%w/v solid) |

**An ideal suspension should have**

Physical properties of well formulated suspension

- Suspensions should possess good pourability leading to ease of removal of dose from container,
- should have good organoleptic properties,
- should have uniform particle size distribution,
- should be ease of redispersion of settled solid particles,
- should be physically and chemically stable,
- should be resistant against microbial contamination.
- Therapeutic active/Chemically / physically stable, and esthetic appeal.
- Consistency should be uniform after shaking
- Should settle slowly and should be redispersible upon gentle container shaking.
- Should not form a hard cake.
- An ideal suspension should have
- Therapeutic active/Chemically / physically stable, and esthetic appeal.
- Consistency should be uniform after shaking
- Should settle slowly and should be redispersible upon gentle container shaking.
- Should not form a hard cake.

## Theories of Suspensions

### Sedimentation Concept

In dispersions the dispersed particles encounter between themselves as a result of Brownian movement. Depending upon the forces of interactions (electrical forces of repulsion, forces of attraction and forces arising due to salvation) the particles aggregate to form collection of particles. The collisions result in permanent contact of particles known as coagulation leading to the formation of larger aggregates, which sediment out known to exhibit flocculation or if the particles rebound they remain freely suspended and form stable system. These particles sediment according to stokes' law.

According to Stokes' law, the sedimentation velocity is expressed by following equation:

$$v = \frac{2r^2(\sigma - \rho)g}{9\eta}$$

where v is velocity of sedimentation, a is the radius of particles, $\rho_s$ density of solid particles, g is acceleration due to gravity and $\rho_l$ is the density of liquid and $\eta$ is the viscosity of the dispersion phase.

The equation of stokes' law reflects that larger particles exhibit greater velocity of sedimentation. The velocity of sedimentation is inversely proportional to the viscosity of dispersion medium.

## Interfacial Phenomenon

Smaller solid particles are used to disperse in a continuous medium. Smaller particle size and large surface area is associated with a surface free energy making it thermodynamically unstable. Thus, the particles possess high energy which leads to grouping together to reduce surface free energy thus leading to formation of floccules. These floccules are held together among themselves and within by weak Van-der-waals forces. However, in cases where particles are adhered by stronger forces to form aggregates forming hard cake. These phenomena occur in order to make system more thermodynamically stable. In order to achieve a state of stability the system tend to reduce the surface free energy, which may be accomplished by reduction of interfacial tension that is achieved by use of surfactants.

## Zeta Potential

It indicates the degree of electrostatic repulsion. For molecules and particles that are small enough, a high zeta potential will confer stability, i.e., the solution or dispersion will resist aggregation. When the potential is small, attractive forces may exceed this repulsion and the dispersion may break and flocculate. So, high zeta potential (negative or positive) electrically stabilizes suspension while low zeta potentials tend to coagulate or flocculate the suspension (**Figure 16.1**).

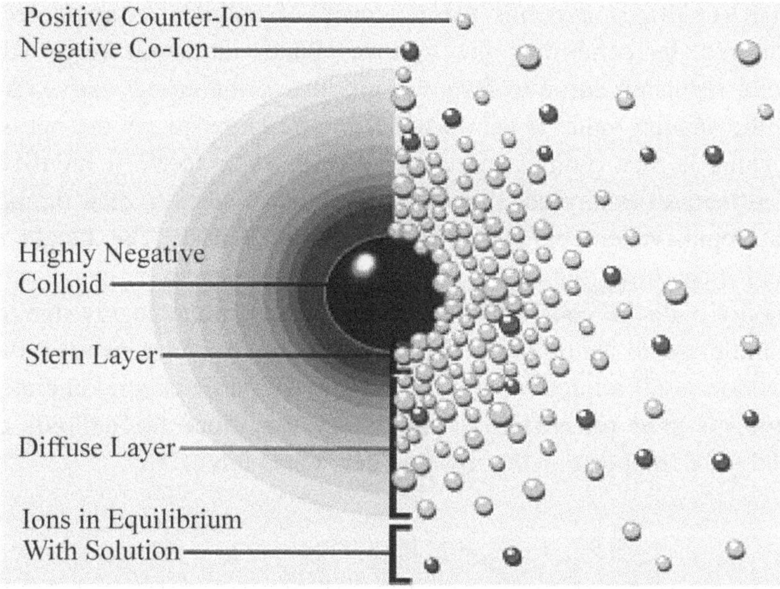


**Figure 16.1** Two Ways to Visualize the Double Layer, The left view shows the change in charge density around the colloid. The right view shows the distribution of positive and negative ions around the charged colloid.

## DLVO theory

The DLVO Theory (named after Derjaguin, Landau, Verwey and Overbeek) is the classical explanation of the stability of colloids in suspension. It looks at the balance between two opposing forces electrostatic repulsion and Van der Waals attraction, to explain why some colloidal systems agglomerate while others do not. Electrostatic repulsion becomes significant when two colloids approach each other and their double layers begin to interfere. Energy is required to overcome this repulsion. An electrostatic repulsion curve is used to indicate the energy that must be overcome if the particles are to be forced together. It has a maximum value when they are almost touching and decreases to zero outside the double layer. The maximum energy is related to the surface potential and the zeta potential.

The theory states that the stability of a suspension depends on Van der Waalsattractive (VA) and electrical double layer repulsive (VR) forces that exist between particles as they approach each other due to the Brownian motion they are undergoing. The Van der Waals forces depend on chemical nature and size of particle. The electrostatic repulsive forces depend on density, surface charge and thickness of double layer.

The DLVO theory explains the tendency of colloids to agglomerate or remain discrete by combining the Van der Waals attraction curve with the electrostatic repulsion curve to form the net interaction energy curve. At each distance, the smaller value is subtracted from the larger to get the net energy. The net value is then plotted and a curve (Fig. 16.2: above if repulsive and below if attractive) is formed. If there is a repulsive section, then the point of maximum repulsive energy is called the energy barrier. The height of the barrier indicates how stable the system is. In order to agglomerate, two particles on a collision course must have sufficient kinetic energy due to their velocity and mass, to "jump over" this barrier. If the barrier is cleared, then the net interaction is all attractive, and as a result the particles agglomerate. This inner region is after referred to as an energy trap since the colloids can be considered to be trapped together by Van der Waals forces.

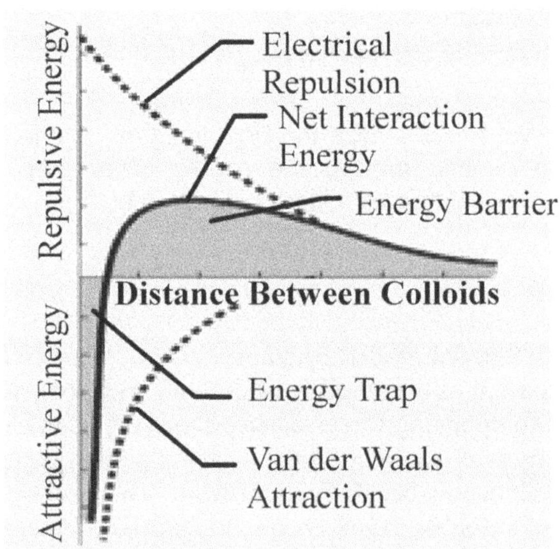


**Figure 16.2** DLVO Theory: The net interaction curve.

In many cases we can alter the environment to either increase or decrease the energy barrier, depending upon our goals. Various methods can be used to achieve this, such as changing the ionic environment, or pH, or adding surface active materials to directly affect the charge of the colloid. In each case, zeta potential measurements can indicate the impact of the alteration on overall stability.

## Brownian Movement

Brownian movement prevents sedimentation by keeping the dispersed material in random motion. Brownian movement depends on the density of dispersed phase and the density and viscosity of the disperse medium.

## Flocculated and Deflocculated Suspension

A suspension may be flocculated or deflocculated type depending on the relative magnitudes of force of repulsion, force of attraction between particles.

## Flocculated System

In this type of system, the solid particles of dispersed phase aggregate leading to network like structure of solid particles in dispersion medium. The aggregates form no hard cake. These aggregates settle rapidly due to their size as rate of sedimentation is high and sediment formed is loose and easily redispersible. The suspension is not elegant, as dispersed phase tends to separate out from the dispersion medium. Therefore, it is desired that flocculation should be carried out in a controlled manner so that a balance exists between the rate of sedimentation and nature of sediment formed and pourability of the suspension.

There are two important steps to formulate flocculated suspension

- The wetting of particles
- Controlled flocculation

The primary step in formulation is that adequate wetting of particles is ensured. Suitable amount of wetting agents solve this problem which is described under wetting agents.

## Controlled Flocculation

A deflocculated system with high viscosity to prevent sedimentation would be an ideal formulation. The next stage of formulation process, after the addition of wetting agent, is to ensure that the product exhibit the correct degree of flocculation. Under flocculation will give those undesirable properties that are associated with the deflocculated system. While an over flocculated product will be inelegant and, to minimize settling, the viscosity of the product may have to be so high that any necessary redispersion would be difficult. Controlled flocculation is usually achieved by a combination of particle size control, the use of electrolytes to control zeta potential, and addition of polymers to enable cross linking to occur between particles. Some polymers have advantage of becoming ionized in an aqueous solution, and can therefore act both electrostatically and sterically. These materials are also termed as polyelectrolyte.

### Properties of Flocculated Suspensions

- Particles in the suspension are in form of loose agglomerates.
- Flocs are collection of particles, so rate of sedimentation is high.
- The sediment is formed rapidly.
- The sediment is loosely packed. Particles are not bounded tightly to each other. Hard cake is not formed.
- The sediment is easily redispersed by small amount of agitation.
- The flocculated suspensions exhibit plastic or pseudo plastic behaviour.
- The suspension is somewhat unsightly, due to rapid sedimentation and presence of an obvious clear supernatant region.
- The pressure distribution in this type of suspension is uniform at all places, i.e. the pressure at the top and bottom of the suspension is same.
- In this type of suspension, the viscosity is nearly same at different depth level.
- The purpose of uniform dose distribution is fulfilled by flocculated suspension.

## Deflocculated System

In this type of system, the solid particles exist as separate entities in dispersion medium. The sediments form hard cake. The solid drug particles settle slowly as rate of sedimentation is low. As sediments are formed eventually there is difficulty of redispersion. The suspension is more elegant as dispersed phase remain suspended for a long-time giving uniform appearance. In deflocculated suspension the individual particle should remain dispersed. In some material where the quantum of surface charge is not sufficient the particle may exhibit the tendency of coming together and forming large particle. To overcome this tendency, some material carrying good charge and which can get easily absorbed on the dispersed phase particle can be added. These additives are referred as dispersants (for example darvans, daxads, marasperses). These are polymerized organic salts of alkyl/aryl substances which increase the zeta potential considerably thus encouraging particles to break energy barrier and comes together.

## Properties of Deflocculated Suspensions

- Particle size is less as compared to flocculated particles. Particles settle separately and hence, rate of settling is very low.
- The sediment after some period of time becomes very closely packed, due to weight of upper layers of sedimenting materials.
- After sediment becomes closely packed, the repulsive forces between particles overcome resulting in a non-dispersible cake.
- More concentrated deflocculated systems may exhibit dilatant behavior.
- This type of suspension has a pleasing appearance, since the particles are suspended for relatively longer period of time.
- The supernatant liquid is cloudy even though majority of particles have been settled.
- There is no clear-cut boundary between sediment and supernatant.

## Formulation of Pharmaceutical Suspensions

The formulator must encounter important problems regarding particle size distribution, specific surface area, inhibition of crystal growth and changes in the polymorphic form. The formulator must ensure that these and other properties should not change after long term storage and do not adversely affect the performance of suspension. Choice of pH, particle size, viscosity, flocculation, taste, color and odor are some of the most important factors that must be controlled at the time of formulation.

## Drug

The drug/API with defined Size distribution of the powder should be used. API with defined chemical/physical stability and defined surface charge should be used.

### Vehicle for suspension

Formulation of suspension includes:

- Structured vehicles
- Other components

## Structured Vehicles

Structured vehicles are used to formulate the stable suspension so that particles remain deflocculated, with ease of dispersibility with a minimum agitation. Structured vehicle concept is applicable only to deflocculated suspensions, where hard solid cake forms due to settling of solid particles and they must be redispersed easily and uniformly at the time of administration. Structured vehicles are prepared with the help of Hydrocolloids. In a particular medium, they first hydrolyzed and swell to great degree and increase viscosity at the lower concentration. In addition, it can act as a 'Protective colloid' and stabilize charge. Density of structured vehicle also can be increased by: Polyvinylpyrrolidone, Sugars, Polyethylene glycols and by using Glycerin.

## Wetting Agents

Some insoluble solids get easily wetted by water, most of them exhibits hydrophobicity and do not get easily wetted by it. Wetting agents are additives which are usually added to decrease this hydrophobicity. These agents generally get adsorbed at the solid-liquid interface and promote wetting of the solid particles by the liquid of the dispersion medium.

- **Surfactants:** Generally, Surfactants possessing HLB values between 7 and 9 have been employed as wetting agents. These orient themselves at solid-liquid interface and decrease the interfacial tension between the particles of the dispersed phase and the dispersed medium. Most surfactants are used at concentration of 0.1 to 0.2%. The minimum concentration that is sufficient to cause wetting should generally be employed since an excess of these agents may cause foaming in the preparation. Examples of surfactants employed for oral preparation include polysorbates, sorbitan, esters, etc; for external preparations, sodium lauryl sulfate, sodium dioctyl sulfosuccinate and quillia extracts can also be used. Ionic as well as non-ionic surfactants may be employed as flocculation agent.
- **Hydrophilic Polymers:** Various hydrophilic colloids such as acacia, bentonite, and colloidal silicon dioxide and cellulose derivatives have also been employed as wetting agents. These act by coating the surface of hydrophobic particles and imparting hydrophilic character to these.
- **Hydrophilic Liquids:** Hydrophilic liquids such as alcohol, glycerol, propylene glycol, are sometimes employed as wetting agents. These

penetrate the loose aggregates of solid particles and displace the air from the pores thus facilitating wetting of the particles by the dispersion medium.

## Flocculating Agents

These are substances added to cause controlled aggregation of the particles of the dispersed phase in a suspension. Examples of such agents include surfactants, electrolytes and hydrophilic polymers.

- **Electrolytes:** Electrolytes such as sodium salt of acetates, phosphates and citrates have been commonly employed as flocculating agents. These act by neutralizing the surface charge on the particles of the dispersed phase thereby reducing the electrical barrier between them. The effectiveness of the electrolytes as flocculating agents depends on the valance of the ions of these electrolytes. Thus, divalent ions are ten times more effective than the monovalent ions while trivalent ones are thousand times more effective. The concentration of the electrolytes used should be minimum that is required to cause flocculation since an excess may cause reversal of this phenomenon.
- **Polymeric Flocculating Agents:** Their linear branched chain molecules form a gel like network within the system and become absorbed on the surface of dispersed particle thus holding them in a flocculated state. E.g. Starch, alginates cellulose derivatives, carbomers, tragacanth, silicates.

## Viscosity Enhancers/ Suspending Agents

They are added with the objective to increase apparent viscosity of the continuous phase thus preventing rapid sedimentation of the dispersed particles. The selection of the type and concentration of a suspending agent depends on sedimentation rate of dispersed particles, pourability and spreadibility (**Table 16.2**). The ideal suspending agent should have a high viscosity at negligible shear i.e., during shelf storage and it should have a low viscosity at high shearing rates i.e., it should be free flowing during agitation, pouring and spreadibility. A suspending agent that is thixotropic as well as pseudoplastic should prove to be useful as it forms a gel on standing and becomes fluid when shaken. They include natural polysaccharides (Gum Acacia, Gum Tragacanth, Guar Gum, Sodium Alginate, Xanthan Gum and Carrageenan), Semi-synthetic polysaccharides (Sodium Carboxymethyl-cellulose, Methyl Cellulose, Hydroxyethyl Cellulose, Hydroxypropyl Cellulose, Hydroxypropyl Methyl Cellulose and Microcrystalline Cellulose),

Clays (Aluminium Magnesium Silicate, Bentonite and Hectorite) and synthetic agents (Carbomer, Colloidal silicon dioxide). Pseudoplastic substances like tragacanth, sodium alginate and sodium carboxymethyl cellulose show these desirable qualities. In cases of combination use of suspending agents like bentonite and CMC dispersions are both pseudoplastic and thixotropic. The suspending agents which gave highest stability are jota carrageenan (having low-temperature gelation characteristics) and MC/CMC (having thixotropic flux).

**Table 16.2** Suspending agents and their properties.

| Suspending agents | Stability pH range | Concentrations used as suspending agent (%) |
|---|---|---|
| Sodium alginate | 4-10 | 1– 5 |
| Methylcellulose | 3-11 | 1– 2 |
| Hydroxyethylcellulose | 2-12 | 1-2 |
| Hydroxypropylcellulose | 6-8 | 1-2 |
| Hydroxypropylmethylcellulose | 3-11 | 1-2 |
| Carboxy methyl cellulose | 7-9 | 1-2 |
| Sodium Carboxy methyl cellulose | 5-10 | 0.1-5 |
| Microcrystalline cellulose | 1-11 | 0.6– 1.5 |
| Tragacanth | 4-8 | 1-5 |
| Xanthangum | 3-12 | 0.05-0.5 |
| Bentonite | > 6 | 0.5– 5.0 |
| Carageenan | 6-10 | 0.5– 1 |
| Guar gum | 4-10.5 | 1-5 |
| Colloidal silicon dioxide | 0-7.5 | 2– 4 |

## Miscellaneous

Other additives to be included in the formulation of a suspension are as followed.

- *Buffers and pH adjusting agents*: They are added to stabilize the suspension to a desired pH range.
- *Osmotic agents*: They are added to adjust osmotic pressure comparable to biological fluid.

- *Coloring agents*: They are added to impart desired color to suspension and improve elegance.
- *Preservatives*: They are added to prevent microbial growth.

### Method of Preparation

There are three precipitation methods: *Organic solvent precipitation, Precipitation affected by changing the pH of the medium and double decomposition.* Water soluble drugs can be precipitated by dissolving them in water-miscible organic solvents and then adding the organic phase to distilled water under standard conditions. Examples of organic solvent include ethanol, methanol, propylene glycol, and polyethylene glycol. The important factor next to particle size control is that the correct polymorphic form or hydrates of crystals are obtained. Besides the influence of the solvent on crystals characteristics the following additional factors may need to be considered: Preparation under sterile conditions, Inherent solvent entrapment, toxicity, volume ratio of the organic to the aqueous phase, Rate and method of addition of one phase to other, temperature control, and finally, the washing of precipitate.

Precipitation affected by changing the pH of the medium and double decomposition is perhaps more readily accomplished and does not present the same difficulties associated with organic solvent precipitation. Although consideration of physical factors is needed for the production of stable suspension.

## Dispersion Method

When the dispersive method is utilized for suspension precipitation, the vehicle must be formulated so that the solid phase is easily wetted and dispersed. The use of surfactant is desirable to ensure uniform wetting of hydrophobic solids. The particle size reduction may or may not result from dispersion process. If particle size reduction occur the particle obtained may have different solubility of a metastable state is involved, and this may lead to transient supersaturation of the system.

### Evaluation of Suspension

Methods used for evaluation of suspension are categorized as :

(a) Sedimentation method

(b) Rheological method

(c) Electrokinetic method

(d) Micromeritic method

(e) Stability study

## Sedimentation Method

Since formation of sediment and its redispersibility are two features related to suspension acceptability. The sediment formed should redisperse by moderate shaking to yield homogenous system. The measurement of the sedimentation volume and its ease of redispersion form two of the most common basic evaluative procedures. The sedimentation volume is the simple ratio of the height of sediment to initial height of the initial suspension. The larger the value better is the suspendability.

The simplest procedure for evaluation is to keep a measured volume of a suspension in a graduated cylinder in an undisturbed state for a certain period of time and note the volume of sediment.

**Sedimentation volume** is a ratio of the final or ultimate volume of sediment ($V_u$) to the original volume of sediment ($V_O$) before settling.

$$F = V_u / V_O$$

Sometime 'F' is represented as 'Vs' and as expressed as percentage. Similarly, when a measuring cylinder is used to measure the volume. The volume of sediment is expressed as ultimate height (Hu) and initial height of suspension (HO).

Sedimentation volume = Hu/Ho

= ultimate height / initial height

Sedimentation volume is dependent on time and likely to vary at different period of time. Sedimentation volume can have values ranging from less than 1 to greater than1; F is normally less than 1. The products for which F = 1, such product is said to be in flocculation equilibrium, and show no clear Supernatant on standing.

Sedimentation volume ($F_d$) for deflocculated suspension

$$F_d = V_d / V_O$$

where, $F_d$ = sedimentation volume of deflocculated suspension

$V_d$ = sediment volume of completely deflocculated suspension. (Sediment volume ultimate relatively small)

$V_O$ = original volume of suspension.

The degree of settling can be related to the amount of sediment that would be produced in the ultimate dispersed state. To obtain the completely dispersed suspension form which represent the least space for the solid phase and hence the smallest sedimentation volume, electrolytes that promotes settling may be added or the preparation may be centrifuged.

Rate of sedimentation can be estimated by the use of an oden's balance. This consists of a pan suspended in the suspension and counterbalanced against weights or attached to a painter which moves on a rotating smoking drum. As more and more particles settle on pan moves down or more weight to keep the original balance.

Redispersibility can be estimated by shaking the suspension with the help of a mechanical device.

## Degree of Flocculation (β)

Degree of flocculation is an expression of the increased sediment volume resulting from flocculation. As the value of β (expressed as followed) approaches unity, the degree of flocculation decreases.

$$\beta = F / F_{\infty}$$

$$= \frac{V_u / V_o}{V_{\infty} / V_o}$$

$$= V_u / V_{\infty}$$

$$= \frac{\text{Ultimate sediment volume of flocculated suspension}}{\text{Ultimate sediment volume of deflocculated suspension}}$$

## Rheological Methods

Rheologic methods can help in determining the settling behaviour of the suspension. In these methods low shear rates are employed and samples are evaluated undisturbed. Evaluation of thixotropy (isothermal slow reversible conversion of gel to sol) in case of parenteral suspensions is most desirable. Properly formulated suspension can prevent sedimentation, aggregation and caking by the virtue of a high yield value/ viscosity at rest which sharp agitation reduces the viscosity to permit pouring and thus dispensing of product.

This technique also indicates in which level of the suspension the structure is greater due to particles aggregates. Data obtained on aged and stored suspension reveals whether changes have taken place.

## Viscosity

Various different viscometers are used to measure viscosity of different fluids and semisolids. Few of them are: Ostwald viscometer, Falling Sphere Viscometer, Cup and Bob Viscometer, Cone and plate viscometer, Falling Sphere Viscometer, Brookefield Viscometer (For details refer: Semalty et al., Essentials of Pharmaceutical Technology, II Edn, 2018, Pharma Med press, Hyderabad, India,).

## Electrokinetic Method

The surface electric charge or zeta potential is instrumental in deciding the stability of disperse phase system. Certain zeta potential produces more stable suspension because of controlled flocculation. The migration velocities of particles can be measured by electrophoretic method and zeta potential can be calculated from it.

## Micromeritic Method

The stability of a suspension is very much dependent on to the particle size and particle size distribution of its disperse phase. A growth in the particle size is a pointer towards its instability since such an occurrence can ultimately results in the formation of lumps or cake destroying the physical structure of suspension.

Particle size analysis is performed by optical microscopy, sedimentation by using Andreasen apparatus and Coulter counter apparatus. None of these methods are direct methods. However microscopic method allows the observer to view the actual particles. The sedimentation method yields a particle size relative to the rate at which particles settle through a suspending medium.

## Stability Testing

It is not possible to conduct accelerated temperature studies as it can be done in solutions a rise in temperature may change the thixotropic properties of the formulations. In this physical form, the preparation would exhibit parameters that could not be extrapolated to those that would exist in the normal system.

The valid temperature data could be obtained that will be useful in the estimation of the physical stability of a product at normal storage conditions. The extended aging tests must be employed under various conditions to obtain the desired information.

As per the WHO guidelines on stability testing, following physical parameters can be studied for accelerated (stress) stability testing of suspension.

- Viscosity, where appropriate
- Resuspendability
- Effects of freezing
- pH
- polymorphic conversion

## Nanosuspensions

Nanosuspensions are the recently developed biphasic dosage forms which have been developed for the delivery of poorly water-soluble and poorly water- and lipid-soluble drugs (belonging to class III as classified in Biopharmaceutical Classification System or BCS).

***Nanosuspensions can be defined as colloidal dispersions of nano-sized drug particles that are produced by a suitable method and stabilized by a suitable stabilizer.***

### Advantages of Nanosuspensions

- Increased dissolution rate and saturation solubility of the drug. The dissolution rate of the nanosuspension increases due to a great increase in the surface area of the drug particles from microns to particles of nanometer size. This effect can be explained by modified Noyes-Whitney's equation, which expresses the rate of drug dissolution at a specific time as following equation.

$$\frac{dx}{dt} = \frac{A.D.K}{h}.C_s - \frac{Xd}{V}$$

where dx/dt is the dissolution rate, A is the surface area of the particle available for dissolution, D is the diffusion rate constant, K is the oil water partition coefficient, h is the thickness of the stagnant layer surrounding the particle, $C_s$ is the saturation solubility of the drug, Xd is the amount dissolved of drug at time t and V is the volume of the dissolution media.

Due to creation of high-energy surfaces when disrupting the more or less ideal drug microcrystals to nanoparticles, saturation solubility of the drug in nanosuspension is also increased.

- **Possible Diversification of Products:** As the flexibility is offered in the modification of surface properties and particle size, and ease of post-production processing of nanosuspensions, the nanosuspension can be incorporated in various dosage forms, such as tablets, pellets, suppositories and hydrogels, for various routes of administration.
- **Improved biological activity:** Improvement in the dissolution rate and saturation solubility of a drug leads to an improvement in the *in vivo* activity of the drug.
- **Easy to manufacture and scale-up:** Nanosuspensions are easy to manufacture. The nanosuspension's production processes (media milling and high-pressure homogenization) are easily scaled up for commercial production.
- **Good stability:** Nanosuspensions show long term physical stability due to the absence of Ostwald ripening. Ostwald ripening has been described for ultrafine dispersed systems and is responsible for crystal growth and subsequently formation of microparticles. The Ostwald ripening leads to the formation of a supersaturated solution around the large particles and consequently to drug crystallization and growth of the large particles leading to adverse effect on long term stability. The nanosuspensions lack the Ostwald ripening due to uniform particle size, which is created by various manufacturing processes. The absence of particles with large differences in their size in nanosuspensions prevents the existence of the different saturation solubilities and concentration gradients in the vicinity of differently sized particles, which in turn prevents the Ostwald ripening effect.

## Packaging and Storage of Suspensions

- Suspensions should be packaged in wide mouth containers. It should have adequate air space above the liquid. Suspensions should be stored in tight containers protected from: freezing, excessive heat & light. These are stored in room temperature if it is dry powder (25 °C). Every effort should be made to avoid temperature fluctuation.

## Further Readings

- "Industrial Pharmacy-I" SWAYAM MOOC: www.swayam.gov.in
- https://www.youtube.com/watch?v=hSUtFDbvqyU

- https://www.researchgate.net/publication/326293246_PHARMACEUTICAL_SUSPENSIONS_PATIENT_COMPLIANCE_ORAL_DOSAGE_FORMS
- https://www.youtube.com/watch?v=15PkDYSoS6s
- https://www.youtube.com/watch?v=CbvzL41WK68

## References


- Semalty et al., Essentials of Pharmaceutical Technology, II Edn, 2019, Pharma Med press, Hyderabad, India, ISBN 9789386819994.
- Attwood D. In: Aulton ME (Editor), Pharmaceutics: The science of dosage form design. 2nd Edn., 2002, Churchil Livingstone, New York, pp. 70-99.
- Billany M. In: Aulton ME (Editor), Pharmaceutics: The science of dosage form design. 2nd Edn., 2002, Churchil Livingstone, New York, pp. 334-58.
- Emsap W, Paeratakul O, Siepmann J, In; Banker GS, Rhodes CT (Eds). Modern Pharmaceutics. 2005(Vol. 121) Marcel Dekker, Inc. New York, Basel, US, pp 237-85.
- Martin A. and Swarbrick J., in sprowls, American Pharmacy, 6 th Edition, Lippincott, Philadelphia, 1966, p.205
- Napper DH, Polymeric Stabilization of Colloidal Dispersions, Academic Press, New York (1983)
- Nash RA. *Suspensions. In*: J Swarbrick, JC Boylan (ed). Encyclopedia of pharmaceutical technology. Second edition vol. 3. New York, Marcel dekker, 2002, p. 2045-3032.
- Patel NK, Kenon L, and Levinson RS. In; Lachman L, Lieberman HA, Kanig JL. Eds. The Theory and Practices of Industrial Pharmacy. (3rd Edition) 1986, Varghese Publishing House, Bombay, pp Pgs. 479 – 501
- Winfield AJ, In: Winfield AJ, Richards RME (Eds). Pharmaceutical Practice, 3rd Edn, 2004, Churchill Livingstone, New York, pp. 191-97.
- World Health Organization, WHO Technical Report Series, No. 953, 2009.
- Zografi G; Schott H. and Swarbrick J., in: Remington's Pharmaceutical Sciences (18th Edition), Philadelphia College of Pharmacy and Science Pg. 257 (1990).

CHAPTER 17

# Parenterals I (Introduction: Preformulation of Parenterals)

**Dr Mona Semalty, Dr Ajay Semalty**
Department of Pharmaceutical Sciences,
H.N.B Garhwal University (A Central University), Srinagar Garhwal-246174

### Learning Outcome

- The fundamentals (concept, advantages and disadvantages)
- The requirements of a parenteral product
- Important preformulation factors to be taken into consideration before for formulating a parenteral product.
- Routes of administration of parenteral products and their suitability.

### Lesson Plan

- Introduction of parenteral and their principal characteristics
- Advantages and disadvantages of parenterals
- Routes of administration of parenterals
- Preformulation of parenterals: crystals characteristics, Chemical modification, polymorphism, pH &pKa

## Introduction

The parenteral or injectables are very popular dosage forms administered in the form of injection and it comes under the category of sterile dosage forms. As this dosage form is administered directly into the systemic circulation i.e., into the blood, sterility is utmost necessary. It shows quick onset of action as compared to other dosage forms and the most useful for the delivery of medicaments which are degraded in the presence of gastric environment.

"The term parenterals is derived from Greek words "para" and "enteron", means outside the intestine." Parenteral products are prepared keeping in view to meet the Pharmacopoeial standards for sterility, pyrogenicity, particulate matter etc. A well designed and maintained manufacturing plant layout is the utmost requirement for formulation of parenterals.

"Parenteral articles are preparations intended for injection through the skin or other external boundary tissue, rather than through the alimentary canal, so that the active substances they contain are administered using gravity or force, directly into a blood vessel, organ, tissue, or lesion."

- ***United States Pharmacopoeia***

## Advantages of Parenterals

The parenteral formulations have various advantages.

- Quick onset of action
- Maximum bioavailability
- Suitable for the drugs which are not administered by oral route
- Useful for unconscious/vomiting/ Non-cooperative patients.
- Duration of action can be prolonged by modifying formulation.
- Suitable for nutritive like glucose & electrolyte.
- Suitable for the drugs which are inactivated in GIT or HCl (GI fluid)

## Disadvantages of Parenterals

- Only trained person is required
- If given by wrong route, difficult to control adverse effect
- Difficult to save patient if overdose
- Sensitivity or allergic reaction at the site of injection
- Requires strict control of sterility & non pyrogenicity than other formulation.

- Once injected cannot be controlled (retreat)
- Injections may cause pain at the site of administration.

## Properties of Parenterals

A parenteral dosage form must have certain characteristics/properties, which are as followed.

- Sterility
- Free from viable and non-viable microorganisms
- Free from any particulate matter (dust, fibre etc.)
- Clear transparent solution
- Stable in different conditions of temperature and humidity
- Should be Isotonic with blood plasma
- Solvents or vehicles used must meet special purity and other standards.
- Must be prepared under aseptic conditions.
- Requires specific and high-quality packaging.

# Routes of Administration

Parenterals can be administered by various routes which can be classified as primary and secondary parenteral routes (**Table 17.1**).

**Table 17.1** Parenteral Routes of Drug Administration.

| Routes | Usual volume (ml) | Needle commonly used | Types of medication administered |
|---|---|---|---|
| **Primary parenteral routes** | | | |
| ***Small volume parenterals*** | | | |
| Subcutaneous | 0.5-2 | 5/8 in., 23 gauge | Insulin, vaccines |
| Intramuscular | 0.5-2 | 1½ in., 22 gauge | Nearly all drug classes |
| Intravenous | 1-100 | 1½-in., 20-22 gauge | Nearly all drug classes |
| ***Large volume parenterals*** | 1000 and larger (infusion units) | 1½ in., 18-19 gauge | Nearly all drug classes like electrolytes and nutrients to restore blood volume & to prevent tissue dehydration. |

**Table 17.1** ***Contd...***

| Routes | Usual volume (ml) | Needle commonly used | Types of medication administered |
|---|---|---|---|
| **Other parenteral routes** | | | |
| ***Intra-arterial:*** directly into an artery (immediate action sought in peripheral area) | 2-20 | 20-22 gauge | Radiopaque media, antineoplastic, antibiotics |
| ***Intrathecal*** (intraspinal) | 1-4 | 24-28 gauge | Local anesthetics, analgesics; neurolytic agents |
| ***Intraepidural*** (into epidural space near spinal column) | 6-30 | 5 in., 16-18 gauge | Local anesthetics, narcotics, steroids |
| ***Intra-articular:*** directly into the joint, usually for a local effect there, as for steroid anti-inflammatory action in arthritis | 2-20 | 1.5-2 in., 18-22 gauge | Morphine, local anesthetics, steroids, NSAIDs, antibiotics |
| ***Intracardial:*** directly into the heart when life is threatened | 0.2-1 | 5 in., 22 gauge | Cardiotonic drugs, calcium |
| ***Intrapeural:*** directly into the pleural cavity or a lung (also used for fluid withdrawal) | 2-30 | 2-5 in., 16-22 gauge | Local anesthetics, narcotics, chemotherapeutic agents |

Subcutaneous (s.c.), Intravenous (i.v.) and Intramuscular (i.m.) routes constitutes primary (Figure 17.1), while Intra-arterial, Intrathecal, Intraarticular, Intrapleural, Intracardial and Intradermal constitutes other routes of parenteral administration.

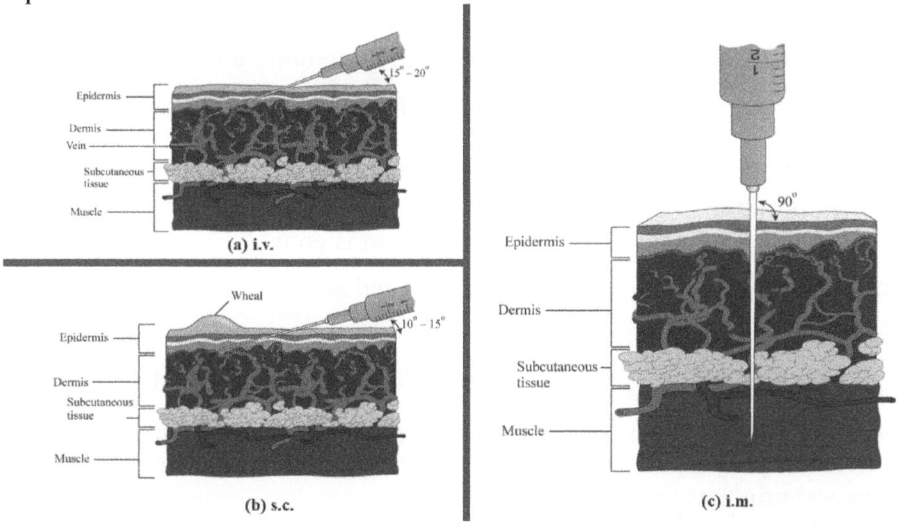


**Figure 17.1** Parenteral Routes of Drug Administration.

## Preformulation

The aim of preformulation study is to develop effective, safe and stable formulation. For that we need to assess physical, chemical and biological properties of the medicament. As it forms basis for the selection of suitable vehicle (aqueous or non-aqueous), excipients (antioxidants, antimicrobials, preservatives, buffers, solubilizing agents and tonicity adjusters) and containers and closures.

The important properties with reference to preformulation of parenterals includes solubility, pKa, pH, solid state characteristics, chemical modification of drug and polymorphism etc.

### Solubility/pKa/pH

Solubility (when a drug substance is dissolved in a unit volume of liquid (solvent) to form a saturated solution under specific condition of temperature and pressure) is one of the important parameter in preformulation of parenterals most of the parenterals dosage form exist in solution form so it should maintain its properties, consistency and stability in liquid form. Solubility is a function of hygroscopicity, chemical nature and pKa of the salt. In general term we state that if the pKa is at least two units lower than the pH of the medium, complete dissolution can be achieved; the opposite holds true for basic compounds. Other considerations like dilution prior to administration, and the rate of administration (dilution factor) should also be simulated using in vitro techniques. Thus, by determining and manipulating the solubility, pH and pKa one can develop a parenteral dosage form with its stability and safety.

When a drug substance is dissolved in a liquid it gets dissociated in ionized and unionized form. The unionized substances are lipid soluble thus dissolve in lipid material of the membrane and transported by passive diffusion and their absorption is rapid. Whereas the ionized substances are a lipid insoluble therefore their permeation is slow and absorption is poor.

The percentage of ionization can be calculated as-

For Acidic compounds: = PH = pKa + log ionized drug/un-ionized drug

For Basic compounds: PH = pKa + log un-ionized drug/ionized drug

For acidic drugs pKa ranges from 3-7.5. for basic drugs pKa ranges from 7-11. Besides, pH plays a vital role in stability of solution and suspension type of parenteral products.

**pH value for parenteral products:**

| | |
|---|---|
| Ideal pH 7 | pH of blood |
| Above pH 9 | Tissue necrosis |
| Below pH 3 | Extreme pain at site of injection |

The methods used to increase solubility are change in pH, cosolvency, dielectric constant, solubilization by surfactant, complexation, hydrotrophy, and chemical modification of drug, etc. Care must be taken when using co solvents although they increase the solubility but as they are conjugate acid base systems there may be a shift of pKa of the buffer or salt results and it may affect the integrity of the formulation like there may be precipitation or degradation of salt.

## Solid State Characteristics

Any active drug substance exists in two types of physical forms crystalline form or amorphous form. Crystalline form is when it exists in crystal form and amorphous form is when it exists in powder form. Both the physical form has its own significance with respect to absorption and bioavailability.

Crystalline characteristics are analyzed by microscopy and X-ray powder diffractometry (XRPD). Crystal habit or the external shape (cubic, tetragonal, hexagonal etc.) of a crystal may be determined by microscopy.

**Crystal → form XRPD → Sharp peak → Slow absorption → prolonged duration of action (e.g. crystalline or ultralente insulin).**

**Amorphous Form → XRPD → Diffused Peak → Rapid Absorption → Short duration of action (e.g. amorphous or semilente insulin).**

Amorphous form of the drug is generally rapidly absorbed but show a short duration of action (e.g. amorphous or semilente insulin). On the other hand crystalline form is slowly absorbed but show a prolonged duration of action (e.g. crystalline or ultralente insulin). So, the combination of crystalline and amorphous form of a same drug may provide a dosage form with combined benefits of rapid onset and prolonged duration of action (e,g. lente insulin, a physical mixture of 70% crystalline ultralente and 30% amorphous semilente insulin). Moreover, the crystalline form of the drug can withstand the high thermal stress (dry heat for several hours) as compared to amorphous form (e.g. Pencillin G).

## Chemical Modification of the Drug

The properties like stability, solubility, and depot action can be improved; while formulation difficulties and pain on injection can be minimized can be improved by the preparation of an ester, salt, or other modification of the parent structure of parenteral drugs. These modified drugs that convert back to the active parent structure are known as a prodrugs. Benzathine penicillin, procaine penicillin, metronidazole phosphate and chloramphenicol sodium succinate are some examples of Antibiotic Prodrugs; while methylprednisolone sodium succinate, hydrocortisone sodium succinate are some steroidal Injectable prodrugs.

The preparation of salts of parenteral drugs is one of the most important and popular tools for improvement of stability and modulating solubility. IV and IM Injectable solutions may require high solubility for loading or incorporating more quantity of drug into acceptable volumes for bolus administration. Sodium and potassium salts of weak acids and hydrochloride and sulfate salts of weak bases are widely used in parenterals requiring highly soluble compounds, based on their overall safety and history of clinical acceptance.

If the solubility of a drug is to be reduced to enhance stability or to prepare a suspension, the formulator may prepare water insoluble salts. Ex: Procaine Penicillin G: decrease solubility (7 mg/ml) of which, when compared with the very soluble penicillin G potassium, is utilized to prepare stable parenteral suspensions. Another alternative to prepare an insoluble drug is to use the parent acidic or basic drug and to buffer the pH of the suspension in the range of minimum solubility.

## Polymorphism

Several crystal forms of a given chemical exhibits different physical properties. The conversion of one polymorph to another may cause a significant change in the physical properties of the drug and it has important formulation, biopharmaceutical, and chemical process implications. The aspect of polymorphism that is of particular concern to the parenteral formulator is the physical stability and bioavailability of the product. For example, cortisone acetate exists in five polymorphic form but first polymorphic form is the most stable one. Indomethacin exists on three polymorphic form but two polymorphic form I and II have higher therapeutic efficacy. Substances that exists different polymorphs must be evaluated for stability in liquid form as well as its thermal stability, as parenteral dosage form must be sterile.

Apart from this we need to analyze the following factors before formulation of a parenteral dosage form.

- Melting point
- Thermal profile
- Particle size and shape
- Hygroscopicity potential
- Ionization constant
- Light stability
- Optical activity
- pH solubility profile
- pH stability profile
- Polymorphism potential
- Solvate formation

## Further Readings

- "Industrial Pharmacy-I" SWAYAM MOOC: www.swayam.gov.in
- https://www.mdpi.com/1420-3049/20/10/18759https://www.taylorfrancis.com/books/e/9781420086447/chapters/10.3109%2F9781420086447-7
- https://www.crcpress.com/Pharmaceutical-Preformulation-and-Formulation-A-Practical-Guide-from-Candidate/Gibson/p/book/9781420025965

- https://www.crcpress.com/Handbook-of-Preformulation-Chemical-Biological-and-Botanical-Drugs/Niazi/p/book/9780849371936

## References


- Akers MJ, Larrimore Daniel S, Guazzo DM. Parenteral Quality Control Sterility, Pyrogen, Particulate, and Package Integrity Testing, III Edn, 2003, Marcel Dekker, Inc. New York, Basel, US.
- Avis KE, In; Lachman L, Lieberman HA, Kanig JL. Eds. The Theory and Practices of Industrial Pharmacy. Varghese Publishing House, Bombay, pp. 430-78.
- Boylan JC, Nail SL, In; Banker GS, Rhodes CT (Eds). Modern Pharmaceutics. 2005 (Vol. 121) Marcel Dekker, Inc. New York, Basel, US, pp 381-414.
- Chapman DG, In: Winfield AJ, Richards RME (Eds). Pharmaceutical Practice, 3rdEdn, 2004, Churchil Livingstone, New York, pp. 247-63.
- Deluca PP, Boylan JC. In; Avis KE, Lieberman HA, Lachman L, (Eds.). Pharmaceutical Dosage Forms: Parenteral Medications vol. 1, 2ndEdn., 1992, Marcel Dekker, New York.
- Grandics P. *Pharmaceutical Technology April 2000.*
- Guide to Good Manufacturing Practice for Medical Products. Pharmaceutical Inspection Convention/ Pharmaceutical Inspection Co-operation Scheme, PE 009-2, 1 July 20044
- Indian Pharmacopoeia, Controller of Publications, Delhi, Vol. II, 1996.
- Remington: The Science and Practice of Pharmacy, Lippincott Williams & Wilkins, New York, Vol.–1, 21st. edn, 2006.
- Sabra K, In: Winfield AJ, Richards RME (Eds). Pharmaceutical Practice, 3rdEdn, 2004, Churchill Livingstone, New York, pp. 298-312.
- The United States Pharmacopoeia (USP), 24th Ed., US Pharmacopoeial Convention, Rockville, MD, 2000.
- Semalty et al., Essentials of Pharmaceutical Technology, II Edn, 2018, Pharma Med press, Hyderabad, India, ISBN 9789386819994.

# CHAPTER 18

# Parenterals I (Formulation of Parenterals)

**Dr Mona Semalty, Dr Ajay Semalty**
Department of Pharmaceutical Sciences,
H.N.B Garhwal University (A Central University), Srinagar Garhwal-246174

## Learning Outcome

After completing this chapter, you will be able to Know:

- Important steps involved in parenteral production
- Components of parenteral formulations
- Methods of preparation and properties of water for injection
- Importance of tonicity and methods of its determination.

## Lesson Plan

- Formulation of parenterals: basic steps of parenteral formulation
- Production of water for injection: Multi-effect still, vapour compression and reverse osmosis
- Formulation components: Vehicles (aqueous and non-aqueous vehicles) other added excipients like preservatives, solubilizers, wetting agents, buffers, antioxidants, chelating agents, suspending agents and tonicity adjuster etc.
- Methods of adjusting tonicity.
- Class I (Freezing point depression and Sodium chloride equivalent method)
- Class II (White-Vincent method and Sprowls method)

## Formulation of Parenterals

The aim of formulation development of parenterals product is to produce a safe effective and stable dosage form. General steps of parenteral formulations are given in Figure 18.1.

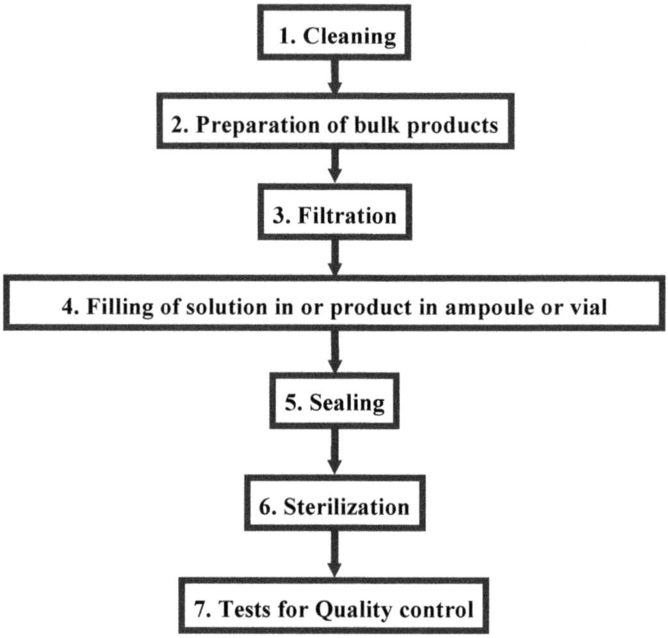


**Figure 18.1** Steps involved in the formulation of parenterals.

The components of parenteral formulations are as followed.

- Therapeutic agents
- Vehicles
    - Water
    - Water miscible vehicles
    - Non- aqueous vehicles
- Added substances (Additives)
    - Antimicrobials
    - Antioxidants
    - Buffers
    - Bulking agents
    - Chelating agents
    - Protectants
    - Solubilizing agents
    - Surfactants
    - Tonicity adjusting agents

## Vehicles

It requires selection of suitable solvent and other added substances as to avoid any formulation difficulty and the component present in the highest proportion is the vehicle (solvent). Vehicle used for parenterals must be -

- Sterile (free from the presence of microbial contamination)
- Pyrogen free
- Free from any particulate matter
- Should be isotonic with blood plasma

The vehicle for parenteral can be classified as aqueous vehicles and non-aqueous vehicles.

Most commonly we use water for injection /sterile water for injections as an aqueous vehicle for preparation of parenteral preparations.

## Non-Aqueous Vehicles

Fixed oils are used as vehicles for non-aqueous injections are of vegetable origin, are odorless and have no odor suggesting rancidity. They meet the requirements of the test for solid paraffin under mineral oil, have a saponification value of between 185 and 200, have an iodine value of between 79 and 128 and meet the requirements of free fatty acids tests. They must be ensured that they exhibit no pharmacological action, non-toxic and none irritating, and are compatible and stable with all ingredients of the formulation. A non-aqueous solvent or a mixed aqueous solvent system may be necessary to stabilize drugs, (such as the barbiturates that are readily hydrolyzed by water) or to improve solubility (e.g. Digitoxin).

Commonly used oils are corn oil, cottonseed oil, peanut oil and sesame oil. Because fixed oils can be quite irritating when injected may cause sensitivity reactions in some patients, the oil used in the product must be stated on the label. Fixed oils must never be administered intravenously and are, in fact, restrict to intramuscular use.

The main use of such oils is with steroids, with which they yield products that produce a sustained-release effect. Ex: sesame oil has also been used to obtain slow release of fluphenazine esters given IM. Benzyl benzoate may be used to enhance steroid solubility in oils if desired. Example of injectable products formulated with nonaqueous solvents are – Diazepam Injection USP and Phenytoin Sodium USP.

## Water-Miscible Vehicles

Water miscible vehicles are used primarily to solubilize certain drugs in an aqueous vehicle and to reduce hydrolysis. They are widely used in parenterals to enhance drug solubility and to serve as stabilizers.

The more common solvents include glycerin, ethyl alcohol, propylene glycol, and polyethylene glycol 300.The most important solvents in this group are ethyl alcohol, liquid polyethylene glycol and propylene glycol. Ethyl alcohol is used particularly in the preparation of solution of cardiac glycosides, certain alkaloids.

### Methods of preparations

Water for Injection can be prepared by distillation or by membrane technologies (i.e., reverse osmosis or ultrafiltration). The EP (European Pharmacopeia) only permits distillation as the process for producing WFI. The USP and JP (Japanese Pharmacopeia) allow all these technologies to be applied.

WFI can be prepared by distillation or by membrane technologies (reverse osmosis or ultrafiltration).USP: "distillation or a purification process that is equivalent of superior to distillation".

Permissible limits for WFI as per USP are

- Conductivity ≤ 1.3 µS/cm @ 25° C
- Total Organic Carbon (TOC) ≤ 500 ppb
- Microbial ≤ 10 cfu / 100 ml
- Endotoxin requirement < 0.25 EU/ml

Distillation is a process of converting water from a liquid to its gaseous form (steam). Since steam is pure gaseous water, all other contaminants in the feedwater are removed (Figure 18.2). A conventional still consists of-

Boiler or evaporator, containing feed water.

- Source of heat to vaporize the water in the evaporator
- Headspace above the level of feed water, with condensing surfaces for refluxing the vapor, thereby returning nonvolatile impurities to the feed water.
- Provision for eliminating volatile impurities before the hot water vapor is condensed.
- Condenser for removing the heat of vaporization, thereby converting the water vapor to a liquid distillate.

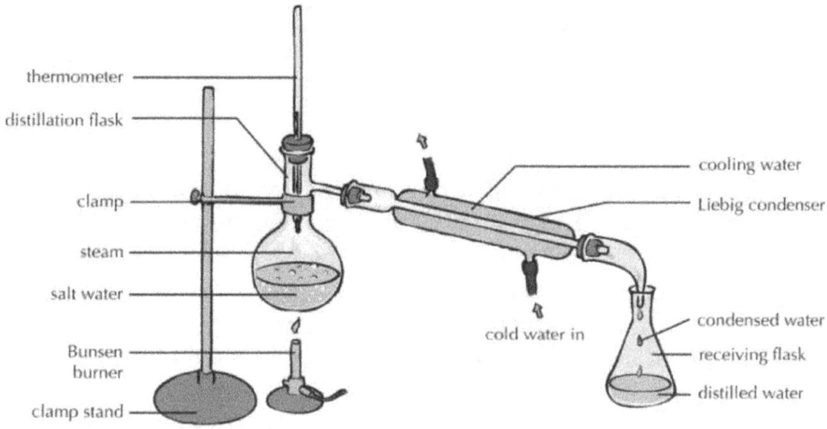


**Figure 18.2** Distillation unit.

There are two basic types of WFI distillation units

- Vapor compression still
- Multiple effect still

## Vapor Compression Distillation

The feed water is heated to boil by applying an external source of heat (**Figure 18.3**). The vapor produced in the tubes is separated from the entrained feed water (distillant) in the separator and lead to a compressor that compresses the vapor and increases its temperature (approximately 107 °C). It then flows to the steam chest, where it condenses on the outer surfaces of the tubes containing the distillant, the vapor is thus, condensed and drawn off as a distillate, while giving up its heat to bring the distillant in the tubes to the boiling point. High electric demand is one of the disadvantages of this method.

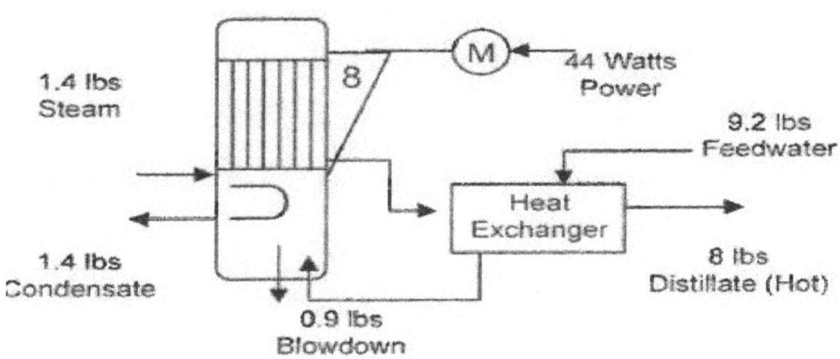


**Figure 18.3** Vapor compression still.

## Multiple-Effect Stills

A multiple-effect still is a simple series of single-effect stills or columns running at different pressures where phase changes of water take place (**Figure 18.4**). A series of up to seven effects can be used, with the first effect operated at the highest pressure and the last effect at atmospheric pressure. Steam from an external source is used in the first effect to generate steam under pressure from feed water and it is used as the power source to drive the second effect. The steam used to drive the second effect condenses as it gives up its heat of vaporization and forms a distillate. This process continues until the last effect when the steam is at atmospheric pressure. It is condensed in a heat exchanger to get distillate.

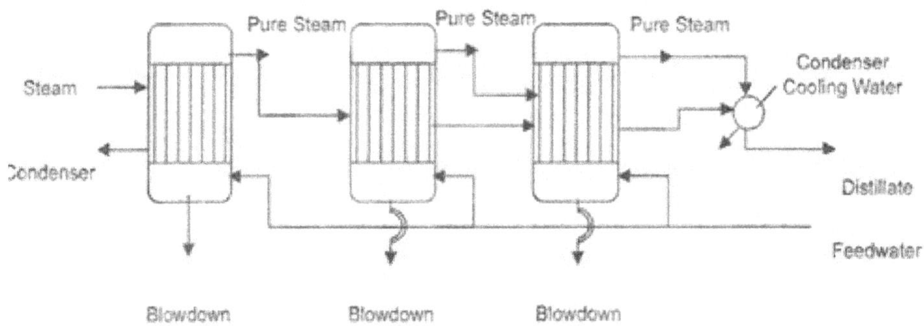


**Figure 18.4** Multi-effect still (MES).

## Reverse Osmosis (RO)

Reverse osmosis is the natural process of selective permeation of molecules through a semi permeable membrane separating two aqueous solutions of different concentrations is reversed (Figure 18.5)

A driving force (usually between 200 and 400 psig) is required to overcome osmotic pressure and to permeate pure water through the membrane. RO membranes are typically either cellulose acetate or polysulfone coated with aromatic polyamides.

The molecules most difficult to remove are small inorganic molecules such as sodium chloride. Sometimes Passage through two membranes in series is used to increase the efficiency of removal of these small molecules and decrease the risk of structural failure of a membrane to remove other contaminants such as bacteria and pyrogens.

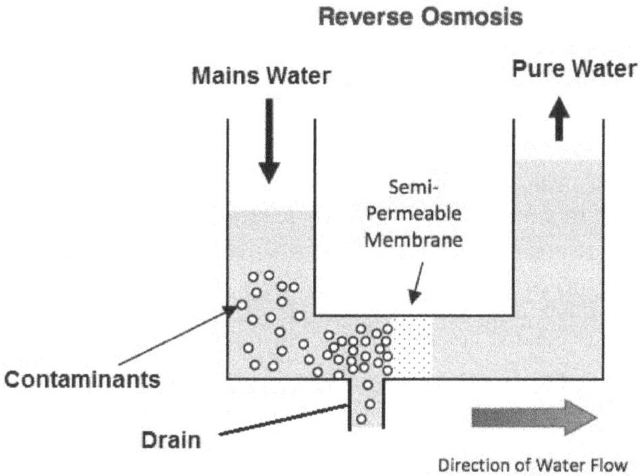


**Figure 18.5** Reverse osmosis.

Sometimes both RO and distillation systems are used for generation of the highest quality water. Since the raw water (with greater impurities) can contaminate the distillation units and affects the operation of the still, thus water is first run through RO units to eliminate contaminants.

Ultrafiltration is a type of membrane filtration in which hydrostatic pressure forces a liquid against semipermeable membrane. In this solid and solutes of high molecular weight are retained, and low molecular weight solutes passes through the membrane. In principle ultrafiltration is not different from reverse osmosis except in terms of size of the molecules it retains.

## Storage and Distribution

As per USP

- WFI should be stored at 80°C for prevention of any contamination When the water cannot be used at 80°C, heat exchangers must be installed to reduce the temperature at the point of use
- The USP also permits the WFI to be stored at room temperature but for a maximum of 24 hrs requires frequent sanitization to minimize the risk of viable microorganisms.

WFI is stored in stainless-steel storage tanks. These tanks are connected to a welded stainless-steel distribution loop supplying the various use sites with a continuously circulating water supply. The tank is provided with a hydrophobic membrane vent filter capable of excluding bacteria and non-viable particulate matter. Such a vent filter is necessary to permit changes in pressure during filling and emptying. Bacterial retentive filters should not be installed in such systems because of the risk of bacterial buildup on the filters and the consequent release of pyrogenic substances.

The Sterile Water for injection (SWFI) requirements differs in that since it is a final product, it must pass USP sterility test (Table 18.1).

Bacteriostatic Water for Injection (BWFI) contains one or more suitable antimicrobial agents in containers 30 ml or less. This restriction is designed to prevent the administration of large quantity of a bacteriostatic agent that probably would be toxic in the accumulated amount of large volume of solution, even though the concentration was low.

**Table 18.1** Specifications for WFI.

| S.No. | Test | Acceptance Criteria |
|---|---|---|
| 1. | Description | Clear, colorless, odorless liquid |
| 2. | Total organic carbon | Not more than 500ppb |
| 3. | Conductivity at 25°C | Less than 1.3 mS/cm |
| 4. | Bacterial endotoxins | Less than 0.25 EU/ml |
| 5 | Total aerobic microbial count | Less than 10 cfu/100ml |
| 6 | Acidity/Alkalinity | No red or blue color should be there |
| 7. | pH | Between 5-7 |
| 8. | Ammonium | Less than 0.2 ppm |
| 9. | Calcium and magnesium | Clear blue color |
| 10. | Heavy metals | Less than 0.1 ppm |
| 11. | Chlorides / Sulphates | Solution shows no change in appearance |
| 12. | Nitrates | Less than 0.2 ppm |
| 13. | Oxidizable substances | Solution should remain faint pink |
| 14. | Residue on evaporation | Less than 0.001 % |

## Isotonicity

The most important thing with respect to parenterals is maintaining the isotonicity of product as to avoid any swelling and contraction of blood cells. 0.9% of NaCl is said to be isotonic and used as a standard in pharmaceutical preparations.

| Hypotonic | isotonic | Hypertonic |
|---|---|---|
| NaCl 0.2% | NaCl 0.9% | NaCl 2% |
| solute > solute<br>Inside outside | solute = solute<br>Inside outside | solute < solute<br>Inside outside |
| swelling | equilibrium | shrinkage |

## Methods of Adjusting Tonicity

Based on the theoretical background provided earlier, individual methods to adjust the tonicity of solution can be devised, based on the principles of colligate properties. However, in the practice of pharmacy, a number of simple methods to adjust the tonicity of a formulation in a prescription order were developed on an extemporaneous basis to help the pharmacist. These methods can be classified into two types.

In Class 1 methods, an inert substance such as sodium chloride or dextrose is added to the solution to lower its freezing point to match that of blood, – 0.52 °C, that is the solution is made isotonic by the addition of an inert excipient.

In Class II methods, a calculated quantity of water is added to the total solute content (drug) of the prescription to make it isotonic and then diluted with sufficient isotonic diluting solution to bring it to the final volume. These methods are explained below followed by a simple example illustrating the method. However, the assumption inherent in all these methods needs to be considered carefully. The first assumption is that colligative properties are additive for mixtures of solutes, and that they are linearly related to their concentration expressed in molarity, molality, or in percentages. This assumption is true in dilute solution of nonelectrolytes and electrolytes. However, for concentrated solutions, this assumption may not be valid. In case if chemical interaction, association, or complexation or micellar interaction between solutes in solution, the colligative properties of solutes may not be additive. The second assumption is that all solutes present in solution contribute to its tonicity. But all biological membranes are not truly semipermeable and hence some solutes do not contribute to the tonicity of the solution across a membrane, for example, boric acid across an erythrocyte membrane. Nevertheless, the errors introduced are small and slight deviations from isotonicity on either side do not result insignificant adverse effect. In the literature, the L-value method or the Liso method can also be found. It is identical to the theoretical method described above for solutes for which the freezing point depression can be calculated based on their molecular weight and ionic nature. Knowing the freezing point depression, any of the Class 1 or Class II methods can then be used to adjust their solution to isotonicity.

- Class I (Freezing point depression and Sodium chloride equivalent method)
- Class II (White-Vincent method and Sprowls method)

## Freezing Point Depression Method

The freezing point depression (f.p.d.) of several drugs and excipients (either experimentally determined by the method described earlier or calculated theoretically using the Liso method) are available in the literature. Basically, the freezing point of the solution is calculated from the percentage of drug present in solution. This number is subtracted from the freezing point of blood (– 0.52 °C) to obtain the freezing point depression to be achieved by the addition of sodium chloride. Knowing that 0.9% sodium chloride is isotonic and freezes at – 0.52 °C, the amount to be added s calculated as shown by Example 1.

In this method any substance is added to lower f.p. of solution to -0.52°. FP of blood and tears is- 0.52°, so any solution having FP 0.52°C is isotonic. The formula for calculating the amount of adjusting substance to make isotonic solution is:

$$w\% = \frac{0.52 - a}{b}$$

W% = conc. gm/100 ml of adjusting substance

a = freezing point depression of 1% of unadjusted substance

b = freezing point depression of 1% of adjusting substance

**Example 1:** How much NaCl is required to render 100 ml of a 1% soln. of apomorphine HCL isotonic?

F.p.d. of 1%NaCl = 0.58°, F.p.d. of 1%drug = 0.08°

***Solution:***

$$w\% = \frac{0.52 - a}{b}$$

W% = 0.76% so, 1 gm of drug and 0.76 g of NaCl and makeup the volume to 100 ml will give isotonic solution.

**Sodium Chloride Equivalent (E) Method.**

The sodium chloride equivalent (E) is the amount of sodium chloride that is equivalent to 1 g of the drug in exerting the same osmotic effect. The E value for a new drug can be calculated from its Liso value or the freezing point depression as shown below.

This method first uses to calculate $E_{NaCl}$ and then calculate the amount of NaCl to reach 0.9%. $E_{NaCl}$ value is generally given to you. And if it is not given it can be calculated by using -

$$E_{NaCl} = 17L_{iso\ (drug)}/M.wt_{drug}$$

$$w\% = 0.9 - (drug\% \times E_{NaCl})$$

W% = weight of NaCl in gm/100 mL (to make solution isotonic)

drug% = wt of drug in gm/100 ml

$E_{NaCl}$ = NaCl equivalent weight to 1 gm of a drug

**Example:** Calculate amount of NaCl needed to adjust 3% $Drug_x$ ($E_{NaCl}$ = 0.12gm)

$$= 0.9 - (W \times E)$$

$$= 0.9 - (3 \times 0.12) = 0.54 \text{ gm of NaCl}$$

So, 0.54gm of NaCl should be added to 3 gm of Drug with 100 ml of water to make an isotonic solution

**White – Vincent method**

This method involves the addition of $H_2O$ to drug to make it isotonic with addition of isotonic vehicle to bring solution to final volume.

$$v = w \times E_{NaCl} \times 111.1$$

V = volume of water

W = weight of drug

111.1 = 100/0.9

## The Sprowls Methods

In the early days of practice of pharmacy, many prescriptions were written to prepare one fluid ounce of a 1% drug solution; thus, the amount of drug (w = 0.3 g) and the final volume were fixed (1 fluid ounce or 30 mL). Sprowls recognizing this fact suggested a modification of the White-Vincent method to further simplify the calculations for the practicing pharmacist.

In this method, the amount of drug is fixed at 0.3 g (30 mL of 1% solution), and the volume of water required to prepare this isotonic solution is calculated using Eq. (4) for all drugs which are commonly used in parental and ophthalmic formulation and for which the sodium chloride equivalents are known. The pharmacist then proceeds to make up the volume of the preparation to 30 mL with an isotonic diluting solution to fill the prescription. For example, if one fluid ounce of 1% physostigmine salicylate solution is to be prepared, 5.3 mL of water is required for 0.3 g of physostigmine salicylate to prepare an isotonic solution. Following its preparation, this 5.3 mL solution can be diluted with any isotonic diluting solution to make up the volume to one fluid ounce.

If 100 mL of a 1% solution are needed, the volume of water (V) should be multiplied by 3.33 to obtain the amount of water necessary to make it isotonic.

## Summary of Methods of Adjusting Tonicity

### A. Freezing Point Depression

- freezing point depressions of 1w/v% drug solutions ($DT_f^{1\%}$)
- choose appropriate solute for adjusting tonicity
  - using $DT_{f,ref}^{1\%}$ determine required amount ($w_{ref}$) to cover remaining $DT_f$

$$w_{ref} = \left[\frac{0.52 - C\Delta T_f^{1\%}}{\Delta T_{f,ref}^{1\%}}\right] V_{req}$$

$V_{req}$ = volume of water required

C = drug concentration (w/v%)

### B. Sodium Chloride Equivalent (E) Method

$$\text{NaCl (w/v\%)} = 0.90 - E \times [\text{drug}]\ (\text{w/v\%})$$

E = NaCl equivalent

### C. White-Vincent Method (USP Method)

Calculates volume (V) in ml of isotonic solution that can be prepared by mixing drug with water/isotonic buffered solution

$$V = w \times E \times 111.1$$

w = wt. of drug (g)

### Parenteral Additives

Various additives are used in parenteral formulations. The various classes of parenteral additives and their examples are listed in Table 18.2.

**Table 18.2** Classes and Examples of Parenteral Additives.

| Additives | Examples | Usual concentration (%) |
|---|---|---|
| Antimicrobials (Protect a preparation against the growth of microorganisms) | Benzalkonium chloride | 0.01 |
| | Benzyl alcohol | 1-2 |
| | Chlorobutanol | 0.25-0.5 |
| | Metacresol | 0.1-0.3 |
| | Butyl p-hydroxybenzoate | 0.015 |
| | Methyl p-hydroxybenzoate | 0.1-0.2 |
| | Propyl p-hydroxybenzoate | 0.2 |
| | Phenol | 0.25-0.5 |
| | Thimerosal | 0.01 |
| Antioxidants, Chelating agents, | Ascorbic acid | 0.01-0.05 |
| | Cysteine | 0.1-0.5 |
| | Monothioglycerol | 0.1-1.0 |
| | Sodium bisulfite | 0.1-1.0 |
| Buffers (Enhance the chemical stability of a solution) | Sodium metabisulphite | 0.1-1.0 |
| | Tocopherols | 0.05-0.5 |
| | Acetates | 1-2 |
| | Citrates | 1-5 |
| | Phosphates | 0.8-2.0 |
| | Salts of ethylenediaminetetraacetic acid | 0.01-0.05 |
| Protectants | Sucrose | 2-5 |
| Prevents loss of activity of drug caused by stress or adsorption | Glucose | 2-5 |
| | Lactose | 2-5 |
| | Maltose | 2-5 |
| | Trehalose | 2-5 |
| | Human serum albumin | 0.1-1.0 |
| Solubilizing agents | Ethyl alcohol | 1-50 |
| | Glycerine | 1-50 |
| Increase and maintain drug solubility | Polyeyhylene glycol | 1-50 |
| | Propylene glycol | 1-50 |
| | Lecithin | 0.2.0 |
| Surfactants (Enhance the physical stability of proteins) | Polyoxyethylene | 0.1-0.5 |
| | Sorbitanmonooleate | 0.05-0.25 |
| Tonicity-adjusting agent Provide patient comfort by reducing pain and tissue irritation | Dextrose<br>Sodium chloride | 4-5<br>0.5-0.9 |

## Further Readings


- "Industrial Pharmacy-I" SWAYAM MOOC: www.swayam.gov.in
- https://www.pharmaguideline.com/2011/03/specification-for-water-for-injection.html
- Deluca PP, Boylan JC. In; Avis KE, Lieberman HA, Lachman L, (Eds.). Pharmaceutical Dosage Forms: Parenteral Medications vol. 1, 2ndEdn., 1992, Marcel Dekker, New York.


## References


- Semalty et al., Essentials of Pharmaceutical Technology, II Edn, 2018, Pharma Med press, Hyderabad, India, ISBN 9789386819994.
- Akers MJ Pharmaceutical Technology 2001; July: 78-79.
- Akers MJ, Larrimore Daniel S, Guazzo DM. Parenteral Quality Control Sterility, Pyrogen, Particulate, and Package Integrity Testing, III Edn, 2003, Marcel Dekker, Inc. New York, Basel, US.
- Avis KE, In; Lachman L, Lieberman HA, Kanig JL. Eds. The Theory and Practices of Industrial Pharmacy. Varghese Publishing House, Bombay, pp. 430-78.
- Boylan JC, Nail SL, In; Banker GS, Rhodes CT (Eds). Modern Pharmaceutics. 2005 (Vol. 121) Marcel Dekker, Inc. New York, Basel, US, pp 381-414.
- Chapman DG, In: Winfield AJ, Richards RME (Eds). Pharmaceutical Practice, 3rd Edn, 2004, Churchill Livingstone, New York, pp. 247-63.
- Deluca PP, Boylan JC. In; Avis KE, Lieberman HA, Lachman L, (Eds.). Pharmaceutical Dosage Forms: Parenteral Medications vol. 1, 2nd Edn., 1992, Marcel Dekker, New York.
- Demorest LJ, Hamilton JG, In; Avis KE, Lieberman HA, Lachman L, Eds. Pharmaceutical Dosage Forms: Parenteral Medications, Vol 1, 2nd Edn, 1992. Marcel Dekker New York,
- Good manufacturing practices for pharmaceutical products. In: WHO Expert Committee on Specification for Pharmaceutical Preparations. Thirty-second Report. Geneva, World Health Organization, 1992, Annex 1 (WHO Technical Report Series, No. 823)
- Indian Pharmacopoeia, Controller of Publications, Delhi, Vol. II, 1996.
- Remington: The Science and Practice of Pharmacy, Lippincott Williams & Wilkins, New York, Vol.–1, 21st. edn, 2006.
- Richards RME. In: Winfield AJ, Richards RME (Eds). Pharmaceutical Practice, 3rd edn, 2004, Churchill Livingstone, New York, pp. 150-60.

CHAPTER 19

# Parenterals I (Types of Parenteral Preparations)

**Dr Mona Semalty, Dr Ajay Semalty**
Department of Pharmaceutical Sciences,
H.N.B Garhwal University (A Central University), Srinagar Garhwal-246174

### Learning Outcome

- Types of parenteral products available and their basic properties like particle size, syringeability, injectability, (injectable suspension) and globule size (injectable emulsion)
- Methods used in preparation of different parenteral products

### Lesson Plan

- Drug injection: Injectable solutions
- Injectable emulsion, suspension and Dry powders
- Characteristics and properties of different types of parenterals
- Methods of preparations of injectable solution, dry powders, suspensions and emulsions

## Types of Parenteral Preparations

1. **Small volume parenterals:** In small volume parenterals the volume of injectables is less than (<100 ml). SVIs include solutions, suspensions, emulsions, and Dry powders.
2. **Large volume parenterals:** In large volume parenterals the volume of injectables is more than (<100 ml). LVIs include electrolytes, carbohydrates, proteins, fatty emulsions, dialysis solutions, and irrigating solutions.
3. Modified release (sustained release) injectables (SVIs delivered by routes other than IV)

## Types of Parenteral Preparation (USP)

Solutions of drugs suitable for parenteral administration are referred as injection. According to USP injections are separated into

- [Drug] Injection: Liquid preparations that are drug substances or solutions thereof, e. g. Insulin.
- [Drug] *for* Injection: Dry solids that, upon addition of suitable vehicles, yield solutions conforming in all respects to the requirements for injections, e.g. Cefamandole Sodium
- [Drug] injectable emulsion: Liquid preparations of drug substances dissolved or dispersed in a suitable emulsion medium, e.g. Propofol
- [Drug] injectable suspension: Liquid preparations of solids suspended in a suitable liquid medium, e.g. Methyl Prednisolone Acetate.
- [Drug] *for* Injectable suspension: Dry solids that, upon the addition of suitable vehicles, yield preparations conforming in all respects to the requirements for injectable suspensions, e.g. Sterile Ampicillin for Suspension

Boylan and Nail has discussed the formulation of major types of parenteral products as solutions, suspensions, emulsions and dry powders.

## Solutions

Solutions are very common preparation for parenteral use. They are ready to use preparations or liquid concentrate to be diluted suitably (packed in ampoules of vials containing suitable antimicrobial agents). Solutions are prepared by mixing accurately weight quantity of API (Added excipients) with aqueous /Non-aqueous/ water miscible vehicles.

As we have mentioned in the previous chapter that for the preparation of WFI/SWFI generally fixed oils are used as a non-aqueous vehicle. The USP provides specifications for such vehicles, indicating that the fixed oils must be of vegetable origin so they will metabolize, will be liquid at room temperature, and will not become rancid readily. The fixed oils should qualify the specific limits for the free fatty acid content, iodine value, and saponification value as per USP. The oils most commonly used are corn oil, cottonseed oil, peanut oil, and sesame oil. Fixed oils are used as vehicles for certain hormone (e.g., progesterone, testosterone, deoxycorticosterone) and vitamin (e.g., Vitamin K, Vitamin E) preparations. A few solvents like liquid polyethylene glycol, propylene glycol, glycerin, sorbitol and ethyl alcohol that are miscible with water have been used as a portion of the vehicle in the formulation of parenterals.

### Solutions: Method of preparations

- Weigh accurate quantity of API
- Addition of suitable excipient
- Adjust pH and tonicity
- Filtration (Sterile filtration using0.22 µm membrane filter membrane)
- Final sterilization by suitable mean
- Packaging and labelling

## Sterile Filtration

Sterile filtration is used for thermolabile substances followed by filling. For sterile filtration, 0.22 µm membrane filter is used. Talc or carbon is also used as a filtration aid (or other filter aids) If talc is used it should be pretreated with a dilute acid solution to remove surface alkali and metals. In filtering protein solutions, the chances of adsorption of protein onto membrane filters must be avoided for that a membrane (such as hydrophilic polyvinyl-idenedifluoride and hydroxyl-modified hydrophilic polyamide membranes) with minimum protein adsorbing properties should be used. Thermostable drugs are sterilized by autoclaving (temp) after filling.

### Small Volume Parenterals

- Ampoules (solutions/ liquid filled concentrate)
- Vials
- Plastic blow-fill-seal ampoules
- Prefilled syringe
- Needle free injection

## Suspensions

Suspension parenteral dosage forms are one of the most difficult formulations due to the requirement of easy resuspendability and syringeability or injectability (so that it can be ejected through an 18 to 21 gauge needle). **Table 19.1** provides the comparison between solution and suspension parenteral dosage forms.

**Table 19.1** Solutions V/S suspension injectables.

| Solutions | Suspensions |
|---|---|
| • The simplest and thus preferred form<br>• Risk of low stability of the active compound<br>• Normally rapid uptake<br>• Important quality parameters<br>  o pH<br>  o Osmolality (ionic strength)<br>  o Sterility<br>  o Content and impurities | • Particles suspended in a solution<br>• Not thermodynamically stable<br>• Used for substances of low solubility or for controlled released formulations<br>• Critical parameter the same as for solutions plus particle size |

Parenteral suspension is dispersions of solids into suitable vehicle (water/oil) depending on the solubility of API. Suspensions are one of the most difficult preparation of parenterals and it cannot be administered by IV route. As it need to fulfil the requirements of Syringeability /injectability.

*Syringeability refers to the handling characteristics of a suspension while drawing it into and manipulating it in syringe. It includes characteristics such as case of withdrawal from the container into the syringe, clogging and foaming tendencies, and accuracy of dose measurement.*

*The term injectability refers to the properties of the suspension during injection; it includes factors as pressure or force required for injection, evenness of flow, aspiration qualities, and freedom from clogging.*

**Requirements of ideal parenterals suspensions**

- Maintenance of particle size distribution
- Surface activity (wetting/contact angle)
- Zeta potential: It is measured by zetasizer (DLS) which is a microelectrophoretic mobility apparatus used to characterize the flocculated and dispersed suspensions and follow changes in physical stability with time.
- Rheological properties/Viscosity-(Stability of the suspension sometime increases on increasing the viscosity (by adding some amount of protective colloid or compounds such as sorbitol).

- Solid content-Solid content ranges from 0.5 to 5% (but may go as high as 30% in some antibiotic preparation).
- Redispersibility (This cake formation may be prevented by the use of surface-active agent which may reduce the interfacial tension between particle and vehicle e.g. Polysorbate 80, lecithin. Hydrocolloids like sodium CMC increase the effect of surfactant.)

**Two basic methods are used to prepare parenteral suspensions.**

**Sterile vehicle and powder are combined aseptically: e.g. Penicillin G Procaine Injectable Suspension USP.**

In the first method (of preparation of Procaine penicillin injectable suspension) an aqueous vehicle containing the soluble components (such as sodium citrate, povidone, lecithin) is filtered through a 0.22 μm membrane filter, heat sterilized, and transferred into a pre-sterilized mixing-filling tank. The sterile antibiotic powder, which has previously been produced by freeze drying, sterile crystallization, or spray drying, is aseptically added to the sterile solution while mixing. After all tests have been completed on the bulk formulation, it is aseptically filled.

In the second method (of preparation of Testosterone suspension) the vehicle is prepared and sterile filtered. The testosterone is dissolved separately in acetone and sterile filtered. The testosterone-acetone solution is aseptically added to the sterile vehicle, causing the testosterone to crystallize. The resulting suspension is then diluted with sterile vehicle, mixed, crystals allowed to settle, and the supernatant solution siphoned off. This procedure is repeated several times until all the acetone is removed. The suspension is then brought to the volume and filled in the normal manner.

**Official preparations of parenteral suspension**

1. Sterile ampicillin suspension USP'95 dispense as powder which is to be rec onstituted at time of administration.
2. Sterile aurothiglucose suspension USP'95 – vegetable oil
3. Tetanus toxoid adsorbed USP'95, IP'96 – aq. Suspension.
4. Betamethasone acetate suspension USP'96 aq. Suspension.
5. Insulin Zinc suspension USP'95, IP'96 aq. S

## Stability and Evaluation of Parenteral Suspension

### Injectability

The syringeability and injectability of suspension are closely related to the viscosity and particle characteristics of the suspension. For syringeability a suitable test is done to ensure that the entire suspension passes through a 25-gauge needle of internal 0.3 mm. A force monitoring device such as instron can be used to determine ejection and injection pressure, and test result can be recorded on a X-Y recorder.

## Freeze-thaw Cycles

It is important for determining the ability of the suspension to withstand thermal shock, retard crystal growth, and to maintain chemical stability of the active ingredient. A total of three complete cycles with each cycle consisting of 24 hours at 40°C followed by 24 hours at 0°C is suggested, although various cycles are suitable.

## Resuspendibility

Resuspendibility describes the ability of the suspension to uniformly disperse with minimal shaking after it has stood for some time. Qualitatively, light transmittance through the upper solution in a cylinder after it has been spun for about 2 minutes at 75 rpm can be used to detect the redispersion properties of the system.

## Sedimentation Volume

The sedimentation volume is defined as the ratio of the final volume, Vu, to the original volume, VO, of the suspension. The larger value of sedimentation volume indicates the better suspendibility.

## Crystal Growth

Crystal growth in suspension is affected by the particle size distribution, changes in pH, temperature, cycle form, and solvate formation and by dissolution and recrystallization of the particle. Crystal growth should be monitored by examining changes in particle size over time and comparing that with the initial particle size distribution.

## Particle size measurements-

Particle size measurements are useful in that they allow aggregation or crystal g rowth to be evaluated there are several methods used for particle size analysis; microscopic determination is preferred over Andersen pipette or subsieve sizer and turbidimetry can be used.

## Zeta Potential Determinations

It is measured by zetasizer (DLS) which is a microelectrophoretic mobility apparatus used to characterize the flocculated and dispersed suspensions and follow changes in physical stability with time.

## Viscosity

An ideal suspension should exhibit a high viscosity at low shear (agitation and syrigeabiltity). The suspension viscosity can change due to concentration of active ingredient(s), particle shape, size, and distribution. And it can be determined by using suitable mean of measurement.

## Emulsions

Parenteral emulsion is dispersed system combined with an oil phase and an aqueous phase. It is oil-in-water emulsion or water-in-oil emulsions. Emulsions are milky white in appearance and have an average globule size of 1 – 5 micrometers. Globules larger than 5 micrometers should be less than 0.05% of the total volume. Propofol and oil soluble vitamins are examples.

Preparing parenteral emulsion is challenging as it need controlled particle size and stability.

- Particle size should be within the permissible limits as to prevent the formation of emboli in blood vessel and preventing the rancidity of oil phase.
- Stability as sterilization should not affect the stability of the product. Small amount of some stabilizers like gelatin, dextran & microcrystalline cellulose are added to stabilize the emulsion.

## Lipid Emulsions for Parenteral

These intravenous emulsions are widely accepted for the patients who are unable to take food themselves. These emulsions consist of a suitable oil, an emulsifier and a balanced blend of amino acids in a continuous phase of distilled water. The composition of the emulsifier is important as it decides the overall stability of the emulsion. These emulsions are injected into the vein and provide a means of administering a nutritive fluid to the patient.

## Perfluorochemical Emulsions

These types of emulsions utilize perfluorocarbon oil (Oxygen carriers), an emulsifier Pluronic F68 was used in the original formulations; hydroxyethyl starch and various salts in water. The perfluorocarbon oil is the oxygen carrier; that is, the oil can dissolve oxygen and carry it through the body. These emulsions have a great deal of potential for the following reasons: non-availability of compatible blood, bloodless surgery and for the treatment various diseases.

## Liposomes

Liposomes are emulsified spherical vesicles composed of a phospholipid bilayer with an aqueous inner phase. Drug can be incorporated in either the liquid or aqueous phases.

## Dry Powders

Dry Powders are parenteral preparations required to be reconstituted before administration. These types of preparations are more suitable for those drugs which are too unstable, either physically or chemically, in an aqueous medium to allow formulation as a solution, suspension or emulsion. The reconstituted product is usually aqueous solution; occasionally it may be an aqueous suspension (e.g. Ampicillin trihydrate).

Dry powders for reconstitution as an injectable product may be produced by following methods:

A. Aseptic Crystallization and Dry Powder Filling

B. Spray Drying

C. Freeze Drying

**A. Aseptic crystallization and dry powder filling**

This method is primarily used for manufacturing of sterile aqueous suspension. In aseptic crystallization the drug is dissolved in a suitable solvent and sterile filtered through an appropriate membrane filter. A second solvent, a sterility filtered nonsolvent for the drug, is then added at a controlled rate causing crystallization and precipitation of the drug. The crystals are collected on a funnel, washed if necessary, and dried by vacuum dryer. After drying it may be necessary to mill or blend the drug crystals. The powder is then transferred to dry powder filling equipment and filled into vials.

**Disadvantages**

- Batch to batch variability in crystal habit and crystal size results in variability in physical properties troublesome consistent product quality.
- Maintenance of asepsis between sterile crystallization and filling of the powder during material handling.
- Maintenance of fill weight uniformity.

**B. Spray Drying**

A solution of drug is sterile filtered and metered into the drying chamber, where it passes through an atomizer that creates an aerosol of small droplets of liquid. The aerosol comes in contact with a stream of hot sterile gas, usually air. The solvent evaporates quickly, allowing drug to be collected as a powder in the form of uniform hollow spheres. The powder is then filled into vials using conventional powder filling equipment. Limitations of spray drying include sterile filtration of very large volumes of air; constructing and maintaining a spray dryer that can be readily sterilized; aseptic transfer of powder from the spray dryer to the powder filling line; and precise control of the drying conditions to prevent overheating of the product while providing adequate drying.

**C. Freeze Drying**

A solution is filled into vials, a special slotted stopper is partially inserted into the neck of the vial, and trays of filled vials are transferred to the freeze dryer. The solution is frozen by circulation of a fluid, such as silicone oil, at a temperature ranging between – 35 °C to – 45 °C through internal channels in the shelf assembly. When the product has solidified sufficiently, the pressure in the freeze dryer chamber is reduced to a pressure less than the vapor pressure of ice at the temperature of the product, and heat is applied to the product by increasing the temperature of the circulating fluid. Under these conditions, water is removed by sublimation of ice.

Freeze drying takes below the triple point of water, at which solid, liquid and vapor all coexist in equilibrium. The most important objective in freeze dried product is to assure that critical quality attributes are met initially and throughout its shelf life. Critical quality attributes include recovery of original chemical or biological activity after reconstitution, rapid and complete dissolution, appropriate residual moisture level and acceptable cake appearance. In addition, process conditions should be those conditions that minimize drying time without adversely affecting product quality. Freeze drying should be carried out at the highest allowable product temperature that maintains the appropriate attributes of a freeze-dried product.

**Advantages**

- Water can be removed at low temperature, avoiding damage to heat sensitive materials.
- Proper freeze drying provides dried product with high specific surface area, which facilitates rapid, complete reconstitution of the solid.
- From operation point of view, freeze dried dosage forms allow drug to be filled into vials as a solution which makes control of the quantity filled into each vial more precise than filling drug into vial as a powder. In addition, there is minimal concern with dust contaminant, cross contamination and potential work exposure to hazardous drugs.

**Limitations**

- Some drugs, particularly biological systems such as proteins, liposomal systems, and vaccines are damaged by freezing, freeze drying or both. Although the damage can be often minimized by using protective agents in the formulation.
- The stability of a drug in a solid state depends on its physical state. If freeze drying produces an amorphous solid and the amorphous form is not stable, then freeze drying will not provide acceptable product.
- Freeze drying is a relatively extensive drying process; it can be an issue for more cost-sensitive products.

While crystallinity of a drug is generally desirable for freeze drying, it is often important for excipients to remain amorphous. In particular, disaccharides (sucrose etc.) are important as formulation additives to stabilize proteins against damage caused by freezing, freeze drying or both. However, in order to be effective stabilizers, it is essential for these compounds to remain amorphous both during freeze drying and subsequent storage.

## Validation of Sterile Products

To ensure the product meets required quality, each manufacturing process should be validated to be sure that it is accomplishing what it is intended to do. FDA provides certain guidelines for Current Good Manufacturing Practice for finished pharmaceuticals under CFR section 211 and its subsections for detailed requirements.

CFR211.25 – personnel qualification requirement based on education, experience and training for the job.

CFR211.80, 211.84, 211.86 – ingredients used in product compounding meet the required identity, quality, and purity

CFR 211.63, 211.65, 211.67, 211.68, 211.182 – validation requirement for processes and equipment used

CFR211.42, 211.46, 211.56, 211.113 – requirements for the production environment preventing any contamination

CFR211.160,211.165,211.167 – requirements for quality control procedures ensuring the finished products have the required potency, purity, and quality until the expiration date

***[For details abut validation of sterile products refer Semalty et al., Essentials of Pharmaceutical Technology, II Edn, 2019, Pharma Med press, Hyderabad, India.]***

## Large Volume Parenterals (LVPs)

LVPs may be of various types and used for various purposes.

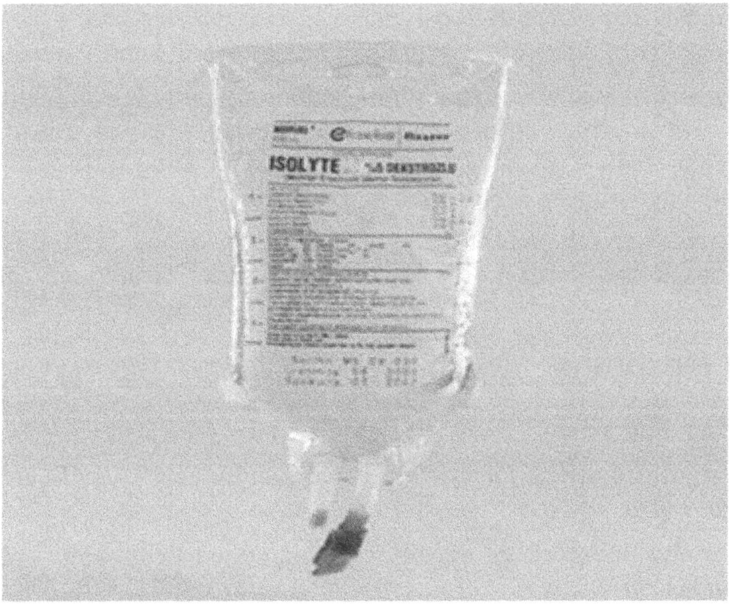


**Figure 19.1** Large Volume Parenterals (LVP).

- Electrolyte solutions – 0.9% NaCl isotonic solutions, 0.45% or 3% NaCl, 20-40 mEq/L KCl, Ringer's lactated Ringer's, etc.

- Carbohydrate solutions – Dextrose 5% in water (D5W)
- Nutritional proteins: 2.5 – 10% synthetic amino acid mixtures used on patients with starvation, renal, hepatic failure or other conditions.
- Fatty Emulsions: Serves as a source of nutrient fat. Composed of 10-20% soybean oil, water and 1.2% egg yolk phospholipids, and 2.5% glycerin.
- Peritoneal Dialysis: Contains large volumes of dextrose to remove waste such as urea and potassium from the blood.
- Irrigating (washing) solutions –Irrigating solutions must be sterile, pyrogen and particulate free.

## Modified Release (Sustained Release) Injectables

- Sustained or controlled release injectable systems are desirable for increased duration of release, reduced number of injections, and increased compliance, localized delivery in the case of cancer therapy and vaccinations, and protection against in vivo degradation of the active ingredient.
- Polymeric implants – sterile, solid drug products manufactured by compression, melting or sintering processes. These have drug and a biodegradable or replaceable polymeric system which controls the sustained or prolonged drug delivery. Example: Norplant (birth control implant)
- Microspheres: injectable suspensions containing particles of diameters of 1 – 100 micrometers. Prior to injection, the particles are mixed with an appropriate vehicle, dispersed and administered. Drug release kinetics are controlled by polymer degradation and diffusion.
- Liposomes - a spherical vehicle having at least one lipid bilayer. The liposome can be used as a vehicle for administration of nutrients and drugs.

## Further Readings


- "Industrial Pharmacy-I" SWAYAM MOOC: www.swayam.gov.in
- https://www.accessdata.fda.gov/scripts/cdrh/cfdocs/cfcfr/CFRSearch.cfm?fr=211.25
- https://study.com/academy/lesson/isotonic-solution-definition-example-quiz.html
- https://media.ahc.ufl.edu/media/Parenteral+Drug+Delivery+6/1_5798eawi/21720711

## References


- Semalty et al., Essentials of Pharmaceutical Technology, II Edn, 2018, Pharma Med press, Hyderabad, India, ISBN 9789386819994.
- Akers MJ Pharmaceutical Technology 2001; July: 78-79.
- Akers MJ, Larrimore Daniel S, Guazzo DM. Parenteral Quality Control Sterility, Pyrogen, Particulate, and Package Integrity Testing, III Edn, 2003, Marcel Dekker, Inc. New York, Basel, US.
- Avis KE, In; Lachman L, Lieberman HA, Kanig JL. Eds. The Theory and Practices of Industrial Pharmacy. Varghese Publishing House, Bombay, pp. 430-78.
- Boylan JC, Nail SL, In; Banker GS, Rhodes CT (Eds). Modern Pharmaceutics. 2005 (Vol. 121) Marcel Dekker, Inc. New York, Basel, US, pp 381-414.
- Chapman DG, In: Winfield AJ, Richards RME (Eds). Pharmaceutical Practice, 3rd Edn, 2004, Churchil Livingstone, New York, pp. 247-63.
- Deluca PP, Boylan JC. In; Avis KE, Lieberman HA, Lachman L, (Eds.). Pharmaceutical Dosage Forms: Parenteral Medications vol. 1, 2nd Edn., 1992, Marcel Dekker, New York.
- Demorest LJ, Hamilton JG, In; Avis KE, Lieberman HA, Lachman L, Eds. Pharmaceutical Dosage Forms: Parenteral Medications, Vol 1, 2nd Edn, 1992. Marcel Dekker New York,
- Good manufacturing practices for pharmaceutical products. In: WHO Expert Committee on Specification for Pharmaceutical Preparations. Thirty-second Report. Geneva, World Health Organization, 1992, Annex 1 (WHO Technical Report Series, No. 823)
- Grandics P. Pharmaceutical Technology April 2000.

# CHAPTER 20

# Parenterals I
# (Plant Layout for Parenterals)

**Dr Mona Semalty, Dr Ajay Semalty**
Department of Pharmaceutical Sciences,
H.N.B Garhwal University (A Central University), Srinagar Garhwal-246174

### Learning Outcome

- Basic designing and layout of a parenteral production unit
- General guidelines required for parenteral production and their structural specifications
- Various facilities required for production of sterile products and their performance (EU guidelines to GMP for manufacturing of sterile products)

### Lesson Plan

- Layout of the parenteral/sterile manufacturing area: Clean-up area, Preparation area, Aseptic area, Quarantine area, Finishing and packaging area
- Production facilities for parenteral/sterile product manufacturing: Principle, Personnel, Premises, Equipment
- Environmental/Air control: HEPA filters /Laminar airflow/Validation of HEPA Filters.

## Production Facilities for Parenterals

The manufacturing of sterile products is subjected to special requirements in order to minimize risks of microbial contaminations **(Figure 20.1)**. General broad guidelines say that that the area should be kept clean (pyrogen free) and strict precaution is taken to prevent contamination from outside. Ceiling & walls & floors sealed & painted or treated with aseptic solution and there should not be any toxic effect of this treatment. High efficiency filter is used (HEPA) which removes particles up to 0.3 micron and are fitted in laminar air flow system, in which air is free from dust & microorganisms flows with uniform velocity. And UV lamps are fitted to maintain sterility.

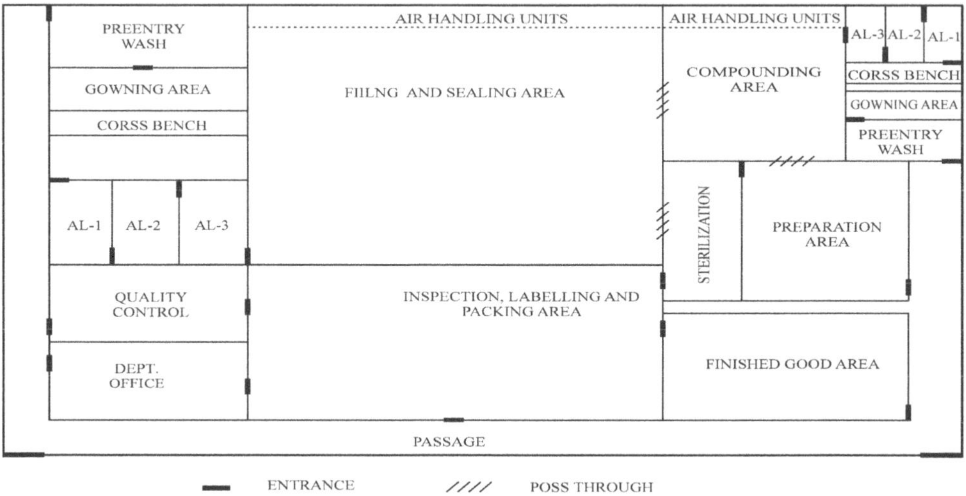


**Figure 20.1** Layout of Sterile Product Manufacturing.

## Different Areas for Production of Sterile Products

- Clean- up area
- Preparation area
- Aseptic area
- Quarantine area
- Finishing and packaging area

## Clean- up Area

- Non-aseptic area
- Free from dust, fibers & micro-organisms and it should withstand moisture, steam & detergent
- Washing is done in this area

## Preparation Area

- The ingredients are mixed & preparation is prepared for filling
- Not essential that the area is aseptic

## Aseptic Area

- Filtration & filling into final containers & sealing is done
- The entry of outside person is strictly prohibited
- To maintain sterility, special trained persons are only allowed to enter & work

## Quarantine Area

- After filling, sealing & sterilization the products or batch is kept in this area
- The random samples are chosen and given for analysis to QC dept.
- The batch is sent to packing after issuing satisfactory reports of analysis from QC
- If any problem is observed in above analysis the decision is to be taken for reprocessing or others.

## Principle

The preparation of sterile products is carried out in specialized designed plant layout as to minimize risks of microbiological and other contaminations. It depends on the facilities of plant and on the skill, training and attitudes of the personnel involved. There are various guidelines by USFDA/ISO/EU. We will be discussing detailed guidelines provided by EU to Good Manufacturing Practice for manufacture of sterile products.

**General guidelines say that**

1. The manufacturing of sterile products should be carried out in clean areas entry to which should be through airlocks for personnel and/or for equipment and materials. Discuss three door air lock system
2. The various operations of component preparation, product preparation and filing should be carried out in separate areas within the clean area.
3. Manufacturing operations are divided in two categories; firstly, those where the product is terminally sterilized, and secondly those which are conducted aseptically at some or all stages.
3. Clean areas for the manufacturing of sterile products are classified according to the required characteristics of the environment.

**For the manufacture of sterile medicinal products 4 grades can be distinguished.**

**Grade A:** The local zone for high-risk operations, e.g. filling zone, stopper bowls, open ampoules and vials, making aspects connections. Normally grade A follows all the specifications for environment control.

**Grade B:** For aseptic preparation and filling, this is the background environment for grade A zone.

**Grade C and D:** Clean areas for carrying out less critical stages in the manufacture of sterile products.

## Personnel

- Only the minimum number of personnel required should be present in clean area and all persons (including those concerned with cleaning and maintenance) employed in such areas should receive initial and regular training in disciplines relevant to the hygiene and the basic elements of microbiology.
- Staff who have been engaged in the processing of biologicals like animal-tissue materials or of cultures of microorganisms should not enter sterile-product areas unless rigorous and clearly defined decontamination procedures have been followed.
- High standards of personal hygiene and cleanliness are essential, and personnel involved in the manufacture of sterile preparations. should be instructed to report any conditions that may cause the shedding of abnormal numbers or types of contaminants; periodic health checks for such conditions are desirable. The action to be taken in respect of personnel who might be introducing undue microbiological hazards should be decided by a designated competent person.
- Outdoor clothing should not be brought into clean areas, and personnel entering changing rooms should already be clad in standard factory protective garments. Changing and washing should follow a written procedure designed to minimize the contamination of clean area clothing or the carry-through of contaminants to clean areas.
- Wristwatches and jewelry should not be worn in clean areas, and cosmetics that can shed particles should not be used.
- The clothing worn and its quality should be appropriate for the process and the grade of the working area (workplace). It should be worn in such a way as to protect the product from contamination. The clothing required for each grade is as follows:
- **Grade D.** The hair and, where relevant, beard and moustache should be covered. Protective clothing and appropriate shoes or overshoes should be worn. Appropriate measures should be taken to avoid any contamination from outside the clean area.
- **Grade C.** The hair and, where relevant, beard and moustache should be covered. A single or two-piece trouser suit, gathered at the wrists and with a

high neck, and appropriate shoes or overshoes should be worn. The clothing should shed virtually no fibers or particulate matter.

- **Grades A/B.** Headgear should totally enclose the hair and, where relevant, beard and moustache. A single or two-piece trouser suit, gathered at the wrists and with a high neck, should be worn. The headgear should be tucked into the neck of the suit. A face mask should be worn to prevent the shedding of droplets. Appropriate, sterilized, non-powdered rubber or plastic gloves and sterilized or disinfected footwear should be worn. Trouser bottoms should be tucked inside the footwear and garment sleeves into the gloves. The protective clothing should shed virtually no fibers or particulate matter and should retain particles shed by the body.
- Outdoor clothing should not be brought into changing rooms leading to grade B and C rooms. For every worker in a grade A/B room, clean sterilized or adequately sanitized protective garments should be provided at each work session, or at least once a day if monitoring results justify this. Gloves should be regularly disinfected during operations. Masks and gloves should be changed at least at every working session. The use of disposable clothing may be necessary.
- Clothing used in clean areas should be laundered or cleaned in such a way that it does not gather additional particulate contaminants that can later be shed. Separate laundry facilities for such clothing are desirable. If fibers are damaged by inappropriate cleaning or sterilization, there may be an increased risk of shedding particles. Washing and sterilization operations should follow standard operating procedures.

## Premises

- All premises should, as far as possible, be designed to avoid the unnecessary entry of supervisory or control personnel. Grade B areas should be designed so that all operations can be observed from outside.
- In clean areas, all exposed surfaces should be smooth, impervious and unbroken in order to minimize the shedding or accumulation of particles or microorganisms and to permit the repeated application of cleaning agents and disinfectants, where used.
- To reduce the accumulation of dust and to facilitate cleaning, there should be no uncleanable recesses and a minimum of projecting ledges, shelves, cupboards and equipment. Doors should be carefully designed to avoid uncleanable recesses; sliding doors are undesirable for this reason.
- False ceilings should be sealed to prevent contamination from the space above them.

- Pipes and ducts and other utilities should be installed so that they do not create recesses, unsealed openings and surfaces that are difficult to clean.
- Sinks and drains should be avoided wherever possible and should be excluded from grade A/B areas where aseptic operations are carried out. Where installed, they should be designed, located and maintained so as to minimize the risks of microbiological contamination; they should be fitted with effective, easily cleanable traps and with air breaks to prevent back-flow. Any floor channels should be open and easily cleanable and be connected to drains outside the area in a manner that prevents the ingress of microbiological contaminants.
- Changing rooms should be designed as airlocks and used to separate the different stages of changing, thus minimizing particulate and microbiological contamination of protective clothing. They should be effectively flushed with filtered air. The use of separate changing rooms for entering and leaving clean areas is sometimes necessary. Hand-washing facilities should be provided only in the changing rooms, not in areas where aseptic work is done.
- Airlock doors should not be opened simultaneously. An interlocking system and a visual and/or audible warning system can be installed to prevent the opening of more than one door at a time.
- A filtered air supply should be used to maintain a positive pressure and airflow relative to surrounding areas of a lower grade under all operational conditions; it should flush the area effectively. Adjacent rooms of different grades should have a pressure differential of approximately 10–15 pascals. Particular attention should be paid to the protection of the zone of greatest risk, i.e. the immediate environment to which the product and the cleaned components in contact with it are exposed. The various recommendations regarding air supplies and pressure differentials may need to be modified where it becomes necessary to contain certain materials, e.g. pathogenic, highly toxic, radioactive or live viral or bacterial materials or products. The decontamination of the facilities and the treatment of air leaving a clean area may be necessary for some operations.
- It should be demonstrated that airflow patterns do not present a contamination risk; for example, care should be taken to ensure that particles from a particle-generating person, operation or machine are not conveyed to a zone of higher product risk.
- A warning system should be included to indicate failure in the air supply. An indicator of pressure difference should be fitted between areas where this difference is important, and the pressure difference should be regularly recorded.

- Consideration should be given to restricting unnecessary access to critical filling areas, e.g. grade A filling zones, by means of a physical barrier.

## Equipment

- A conveyor belt should not pass through a partition between a grade A or B clean area and a processing area of lower air cleanliness, unless the belt itself is continuously sterilized (e.g. in a sterilizing tunnel).
- Whenever possible, equipment used for processing sterile products should be chosen so that it can be effectively sterilized by steam or dry heat or other methods.
- As far as possible, equipment fittings and services should be designed and installed so that operations, maintenance and repairs can be carried out outside the clean area. Equipment that has to be taken apart for maintenance should be re-sterilized after completing reassembly, wherever possible.
- When equipment maintenance is carried out within a clean area, clean instruments and tools should be used, and the area should be cleaned and disinfected again, where appropriate, before processing recommences if the required standards of cleanliness and/or asepsis have not been maintained during the maintenance work.
- All equipment, including sterilizers, air-filtration systems, and water treatment systems, including stills, should be subject to planned maintenance, validation and monitoring; its approved use following maintenance work should be documented.
- Water-treatment plants and distribution systems should be designed, constructed and maintained to ensure a reliable source of water of an appropriate quality. They should not be operated beyond their designed capacity.
- Consideration should be given to include a testing programme in the maintenance of a water system. Water for injection should be produced, stored and distributed in a manner which prevents the growth of microorganisms, e.g. by constant circulation at a temperature above 70 °C or not more than 4 °C.

## Environment control/Air control

As we know that preparation of sterile product requires strict control over protection against microbial contaminations. Surrounding environment and air can be greatest source of contamination. It can be mi- nimised by using special bacterial and particulate filters. Air for aseptic area is then passed through high efficiency particulate air (HEPA) filters. HEPA filters are highly efficient it can remove 99.7% of all particles 0.3 µm or larger. A positive pressure is maintained relative to corridors, to prevent outside air from entering aseptic areas.

A Laminar air flow system is used. It provides an effective means for environment control of an aseptic area. Laminar air flow system contains three basic elements-a blower, a high efficiency air filter, and a plenum. The flow is called laminar because the turbulent air upstream is changed by the filter into a straight-line flow off the downstream face of the filter. Many blowers, many filters, and very large plenums but all have the same basics. The necessity of laminar air flow is to remove most of the particulate matter, as a matter of fact 99.99% of everything air-borne down to 0.3 microns should be screened out to have an environment whose air supply is free of bacteria, fungi, pollen, and practically all air-borne dirt.

These Laminar air flow may be of two types.

**Type 1:** Horizontal Flow (Laminar Flow Hood), in which air blows towards worker and; which is used for non-chemotherapy preparations (Figure 20.2).

**Type 2:** Vertical Flow: in which air blows from top down to maintain sterility and protect the worker. These are used as Biological Safety Cabinet or Chemotherapy Hood.

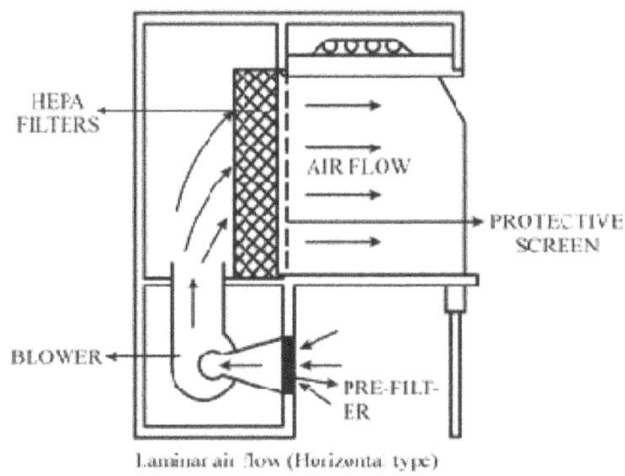


**Figure 20.2** Horizontal laminar air flow system.

The HEPA filters validated by DOP-dioctylphthalate-method.

When manufactured, DOP liquid plasticiser, heated to the point of vaporization and reconstituted into 0.3-micron particles to form a monodisperse aerosol. These single size particles are diluted with air until a conc. of 100 µg per litre is reached and aerosol mixture allow to be passed through the filter. The amount of penetration is measured on the downstream side with a forward light scattering photometer, giving the familiar reading of 0.03% or better studies were made of the effect of different size leaks on typical types of work such as photoresist, microweld, sterile transfers, and the like where it was shown that a leak of 0.01% was the border at which reject rates began to increase and excessive contamination was detected for in-situ DOP test this also represents the linear mass photometer threshold accuracy.

## Air Classification Technique of Environmental Control

Air Classification system monitors the numbers of particle accepted and permitted in the manufacturing area (**Table 20.1**). (It is defined as the number of particles per cubic foot of air that are larger than 0.5 μm in diameter. e.g. Class 100, Class 1000, Class 10000). In the same way the air borne particulate classification system may be Grade A, B, C and D (**Table 20.2**)

**Table 20.1** Clean Room Classification.

| FS209 cleanroom classification | ISO 14644-1 cleanroom classification | NMT 0.5 um particles/ $m^3$ | Viable microbes (cfu/$m^3$) | Average airflow velocity (fpm) | Air change/hr |
|---|---|---|---|---|---|
| 100,000 | 8 | 3,520,000 | 100 | 5-10 | 5-48 |
| 10,000 | 7 | 35,200 | 10 | 10-15 | 60-90 |
| 1000 | 6 | 35,200 | 7 | 25-40 | 150-240 |
| 100 | 5 | 3,520 | 1 | 40-80 | 240-480 |

**Table 20.2** Air Borne Particulate Classification.

| | Maximum permitted number of particles/$m^3$ | | | |
|---|---|---|---|---|
| Grade | At rest | | In n operation | |
| | 0.5mm | 5mm | 0.5mm | 5mm |
| A | 3500 | 0 | 3500 | 0 |
| B | 3500 | 0 | 350,000 | 2000 |
| C | 350,000 | 2,000 | 3,500,000 | 20,000 |
| D | 3,500,000 | 20,000 | Not defined | Not defined |

## Further Readings

- "Industrial Pharmacy-I" SWAYAM MOOC: www.swayam.gov.in
- https://www.terrauniversal.com/uploads/tech_resources/verticalvshorizontal laminarflow150121_052815154749.pdf

- Federal standard 209 E: Clean room and workstation requirements: Controlled Environment

## References


- Semalty et al., Essentials of Pharmaceutical Technology, II Edn, 2019, Pharma Med press, Hyderabad, India, ISBN 9789386819994.
- Good manufacturing practices for sterile pharmaceutical products. In: WHO Expert Committee on Specifications for Pharmaceutical Preparations. Thirty-sixth report. Geneva, World Health Organization, 2002 (WHO Technical Report Series, No. 902), Annex 6; and in Quality assurance of pharmaceuticals. A compendium of guidelines and related materials. Vol. 2. 2nd updated ed. Good manufacturing practices and inspection. Geneva, World Health Organization, 2007; and in Quality Assurance of Pharmaceuticals. A compendium of guidelines and related materials. Geneva, World Health Organization, 2010 (CD-ROM).
- Federal standard 209 E: Clean room and workstation requirements: Controlled Environment
- ISO 14644-1. Clean rooms and associated controlled environments. Part 1: Classification of airborne particles. Geneva, International Organization for Standardization.
- ISO 14644-3. Clean rooms and associated controlled environments. Part 3: Test methods. Geneva, International Organization for Standardization.
- ISO 1822-4. High efficiency air filters (HEPA and ULPA). Determining leakage of filter elements (scan method).
- ISO 14644-4. Clean rooms and associated controlled environments. Part 4: Design, construction and start-up. Geneva, International Organization for Standardization.
- ISO 14644-2. Clean rooms and associated controlled environments. Part 2: Monitoring for continued compliance with ISO 14644-1. Geneva, International Organization for Standardization.
- ISO 14644-5 Clean rooms and associated controlled environments. Part 5: Cleanroom operations. Geneva, International Organization for Standardization.
- Remington: The Science and Practice of Pharmacy, Lippincott Williams & Wilkins, New York, Vol.–1, 21st. edn, 2006.
- Boylan JC, Nail SL, In; Banker GS, Rhodes CT (Eds). Modern Pharmaceutics. 2005 (Vol. 121) Marcel Dekker, Inc. New York, Basel, US, pp 381-414.

# CHAPTER 21

# Parenterals II (Pyrogens and Pyrogenicity)

**Dr Mona Semalty, Dr Ajay Semalty**
Department of Pharmaceutical Sciences,
H.N.B Garhwal University (A Central University), Srinagar Garhwal-246174

### Learning Outcome

- Pyrogens and pyrogenicity
- Endotoxins its structure
- Sources of contaminations /elimination of pyrogens

### Lesson Plan

- Introduction to pyrogens/importance
- Endotoxins (classification and structure)
- Bioactivity of endotoxins
- Sources of pyrogen contamination
- Elimination of pyrogens

## Quality Control Test for Parenterals

### Pyrogens

Pyrogens are the metabolic products of microorganisms. Parenteral product must be free from pyrogens. If it is injected it causes increase in body temperature (causes fever), reduction of the blood pressure, shock, tissue damage, inflammation, thrombosis, hemorrhages of the skin and mucous membranes, sepsis, death. These types of symptoms may result from the harmful effects of bacterial endotoxins. Endotoxin, also referred as lipopolysaccharide (LPS), they are complex of pyrogenic lipopolysaccharide, a protein and inert lipid. Bacteria are prokaryotic organisms and based on their behavior against different staining methods (Gram-staining), they can be grouped in Gram-negative and Gram-positive bacteria.

## Gram-positive Bacteria

They have a thick, mesh-like cell wall, consisting mainly of peptidoglycan, that surrounds the cytoplasmic membrane. This peptidoglycan layer (formerly known as murein) serves as an exoskeleton and contain teichoic and lipoteichoic acids. Examples Streptococcus species (pneumonia causing), Bacillus anthracis (anthrax causing) and the Clostridium species (botulism- and tetanus-causing)

The Gram-negative cell wall is more complex the peptidoglycan layer is much thinner, and an outer membrane can be found on its external surface. This is basically a non-symmetric double phospholipid-layer, whose outer layer is formed by lipopolysaccharides (LPSs) and proteins examples are Vibrio, Salmonella and Shigella species and Escherichia coli.

### Structure of Endotoxins

The endotoxins (also known as lipopolysaccharides or LPSs) are heat-stable, resistant to proteolytic enzymes, immunogenic, cannot be converted to toxoids and are produced by Gram-negative bacteria. They exist in high molecular weight aggregate forms. However, the monomer unit of LPS is less than 10,000 Daltons, enabling endotoxin to easily pass through sterilizing 0.2-micron filters. The LPSs can be divided into three distinct regions:

- The lipid A
- The R-core and
- The O-specificchain

The lipid a part is responsible for the toxic biological effect it has hydrophobic structure directed towards the interior of the cell. It is a specific glycophospholipid (usually a bis-phosphorylated disaccharide backbone acylated with fatty acid chains).

The R-core is an oligosaccharide and can be divided into two subunits: (inner core) and (outer core). The inner core has the same composition in all Gram-negative bacteria, containing rarely occurring components [heptose (Hep) and 3-deoxy-d-manno-2-octulonic acid (Kdo)] and is linked to the lipid A part. The outer core is made of up to six hexose components and is linked to the O-specific side chain.

The outermost element of the LPS structure is the hydrophilic O-specific chain, which is built up from 1-40 repeating units of 2-7 sugar components.

## Bioactivity of Endotoxins

The toxicity of LPS is associated with the lipid A part. However, most of the toxicity is brought about by mediators, instead of the LPSs directly destroying the host cells and tissues. The bioactivity of endotoxins depends on its concentration. It shows immune response after releasing from the surface of the bacteria. As LPSs, releases it binds to the LPS-binding protein (LBP), this complex is transferred to CD14 on the surface of monocytes and macrophages and to receptor-4 (TLR4) on the surface of macrophages and endothelial cells. The activated macrophages induce the production of cytokines (eg IL-1, IL-6, IL-8, TNF-α, IFN-γ, etc.), prostaglandin and leukotriene, which are powerful inflammation- and septic shock-causing mediators and are required for the adaptive immune response.

The release of large amounts of endotoxin into the blood stream induces endotoxemia, causing a wide variety of symptoms such as chills, fever, septic shock, circulatory failure and even death. The characteristics of endotoxic shock are hypotension, disturbances of organ functions, metabolic acidosis, thrombocytolysis and disseminated intravascular coagulation (DIC). During pregnancy, the increased secretion of opioid peptides may cause decidual hemorrhage, premature birth or abortion.

Sources of pyrogen contamination

- Solvent
- The medicament
- The apparatus
- The method of storage between preparation and sterilization

## Elimination of Pyrogens

Pyrogens can be eliminated by

- Adsorption on the surface of selective adsorbents, but the often-concurrent phenomenon of the adsorption of solute ions or molecules may prevent the use of such method.
- Solvent extraction methods are useful in the production of antibiotics where heavy pyrogen contamination results from the fermentation process.
- Pyrogens can be destroyed by heating at high temperatures. A typical procedure for depyrogenation of glassware and equipment is maintaining a dry heat temperature of 250°C for 45 min. Exposure of 650°C for 1 min or 180°C for 4 hours, like- wise, will destroy pyrogens.
- Other in-process methods for their destruction or elimination include selective extraction procedures and careful heating with dilute alkali, dilute

acid, or mild oxidizing agents. Ultrafiltration is also sometimes used to eliminate pyrogens.

### Control of Pyrogens

It is very difficult to eliminate pyrogens from contaminated injections. Certain precautions must be taken to control pyrogen contamination throughout the entire process of product manufacturing.

- Therefore, compounding and manufacturing processes should be carried out as expeditiously as possible.
- The manufacturing process must be carried out with great care and as rapidly as possible, to minimize the risk of microbial contamination. Preferably, no more product should be prepared than can be processed completely within one working day, including sterilization

## Pyrogen Detection

Both the United States Pharmacopeia and the European Pharmacopoeia specify the rabbit pyrogen test and the Limulus amebocyte lysate (LAL) test. However, the LAL test detects only LPS and results in false negatives with certain products. Technically, the rabbit test is an acute toxicity test with an arbitrarily selected end point. There are reports that some parenteral products (e.g. human serum albumin) have caused pyrogenic reactions in patients even after passing the rabbit and LAL tests. Therefore, it is possible that even the rabbit test cannot detect all pyrogenic bacterial products.

There are 6 methods of pyrogen detection.

Method A. Gel-clot method: limit test

Method B. Gel-clot method: semi-quantitative test

Method C. Turbidimetric kinetic method

Method D. Chromogenic kinetic method

Method E. Chromogenic end-point method

Method F. Turbidimetric end-point method

An alternative pyrogen test is the monocyte activation cytokine assay. In this assay, monocytes isolated from human peripheral blood are incubated with test samples and their supernatant assayed for pyrogenic cytokines such as IL-1 or TNF-α. A variation of this test is the whole blood-IL-6 assay. A monocytic cell-based assay also has been developed. The disadvantage of the monocyte activation-cytokine assay is that the sensitivity of freshly isolated monocytes can vary depending on the immunological responsiveness of the donors. To make this assay suitable for quality control purposes, a well-defined monocytic cell line, which retains its ability to synthesize and secrete cytokines, is needed. This could lead to the development of a quantitative pyrogen test with a broader range of applicability. The Mono-Mac-6 and THP-1 cell lines have been characterized for their suitability in a cell-based pyrogen assay and were found to have the ability to detect bacterial pyrogens.

**Quality control of parenteral includes:**

- Test for pyrogens: Rabbit test and Bacterial endotoxins test (BET).
- Particulate evaluation
- Leakers Test
- Sterility test

## Test for Pyrogens (Rabbit Test)

### Preliminary Test (Sham Test)

Intravenous injection of sterile pyrogen-free saline solution is given to the animal to exclude any animal showing an unusual response to the trauma (shock) of injection any animal showing a temperature variation greater than 0.6°C is not used in the main test.

**Main test:**

- Group of 3 rabbits
- Preparation and injection of the product:
    - Warming the product
    - Dissolving or dilution
    - Duration of injection: not more than 4 min
    - The injected volume: not less than 0.5 ml per 1 kg and not more than 10 ml per kg of body mass
- Determination of the initial and maximum temperature
- All rabbits should have initial T: from 38.0 to 39.8°C
- The differences in initial T should not differ from one another by more than 1°C

## Interpretation of the Results

If the sum of the responses of the group of three rabbits does not exceed 1.4° and if the response of any individual rabbit is less than 0.6°, the preparation under examination passes the test. If the response of any rabbit is 0.6° or more, or if the sum of the response of the three rabbits exceeds 1.4°, continue the test using five other rabbits. If not more than three of the eight rabbits show individual responses of 0.6° or more, and if the sum of responses of the group of eight rabbits does not exceed 3.7°, the preparation under examination passes the test. (**Table 21.1**)

**Table 21.1** Interpretation of results (Sham test).

| No. of Rabbits | Individual Temp. rise (°C) | Temp. rise in group (°C) | Test* |
|---|---|---|---|
| 3 rabbits | <0.6 | ≤ 1.4 | Passes |
| If above not passes take additional 5 rabbits (for 3+5 = 8 rabbits) | <0.6 (not more than 3 should show ≥ 0.6) | ≤ 3.7 | Passes |

*If above test does not pass the sample is said to be pyrogenic perform the test again

**Limulus Amebocyte Lysate (LAL) test or Bacterial Endotoxins Test (Official in I.P. and B.P.).**

The test is used to detect or quantify endotoxins of gram-negative bacterial origin. LAL test is based on the primitive blood-clotting mechanism of the horseshoe crab (**Figure 21.1**). The presence of pyrogen is indicated by the formation of a proteinaceous gel, upon incubation of the mixture of LAL reagent and test solution.

**Figure 21.1** Limulus polyphemus or horseshoe crab.

**LAL Test performance (The key points)**

- Avoid endotoxin contamination

- Before the test:
    - interfering factors should not be present
    - equipment should be depyrogenated
    - the sensitivity of the lysate should be known
- Test:
    - equal volume of LAL reagent and test solution (usually 0.1 ml of each) are mixed in a depyrogenated test-tube
    - incubation at 37°C, 1 hour
    - remove the tube, invert in one smooth motion (180°), read (observe) the result
    - pass-fail test
- If a firm gel is formed- Pyrogen present.
- If an intact gel is not formed – Pyrogen absent.

**Note:**

1. A lysate of amoebocytes from either of the species of the horseshoe crab, Limulus polyphemus, Tachypleusgigas, Tachypleus tridentatus or Carcinoscorpius rotundicauda may be used for the LAL test. The species from which the lysate is obtained is mentioned on the label and reconstituted as stated on the label.
2. The LAL test or BET may be used as qualitative as well as quantitative (and also semi-quantitaive) measure of detecting the presence of pyrogens. IP and BP may be referred for further studies about the same.

**Limit test (method A)**

- A firm gel - positive result.
- An intact gel is not formed - negative result.
- The interpretation of the results

## Semi-quantitative Test (method B)

Quantification of bacterial endotoxins in the test solution is done by titration to an endpoint. This procedure is similar as in the limit test. The results are expressed as concentration of endotoxin as less, equal or greater than the labeled lysate sensitivity (photometric test to measure the increase in turbidity).

**End-point test (Method F)**: Quantitative relationship between the endotoxin concentration and the turbidity (absorbance or transmission) of the reaction mixture at the end of an incubation period.

**Kinetic test (Method C):** This method to measure either the time (onset time) needed for the reaction mixture to reach a predetermined absorbance, or the rate of turbidity development.

Measuring the chromophore released from a suitable chromogenic peptide by the reaction of endotoxins with the lysate.

**End-point test (Method E):** This active relationship between the endotoxin concentration and the quantity of chromophore released at the end of an incubation period.

**Kinetic test (Method D):** A method to measure either the time (onset time) needed for the reaction mixture to reach a predetermined absorbance, or the rate of color development Fast - 60 minutes vs. 180 minutes

**Advantages of LAL Test**

- Greater Sensitivity
- Less Variability
- Much Less False Positives
- Much Less Expensive
- Alternative to Animal Model
- cheaper,
- more accurate than other
- performed in the pharmaceutical laboratory
- specific for endotoxins of gram-negative origin
- particularly useful for:
- Radiopharmaceuticals and cytotoxic agents
- Products with marked pharmacological or toxicological activity in the rabbit (e.g. insulin)
- Blood products which sometime give misleading results in the rabbit
- Water for injection where LAL test is potentially more stringent and readily applied

## Particulate Evaluation

The entire product should be inspected by human inspectors under good light baffled against reflection into the eye and against black and white background (**Figure 21.2**). Any container with visible particle if seen is discarded.

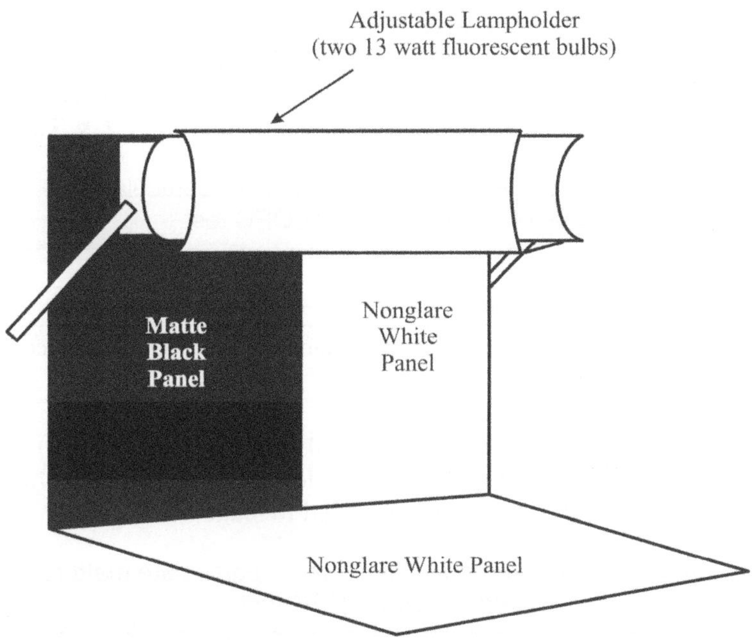


**Figure 21.2** Apparatus for visible particle inspection as presented.

**Limitations**

- Size of the particles that can be seen (Visible in unaided eye: 50 µm) only be observed
- Variations of visual acuity from inspector
- Emotional stress
- Eye Strain
- Fatigue

For the assessment of particulate matter below visible size like in all large volume parenterals (LVP) for single use and small volume parenterals (SVP), excluding IM and SC injections light obscuration and microscopic particle count test is done. For small-volume parenterals less than 25 mL in volume, the contents of 10 or more units are combined in a cleaned container to obtain a volume of not less than 25 mL; where justified and authorized, the test solution may be prepared by mixing the contents of a suitable number of vials and diluting to 25 mL with particle-free purified water or with an appropriate solvent without contamination of particles when particle-free purified water is not suitable. Light obscuration is referred as Stage 1 and microscopic particle count is referred as stage 2.

**In light obscuration method** equipment used to count and measure the size of particles by means of a shadow cast by the particle as it passes through a high-intensity light beam. BP, JP and USP limits for particulate matters determined by LOPC and MPC test is mentioned in **Table 21.2 & Table 21.3.**

**Table 21.2** BP, JP and USP limits for particulate matters determined by LOPC test.

| Nominal Volume | ≥ 10 μm | ≥ 25 μm |
|---|---|---|
| More than 100 mL | 25 particles/mL | 3 particles/mL |
| 100 mL or less than 100 mL | 6000 particles/container | 600 particles/container |

In microscopic method sample is filtered through membrane filter (under ultra clean condition) and counting the particles on the surface of filter. If limit is exceeded for stage 1 the sample is subjected to stage.

**Table 21.3** BP, JP and USP limits for particulate matters determined by MPC test.

| Nominal Volume | ≥ 10 μm | ≥ 25 μm |
|---|---|---|
| More than 100 mL | 12 particles/mL | 2 particles/mL |
| 100 mL or less than 100 mL | 3000 particles/container | 300 particles/container |

## Leakers Test

Ampoules sealed by fusion are subjected for leakers test. Negative pressure is built within an incompletely sealed ampoule (submerged entirely in deeply colored solution, i.e. methylene blue solution). All leakers are discarded

**Note:** Vials and bottles are not subjected to leakers test because the sealing material is not rigid.

## Further Readings

- Industrial Pharmacy-I" SWAYAM MOOC: www.swayam.gov.in
- http://library.open.oregonstate.edu/microbiology/chapter/bacteria-cell-walls/
- Depyrogenation, https://youtu.be/cWwi2Yq7P-s
- https://slideplayer.com/slide/5271865/
- Endotoxin Testing, https://youtu.be/v2ZiqFLuAg4
- Endotoxin detection, https://youtu.be/5Zi2Rl-bI7E

## References


- Semalty et al., Essentials of Pharmaceutical Technology, II Edn, 2019, Pharma Med press, Hyderabad, India, ISBN 9789386819994.
- Remington: The Science and Practice of Pharmacy, Lippincott Williams & Wilkins, New York, Vol.–1, 21st. edn, 2006.
- Boylan JC, Nail SL, In; Banker GS, Rhodes CT (Eds). Modern Pharmaceutics. 2005 (Vol. 121) Marcel Dekker, Inc. New York, Basel, US, pp 381-414.
- Akers MJ, Larrimore Daniel S, Guazzo DM. Parenteral Quality Control Sterility, Pyrogen, Particulate, and Package Integrity Testing, III Edn, 2003, Marcel Dekker, Inc. New York, Basel, US.
- Avis KE, In; Lachman L, Lieberman HA, Kanig JL. Eds. The Theory and Practices of Industrial Pharmacy. Varghese Publishing House, Bombay, pp. 430-78.
- Chapman DG, In: Winfield AJ, Richards RME (Eds). Pharmaceutical Practice, 3rd Edn, 2004, Churchil Livingstone, New York, pp. 247-63.
- Deluca PP, Boylan JC. In; Avis KE, Lieberman HA, Lachman L, (Eds.). Pharmaceutical Dosage Forms: Parenteral Medications vol. 1, 2nd Edn., 1992, Marcel Dekker, New York.

CHAPTER 22

# Parenterals II (Sterility Test and Sterilization)

**Dr Mona Semalty, Dr Ajay Semalty**
Department of Pharmaceutical Sciences,
H.N.B Garhwal University (A Central University), Srinagar Garhwal-246174

### Learning Outcome

After reading this chapter, you will be able to know

- Sterility tests procedures and official guidelines
- Different methods of sterilization
- Container (glass and plastic) and closures used for parenterals

### Lesson Plan

- Sterility tests: basics, compendial requirements, tests methods and results interpretation
- Sterilization/sterility
- Methods of sterilization
- Direct transfer method
- Membrane tests method
- Containers for parenterals
- Filling and sealing of ampules and closures system

## Sterility and Sterility Test

Sterility is the most important and essential characteristic of a parenteral product. Sterility means the complete absence of all viable microorganisms. It is an absolute term; that is, a product is either sterile or not sterile. Building sterility into a product through meticulously validated cleaning, filtration, and sterilization procedures is preferable than testing for sterility of a product subjected to marginal or inadequate production processes. The sterility test should never be employed as an evaluation of the sterilization process.

Sterility and quality cannot be tested into a product; they can only be components of controlled processes throughout the production sequence. The sterility test, however, should be employed as the last of several checkpoints in reaching a conclusion that the production process has removed or destroyed all living microorganisms in the product. The USP chapter 1 on injections states that preparations for injection meet the requirements under "Sterility Tests." After meeting these requirements—that is, all media vessels incubated with product sample reveal no evidence of microbial growth (turbidity)—the tested product may be judged to meet the requirements of the test. If evidence for microbial growth is found, the material tested has failed to meet the requirements of the test for sterility. Retesting is only allowed if there is unequivocal proof that the failed result was due to operator or accidental contamination. The FDA has stringent requirements for sterility retesting.

Evidence for microbial growth is determined by visual evaluation of a vessel containing the product sample in the proper volume and composition of nutrient solution. Provided that the growth conditions are optimal—proper nutrients, pH, temperature, atmosphere, sufficient incubation time, and so on—a single microbial cell will grow by geometric progression until the number of microbial cells and their metabolic products exceed the solubility capability of the culture medium. Manifestation of this "overgrowth" is visualized by the appearance of a cloudy or turbid solution of culture medium. A noxious odor may also accompany the turbid appearance of the contaminated medium. The sterility test is a failure when a product generates turbidity in a vessel of culture medium while the same lot of medium without the product sample shows no appearance of turbidity.

## Sterility Test Methods

The USP and EP sterility tests specify two basic methods for performing sterility tests, the direct transfer (DT) or direct inoculation method and the MF method, with a statement that the latter, when feasible, is the method of choice. In fact, in some cases, membrane filtration may be the only possible choice. IP, USP and EP provide the detailed SOPs of these tests.

### Direct Transfer Method

The DT method is the more traditional sterility test method. Basically, the DT method involves three steps:

- Aseptically opening each sample container from a recently sterilized batch of product

- Using a sterile syringe and needle to withdraw the required volume of sample for both media from the container
- Injecting one-half of the required volume sample into a test tube containing the required volume of Fluid Thioglycolate medium (FTM) and the other half volume of sample into a second test tube containing the required volume of trypticase soy broth (TSB)

The sample volume must be a sufficient representation of the entire container volume and the volume, of medium must be sufficient to promote and expedite microbial growth, if present. Adequate mixing between the sample inoculum and the culture medium must take place to maximize interaction and facilitate microbial growth.

## Membrane Filtration Method

The successful employment of this technique requires more skill and knowledge than that required for the DT method. Five basic steps are involved in the use of the MF sterility test method.

1. The filter unit must be properly assembled and sterilized prior to use.
2. The contents of the prescribed number of units are transferred to the filter assembly under strict aseptic conditions. The contents are filtered with the aid of a vacuum or pressure differential system.
3. The membrane is removed aseptically and cut in half.
4. One-half of the membrane is placed in a suitable volume (usually 100 ml) of FTM, and the other membrane half is placed in an equal volume of TSB.

A suitable membrane filter unit consists of an assembly that facilitates the aseptic handling of the test articles and allows the processed membrane to be removed aseptically for transfer to appropriate media or an assembly by which sterile media can be added to the sealed filter and the membrane incubated in situ. A membrane suitable for sterility testing has a rating of 0.45 μm and a diameter of approximately 47 mm.

**Advantages**

- Greater sensitivity.
- The antimicrobial agent and other antimicrobial solutes in the product sample can be eliminated by rinsing prior to transferring the filter into test tubes of media, thereby minimizing the incidence of false-negative test results.
- The entire contents of containers can be tested, providing a real advantage in the sterility testing of large volume parenterals and increasing the ability

to detect contamination of product lots containing very few contaminated units.

- Low-level contamination can be concentrated on the membrane by filtering large volumes of product. This results in faster reporting of test results since MF requires only 7 days incubation (for most terminally sterilized products).
- Organisms present in an oleaginous product can be separated from the product during filtration and cultured in a more desirable aqueous medium.

**Disadvantages**

- There exists a higher probability of inadvertent contamination in manual operations because of the need for greater operator skill and better environmental control in disassembling the filtration unit and removing, cutting, and transferring the membrane.
- The method is unable in differentiate the extent of contamination between units, if present, because all product contents are combined, filtered through a single filter, and cultured in single test tubes. Also, if accidental contamination has occurred, rather than this being detected in one or more vessels of the DT method, it manifests itself in the only container used per culture medium.

## Interpretation of Results

If there is no visible evidence of microbial growth in a culture medium test tube, after subjecting the sample and medium to the correct procedures and conditions of the USP and EP sterility test, it may be interpreted that the sample representing the lot is without intrinsic contamination.

If microbial growth is found or if the sterility test is judged to be invalid (because of inadequate environmental conditions), the sterility test may be repeated.

### Methods of Sterilization

"Sterilization can be defined as any process that effectively kills or eliminates transmissible agents (such as fungi, bacteria, viruses and prions) from a surface, equipment, foods, medications, or biological culture medium. In practice sterility is achieved by exposure of the object to be sterilized to chemical or physical agent for a specified time. Various agents used as sterilant are: elevated temperature, ionizing radiation, chemical liquids or gases etc. The success of the process depends upon the choice of the method adopted for sterilization."

Terms commonly used Survivor curves

"They are plots of the logarithm of the fraction of survivors (microorganisms which retain viability following a sterilization process) against the exposure time or dose".

## D-value

D-value is indicative of the resistance of any organism to a sterilizing agent. For radiation and heat treatment, D-value is the time taken at a fixed temperature or the radiation dose required to achieve a 90% reduction in viable count.

## Z-value

Z-value represents the increase in temperature needed to reduce the D-value of an organism by 90%.

### Methods of Sterilization-

1. Physical Method
- Thermal (Heat) methods
- Radiation method
- Filtration method
2. Chemical Method
3. Gaseous method

## Heat Sterilization

Heat sterilization is the most widely used and reliable method of sterilization, involving destruction of enzymes and other essential cell constituents. The process is more effective in hydrated state where under conditions of high humidity, hydrolysis and denaturation occur, thus lower heat input is required. Under dry state, oxidative changes take place, and higher heat input is required.

This method of sterilization can be applied only to the thermostable products, but it can be used for moisture-sensitive materials for which dry heat (160-180 °C) sterilization, and for moisture- resistant materials for which moist heat (121-134 °C) sterilization is used.

The efficiency with which heat can inactivate microorganisms is dependent upon the degree of heat, the exposure time and the presence of water. The action of heat will be due to induction of lethal chemical events mediated through the action of water and oxygen. In the presence of water much lower temperature time exposures are required to kill microbe than in the absence of water.

## Dry Heat Sterilization

- Incineration
- Red heat
- Flaming
- Hot air oven

It employs higher temperatures in the range of 160-180 °C and requires exposures time up to 2 hours, depending upon the temperature employed. The benefit of dry heat includes good penetrability and non-corrosive nature which makes it applicable for sterilizing glassware and metal surgical instruments. It is also used for sterilizing non-aqueous thermostable liquids and thermostable powders. Dry heat destroys bacterial endotoxins (or pyrogens) which are difficult to eliminate by other means and this property makes it applicable for sterilizing glass bottles which are to be filled aseptically.

Hot-air oven Dry heat sterilization is usually carried out in a hot air oven, which consists of the following: (i) An insulated chamber surrounded by an outer case containing electric heaters. (ii) A fan iii) Shelves (iv) Thermocouples (v) Temperature sensor (vi) Door locking controls.

**Procedure**

- Articles to be sterilized are first wrapped or enclosed in containers of cardboard, paper or aluminum.
- Then, the materials are arranged to ensure uninterrupted air flow.
- Oven may be pre-heated for materials with poor heat conductivity.
- The temperature is allowed to fall to 400°C, prior to removal of sterilized material.

## Moist Heat Sterilization

Moist heat may be used in three forms to achieve microbial inactivation.

- Dry saturated steam – Autoclaving
- Boiling water/ steam at atmospheric pressure

- Hot water below boiling point

Moist heat sterilization involves the use of steam in the range of 121-134°C. Steam under pressure is used to generate high temperature needed for sterilization. Saturated steam (steam in thermal equilibrium with water from which it is derived) acts as an effective sterilizing agent. Steam for sterilization can be either wet saturated steam (containing entrained water droplets) or dry saturated steam (no entrained water droplets).

Autoclaves use pressurized steam to destroy microorganisms and are the most dependable systems available for the decontamination of laboratory waste and the sterilization of laboratory glassware, media, and reagents.

For efficient heat transfer, steam must flush the air out of the autoclave chamber. Before using the autoclave, check the drain screen at the bottom of the chamber and clean if blocked. If the sieve is blocked with debris, a layer of air may form at the bottom of the autoclave, preventing efficient operation. Autoclaves should be tested periodically with biological indicators like cultures of Bacillus stearothermophilus to ensure proper function.

This method of sterilization works well for many metal and glass items but is not acceptable for rubber, plastics, and equipment that would be damaged by high temperatures.

**Autoclaves, or steam sterilizers essentially consist of following:**

- A cylindrical or rectangular chamber, with capacities ranging from 400 to 800 liters.
- Water heating system or steam generating system
- Steam outlet and inlet valves
- Single or double doors with locking mechanism.
- Thermometer or temperature gauge
- Pressure gauges

## Gaseous Sterilization

The chemically reactive gases such as formaldehyde, (methanol, H.CHO) and ethylene oxide $(CH2)2O$ possess biocidal activity. Ethylene oxide is a colorless, odorless, and flammable gas.

The mechanism of antimicrobial action of the two gases is assumed to be through alkylations of sulphydryl, amino, hydroxyl and carboxyl groups on proteins and amino groups of nucleic acids. The concentration ranges (weight of gas per unit chamber volume) are usually in range of 800- 1200 mg/L for ethylene oxide and 15-100 mg/L for formaldehyde with operating temperatures of 45-63°C and 70-75°C respectively.

Both gases being alkylating agents are potentially mutagenic and carcinogenic. They also produce acute toxicity including irritation of the skin, conjunctiva and nasal mucosa.

## Ethylene Oxide Sterilizer

An ethylene oxide sterilizer consists of a chamber of 100-300- Litre capacity and surrounded by a water jacket. Air is removed from sterilizer by evacuation, humidification and conditioning of the load is done by passing sub-atmospheric pressure steam, then evacuation is done again and preheated vaporized ethylene oxide is passed.

After treatment, the gases are evacuated either directly to the outside atmosphere or through a special exhaust system. Ethylene oxide gas has been used widely to process heat-sensitive devices, but the aeration times needed at the end of the cycle to eliminate the gas made this method slow.

## Low Temperature Steam Formaldehyde (LTSF) Sterilizer

An LTSF sterilizer operates with sub atmospheric pressure steam. At first, air is removed by evacuation and steam is admitted to the chamber. Liquid Sterilization a. Peracetic Acid liquid sterilization: Peracetic acid was found to be sporicidal at low concentrations.

It was also found to be water soluble and left no residue after rinsing. It was also shown to have no harmful health or environmental effects. It disrupts bonds in proteins and enzymes and may also interfere with cell membrane transportation through the rupture of cell walls and may oxidize essential enzymes and impair vital biochemical pathways.

In a low-temperature liquid chemical sterile processing system, several steps must be followed for effective sterilization:

- Pre-cleaning of the devices is necessary because many devices have small connected lumens.
- Leak testing is done to ensure there are no leaks that could allow fluid to enter/leak the ampoules/vials and cause damage.

- The appropriate tray/container must then be selected, and if the device has lumens, the appropriate connector attached.
- The sterilant concentrate is provided in a sealed single- use cup and requires no pre-mixing or dilution.

The disadvantages of this method of sterilization are that the devices must be immersible, must fit in the appropriate tray, and must be able to withstand the 55°C temperature the process uses.

## Hydrogen Peroxide Sterilization

This method disperses a hydrogen peroxide solution in a vacuum chamber, creating a plasma cloud. This agent sterilizes by oxidizing key cellular components, which inactivates the microorganisms.

The plasma cloud exists only while the energy source is turned on. When the energy source is turned off, water vapor and oxygen are formed, resulting in no toxic residues and harmful emissions.

The temperature of this sterilization method is maintained in the 40-50°C range, which makes it particularly well-suited for use with heat-sensitive and moisture-sensitive medical devices. The instruments are wrapped prior to sterilization and can either be stored or used immediately.

**Five phases of the hydrogen peroxide processing cycle:**

- A vacuum phase creates a vacuum in the chamber and the pressure drops to less than one pound per square inch. This phase lasts about 20 minutes.
- In the injection phase, the aqueous hydrogen peroxide is introduced into the vacuum chamber and is vaporized into a gas, which creates a rise in pressure due to the increase of molecules.
- During the diffusion phase the hydrogen peroxide vapor spreads throughout the chamber and the increased pressure drives the sterilant into the packs, exposing the instrument surfaces to the sterilant and killing the microorganisms.
- During the plasma phase the radio frequency energy is applied, stripping the electrons from some of the molecules and producing a low-temperature plasma cloud. Following this reaction, the activated compounds lose their high energy and recombine to form oxygen and water.
- The purpose of the venting phase is to introduce filtered air into the chamber and return the chamber to atmospheric pressure so that the door can be opened. It lasts about one minute.

# Radiation Sterilization

Many types of radiation are used for sterilization like electromagnetic radiation (e.g. gamma rays and UV light), particulate radiation (e.g. accelerated electrons). The major target for these radiations is microbial DNA. Gamma rays and electrons cause ionization and free radical production while UV light causes excitation. Radiation sterilization with high energy gamma rays or accelerated electrons has proven to be a useful method for the industrial sterilization of heat sensitive products. But some undesirable changes occur in irradiated products, an example is aqueous solution where radiolysis of water occurs.

Radiation sterilization is generally applied to articles in the dry state; including surgical instruments, sutures, prostheses, unit dose ointments, plastic syringes and dry pharmaceutical products. UV light, with its much lower energy, and poor penetrability finds uses in the sterilization of air, for surface sterilization of aseptic work areas, for treatment of manufacturing grade water, but is not suitable for sterilization of pharmaceutical dosage forms.

## Gamma Ray Sterilizer

Gamma rays for sterilization are usually derived from Cobalt-60 source, the isotope is held as pellets packed in metal rods, each rod carefully arranged within the source and containing 20 KCi of activity. This source is housed within a reinforced concrete building with 2 m thick walls. Articles being sterilized are passed through the irradiation chamber on a conveyor belt and move around the raised source.

**Ultraviolet Irradiation:** The optimum wavelength for UV sterilization is 260 nm. A mercury lamp giving peak emission at 254 nm is the suitable source of UV light in this region. Electron Accelerator There are two types of electron accelerator machines, the electrostatic accelerator which produces electrons with maximum energies of 5 MeV, and the microwave linear accelerator which produces electrons with maximum energies of 10 MeV. Higher energies cause better penetration into the product but there is a risk of induced radiation.

A high energy electron beam is generated by accelerating electrons from a hot filament down an evacuated tube under high potential difference, and then additional energy is imparted to this beam in a pulsed manner by a synchronized traveling microwave. Articles to be sterilized are arranged on a horizontal conveyor belt and are irradiated from one or both sides.

## Filtration Sterilization

Filtration process does not destroy but removes the microorganisms. It is used for both the clarification and sterilization of liquids and gases as it can prevent the passage of both viable and non-viable particles. The major mechanisms of filtration are sieving, adsorption and trapping within the matrix of the filter material. Sterilizing grade filters are used in the treatment of heat sensitive injections and ophthalmic solutions, biological products and air and other gases for supply to aseptic areas. They are also used in industry as part of the venting systems on fermenters, centrifuges, autoclaves and freeze driers. Membrane filters are used for sterility testing.

**Application of filtration for sterilization of gases:**

HEPA (High efficiency particulate air) filters can remove up to 99.97% of particles >0.3 micrometer in diameter. Air is first passed through prefilters to remove larger particles and then passed through HEPA filters. The performance of HEPA filter is monitored by pressure differential and airflow rate measurements.

There are two types of filters used in filtration sterilization

- Depth filters: Consist of fibrous or granular materials so packed as to form twisted channels of minute dimensions. They are made of diatomaceous earth, unglazed porcelain filter, sintered glass or asbestos.
- Membrane filters: These are porous membrane about 0.1 mm thick, made of cellulose acetate, cellulose nitrate, polycarbonate, and polyvinylidene fluoride, or some other synthetic material. The membranes are supported on a frame and held in special holders. Fluids are made to transverse membranes by positive or negative pressure or by centrifugation.

**Application of filtration for sterilization of liquids:** Membrane filters of 0.22 micrometer nominal pore diameter are generally used, but sintered filters are used for corrosive liquids, viscous fluids and organic solvents. The factors which affects the performance of filter is the titer reduction value, which is the ratio of the number of organisms challenging the filter under defined conditions to the number of organisms penetrating it. The other factors are the depth of the membrane, its charge and the tortuosity of the channels.

**Containers and closures systems for parenteral doses form**

So, injectable formulations, they are packed into containers made up of glass or plastic containers. And it includes ampoules, vials, syringes, cartridges, bottles, and bags. So, ampoules are glass whereas bags are all plastics. The other containers that can be composed of glass or plastic and must include rubber material such as rubber stoppers for vials and bottles. Rubber plungers and rubber seals for syringes and cartridges.

And irrigating solution, these are packed in glass bottles with aluminum screw caps. So, the USP provides classification system for glass container- type I, type II, type III, and soda-lime glass. So

- Type I- borosilicate glass
- Type II- soda lime treated glass
- Type III- soda lime glass, and
- Soda lime glass which is not suitable for containers for parenterals
- So these are four classes of glass containers as per United States Pharmacopoeia.
- Type I glass, it is composed of silicone dioxide, nearby 81% and boric oxide with sodium and aluminum oxides. It is a chemically resistant glass with low leachability and also having a low thermal coefficient of expansion. The lower the thermal coefficient of expansion the more dimensionally stable the glass is against the thermal expansion stress that can result in cracking.
- So type II and type III glass compounds, they are composed of relatively high proportion of sodium oxide near by 14% and calcium oxide. This makes the glass chemically less resistant. So both types melts at a lower temperature and are easier to mold into various shapes, and have a higher thermal coefficient of expansion.

So USP provides different glass test for its evaluation.

USP tests

- The powdered glass test
- The water attack test
- Hydrolytic resistance test, and
- Light transmission test

So, these are the tests for glass containers and in the coming module of packaging we will be discussing the details of these glass tests.

Now moving to the

Plastic material

Thermosetting plastic and thermoplastics. Thermosetting plastics- that cannot be remelted. And thermoplastics that can be reprocessed. So polymers which are used for packing of large volume parenterals ophthalmic solutions, they are plastics.

What are the principal problems exist with these materials? The plastics

- The very first permeation of vapors and the other molecules in either direction through the walls of the plastic containers. This is problem with plastic container. And
- Leaching of constituents and sorption that is adsorption or absorption of drug molecules or ions on the plastic material.

Now the principle

Advantages of plastic packaging material

What are the advantages?

- They are not breakable.
- There is a substantial weight reduction. So it reduces the overall cost of manufacturing.
- No air interchange is required in the flexible bag of polyvinyl chloride and polyolefins..

Now,

What is the disadvantage?

- They are not clear as glass containers.

**Test for plastic packaging**

- Leakers test
- Collapsibility test
- Clarity of aqueous extract
- Transparency, and
- Water vapor permeability test

These are the evaluation parameters for plastic containers.

Now moving to the filling and sealing of parenteral doses form.

**Filling and sealing**

So, these two operations- filling and sealing are carried out aseptically with great care to control any type of contamination.

For filling as per the suitability of the preparation the container system has been specified. And the next step is the validation of the vial and of the cleaning, sterilization, and depyrogenation processes. So we need to do the validation of these processes before filling and sealing.

**Sealing of ampoules**

Sealing of ampoules is done by using automated machine system for both glass and plastic container. So, glass ampoules they are sealed by melting a portion of glass of neck to form either beads seal that is tip sealing or pull seal. Now, what is tip sealing?

*Tip sealing* is done by melting sufficient glass at the tip of the ampoule neck to from a bead of glass and close the opening. So, by this way we close the opening of the ampoule by forming a bead of glass.

*Pull seals* are done by heating the neck of rotating ampoules below the tip and then pulling the tip away to form a small, twisted capillary just prior to being melt closed.

**Closure system for parenteral dosage form**

The closure is normally the most vulnerable and critical component of the container as far as the stability and compatibility of the product is concerned. Rubber closures are used to seal the cartridges, vials, and bottles providing a material, soft and elastic enough to permit the entry and withdrawal of hypodermic needle without the loss of integrity of sealed container.

So, suitable closing of the container is necessary because

- It prevents the loss of material by spilling and volatilization.
- It prevents the deterioration of the product from the effect of environment such as moisture, oxygen, or carbon dioxide attack.
- And it avoids contamination of the product from dirt, microorganism, or from insect or by any other mean.

**Tests for rubber closures**

The rubber closures are tested for

- Self sealibility test
- Extractive test
- Penetrability
- Fragmentation test
- Light absorption test, and
- Compatibility test

So, these all tests are official in Indian Pharmacopoeia. All these evaluation parameters and the acceptance criteria have been discussed in detail in the last chapter dealing with the evaluation of packaging materials.

## Summary

Dear learners, with this chapter, we finish our parenteral doses form here. We have covered: -

- Introduction of parenterals, advantages, disadvantages, properties, and Preformulation of parenterals in the very first module
- Formulation of parenteral, methods of adjustment of isotonicity
- Different types of parenteral preparation that is solutions, emulsions, suspension, dry powders. Then method of preparation
- Plant layout and production facilities for parenteral doses form
- Pyrogens, pyrogenicity, and
- Evaluation of parenteral doses form including different tests of evaluation, sterility testing, leakers test, and clarity testing, and tests for sterility
- And methods for sterilization, container, and closure systems. And finally filling and sealing of ampoules.

The container and closure system, we will be covering in detail in our packaging module.

## Further Readings

- "Industrial Pharmacy-I" SWAYAM MOOC: www.swayam.gov.in
- https://www.youtube.com/watch?v=Ztl7_5xK2Zc
- https://www.youtube.com/watch?v=Ao2p19NkcQI
- https://www.youtube.com/watch?v=ygwca5oDPZI

## References


- Semalty et al., Essentials of Pharmaceutical Technology, II Edn, 2019, Pharma Med press, Hyderabad, India, ISBN 9789386819994.
- Sterilisation and disinfection, Microbiology, DMLT. Lesson 4, https://nios.ac.in/media/documents/dmlt/Microbiology/Lesson-04.pdf
- Remington: The Science and Practice of Pharmacy, Lippincott Williams & Wilkins, New York, Vol.–1, 21st. edn, 2006.
- Boylan JC, Nail SL, In; Banker GS, Rhodes CT (Eds). Modern Pharmaceutics. 2005 (Vol. 121) Marcel Dekker, Inc. New York, Basel, US, pp 381-414.
- Akers MJ, Larrimore Daniel S, Guazzo DM. Parenteral Quality Control Sterility, Pyrogen, Particulate, and Package Integrity Testing, III Edn, 2003, Marcel Dekker, Inc. New York, Basel, US.

- Avis KE, In; Lachman L, Lieberman HA, Kanig JL. Eds. The Theory and Practices of Industrial Pharmacy. Varghese Publishing House, Bombay, pp. 430-78.
- Chapman DG, In: Winfield AJ, Richards RME (Eds). Pharmaceutical Practice, 3rd Edn, 2004, Churchill Livingstone, New York, pp. 247-63.
- Deluca PP, Boylan JC. In; Avis KE, Lieberman HA, Lachman L, (Eds.). Pharmaceutical Dosage Forms: Parenteral Medications vol. 1, 2nd Edn., 1992, Marcel Dekker, New York.

## CHAPTER 23

# Capsule I

**Dr Lokesh Adhikari, Dr Ajay Semalty**
Department of Pharmaceutical Sciences,
H.N.B Garhwal University (A Central University), Srinagar Garhwal-246174

### Learning Outcome

After learning this chapter, you will be able to develop your understanding of:

- Capsule dosage forms
- Advantages and disadvantages of capsule dosage forms
- Composition, production of capsule shells
- Shorting, printing, and storage of empty capsule shells
- Hard gelatin capsules

### Lesson Plan

- Definition and basic concept of capsule dosage forms
- Advantages and disadvantages of capsules
- Capsule shell production
- Capsule shell storage
- Hard gelatin capsules

## Capsule

Capsules are solid dosage forms in which the drug substance is enclosed within either a hard or soft soluble shell, usually formed from gelatin. The term capsule is derived from the Latin word *capsula*, meaning a small container.

Today capsules may be classified as either hard or soft, depending on the nature of the shell. Most capsules of both types are intended to be swallowed whole.

However, some soft gelatin capsules are intended for rectal or vaginal insertion as suppositories.

**"Capsules are solid preparations with hard or soft shells of various shapes and capacities, usually containing a single dose of the active substance(s). They are intended for oral administration."**

***-British Pharmacopoeia***

## Unit Dosage Form

- The solid and liquid material both can be used as filling material (Figure 23.1).
- Capsules are meant for the oral route of administration.
- Capsules were firstly developed in 1834 by a Persian pharmacist.
- Capsule covers an approximate 20% worldwide share in prescribed drugs.

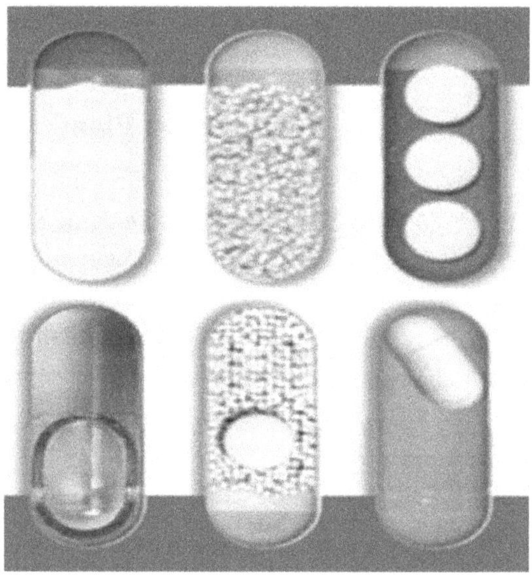

**Figure 23.1** Types of filling material in capsules.

**Material to be filled:** A wide range of filling material is covered by capsules (). We can categories the filling material in the following classes on the basis of their physical state-

- Dry powder
- Semisolids
- Non-aqueous liquids
- Beads
- Mini tablets
- Mini capsules

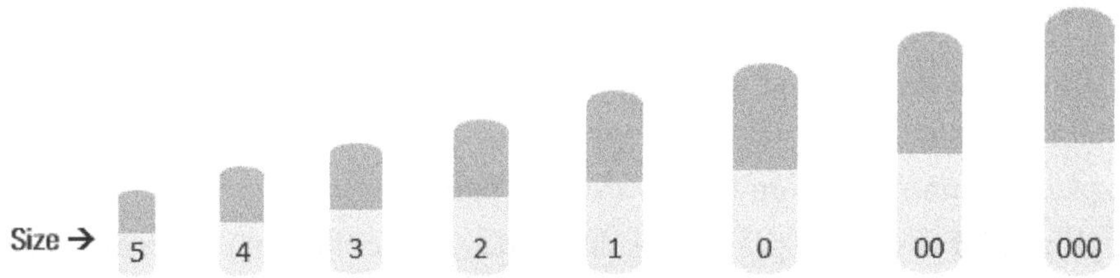


Formulation Capacity

| | | | | | | | | | |
|---|---|---|---|---|---|---|---|---|---|
| Volume | 0.13 | 0.21 | 0.27 | 0.37 | 048 | 0.67 | 0.95 | 1.36 | ml |
| Mass | 100 | 160 | 200 | 300 | 365 | 530 | 775 | 1110 | mg |

**Figure 23.2** Size and capacity of various capsule types.

## Advantages of capsules

Capsules have following benefits over other solid dosage forms:

- Capsules have a higher rate of dissolution as disintegration is only limited to solubilization of shell.
- Capsules have better taste masking.

Over liquid dosage form:

- Uniform dosing is possible with capsules.
- Capsules show better stability profile.
- The modified release is possible using capsules.

## Advantages of capsules

- Capsules are easy to swallow.
- The protection of medicament it is possible with capsules.
- Capsules are therapeutically inert & easy to digest.
- It is easy to handle and carry capsules.
- capsules are available in different sizes.
- Weekend easily identify the product in capsule dosage form.
- No need for complicated machinery
- Filling of incompatible substance in the same

## Disadvantages

- In comparison to tablets, the stability of capsules is low as the material for shell i.e., gelatin is very hygroscopic.
- Capsules cannot be given to unconscious patient.
- Highly soluble salts (e.g., iodides, bromides, and chlorides) generally should not be dispensed in hard gelatin capsules.
- Their rapid release may cause gastric irritation.
- The rate of production of the capsule is slower as compared to the tablet.
- The efflorescent substance may cause to capsule too soft.
- Deliquescent material may dry to the capsule shell to excessive.

# Capsule Shell Production

## Capsule Material

**Gelatin** is the most used, most acceptable shell material with excellent performance. Hypromellose is a carbohydrate that is used as a replacement of gelatin as shell material. It is less hygroscopic and suitable for vegetarian patients. It has no stability issue as such.

**Gelatin type (Figure 23.3):** There are two types of gelatin, type A and type B.

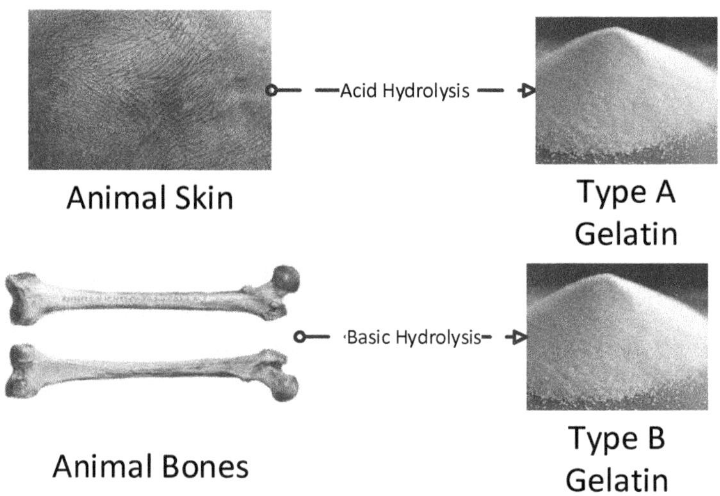


**Figure 23.3** Type of gelatin.

**Evaluation of Raw Material:** Before preparing capsule shells, gelatin is tested for bloom strength (gelling properties), viscosity, solubility, pH value, chemical purity, heavy metals, and microbial count. All these tests are done according to the monographs/standards.

**Evaluation of Raw Material:** Water is tested for electrolyte content, pH value and microbial count as per pharmacopeia.

The final gelatin solution is tested for viscosity, temperature, color composition and color shade.

**Controlled manufacturing environment:** Capsule shell production (Figure 23.4**Error! Reference source not found.**) requires a controlled environment which includes the relative humidity with the variation of ± 0.5%, temperature with the variation of ± 0.5°C and air circulation with the variation of 8 to 10 changes per hour,

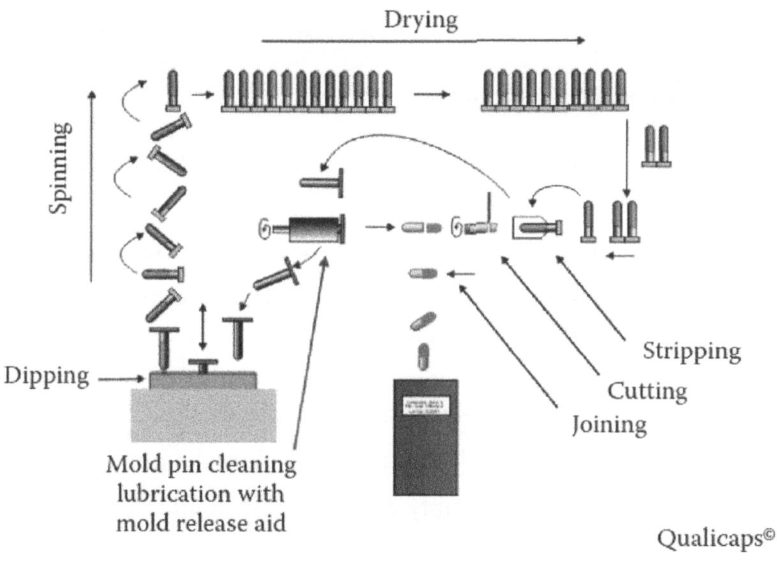


**Figure 23.4** Unit operation of capsule shell formation.

**Mold:** The molds are made up of stainless steel.

Molds are also known as pins.

Moles are cylindrical in shape with a hemispherical end.

Molds are mounted 30 in a line on metal bars.

The temperature of molds is kept 22°C.

**Shaft:** Taper along its length toward the end of 0.1–0.3 mm $cm^{-1}$

This makes it easier to remove the dried films from the pins.

There is a set of pin bars, ≥5, assembled in a rack is used which is dipped into the gelatin solution.

**Solution temperature:** The temperature of the solution is kept approximately about 45–50°C.

The mold pin temperature should be lower than the gelling point of the solution.

Sol is formed which is converted to gel which is subsequently gets turned into a homogeneous film **(Figure 23.5)**.

**Figure 23.5** Formation of the gelatin film.

**Important points to be considered:** The rate of the drain of the wet film is directly proportional to the viscosity of the solution.

Rate of drain – from wet film $\alpha$ solution viscosity

The amount retained on the pin is also proportional to the solution viscosity. The amount retained on the pin $\alpha$ solution viscosity.

An increase in viscosity will increase the amount of gelatin retained on the pin. This is used to control the thickness of capsule shells.

↑ viscosity = ↑ amount retained on the pin

The moisture content of the empty capsule shell should be in the range of 13 to 16 %.

The average production cycle time is about 45 min.

Prepared empty shells go through further processing steps **(Figure 26.6)**:

- Capsule shorting
- Capsule printing
- Packaging and storage

Moisture content is the most important parameter. The moisture content of the empty capsule shell should be in the range of 13.0% to 16.0% w/w. For every 1% change in moisture, there is a 0.5% change in capsule shell dimension.

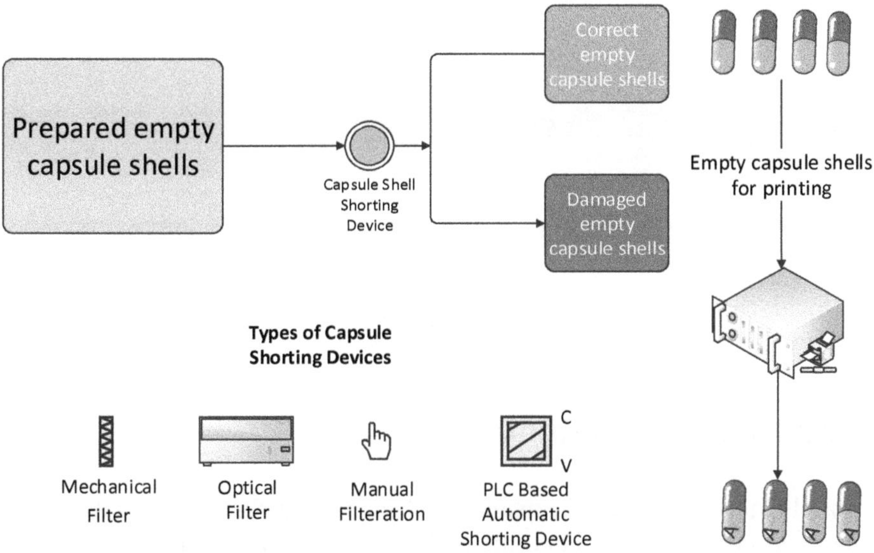


**Figure 23.6** Preparation of empty capsule shells.

Defects of hard gelatin capsule shells **(Figure 23.7)**:

**Cracked:** Body or caps with many splits

**Double cap:** Capsule with an additional cap covering the body.

**Double-dipping:** Extra thick cap due to double-dipping

**Failure to separate:** Cap and body may not separate properly.

**Hole:** Irregular opening in cap or body

**Joined in the lock:** Capsule in the locked position.

**Long cap/body:** Length cap or body 1 mm more than specification

**Mashed:** Mechanically damaged, squashed flat

**Pinched:** Cap or body damaged in collets, pinch > 3 mm

**Short body:** Length 0.4 mm less than specification

**Trimming:** Whole or piece of trimmed end cap or body inside the capsule

**Uncut cap/body:** Untrimmed cap or body

**Un-joined:** Single cap or body.

**Dye speck:** A Colored spot of pigment, different from cap or body-color

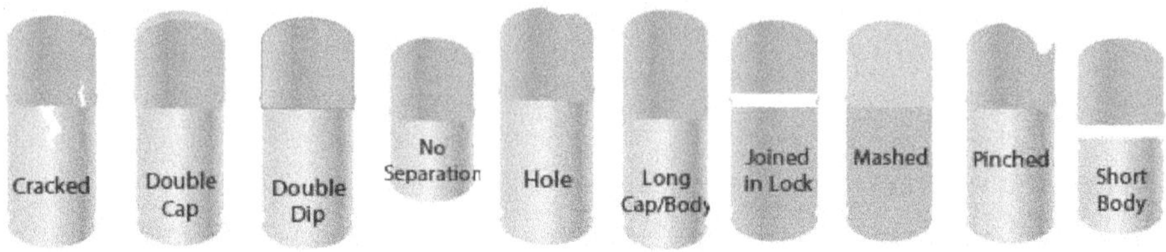


**Figure 23.7** Formulation defects of the capsule shell.

An ideal condition for temperature is between 15°C and 30°C. For this method, raw material with thermoplastic property required.

## Injection Molding Method

It is an advanced method of capsule shell manufacturing, though its practical applications are limited. This method is preferred for the thermoplastic material. The unit operation of this method has been illustrated in Figure 23.8.

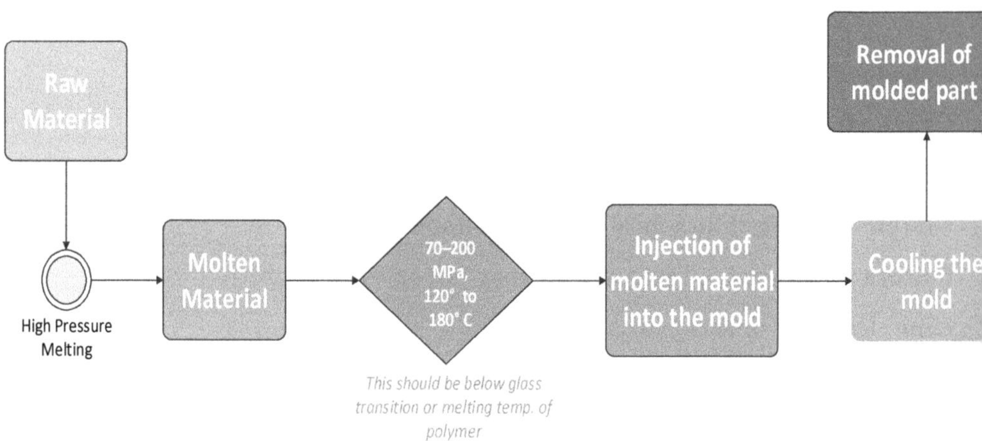


**Figure 23.8** Injection molding method.

## Advantages

Starting materials have a lesser water content.

Low production cost as no drying step involved.

Minimum chances of microbial contamination

Produce capsule with precise dimensions.

## Hard Gelatin Capsule

Hard gelatin capsules are consisting of two pieces in the form of cylinders closed at one end (Figure 23.9). The shorter piece is called the cap. This cap fits over the open end of a longer piece called the body.

Hard gelatin capsules are also known as dry-filled capsules or two-piece capsules. The drug substance placed in the body and the caps are slid over it, hence enclosing the drug substance.

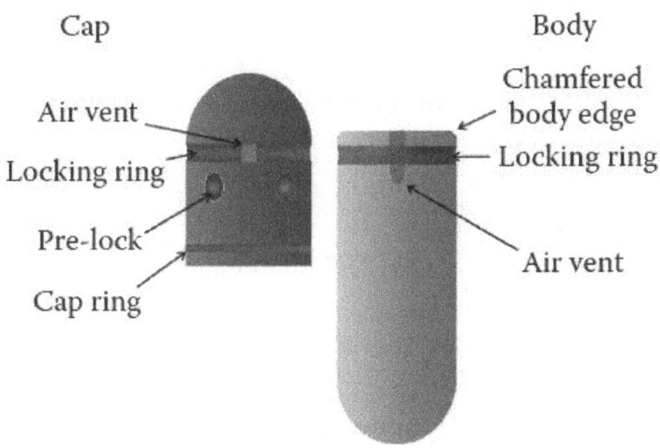


**Figure 23.9** Hard gelatin capsule.

## Summary

In this chapter, we learned about capsules as dosage form, official definition, advantages and disadvantages over the tablet and other formulations. We also discussed the production of capsule shells including shorting, printing and storage of prepared empty capsule shells. And lastly, we had gone through the introduction of hard gelatin capsules.

## Further Readings

- "Industrial Pharmacy-I" SWAYAM MOOC: www.swayam.gov.in

- Pharmaceutical Capsules. Edited by Fridrun Podczeck, Brian E. Jones. Pharmaceutical Press. ISBN: 9780853695684
- Pharmaceutical Dosage Forms: Capsules. Edited by Larry L. Augsburger, Stephen W. Hoag. CRC Press. ISBN: 9781351620390
- Banker GS, Rhodes CT, Modern Pharmaceutics, CRC Press.
- Augsburger, L. L., & Hoag, S. W. (2017). Pharmaceutical Dosage Forms: Capsules. CRC Press.
- Qiu, Y., Chen, Y., Zhang, G. G. Z., Liu, L., & Porter, W. (2009). Developing Solid Oral Dosage Forms: Pharmaceutical Theory and Practice. Academic Press.

## References

- Semalty et al., Essentials of Pharmaceutical Technology, II Edn, 2019 (Reprint), Pharma Med press, Hyderabad, India
- Swarbrick, J. (2013) Encyclopedia of pharmaceutical technology. CRC Press.
- Indian Pharmacopoeia 2018. (2018). Indian Pharmacopoeia Commission.
- Tovey, G. D. (2018). Pharmaceutical Formulation: The Science and Technology of Dosage Forms. Royal Society of Chemistry.
- Aulton ME (ED), Pharmaceutics: The science of Dosage form design, II edn, Churchill Livingstone, London, 2002.

CHAPTER 24

# Capsule II

**Dr Lokesh Adhikari, Dr Ajay Semalty**
Department of Pharmaceutical Sciences,
H.N.B Garhwal University (A Central University), Srinagar Garhwal-246174

### Learning Outcome

After learning this Chapter, you will be able to develop your understanding about:

- Hard Gelatin Capsules
- Hard Gelatin Capsule Filling
- Various principle and methods of capsule filling
- Formulation principles of hard gelatin capsules

### Lesson Plan

- Introduction to hard gelatin capsules
- Methods of filling hard gelatin capsules
- Advancements in filling of hard gelatin capsules
- Formulation aspects of hard gelatin capsule

## Hard Gelatin Capsules

These are also known as two-piece capsules or dry powder capsules. More than 85% of hard capsule shells are made up of gelatin. Gelatin based capsules are elegant in appearance and easy to swallow. The medicament is protected from external environment with a faster release in comparison with tablet.

James Murdock of London patented the two-piece telescoping gelatin capsule in 1847.The capsule is filled with powder or more normally pellets made by the process of Extrusion & Spheronization (either by placing a compressed slug of powder into one half of the capsule, or by filling one half of the capsule with loose powder) and the other half of the capsule is pressed on. With the compressed slug method, weight varies less between capsules. However, the machinery required to manufacture capsule is more complex.

Hard gelatin capsules can be filled either by manual method or mechanical method. Any method of filling comprises of five necessary steps.

- Feeding and rectification
- Separation
- Filling
- Joining
- Ejection

## Hand-Operated Filling Devices

Empty capsules are hand fed into an orienter, which rectifies the capsules. The orienter is positioned over a two-part filler plate to house the oriented cap and body. The body section has a locking mechanism to secure the capsule body while the caps are removed into the upper section cap tray. The locking mechanism is then released, allowing the bodies to drop flush into the lower filler plate. A powder tray is positioned on top of the lower filler plate. Premeasured powder is poured into the powder tray and a powder spreader manually dispenses the powder into the capsule bodies. A tamper plate packs the powder into the capsule bodies. The cap tray is then placed over the filled capsule bodies, and the cap and body plates are manually pressed together to join and eject the capsules. Some of the devices are available as bench top fillers with a semiautomatic orienter and an optional vibrator for faster filling of powders (Figure 24.1).

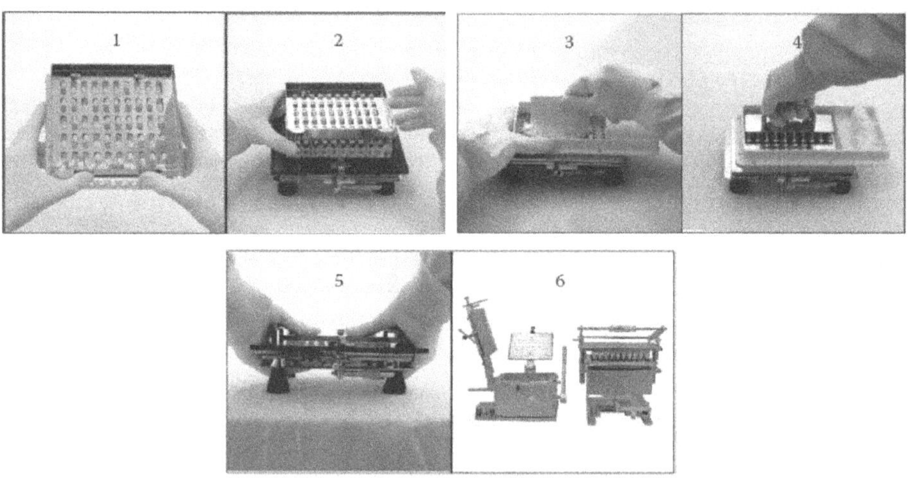


**Figure 24.1** Hand filling method of hard gelatin capsule.

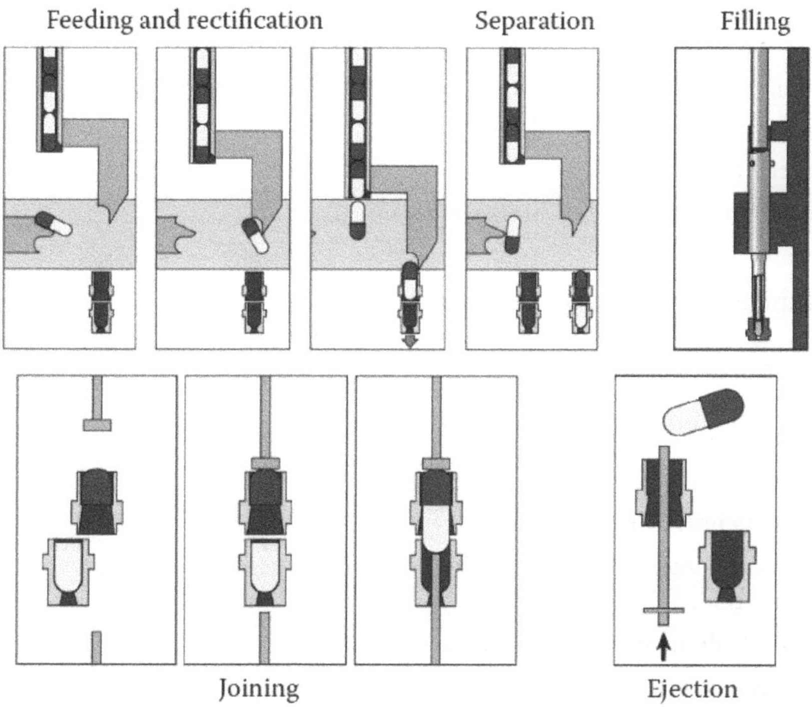


**Figure 24.2** Hard gelatin capsule filling method.

## Feeding and Rectification

Capsules fall by gravity into feeding tubes or chutes. Uniform aligned by mechanically gauging the diameter differences between the cap and the body. Rectified capsules fed, in proper orientation, into a two-section housing or bushing (**Figure 24.2**).

## Separation

- The diameter of the upper bushing or housing is larger than the diameter of the capsule body bushing.
- The capsule cap is retained within the upper bushing.
- The body is pulled into the lower bushing by vacuum.
- Once the capsule is opened/separated.
- The upper and lower housing or bushing is separated to position the capsule body for filling.

## Filling

The open capsule body is then dosed with the medicament. Types of methods used for filling capsule shells:

- Auger Fill Method
- Mechanical Vibration Filling Method
- Dosator Method
- Tamping Pin/Dosing Disc Method
- Compression Filling Method

## Auger Fill Method

- Semiautomatic method
- Filling is primarily volumetric.
- A rotating auger blade forces the powder through a feed shoe into the open capsule bodies.
- Dosing volume can be controlled by
- Rotation speed of the body ring
- Rotation speed and design or pitch of the auger
- Level of powder within the drug hopper reservoir

## Mechanical Vibration Fill Method

- A level sensor located in the powder supply chute maintains a stable powder layer.
- This layer fills directly into the capsule body facilitated by a vibration plate.
- The accuracy of the filled powder is improved by the use of an adjustable spring plunger.
- It removes air from the powder, creating uniform density.
- A scraper removes any excess fill material before capsule joining.

## Dosator Method

- The dosator consists of a hollow metal tube with a spring-loaded adjustable piston.
- It is adjusted volumetrically to capture the powder dose.
- The dosator descends into a rotating dosing bowl of powder that is being maintained at a constant level.

- Once the dosator reaches the bottom of the powder bed, the powder dose is pre-compressed and then the piston moves downward forming a plug.
- The dosator moves out of the powder bed and then aligns over the open capsule body.
- The piston descends to the bottom of the dosing tube, discharging the dosage plug into the capsule body.

## Tamping Pin/Dosing Disk Method

- It is fully automatic method.
- A rotating steel dosing disc is mounted at the base of a dosing bowl.
- The dosing disc has six sets of precisely bored holes.
- As the rotating dosing disc indexes, the holes beneath five sets of spring-loaded tamping pins → a stationary tamping ring seated below the dosing disc retains the powder.
- After five tamps, a deflector isolates the powder from the disc.
- A set of transfer pins push the powder plug out of the holes into the capsule bodies.

## Compression Fill Method

- It is a modified version of the Tamping Pin/Dosing Disc method.
- It employs four sub hoppers, tapping rods, and a powder molding plate.
- In the first sub hopper, a powder stirring agitator feeds the powder into the bores of the molding plate.
- In the second and third sub hoppers, tapping rods compress the filling powder into the molding plate→ forming a powder slug.
- In the fourth sub hopper, a weight ad.justment pusher raises the molded slug to a set height above the plate.
- At the fifth section, a transfer rod places the finished slug into the capsule body.

## Joining

- The cap and body housings or bushings are then realigned for capsule closing.
- An upper plate or pin will hold the cap stationary in the housing.

- Lower closing shaft rods will push the bodies upward into the caps until the capsules are completely joined.
- This will engage the locking mechanism of the capsule shell.

## Ejection

- The lower closing rod or shaft will ascend.
- This will eject the capsule from the housing or bushing into an exit chute.
- Compressed air nozzles are frequently used to assist the ejection of capsules from the machine, particularly with fully automatic filling machines.

## Sealing

- Sealing can be automatic or manual.

It can be:

  - Heat welding method
  - Liquid welding method

- Spraying → Warming → Setting
- Heat weld method is most suitable for gelatin-based capsules.

# Biopharmaceutical

Formulation factors influencing the bioavailability of drugs from hard gelatin capsules:

- Surface area and particle size of the drug
- A reduction in particle size is not a solution for all problems because agglomeration effects may prevail.
- Use of the salt form of a drug in preference to the parent weak acid or base.
- Crystal form of the drug
- Chemical stability of the drug (in the dosage form and GI fluids)
- Nature and quantities of the diluent, lubricant, and wetting agent
- Drug–excipient interactions (e.g., adsorption, complexation)
- Type and conditions of the filling process
- Packing density of the capsule contents
- Composition and properties of the capsule shell
- Interactions between the capsule shell and contents

- Formulation Principle of Hard Gelatin Capsule
- Section of diluent/filler related to solubility of active ingredient to aid and not interfere with dissolution.
    - for poorly soluble active, select a soluble excipient (e.g., lactose)
    - for soluble active, select an insoluble excipient (e.g., starch)

Choice of diluent/filler dictates plug-forming capability at low compression forces (10 to 100 N).

Such fillers modified for direct compression tableting have enhanced flowability and compactibility and may be of special advantage in automatic filling machine that form plugs by tamping or compression.

## Formulation Principle of Hard Gelatin Capsule

Laminar lubricants like magnesium stearate should not be over-blended. Particles delaminate under the shearing of blending to produce more hydrophobic particles in the blend. If too much glidant is used, they can act as an anti-glidant.

As a general rule, the water content of the fill should not exceed a critical value of about 5%. Doses > 600 mg in powder form are virtually impossible to fill into capsules of acceptable size. It may be possible to produce such doses in hard gelatin capsule form by increasing the density of the formulation, for instance, by granulation.

## Important Capsule Blend Properties

- **Density:** This affects fill weight and size of capsule.
- **Flow:** This affects bed recovery and segregation.
- **Adhesion:** This affects the fill weight uniformity, potency drop, segregation, and electrostatic interactions.
- **Water content:** This can affect wettability, dissolution, and shell and content stability.
- **Compactibility:** This can affect fill weight uniformity, plug formation, tamp/compression pressure, plug retention in dosing tubes and dosing discs, and dissolution.
- **Compressibility:** This affects fill weight, tamp/compression pressure, and capsule size selection.

## Summary

In this chapter, we learnt about hard gelatin capsules as dosage form and their importance. We also discussed about various methods of filling of hard gelatin capsules including handheld method. The advancement of capsule filling technology was also discussed in this module. And lastly, we had gone through formulation consideration of hard gelatin capsules.

## Further Readings

- "Industrial Pharmacy-I" SWAYAM MOOC: www.swayam.gov.in
- Pharmaceutical Capsules. Edited by Fridrun Podczeck, Brian E. Jones. Pharmaceutical Press. ISBN: 9780853695684
- Pharmaceutical Dosage Forms: Capsules. Edited by Larry L. Augsburger, Stephen W. Hoag. CRC Press. ISBN: 9781351620390
- Banker GS, Rhodes CT, Modern Pharmaceutics, CRC Press.
- Augsburger, L. L., & Hoag, S. W. (2017). Pharmaceutical Dosage Forms: Capsules. CRC Press.
- Qiu, Y., Chen, Y., Zhang, G. G. Z., Liu, L., & Porter, W. (2009). Developing Solid Oral Dosage Forms: Pharmaceutical Theory and Practice. Academic Press.

## References

- Semalty et al., Essentials of Pharmaceutical Technology, II Edn, 2019 (Reprint), Pharma Med press, Hyderabad, India
- Swarbrick, J. (2013) Encyclopedia of pharmaceutical technology. CRC Press.
- Indian Pharmacopoeia 2018. (2018). Indian Pharmacopoeia Commission.
- Tovey, G. D. (2018). Pharmaceutical Formulation: The Science and Technology of Dosage Forms. Royal Society of Chemistry.
- Aulton ME (ED), Pharmaceutics: The science of Dosage form design, II edn, Churchill Livingstone, London, 2002.

# CHAPTER 25

# Capsule III

**Dr Lokesh Adhikari, Dr Ajay Semalty**
Department of Pharmaceutical Sciences,
H.N.B Garhwal University (A Central University), Srinagar Garhwal-246174

### Learning Outcome

After learning this chapter, you will be able to develop your understanding about:

- Soft Gelatin Capsules
- Soft Gelatin Capsule Filling
- Various principle and methods of soft gelatin capsule filling
- Formulation principles of soft gelatin capsules

### Lesson Plan

- Introduction to soft gelatin capsules
- Methods of filling soft gelatin capsules
- Advancements in filling of soft gelatin capsules
- Formulation aspects of soft gelatin capsule

## Soft Gelatin Capsules

### Definition

Soft capsules are a single-unit solid dosage form, consisting of a liquid or semi-solid fill enveloped by a one-piece hermetically sealed elastic outer shell. Formed, filled and sealed in one continuous operation, preferably by the rotary die process.

### Reason for Selection

- **Strategic reasons:** When you have to create a new product for market with minimum resource application, only changing the production strategy can be helpful like line extension.

- **Technological issues:** When there is a technical issue in the development of the drug in the form of tablet or any other solid dosage form and the problem can be resolved by capsule formulation development. Such type of issue includes high content uniformity of low-dose drugs.
- **Safety aspects:** When it is unsafe to formulate the drug in other solid dosage form and developing the drug as capsules will lead to reduced operator and environmental contamination with highly potent or cytotoxic compounds.
- **Consumer preference:** It is easy to swallow capsules in comparison with administering powdered drug.

**Advantages**

- Easy to swallow.
- No taste leading to the better patient compliance.
- Unit dose delivery is possible.
- Tamper-proofing is possible.
- Wide variety of colors, shapes, and sizes can be achieved.
- Accommodates a wide variety of compounds filled as a semi-solid, liquid, gel or paste.
- Immediate or delayed drug delivery can be formulated as capsules.
- Can be used to improve bioavailability by delivering drug in solution or other absorption enhancing media.

**Disadvantages**

- Requires special manufacturing equipment.
- Stability concerns with highly water-soluble compounds, and compounds susceptible to hydrolysis.
- Limited choices of excipients/carriers compatible with the gelatin.

## Composition (Figure 25.11)

**On the basis of formulation category**

- Shell material (Gelatin/PVA/carrageenan)
- Plasticizer (single or a combination of plasticizers)
- Water as solvent
- Preservatives

- Colouring agents
- Opacifying agents
- Flavourings and sweeteners

**On the basis of solubility**

- Hydrophilic solvents
- Lipophilic materials
- Hydrophilic surfactants
- Lipophilic surfactant
- Cosolvents

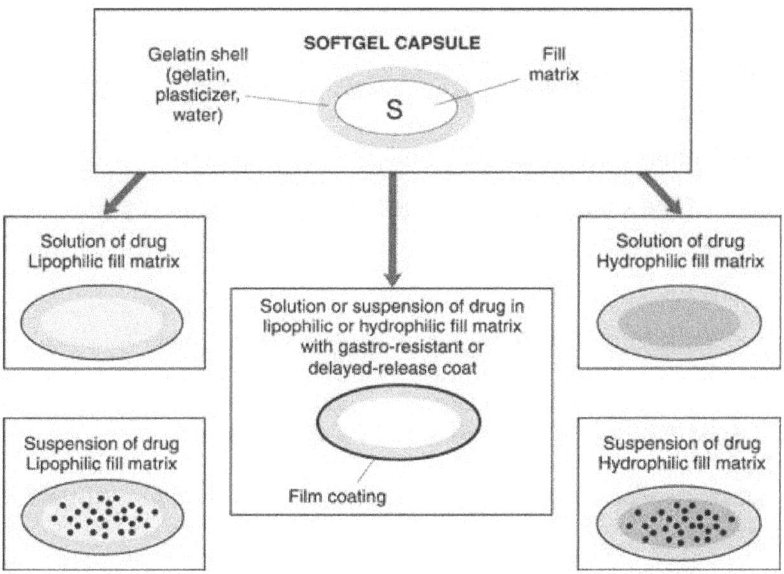


**Figure 25.1** Soft gel capsule filling material.

## Pre-requisite

- Selection of appropriate shell material as a variety of shell material has been developed and each of these has unique formulational characteristics.
- Selection of appropriate fill composition as it changes the size of shell.
- Optimization of these two for physical and chemical stability

**Gelatin:** Most used shell forming agent, obtained from animal bone and skin. It has following film forming properties which makes it best for shell formation:

- Gel strength: 150–200 Bloom

- Viscosity (60°C/6–23% w/w in water): 2.8–4.5 mPa
- Well-controlled degree of viscosity breakdown
- Well-defined particle size to allow fast dissolution and deaeration of the molten mass, even at high gelatin concentrations.
- A broad molecular weight distribution to provide a fast setting and the fusion temperature being well below the melting temperature of the plasticized wet film.

## Plasticizers

- Glycerol (85% and 98% w/w)
- Sorbitol
- Sorbitan solutions
- Propylene glycol
- Low molecular weight polyethylene glycol (PEG 200)

Strength of the shell depends on the ratio by weight of dry plasticizer to dry gelatin (P/G)

Drug : Plasticizer:: 1: 0.4 -------For hard gelatin capsule

Drug : Plasticizer:: 1: 0.8 -------For soft gelatin capsule

## Directly Interacting Plasticizer causes

- Higher degree of reduction in glass transition temperature of gelatin during preparation
- Maintaining crystal formation within the sol-gel network
- Most effective and stable
- Slight increase in hygroscopicity

Eg.: Glycerol

## Indirectly Interacting Plasticizer causes

- Small reduction in glass transition temperature of gelatin during preparation
- Causes moisturizing effect.
- Doesn't maintain crystal formation within the sol-gel network.
- Less effective and unstable

- Mostly used in combination

  Eg.: Sorbitol &sorbitan combination

**Factors to be considered for fill materials:**

- Temperature should be in the range of 37 to 40°C.
- Viscosity.
- Surface activity.
- Particle size of the suspended drug (in case of suspension), it should have less than 200 μm

**Formulation consideration**

Possible interactions

- Chemical reactions of fill components with the gelatin and the plasticizer.
- Physical interactions, i.e., migration of fill components in or through the shell and vice versa.
- To be noted that water content of the fill should not exceed a critical value of about 5%.
- For minimizing the hydrolysis/oxidation of formulation we use gelatin with high-Bloom, low-viscosity, for faster drying.
- Replacement of single plasticizer by blends of two or more; to minimize diffusion of API into the shell.
- Coating of drug particles to inhibit the browning reaction.
- Post treatments and coating enhances the stability of the formulation. It includes aldehyde treatment but it's difficult because low surface roughness intrinsic insolubility of the shell components in organic solvents resulting to non-adherence of coating material to shell.

## Gelatin Preparation

The process of blending and heating granulated gelatin and other ingredients in warm water in a gelatin melting tank. Color may be added during the melting process or in a separate machine (Figure 25.22).

### Fill Material Preparation

Preparation equipment may include processing tanks, mixers, vacuum homogenizers, sieves and mills.

## Encapsulation

Converting the gel mass into a thin layer of gelatin and wrapping it around the fill material to form a softgel.

## Drying

Removes excess moisture from the gelatin shell to shrink and firm up the softgel, either by tumbling or by a combination of tumbling and tray drying.

## Cleaning, Inspection and Sorting

Often required prior to packaging based upon the intended use of the softgel.

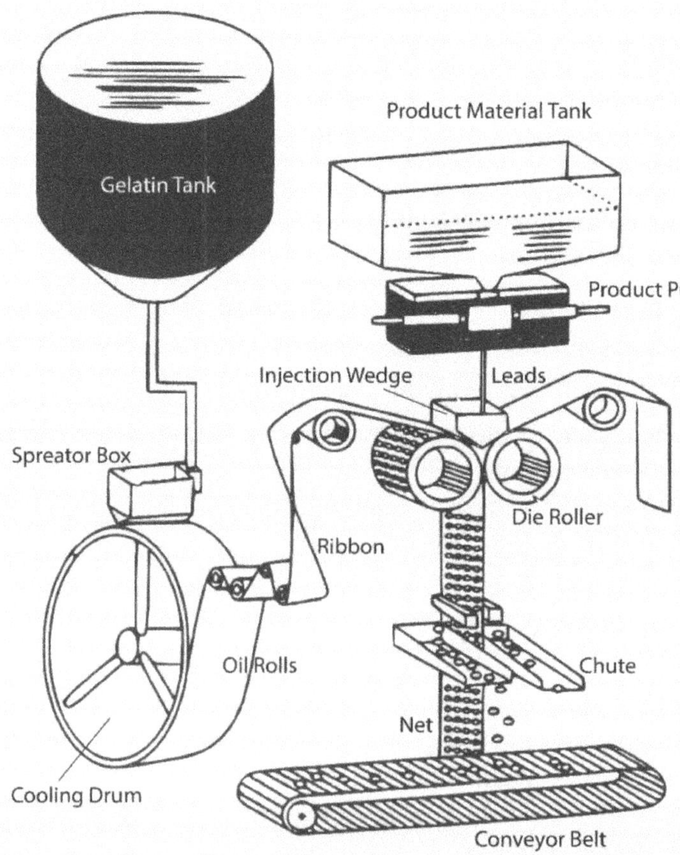


**Figure 25.2** Softgel filling equipment

## Equipment

Product Pump for feeding the shell material:

- Separate or attached.

  Injection time adjustment for time regulated feeding
- Electronic or manual

  Injection wedge for shape creation
- Manual or pneumatic

  Rollers for filling material
- Electronic or pneumatic pressure based.

  Ribbon system for film formation
- Electronic or pneumatic

  Oil quantity adjustment for core material feeding.
- Electronic or manual

  Collection assembly for separating soft gels
- Chute or divider

  Speed
- Fixed or variable.

  Conveyer
- Unidirectional or bidirectional

**In-process tests** are done to minimise the risk of product failure by checking it within the process for related parameters.

- The gel ribbon thickness for assessment of pharmacokinetic profiling of formulation.
- Soft gel seal thickness at the time of encapsulation for any leakage of the filling material from the formulation.
- Fill matrix weight & capsule shell weight for uniformity of dose and dosage form.
- Soft gel shell moisture level and soft gel hardness at the end of the drying stage for assessment of stability.

### Finished Product Tests

- Capsule appearance for elegance and better patient compliance.
- Active ingredient assay & related substances assay for uniformity of dosing and dosage form.

- Fill weight
- Content uniformity
- Microbiological testing for safety purpose.

**Limitations**

- Liquids that can easily migrate through the gelatin shell, such as water (more than 5 percent of the fill), and hygroscopic and volatile compounds.
- Aldehydes, which have the ability to harden the shell and hence affect its dissolution property.
- Acidic or alkaline solutions should be avoided, unless they are pictures on a blackboard. adjusted to become neutral; acids and alkalis can cause hydrolysis and leakage of the gelatin shell.
- Water-soluble solid compounds that may affect the gelatin shell unless they are minor constituents of a formula or combined with a carrier that reduces their effect on the shell.

## Summary

In this lecture, we learnt about soft gelatin capsules as dosage form and their importance. We also discussed about the method of filling of soft gelatin. The advancement of soft gelatin capsule filling technology was also discussed in this module. And lastly, we had gone through formulation consideration of soft gelatin capsules.

## Further Readings

- "Industrial Pharmacy-I" SWAYAM MOOC: www.swayam.gov.in
- Pharmaceutical Capsules. Edited by Fridrun Podczeck, Brian E. Jones. Pharmaceutical Press. ISBN: 9780853695684
- Pharmaceutical Dosage Forms: Capsules. Edited by Larry L. Augsburger, Stephen W. Hoag. CRC Press. ISBN: 9781351620390
- Banker GS, Rhodes CT, Modern Pharmaceutics, CRC Press.
- Augsburger, L. L., & Hoag, S. W. (2017). Pharmaceutical Dosage Forms: Capsules. CRC Press.
- Qiu, Y., Chen, Y., Zhang, G. G. Z., Liu, L., & Porter, W. (2009). Developing Solid Oral Dosage Forms: Pharmaceutical Theory and Practice. Academic Press.

## References


- Semalty et al., Essentials of Pharmaceutical Technology, II Edn, 2019 (Reprint), Pharma Med press, Hyderabad, India
- Swarbrick, J. (2013) Encyclopedia of pharmaceutical technology. CRC Press.
- Indian Pharmacopoeia 2018. (2018). Indian Pharmacopoeia Commission.
- Tovey, G. D. (2018). Pharmaceutical Formulation: The Science and Technology of Dosage Forms. Royal Society of Chemistry.
- Aulton ME (ED), Pharmaceutics: The science of Dosage form design, II edn, Churchill Livingstone, London, 2002.

# CHAPTER 26

# Capsule IV

**Dr Lokesh Adhikari, Dr Ajay Semalty**
Department of Pharmaceutical Sciences,
H.N.B Garhwal University (A Central University), Srinagar Garhwal-246174

## Learning Outcome

In this lecture, we would like to find some answers for the questions regarding the evaluation tests for capsules such as:

- What are general acceptance criteria for capsules?
- How do we evaluate the raw material being used?
- How we ensure that the process we opted will give us the best possible formulation?

What are the necessary criteria to be met by finished product before going to the consumer?

## Lesson Plan

- General acceptance criteria for capsules
- Evaluation of raw material
- Evaluation of in process material
- Evaluation of finished product

Capsules are two main types. They are classified according to the nature and flexibility of the capsule shell. Hard gelatin capsules contain powder or beads as filling material with equilibrium moisture content is between 13% and 16% and no plasticizer.

Soft gelatin capsules: containing liquid or semisolid as filling material with equilibrium moisture content is between 6% and 10% and 20% and 30% w/w of plasticizers.

Now the question arises:

How we ensure the quality?

Do we have any criteria to judge?
If yes, for which part of operation it is suitable for?

For raw material?

For in process material?

For finished product?

What are the limits?

Are these evaluation parameters, official?

## Evaluation

We can categorize the evaluation tests in three categories:

- For raw material
- For in process material
- For finished products

## Evaluation for Raw Material

In this category, shell forming agent is prime focus of evaluation. Though, APIs are also tested for general tests of purity as per the monographs.
API testing involves:

- FTIR,
- Assay,
- Limit test
- Or any other, if stated in monograph.

In case of shell forming agents, evaluation parameter includes:

- Bloom strength (in case of gelatin),
- Viscosity (in solution form),
- Antimicrobial test etc.

Official tests for shell forming agents include:

- Identification,
- Microbial contamination,
- Loss on drying,
- Isoelectric point,
- Conductivity etc.

## Evaluation for Raw Material

All the tests should be done according to the procedure given in pharmacopoeias and the results should be under permissible limits of monograph in pharmacopoeias.

There are two mostly used shell forming agents:

- Gelatin
- Hypermellose

## Evaluation for Raw Material: Gelatin

**Bloom strength:** Bloom Gelometer is used which is named after inventor Oscar T. Bloom. It is used in a controlled process to measure the rigidity of a gelatin film. A higher number indicates a stiffer product. Gelatin used in food usually runs from 125 Bloom to 250 Bloom.

**Gelling strength:** Rheometer is used for the test and it should be in range of 200-300 (for hard gelatin capsule) and 125-200 (for soft gelatin capsule).

**Viscosity:** Viscometer is used, and the results should be in range of 45-60 (for hard gelatin capsule) and 25-45 (for soft gelatin capsule).

**pH:** Gives the direction about chemical interaction of shell & excipient. The pH should be in range of 4.5-6.5 (for both, hard gelatin capsule and soft gelatin capsule).

**Antimicrobial test:** The results should be negative for *E. coli* and *Salmonella* (for both, hard gelatin capsule and soft gelatin capsule). Yeasts & Molds presence in the results should be <1000 cfu/g.

## Evaluation for Raw Material: Hypromellose

**pH (2% w/w solution):** This should be in range of 5.8-8.0 (for both, hard gelatin capsule and soft gelatin capsule).

**Viscosity:** Should be in range of 80–120 (for both).

**Loss on drying:** Should not be more than 5% at 105°C, for both.

## Evaluation for in Process Material

### Moisture Content

- Weigh the substance about 1 to 2 g.
- Reduce the particle size to about 2 mm.
- Put the test specimen in the glass stoppered bottle.
- Accurately weigh the bottle and the contents.
- Place the loaded bottle in the drying chamber, removing the stopper.
- Dry the test specimen at the temperature and for the time specified in the monograph.

### Gel ribbon thickness

- Measured using caliper gauge.
- Should be in the range of 0.022 inches to 0.045 inches, when wet.
- Deviation from the limit should not be >±10% of stated, if any.

### Gel seal thickness

- Should be in the same range as the ribbon thickness.
- Also measured using caliper gauge
- This range is based on the requirement that 20 capsules, or such other number as may be indicated in the monograph, are used in the Assay.
- Where 20 capsules cannot be obtained, a smaller number, which must not be less than 5, may be used.
- To allow for sampling errors the tolerances are widened.
- The requirements stated in pharmacopoeias apply when the stated limits are between 90 and 110 per cent.
- For limits other than 90 to 110 per cent, proportionately smaller or larger allowances should be made.

## Uniformity of Weight

- Weigh an intact capsule.
- Open the capsule without losing any part of the shell.
- Remove the contents as completely as possible.
- Weigh the shell. The weight of the contents is the difference between the weighing.
- Repeat the procedure with a further 19 capsules. (For number of samples refer Table 26.1). Determine the average weight.

**Table 26.1** Content of active ingredient in each capsule.

| Weigh of Active ingredients in each capsule | Subtract from the lower limit for samples of | | | Add to the upper limit for samples | | |
|---|---|---|---|---|---|---|
| | 15 | 10 | 5 | 15 | 10 | 5 |
| **0.12 g or less** | 0.2 | 0.7 | 1.5 | 0.3 | 0.8 | 1.8 |
| **More than 0.12 g and less than 0.3 g** | 0.2 | 0.5 | 1.2 | 0.3 | 0.6 | 1.5 |
| **0.3 g or more** | 0.1 | 0.2 | 0.8 | 0.2 | 0.4 | 1.0 |

- Not more than two of the individual weights deviate from the average weight by more than the percentage deviation given in monograph and none deviates by more than twice that percentage ().

**Table 26.2** Weight variation limit for capsules.

| Average weight of capsule contents | Percent deviation limit |
|---|---|
| Less than 300 mg | 10 |
| 300 mg or more | 7.5 |

## Uniformity of Dosage Units

- Capsules comply with the test for uniformity of dosage units or, where justified and authorized, with the tests for uniformity of content and/or uniformity of mass shown below.
- Herbal drugs and herbal drug preparations present in the dosage form are not subject to the provisions of this test.

## Disintegration Testing for Hard Capsules

- Comply with the general disintegration test.
- Unless otherwise directed in the individual monograph use water as the medium.
- If the capsules float on the surface of the medium, a disc may be added.
- If the capsules adhere to the discs, attach a removable piece of stainless-steel woven gauze with mesh aperture of 2.00 mm to the upper plate of the basket rack assembly and carry out the test omitting the discs.
- Operate the apparatus for 30 minutes unless otherwise directed.

## Disintegration Testing for Soft Capsules

- Comply with the general disintegration test.
- Unless otherwise directed in the individual monograph use water as the medium and add a disc to each tube.
- Operate the apparatus for 60 minutes unless otherwise directed.

## Dissolution Testing

- Comply with the general dissolution test using the basket type apparatus (Figure 26.1).

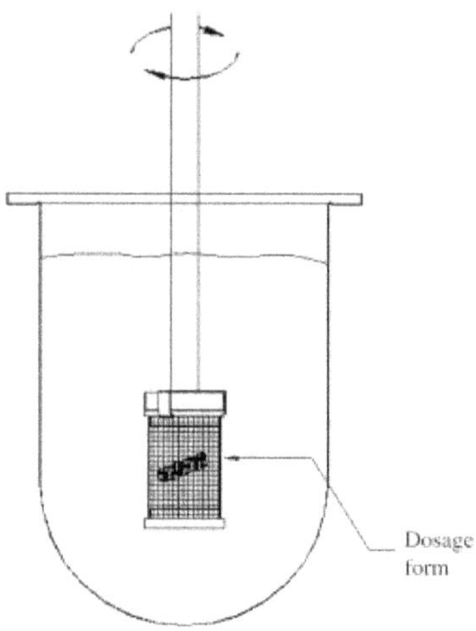


**Figure 26.1** Dissolution test apparatus for capsule dosage forms.

- Place the stated volume of the Dissolution Medium (±1%) in the vessel of the specified apparatus given in the individual monograph.
- Assemble the apparatus, equilibrate the Dissolution Medium to 37 ± 0.5, and remove the thermometer.
- Place 1 dosage unit in the apparatus, taking care to exclude air bubbles from the surface of the dosage unit.
- Immediately operate the apparatus at the specified rate given in the individual monograph.
- Within the time interval specified, or at each of the times stated, withdraw a specimen from a zone midway between the surface of the Dissolution Medium and the top of the rotating basket or blade, not less than 1 cm from the vessel wall.
- Where multiple sampling times are specified, replace the aliquots withdrawn for analysis with equal volumes of fresh Dissolution Medium at 37°C.
- Where it can be shown that replacement of the medium is not necessary, correct for the volume change in the calculation.
- Unless otherwise specified in the individual monograph, the requirements are met if the quantities of active ingredient dissolved from the dosage units tested conform to pharmacopeial standards (**Table 26.3**).

**Table 26.3** USP Dissolution test for capsules: acceptance criteria.

| Stage | Number Tested | Acceptance criteria |
|---|---|---|
| S1 | 6 | Each unit is not less than Q+5% |
| S2 | 6 | Average of 12 units (S1+S2) is equal to or greater than Q, and no unit is less than Q-15%. |
| S3 | 12 | Average of 24 units (S1+S2+S3) is equal to or greater than Q, not more than 2 units are less Q-15%, and no unit is less than Q-25%. |

## Evaluation for in Finished Material

### Disintegration Testing

- The disintegration test is not applicable to Modified-release Capsules.
- For those Hard Capsules and Soft Capsules for which the general dissolution test is included in the individual monograph, the test for Disintegration is not required.

## Physicochemical Testing

- Done for color, opacity, shape.
- By visual observation
- Change in color or opacity or shape leads to the discard of the formulation.
- Sensor based inspection systems are also available.
- These systems are attached with the conveyer belts and checks the individual formulation.

## Packaging

- Similar to tablet, capsules are packaged in blister packing as well as alu-alu packing.
- Blister packaging is preferred for soft gelatin capsules.

## Storage

- Should be stored in a cool and dark place.

## Labelling

- Label should necessarily state about the concentration of preservatives, if there any.

## Capsules: Recap

In this Chapter, we learnt about the evaluation parameters of capsules dosage form. We also discussed about the raw material testing. The testing of in process material was also discussed in this module. And lastly, we had gone through the evaluation methods for finished products.

## Further Readings

- "Industrial Pharmacy-I" SWAYAM MOOC: www.swayam.gov.in
- Pharmaceutical Capsules. Edited by Fridrun Podczeck, Brian E. Jones. Pharmaceutical Press. ISBN: 9780853695684
- Pharmaceutical Dosage Forms: Capsules. Edited by Larry L. Augsburger, Stephen W. Hoag. CRC Press. ISBN: 9781351620390
- Banker GS, Rhodes CT, Modern Pharmaceutics, CRC Press.

- Augsburger, L. L., & Hoag, S. W. (2017). Pharmaceutical Dosage Forms: Capsules. CRC Press.
- Qiu, Y., Chen, Y., Zhang, G. G. Z., Liu, L., & Porter, W. (2009). Developing Solid Oral Dosage Forms: Pharmaceutical Theory and Practice. Academic Press.


## References


- Semalty et al., Essentials of Pharmaceutical Technology, II Edn, 2019 (Reprint), Pharma Med press, Hyderabad, India
- Swarbrick, J. (2013) Encyclopedia of pharmaceutical technology. CRC Press.
- Indian Pharmacopoeia 2018. Indian Pharmacopoeia Commission.
- Tovey, G. D. (2018). Pharmaceutical Formulation: The Science and Technology of Dosage Forms. Royal Society of Chemistry.
- Aulton ME (ED), Pharmaceutics: The science of Dosage form design, II edn, Churchill Livingstone, London, 2002.

# CHAPTER 27

# Pellets and Pelletization

**Dr Lokesh Adhikari, Dr Ajay Semalty, Dr Mona Semalty**
Department of Pharmaceutical Sciences,
H.N.B Garhwal University (A Central University), Srinagar Garhwal-246174

### Learning Outcome

After learning this chapter, you will be able to develop your understanding about:

- Pellet
- Pelletization technique
- Various methods of pelletization

### Lesson Plan

- Introduction to pellet
- Methods of pelletization
- Equipment

Pellet has been described as a variety of agglomerates which are produced from diverse raw materials by using different pieces of manufacturing equipment.

Pellets are small, free-flowing, spherical particulates manufactured by the agglomeration of fine powders or granules of drug substances and excipients.

Pellets are described as small rods with aspect ratios of close to unity with a high degree of flexibility in the design and development of oral dosage forms. In the case of pellets, we can achieve desired dose strengths without formulation or process changes and easy to deliver incompatible bioactive agents simultaneously.

With minor modifications in the formulations, pellets can have different release profiles at the same or different sites in the gastrointestinal (GI) tract.

Generally, pellets are taken by the oral route which gets disperse freely in the GI tract with maximise drug absorption and minimise local irritation of the mucosa by certain irritant drugs reducing inter- and intra-patient variability.

**Pelletization:** Several techniques have been developed for pelletization. We are going to discuss them one by one-

The process of blending and heating granulated gelatin and other ingredients in warm water in a gelatin melting tank. Color may be added during the melting process or in a separate machine (Chapter 25).

## Powder Layering

This technique involves the deposition of successive layers of dry powder of drug or excipients or both on preformed nuclei or cores with the help of a binding liquid. The deposition occurs as the binding liquid gets dried, and a solid bridge is formed between the core and covering material.

The simultaneous application of the binding liquid and dry powder is not possible with conventional equipment, so powder layering involves, specialized equipment. The product container is made up of solid SS walls with no perforations.

The first equipment used for pelletization with the powder layering technique is a conventional coating pan with either an elliptical or cylindrical shape. In comparison with cylindrical pans, the elliptical pans tend to have fewer motionless spots. The reason behind this is the decrease in the tilt angle causes a decrease in the formation of dead spots.

With decreasing rotation speed, the segregation of particles increases so the speed should be optimum. Particles get agglomerated if they get in contact with each other for a longer duration of time.

In the initial stage of powder layering, the starter seed or nuclei are introduced in the equipment. After that, the simultaneous addition of a binding solution and a finely milled powder takes place at a controlled rate.

At first, the drug particles are bound to the starter seeds. Liquid bridges originated from the sprayed liquid helps the bounded drug particles to form pellets. These bridges can be formed either from a binder in the application medium or from any eutectic or low melting point material.

The successive layering of the drug and binder solution continues until the desired pellet size is achieved. The equilibrium between the binder liquid application rate and the powder delivery rate is maintained by controlling the delivery rate of the powder.

## Optimizable Properties

The rheological properties of the binding liquid, the liquid application rate, and drying air temperature should be optimized. The powder should be delivered at a rate that maintains a balance. between the surface wetness of the cores and powder adhesion. If the product bed temperature is high, the powder is lost to the exhaust system. If it is too low, it leads to agglomeration and the formation of new nuclei that serve as cores for further layering.

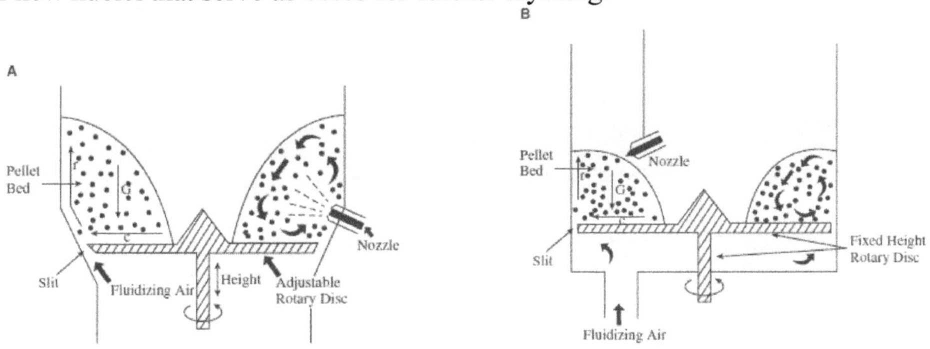


**Figure 27.1 & 27.2** Centrifugal fluid-bed equipment.

## Wurster Coating Process

This process was invented about 30 years ago. The cylindrical partition located in the product chamber and the configuration of the air distributor plate, also known as the orifice plate.

The air distribution plate allows most of the fluidization or drying air carrying the layered particles to pass at high velocity around the nozzle towards the partition (Figure 27.1 & 27.2).Once the particles exit the partition, they enter the expansion chamber. Here the velocity of the air is reduced below the entrainment velocity (Figure 27.3 & 27.4).

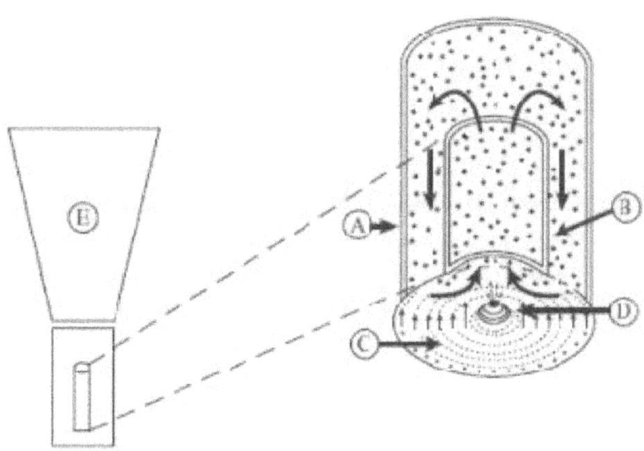


**Figure 27.3** Wurster Product Chamber and Process; A: product chamber, B: partition; C: Orifice plate; D: Nozzle; E: Expansion chamber.

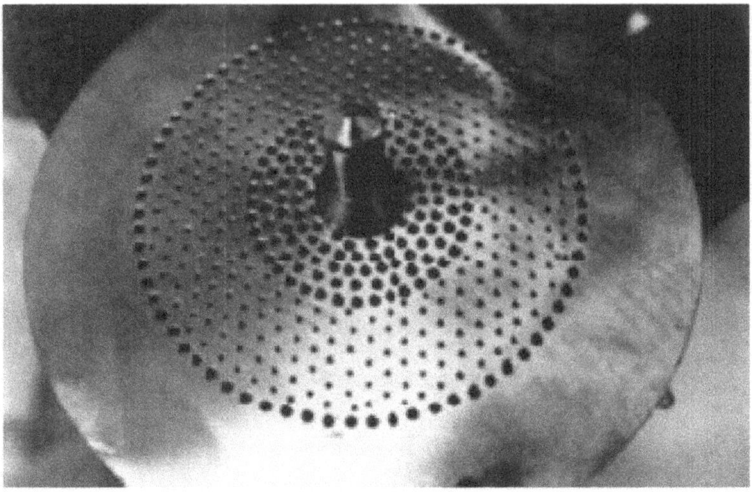

**Figure 27.4** Air distributor or orifice plate of a Wurster coater.

The particles fall back to the area surrounding the partition (referred to as the down bed). The down bed is kept aerated by the small fraction of air that passes through the small holes on the periphery of the orifice plate at a given load size and fluidization air volume. The partition height can be reduced or increased to provide either a well-controlled particle motion. It produces the desired pellet movement or a bubbling down bed which leads to disorganized particle movement and inefficient process.

The disadvantage of the Wurster process is the inaccessibility of the nozzles. If the nozzles are clogged at any time during the layering process. In such conditions, the operation has to be interrupted, and the spray guns must be removed for cleaning. Multiple nozzles are used the potential overlap of adjacent spray zones.

## Solution/Suspension Layering

This process is generally used when the desired drug loading of the pellets is low because the production of high-potency pellets from a low solids content formulation is not economically feasible.

## Extrusion–spheronization

The technology is unique in that it is not only suitable for the manufacture of pellets with a high drug loading. It also can be used to produce extended-release pellets in certain situations in a single step. It can obviate the need for subsequent film coating. A variety of extruders are currently on the market which differs in design features and operational principles (**Table 27.1**). These extruders can be classified as

- Screw-fed extruders
- Gravity-fed extruders
- Ram extruders

**Table 27.1** Important factors in extrusion-spheronization pallet manufacturing.

| | Characteristic | Significance |
|---|---|---|
| **Drug substance** | Particle size | High |
| | Particle size distribution | Medium |
| | Particle shape | High |
| | Solubility | Medium |
| **Formulation** | Water content | High |
| | Water temperature | Low |
| | Excipient type | High |
| | Excipient concentration | Medium |
| | Excipient particle size | Medium |
| **Extrusion** | Extruder type | Medium |
| | Extruder speed | Medium |
| | Extrusion screen size | High |
| | Thickness of the die plate | Low |
| **Spheronization** | Spheronizer speed (rpm) | High |
| | Spheronizer load | Low |
| | Spheronization time | High |
| | Friction plate design | Low |

## Screw-fed Extruders

These equipment have screws that rotate along the horizontal axis, transporting the material horizontally (Figure 27.5). In this equipment, product temperature is controlled during extrusion by jacketed barrels.

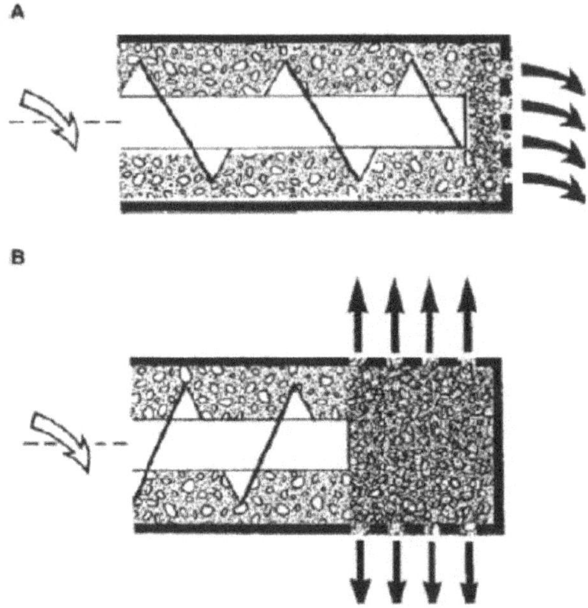


**Figure 27.5** Screw Fed Extruder A: axial; B: radial extruder.

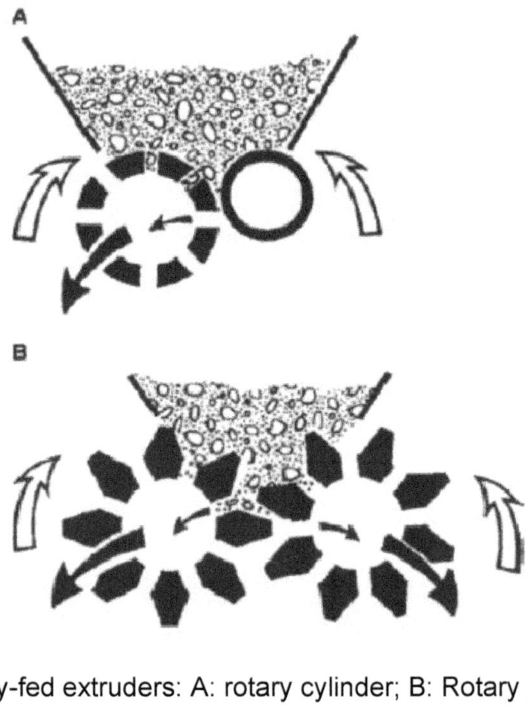


**Figure 27.6** Gravity-fed extruders: A: rotary cylinder; B: Rotary gear extruders.

## Gravity-fed Extruders

It includes the rotary cylinder and rotary gear extruders (Figure 27.6). The rotary-cylinder extruder has two rotating cylinders- one hollow and perforated cylinders and another solid cylinder. These cylinders rotate in the opposite direction to each other, and the solid cylinder works as a pressure roller. Another equipment with two hollow counter-rotating gear cylinders with counterbored holes is known as a rotary-gear extruder.

## Ram Extruders

In this equipment, a piston displaces and forces the material through a die at the end. It is preferred during formulation development because itis designed to allow for the measurement of the rheological properties of formulations.

Formulation components such as fillers, lubricants, and pH modifiers play a critical. The granulated mass must be plastic and sufficiently cohesive and self-lubricating. During the spheronization step, the extrudates must break at the appropriate length and have sufficient surface moisture.

## Spherical Agglomeration

It is a process in which powders on the addition of an appropriate quantity of liquid gets treated to high temperatures and converted to spherical particles by a continuous rolling or tumbling action (Figure 27.7).

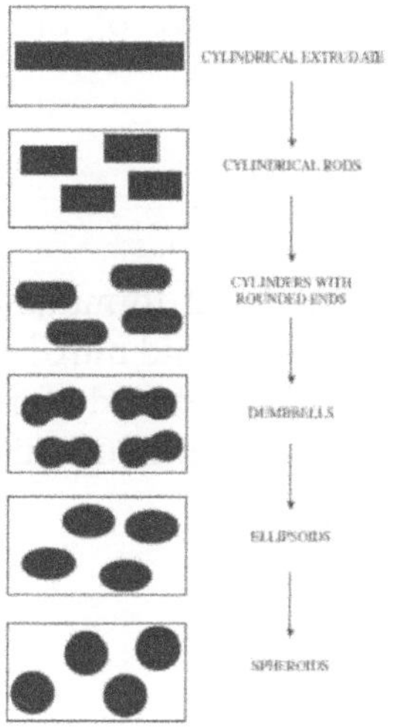


**Figure 27.7** Shape transition during spheronization process.

There are two types of the mechanism involved in spherical agglomeration—

- Liquid-induced
- Melt-induced agglomerations

## Liquid-induced Agglomeration

Agglomerates or nuclei formation occurs with the help of liquid. The powders form after coming in contact with a liquid phase. The particles initially bound together by liquid bridges. A phase transformation of the bridges from liquid to solid occurs due to the collision of the nuclei forming larger nuclei or pellets. The coalescence process continues for some time Coalescence is replaced by layering increasing the size of the latter until pelletization is completed. Some particles may undergo nucleation due to the change in surface moisture and coalescence at different rates.

Forming different sizes of nuclei admixed with the larger pellets. As a result, spherical agglomeration tends to produce pellets with a wide particle size distribution.

## Spray Drying and Spray Congealing

It is also known as globulation processes and widely used for tablet coating purposes. It is an automated process that uses hot melts, solutions, or suspensions to generate spherical particles or pellets. The maximum rate of evaporation or to congeal is achieved by reducing the droplet size in both processes. Consequently, the particle size of the pellets produced is usually very small.

## Cryopelletization

A process whereby droplets of a liquid formulation are converted into solid spherical particles or pellets by using liquid nitrogen as the fixing medium. The technology, which was initially developed for lyophilization of viscous bacterial suspensions can be used to produce drug-loaded pellets in liquid nitrogen at 160°C.

## Melt Spheronization

It is a process whereby a drug substance and excipients it into a molten or semi-molten state. Subsequently shaped using appropriate equipment to provide solid spheres or pellets. The process requires several pieces of equipment such as blenders, extruders, cutters (known as pelletizers in the plastics industry), and spheronizers.

## Summary

In this chapter, we learned about pellets as a dosage form and their importance.

We also discussed various methods of preparation of pellets.

The advancement of pelletization techniques has been discussed in the chapter. Refer newer advancement of pelletization techniques.

## Further Readings

- "Industrial Pharmacy-I" SWAYAM MOOC: www.swayam.gov.in

## References


- Indian Pharmacopoeia 2018. (2018). Indian Pharmacopoeia Commission.
- Banker, G. S., Siepmann, J., & Rhodes, C. (2002). Modern Pharmaceutics. CRC Press.
- Organization, W. H. (2006). The International Pharmacopoeia. World Health Organization.
- Ghebre-Selassie, I. (1989). Pharmaceutical Pelletization Technology. Taylor & Francis.

CHAPTER 28

# Ophthalmic Preparations: Introduction, Absorption through Eye, Formulation Considerations

**Dr Lokesh Adhikari, Dr Ajay Semalty**
Department of Pharmaceutical Sciences,
H.N.B Garhwal University (A Central University), Srinagar Garhwal-246174.

### Learning Outcome

After learning this chapter, you will be able to develop your understanding of:

- Ocular route
- Drug absorption
- General properties of ophthalmic products

### Lesson Plan

- Introduction to ophthalmic dosage forms
- Ocular route and absorption
- General properties of ophthalmic products

## Definition

Three ways can be used for the instillation of the specialized dosage forms into the eyes: 1. topical (onto the external surface of the eye), 2. intraocular (administered inside) and 3. periocular (adjacent to the eye). Sometimes, these formulations are also used in conjunction with an ophthalmic device. These are known as ophthalmic dosage forms.

Ophthalmic dosage forms can be of the semisolid or liquid type, including solutions, suspensions, and ointments. Gel, gel-forming solution, ocular insert, intravitreal injections, and implants are few newly developed forms of ophthalmic drug delivery.

**Examples:**

- Miotics, e.g. pilocarpine HCl

- Mydriatics, e.g., Atropine
- Cycloplegics, e.g., atropine
- Anti-inflammatories, e.g., corticosteroids
- Anti-infectives (antibiotics, antivirals and antibacterials)
- Anti-glaucoma drugs, e.g., pilocarpine HCl
- Adjuncts, e.g., Irrigating solutions
- Diagnostic drugs, e.g., sodium fluorescein
- Anesthetics, e.g., Tetracaine

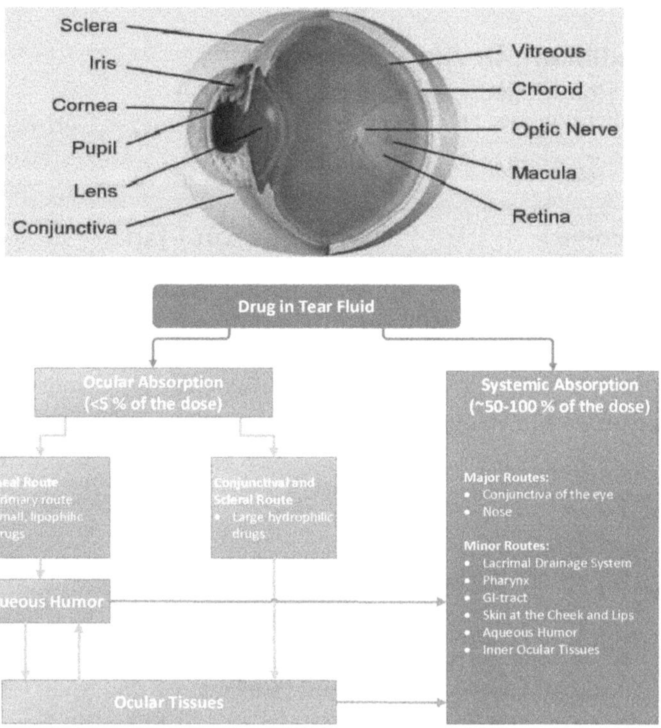


**Figure 28.1** Absorption through eye.

## Anatomy & Physiology of the eye

- In the human eye, the protective outer layer is known as the **sclera,** also called "white of the eye" which helps in maintaining the **shape of the eye** (Figure 28.1 & Figure 28.2).
- The front transparent portion of the sclera is called the **cornea**. It passes the light into the eye. The cornea provides the focusing power of the eye with its sturdy **refracting surface**.

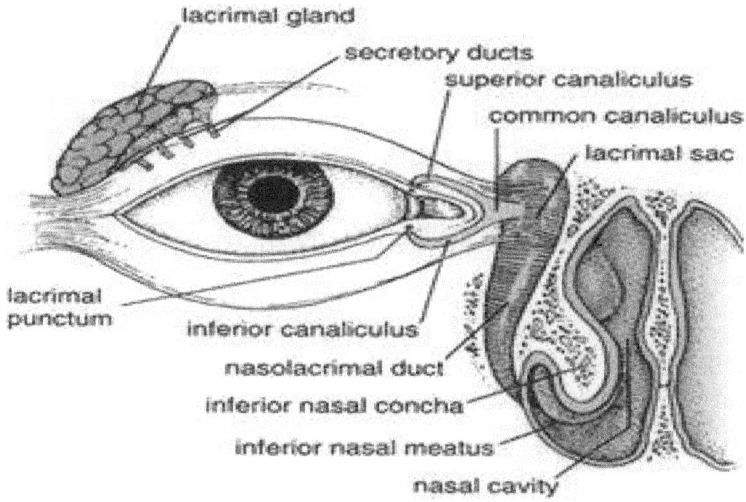


**Figure 28.2** Anatomy of human eye.

Another layer between the sclera and the retina is present, which is named as **the choroids**. Retina gets nourishment from the choroids, which contain the blood vessels.

- The colourful portion of the eye, the **iris,** is made up of muscular tissues. Iris has a property to respond to the surrounding light subsequent opening of the pupil, which is present in the center of the iris. The pupil changes its shape with the change in the brightness of the light.
- A transparent, biconvex **lens** is encased in a thin transparent covering which refracts the incoming light. It also helps in focusing the light onto the retina.
- The innermost layer in the eye is called the **retina,** which converts images into electrical impulses. These impulses are sent along the optic nerve to the brain. The brain interprets these impulses into an image.
- In the center of the retina, the **macula** is located, which produces the sharpest vision. The lens divides the eyeball from inside into two fluid-filled sections.
- At the back of the eye, a larger section is filled with **vitreous humor,** which is a colourless gelatinous mass called the.
- A transparent, water-like material called **aqueous humor** is filled in the front of the eye.
- The mucous membrane, **conjunctiva,** begins at the edge of the cornea and lines the inside surface of the eyelids and sclera, which serves to lubricate the eye.

## Factors Affecting Drug Availability

- Gravity, lachrymation, blinking, and tear turnover are some common factors which result in rapid solution drainage from the eye (Figure 28.3). The normal volume of tears = 7 μl, the blinking eye can accommodate a volume of up to 30 μl without spillage, the drop volume = 50 μl.

  Low corneal permeability (act as lipid barrier)

  Transport of hydrophilic and macromolecular drugs occurs through scleral route.

  Lipophilic agents of low molecular weight follow trans corneal transport by passive diffusion and obey.

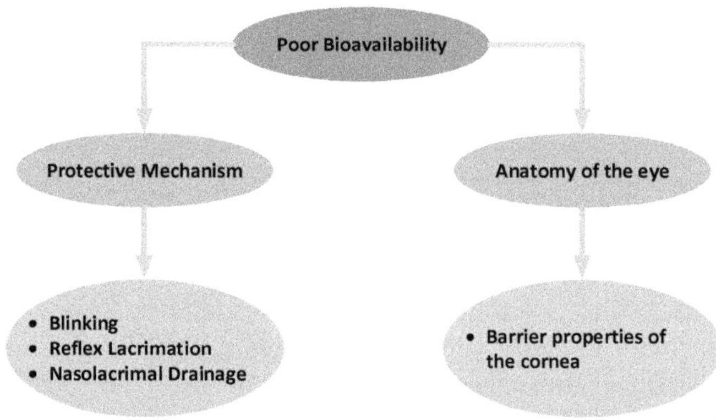


**Figure 28.3** Factors affecting bioavailability of ophthalmic products.

## Fick's First Law of Diffusion

$$J = -D \times \frac{dC_m}{dx}$$

J = The flux rate across the membrane

D = diffusion coefficient which increases with the decrease of molecular size of the drug

$C_m$ = concentration gradient, as the drug solubility increases, the gradient also increases resulting an increase in the driving force for drug entry into the aqueous humour.

As the drug solubility increases, the gradient increases, the driving force for drug entry into the aqueous humour increases.

Drug delivery in ocular therapeutics is a challenge. Why?

A. **Sterility:** Ideally, sterilization of all ophthalmic products is done in the final packaging.

The formulation in simple aqueous vehicles of few ophthalmic drugs are stable to normal autoclaving temperatures and times (121°C for 20-30 min) **Figure 28.4**. Glass or other heat-deformation-resistant packaging is used to pack such heat-resistant drugs so these can be sterilized in this manner.

**Figure 28.4** Autoclave apparatus.

Sterilization by heat cannot be used for most ophthalmic products (Figure 28.5). The reason behind this is the instability of active principle or polymers used to increase viscosity at high temperature. Aseptic manufacturing, followed by aseptic filling-and-capping techniques in aseptic environments is the most suitable technique for the majority of ophthalmic products.

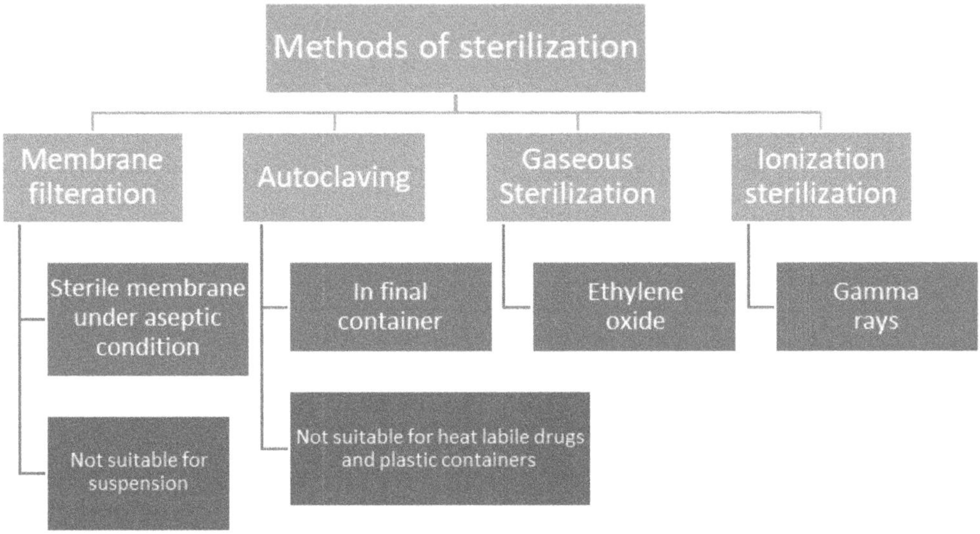


**Figure 28.5** Methods of sterilization.

**Ocular toxicity and irritation:** the ocular toxicity and irritation of ophthalmic formulations is tested in albino rabbits. The observation of changes in the conjunctiva, the cornea or the iris is the basis of this testing.
For example, the USP test of plastic containers:

- Containers are cleaned and sterilized as in the final packaged product.
- It is extracted by submersion in saline and cottonseed oil.
- The rabbit eye test is performed for topical ocular instillation of the extracts and samples.

## Preservation and Preservatives

A multiple-dose eye solution requires product sterility and stability maintained during its use. This specific purpose is solved by using preservatives in the formulation (**Table 28.1**). However, preservatives not needed in case of the unit-dose package. For the products with surgical applications, the use of preservatives is prohibited as the cells of the corneal endothelium can become damaged when gets contacted with a high concentration of the preservative. It may result in clouding of the cornea and possible loss of vision. So, the sterility of the product should be maintained during the production, packaging to the application and sterile, unit-of-use containers are used to achieve the desired sterility.

**Examples:**

**Table 28.1** Types of excipients of ophthalmic dosage forms.

| Category | Example | Properties |
|---|---|---|
| Cationic wetting agents | Benzalkonium chloride | • 0.01-0.1% |
| | Disodium edetate (EDTA) | • Ability to render the resistant strains of PS aeruginosa.<br>• More sensitive to benzalkonium chloride |
| Organic mercurial | Phenylmercuric nitrate | • 0.002-0.004% |
| | Phenylmercuric acetate | • 0.005-0.02%. |
| Esters of p-hydroxybenzoic acid | Methyl and propyl hydroxybenzoate | • 2 :1, 0.1% mixture |
| Alcohol Substitutes | Chlorobutanol | • 0.5%<br>• pH 5-6. |
| | Phenyl ethanol | • 0.5% |

## Foreign Particles

Similar to the parenteral products, foreign particles, fibers and filaments should not be present or within the limit in all the ophthalmic products. Bacteria proof filters (membrane filters, sintered glass filters) are applied to attain the desired clarity. in ophthalmic products. The particle size of the eye suspension should be in an ultrafine state of subdivision to minimize irritation. To avoid the contamination within the products during the filtration, for every ophthalmic product, a separate filter should be used.

## Viscosity

Optimum viscosity is an essential character for any ophthalmic formulation which prolongs the contact time of the drug in the eye. To achieve the desired viscosity, we add one or more thickening agent in the ophthalmic preparations.

Some of the commonly used viscosity enhancers are polyvinyl alcohol (1-4%), polyethylene glycol, methylcellulose, carboxymethylcellulose.

Desired properties an ideal thickening agent:

1. Easy to filter.
2. Easy to sterilize.
3. Compatible with other ingredients.
4. Must have requisite refractive index and clarity level.

Due to some possible adverse effects, in the formulation of eye drops and eye lotions which are required to be used during or after surgery on the interior of the eye, thickening agents are not included.

### Tonicity

Isotonicity with lachrymal secretions is very much desirable in all the ophthalmic products to avoid discomfort and irritation. On average, an eye can only tolerate a range of tonicity equivalent to 0.5-2% solution of NaCl. To adjust tonicity, we prepare ophthalmic products with certain isotonic vehicles such as 1.9% boric acid, sodium acid phosphate buffer.

### pH

The pH of the product has a vital role in the therapeutic activity, solubility, stability, and comfort to the patient. Tears have a pH of about 7.4. An eye can tolerate solutions of wide pH range as eyes have its control system for pH. Alkaloid salt solutions are stable at pH 2-3 pH, which is irritant to eye. The alkaloids get precipitated at pH above 7 and create several formulation problems. Benzalkonium chloride, polysorbate 20, polysorbate 80, dioctyl sodium succinate are some of the surfactants which are commonly used.

## Summary

In this chapter, we learnt about absorption and factors affecting drug delivery from the ocular route. Ophthalmic formulation, definition, and their application was discussed. The factor of interest in the ophthalmic formulation were also discussed.

## Further Readings

- "Industrial Pharmacy-I" SWAYAM MOOC: www.swayam.gov.in

- Reynolds, L. A. (1993). Extemporaneous Ophthalmic Preparations. Applied Therapeutics.
- Banker, G. S., Siepmann, J., & Rhodes, C. (2002). Modern Pharmaceutics. CRC Press.
- Ghebre-Selassie, I. (1989). Pharmaceutical Pelletization Technology. Taylor & Francis.

## References

- Banker, G. S., Siepmann, J., & Rhodes, C. (2002). Modern Pharmaceutics. CRC Press.
- Indian Pharmacopoeia 2018. (2018). Indian Pharmacopoeia Commission.
- Reddy, I. K. (1995). Ocular Therapeutics and Drug Delivery. CRC Press.
- Reynolds, L. A. (1993). Extemporaneous Ophthalmic Preparations. Applied Therapeutics.
- Organization, W. H. (2006). The International Pharmacopoeia. World Health Organization.

CHAPTER 29

# Ophthalmic Preparations: Dosage Form

**Dr Lokesh Adhikari, Dr Ajay Semalty**
Department of Pharmaceutical Sciences,
H.N.B Garhwal University (A Central University), Srinagar Garhwal-246174.

### Learning Outcome

After learning this chapter, you will be able to develop your understanding about:

- Preparation of ocular drug delivery systems
- Containers for ocular drug delivery systems
- Packaging of ocular drug delivery systems

### Lesson Plan

- Manufacturing of ophthalmic preparations
- Packaging of ophthalmic preparations

## Preparation of Eye Drops involves Four Steps:

- Preparation of the solution
- Clarification of the solution
- Filling into the container
- Sterilization of the formulation

## Preparation of the Solution

In the eye drops, a vehicle is the most critical component. Mostly aqueous vehicles containing any necessary preservatives, antioxidant, stabilizer, tonicity modifier, viscosity enhancer or buffer are preferred and should be prepared first. The addition of API and making up the final volume is the subsequent steps.

## Manufacturing of Ophthalmic Preparations

### Clarification

All the ophthalmic formulations should be free from particulate matter & bacterial endotoxins have a stringent requirement for their absence. Sintered glass filter or membrane filter of 0.25 μm or lees pore size are suitable. The clarified solution is now filled into the container. One way to achieve that is to fill the clarified solution directly into the final container which is sealed before heat sterilization Another way to do the filling is to fill the clarified solution into a suitable container to filtration sterilization. These clarified solutions prepare eye drops suspensions. These suspensions are filled into a final container and kept sealed before sterilization. The sterilization is done by an autoclaving method with a specified range of temperature and time at 115$^0$C for 30 min or 121$^0$C for 15 min. Another method is to heat the solution packed and sealed at 60$^0$C for 30 min together with either be the benzalkonium Chloride or phenylmercuric acetate or nitrate or thiomersal according to BP, but nowadays this method is not recommended.

## Filtration through a Membrane Filter

Filtration through a membrane filter having 0.22 μm pore size into the sterile container using strict aseptic technique. Dry heat sterilization at 160$^0$C for 2 hours employed for non-aqueous preparation, Silicone rubber teat must be used. Immediately the following sterilization, the eye containers must be covered with a readily breakable seal to distinguish btw opened & unopened containers.

**Ophthalmic Suspensions:** Used to increase the corneal contact time of a drug substance providing more sustained action. The ophthalmic suspension includes those solid preparations that, when reconstituted according to the label instructions — required when the active ingredient is insoluble or is unstable in solution form — and commonly formulated by dispersing micronized drug powder (less than ten μm in diameter). In the powdered form, the drug may have a much longer shelf life than in solution or suspension.

Disadvantage: concentration of dissolved drug cannot be manipulated due to their relative insolubility

**Ophthalmic Gels:** are composed of mucoadhesive polymers and provide localized delivery of API to the eye. Bio adhesion is the property of such polymers. These polymers can extend the contact time of the drug with the biological tissues resulting in improved ocular bioavailability. In the release kinetics, the choice of the polymer plays a critical role.

## Formulation of Eye Lotions

Eye lotions used to clean off the external surface of the eye. Removes non-impacted foreign body or clean away conjunctival discharge. For surgical use in surgical or, first aid procedure should not contain antimicrobial preservative & should be in a single-use container. Preparation of eye lotion is rather easy, most commonly consist of NS.

## Requirements of Eye Lotions

- Sterile
- Preservative-free
- Isotonic to the lacrimal fluid
- Neutral pH
- Large vol. not exceeding more than 200 ml.
- Non-irritant to ocular tissue

## Label Requirements: A Label must include:

- Title identifying the product.
- Conc. of contents
- Sterile until open
- Not to be taken
- Use once & discard the remaining solution.
- Expiry date

## Preserved Eye Lotions would need:

## Additional label which includes

- Avoid contamination of contents during use.

- Discard remaining solutions not more than four weeks after first opening.
- Lotions should be supplied in coloured fluted bottles & sealed.

## Formulation of Eye Ointments

**Advantage:**

Provide greater total drug bioavailability.

However, they take a longer time to reach peak absorption.

**Disadvantage**

Temporarily interfering with vision

## Requirements of Eye Ointments

The formulation must be sterile and should necessarily contain suitable antimicrobial preservative, antioxidant & stabilizer. USP offers chlorobutol, parabens, organic mercurial as preservatives for such products. It also must be free from particulate matter, and the particle size of the formulation must be reduced to <25 μm.

## Basic Components

Liquid paraffin → 1part

Wool fat → 1 part

Yellow soft paraffin →8 parts

Hard paraffin as required to produce required consistency in hot climates.

## Preparation of Eye Ointments

Prepared using aseptic techniques to incorporate the finely powdered active ingredient or a sterilized concentrated solution of the medicament into the sterile eye ointment basis. Immediately after preparation, the eye ointment is filled into the sterile container which is then sealed. The screw cap should be covered with a readily breakable seal. Certain eye ointment can be sterilized in their final container using ionizing radiation.

## Preparation of Eye Ointment Basis

The paraffin & wool fat are heated together & filtered, while molten, through a coarse filter paper in a heated funnel into a container which can withstand dry heat sterilization temp. The container is closed & contents are maintained at 160 $^0$C for 2 hrs.

### The General Method of P

Load liquid paraffin, cetostearyl alcohol, hard paraffin, soft paraffin in a melting vessel. Then heat to 145°C and keep it at this temperature for 45 minutes. Afterwards, allow cooling to room temperature. In a separate vessel, dissolve item drug in 200 mL of water for injection and add to prepared base under aseptic conditions. Finally, fill in tubes and sterilize with gamma radiation.

## Solid Dosage Forms Ocular Inserts

Ophthalmic inserts are defined as sterile solid or semisolid preparations, with a thin, flexible, and multi-layered structure, for insertion in the conjunctival sac.

**Advantages:**

- Increasing contact time
- Improving bioavailability
- Providing a prolong drug release.
- Better efficacy
- Reduction of adverse effects
- Reduction of the number administrations
- Better patient compliance

### Insoluble Inserts

The insoluble insert is a multi-layered structure consisting of a drug-containing core surrounded on each side by a layer of copolymer membranes through which the drug diffuses at a constant rate.

The rate of drug diffusion is controlled by:

- The composition of the polymer
- The thickness of the membrane
- The drug solubility

The Ocusert® Pilo-20 and Pilo-40 Ocular system designed to be placed in the inferior cul-de-sac between the sclera and the eyelid and to release pilocarpine continuously at a steady rate for seven days for treatment of glaucoma.

Consists of

**A drug reservoir**, pilocarpine (free base), and a carrier material, alginic acid

**A rate controller membrane** ethylene vinyl acetate (EVA) copolymer

## Soluble Ocular Inserts

Soluble inserts consist of all monolytic polymeric devices that at the end of their release, the device dissolves or erode.

**Types**

- Based on natural polymers, e.g., collagen
- Based on synthetic or semi-synthetic polymers, e.g., Cellulose derivatives – Hydroxypropyl cellulose, methylcellulose or Polyvinyl alcohol, ethylene-vinyl acetate copolymer

## Soluble Ocular Inserts

The system softens in sec after introduction into the upper conjunctival sac which gradually dissolves within one hour, while releasing the drug.

Advantage: being entirely soluble so that they do not need to be removed from their site of application.

## Ophthalmic Implants

Implants are used to extend the release of drugs in ocular fluids and tissues, particularly in the posterior segment. Classified into two categories based on their degradation properties: 1. biodegradable and 2. nonbiodegradable. Implants can be solids, semisolids, or particulate-based delivery systems. Particulate systems can be injected through thin needles and have different behaviour and distribution in the ocular media depending on their size and composition. Biodegradable polymers include polylactic acid (PLA), polyglycolic acid (PGA), poly(lactic-co-glycolic acid) (PLGA). Bulk erosion occurs, causing a burst of the encapsulated drug caused by the cleavage of polymeric chains by enzymatic and nonenzymatic hydrolysis Manufactured in various shapes including rods, plugs, pellets, discs, and sheets. Implanted into the anterior chamber, the vitreous cavity through the pars plana, or into the intrascleral space.

# Packaging of Ophthalmic Preparations

## Containers

Ophthalmic liquid products were packed in glass containers fitted with an eye dropper. Today, glass containers have limited use where product stability or compatibility issues exclude the use of flexible plastic containers made of polyethene or polypropylene. Most liquid ophthalmic products on the market are packaged in plastic containers fitted with nozzles from which, by gentle squeezing, the contents may be delivered as drops.

Plastic containers have several advantages over the glass-dropper combination minimizing the risk of the contents being contaminated with microorganisms by the replacement of the dropper which may have become contaminated by touching the infected eye or any other surfaces. Plastic containers are cheap, light in weight, more robust to handle and easier to use than glass-dropper type containers.

## Disadvantages of Plastic Eye-drop Containers

Some plastic materials such as polyethene can absorb some antimicrobial preservatives (e.g., benzalkonium chloride), or some drugs. They may also leach plasticizers into the product, and printing inks from the label can migrate through the plastic into the product. It is necessary to conduct compatibility and stability studies to ascertain whether this is likely to be a problem. Alternatives are to use glass or a preservative-free product.

The challenge is to develop a packaging system for preservative-free products that maintains the sterility of the product throughout its shelf-life and during use.

## Packaging of Ophthalmic Preparations

Plastic containers can also be permeable to water vapor and oxygen over prolonged periods of storage. This can lead to the gradual loss of liquid product or oxidation of an unstable drug over time. Polyethylene containers are not able to withstand autoclaving and are usually sterilized by ethylene oxide or by irradiation before being filled aseptically with presterilized product. Polypropylene containers can be autoclaved but are not as flexible as polyethylene for eyedropper use.

## Summary

In this chapter, we learnt about various types of ophthalmic formulations.

We also discussed the method of preparation of a few formulation aspects.

We also covered the merits and demerits of various formulations.

At last, we had gone through the packaging techniques with specific to the ophthalmic dosage forms.

## Further Readings

- "Industrial Pharmacy-I" SWAYAM MOOC: www.swayam.gov.in
- Reynolds, L. A. (1993). Extemporaneous Ophthalmic Preparations. Applied Therapeutics.
- Banker, G. S., Siepmann, J., & Rhodes, C. (2002). Modern Pharmaceutics. CRC Press.

## References


- Banker, G. S., Siepmann, J., & Rhodes, C. (2002). Modern Pharmaceutics. CRC Press.
- Indian Pharmacopoeia 2018. (2018). Indian Pharmacopoeia Commission.
- Reddy, I. K. (1995). Ocular Therapeutics and Drug Delivery. CRC Press.
- Reynolds, L. A. (1993). Extemporaneous Ophthalmic Preparations. Applied Therapeutics.
- Organization, W. H. (2006). The International Pharmacopoeia. World Health Organization.

# Chapter 30

# Ophthalmic Preparations: Evaluation

**Dr Lokesh Adhikari, Dr Ajay Semalty**
Department of Pharmaceutical Sciences,
H.N.B Garhwal University (A Central University), Srinagar Garhwal-246174.

## Learning Outcome

After learning this chapter, you will be able to develop your understanding about:

- Evaluation of ocular drug delivery systems

## Lesson Plan

- Evaluation of ophthalmic preparations

Types of evaluation tests for ophthalmic products.

There are two major types of tests for ophthalmic products. Few formulations based specific tests are also mentioned in the monograph of different formulations **Figure 30.1**.

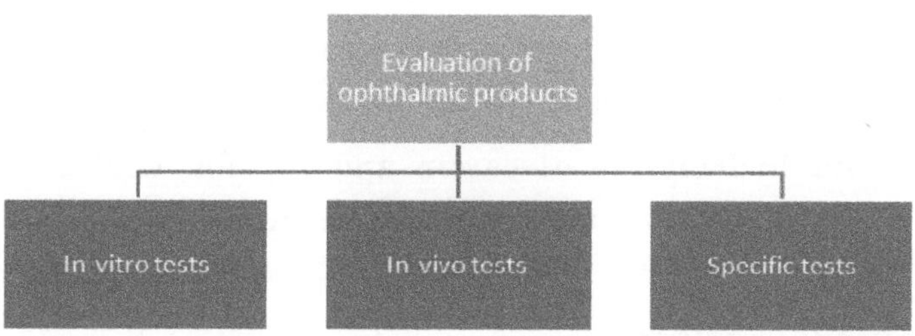


**Figure 30.1** Types of evaluation methods of ophthalmic preparations.

*In vitro* tests include-

- Sterility
- pH

- Clarity of solutions
- Visual assessment
- Size of the particles,
- Tonicity/osmolarity
- Viscosity
- Amount of substance
- Amount of preservative
- Stability
- In vitro release

***In vivo*** tests include-

- Draize eye test
- *In vivo* release

**Specified (Other) tests include-**

- Analysis of ions (for contact lenses)
- Oxygen permeability (for contact lenses)
- Determination of encapsulation efficiency (for multicompartment drug delivery systems and emulsions)

**Sterility Examination** is the primary type of in-vitro test. It involves inoculation of the sample at aseptic conditions (Figure 30.2). The sample can be examined on one of the two microbiological media,

1. **Thioglycolate medium** for aerobic and anaerobic bacteria. It is also known as fluid sodium mercapto acetate or sodium thioglycolate.
2. **Medium with hydrolysate of casein and soy** for aerobic bacteria and fungi. It is also called soya-bean casein digest media.

## Sterility Examination

The first step of the test is to perform the test either with thioglycolate medium or with medium with hydrolysate of casein and soy, which is then incubated at the temperature of 30–35°C. The time duration for the test is not less than 14 days, which means the samples are at least kept for such duration.

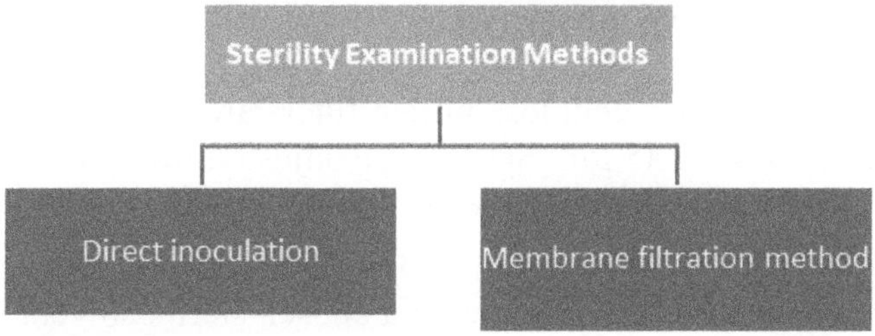


**Figure 30.2** Sterility examination methods.

## Direct Inoculation Method

This process involves the transfer of the prepared sample to the medium **(Figure 30.3 & Figure 30.4)**. A limitation of sterility testing is that product containing antimicrobial properties should be neutralized for such effects these properties may interfere with results. The diluted solution of ointment formulation with a sterile solvent containing the chosen surface-active agent is necessary before the test.

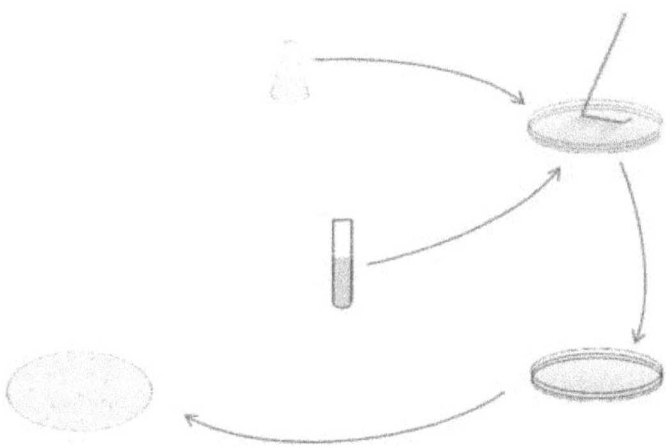

**Figure 30.3** Direct inoculation method: spreading over the medium.

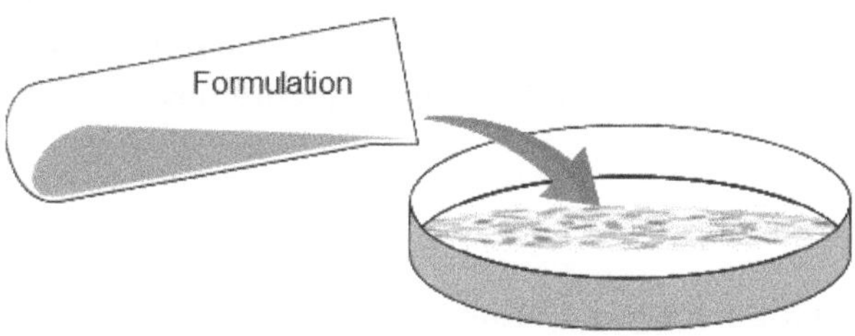


**Figure 30.4** Direct inoculation method: direct transfer.

## Membrane Filtration Method

For water and oil solutions, cellulose nitrate filters are used for this test having a size of pores less than 0.45 $\mu$m. Specialized adjusted filter is used for specific products like antibiotics. In the case of testing products with antimicrobial effects

The membrane should be washed with a chosen sterile solvent at least three times limiting with not exceeding the fivefold cycle of filter washing for each 100ml of the solvent sample (**Figure 30.5**).

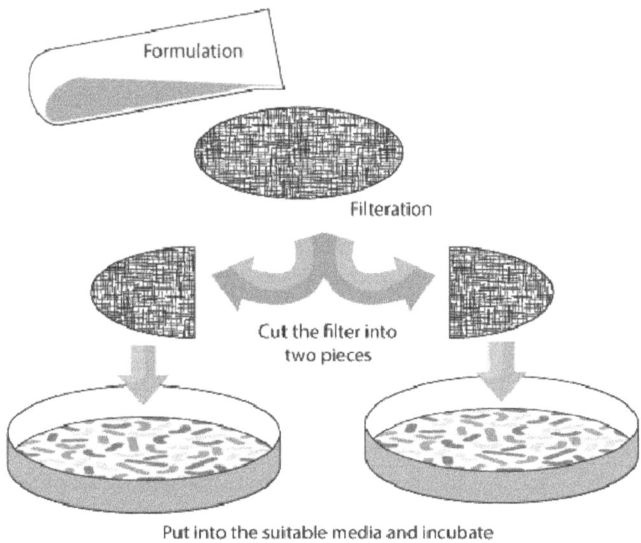


**Figure 30.5** Membrane filtration method.

The indirect method can also be used for ointments. Isopropyl myristate is used to dilute the fatty base ointments at the temperature not more than 40°C.The product is filtered as quickly as possible. For every drug form, after filtration and washing, the membrane is either transferred to the medium, or the medium introduced to the filtration set on the membrane.

## pH Testing

A suitable formulation for pH testing is solutions, drops, suspensions and in situ gels. The test is performed by using a potentiometer using the potential difference measurement principle. In this method, the sample is kept separately at the sample electrode, and a reference of known pH is used on the other electrode. Another method which can be used for this purpose is by measuring the potential difference between measurement (glass) electrode and reference (calomel or silver chloride) electrode, both placed in examined preparation.

## Clarity Testing (Visual Method)

It involves the visual assessment of formulation in suitable lighting on white and black background. The test is performed for liquid forms but not for the suspensions. Eye drops are tested for clarity while in situ gels are tested two times, one before and one after gelling.

Various other evaluation test which are specific to particle size and shape are mentioned in **Figure 30.6.**

## Clarity Testing by UV Transmittance

Another method of testing for clarity by transmittance measurement using a UV-Vis spectrophotometer. This method employed on contact lenses filled with active ingredients where the formulation is of solid type. The lenses are hydrated in physiological saline at the initial stage of the test followed by placing on the surface of a quartz cuvette. In the final step, the transmittance is measured afterwards from 200 to 1000 nm wavelength.

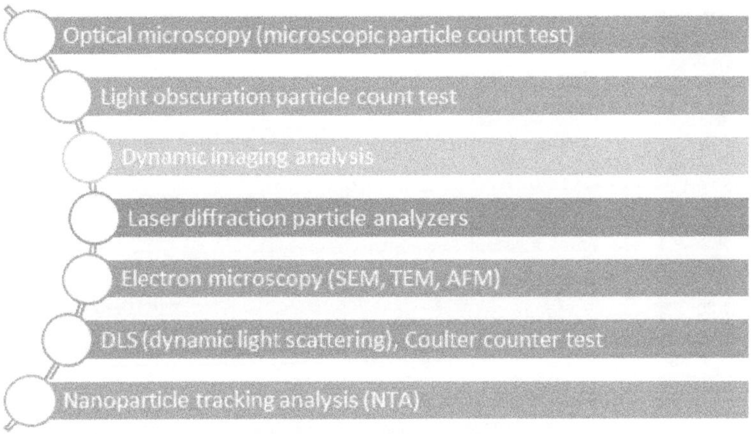


**Figure 30.6** Evaluation of ophthalmic preparations.

## Content of Substance or Preservative Analysis

The examination of drug or preservative content should be done by testing parameters given as per the label with relevant analytical technique, i.e., Spectrophotometric method, HPLC.

## Viscosity Analysis

This test is done by using viscometer. Choice of viscometer is based on the type and amount of sample.

## Tonicity Analysis

Three primary methods are used to assess the tonicity of any ophthalmic formulation.

- Freezing point depression method
- Electrical impedance method
- Vapour pressure method

## Stability Analysis

This test provides the information on changes in the quality of active ingredient or medicinal product over the time due to the environmental factors.

## *In Vitro* Drug Release Analysis

*In vitro* drug release analysis is done through various methods (**Figure 30.7**).

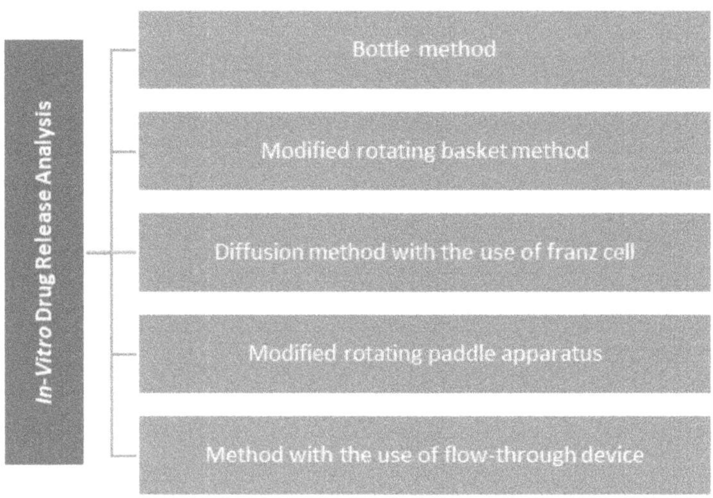


**Figure 30.7** Types of *in-vitro* analysis methods.

## Bottle Method

In this method, the formulations are placed in culture bottles or vials containing phosphate buffer at pH 7.4 or artificial isotonic tear fluid. The bottles and vials are shaken in water baths or incubated under magnetic stirring at 37°C. The samples are withdrawn at specified time intervals and afterwards examined for drug amount.

## Franz Diffusion Cell Method

The test requires equipment consisting of two separate compartments, one donor and one receiver. The formulation is placed in a donor compartment of Franz cell, and a thermostated (37°C ± 0.5°C) the receiver compartment contains dissolution medium. Continuous stirring is applied in the receiver compartment using a magnetic stirrer (50 rpm). Both the compartments are separated with a dialysis membrane (cellophane). Samples are taken from the receiver compartment at specified time intervals, and the drug is marked using a suitable analytical technique.

## Rotating Basket Method

In this test, the formulation is placed in a set of baskets or substitutes cylindrical glass pipes. These pipes are connected with a stirrer on one side and the other side is attached to shafts of the apparatus, covered with a dialysis membrane. The components are put in a beaker with a water jacket, containing a buffer solution (35°c ± 1°c), a simulated tear fluid (STF) and the rotation is set at 50 rpm. A sample of the solution is taken in specified time intervals, and it is examined for drug amount.

## Draize Eye Test

The test subject for this test should be rabbits, as their vision organ anatomy and physiology are well described in the literature. Susceptibility of the eye to irritating compounds is higher in case of rabbits in comparison with humans. Rabbits are taken into the group of 3 to 6 and placed in cages, adapted explicitly for them. The site of administration of the drug for this test is either conjunctival sac or applied directly on the cornea. The initial amount of the formulation being applied on the eyeball was set about 0.1ml, but various after attempts pointed to reducing the amount. The left eyeball is used as a control. The eyeball condition is observed using a magnifying glass before and after administering the formulation. The eyeball is monitored for the blinking or rubbing of the eye as an indication of the discomfort level after application. The evaluation takes place usually after one h, 24 h, 48 h, and 72 h.

## Transcorneal Permeation Test

This test includes healthy albino rabbits as test subjects. The formulation is applied Using a syringe with needle, after intramuscular or intravenous anesthetic injection a sample of aqueous humor is taken (150–200 $\mu$L)Stored at negative temperature (−20 °C) before HPLC analysis

## Summary

In this chapter, we learnt about evaluation tests for ophthalmic products.

We also discussed various in-vitro testing methods.

## Further Readings

- "Industrial Pharmacy-I" SWAYAM MOOC: www.swayam.gov.in
- Reynolds, L. A. (1993). Extemporaneous Ophthalmic Preparations. Applied Therapeutics.
- Banker, G. S., Siepmann, J., & Rhodes, C. (2002). Modern Pharmaceutics. CRC Press.
- Ghebre-Selassie, I. (1989). Pharmaceutical Pelletization Technology. Taylor & Francis.

## References


- Banker, G. S., Siepmann, J., & Rhodes, C. (2002). Modern Pharmaceutics. CRC Press.
- Indian Pharmacopoeia 2018. (2018). Indian Pharmacopoeia Commission.
- Reddy, I. K. (1995). Ocular Therapeutics and Drug Delivery. CRC Press.
- Reynolds, L. A. (1993). Extemporaneous Ophthalmic Preparations. Applied Therapeutics.
- Organization, W. H. (2006). The International Pharmacopoeia. World Health Organization.

CHAPTER 31

# Pharmaceutical Aerosols I (Introduction and Classification)

**Dr Ajay Semalty**
Department of Pharmaceutical Sciences,
H.N.B Garhwal University (A Central University), Srinagar Garhwal-246174

### Learning Outcomes

After learning this chapter, you will be able to understand

- Basic principle of Aerosol
- Advantages, Limitation of aerosol
- Uses of aerosol

### Lesson Plan

- Aerosol: Definition
- Advantages,
- Limitation
- Uses of aerosol

## Aerosols

You know it very well, but you just don't know that it is aerosol. Can you guess? We use/see it almost daily. Not necessarily for medical use. E.g. Deospray, perfume spray, Mosquito/cockroach repellant spray. Yes, these are aerosols.

The beautiful rainbow is the best example from the nature. It is a quite stable liquid aerosol. On the other hand, Irrigation fountain is the example of coarse unstable liquid aerosol.

## Pharmaceutical Aerosols

Aerosols are being used from decades for therapeutic purpose globally e.g. pressurized metered dose inhalers (MDIs), dry powder inhalers (DPIs), nebulizers, skin sprays (pain killer spray) etc. Ever increasing incidence of asthma globally is increasing the demand of aerosols.

The technology's continual advancement, the ease of use and the more desirable pulmonary-rather-than-needle delivery for systemic drugs has increased the attraction for the pharmaceutical aerosol in recent years. Moreover, the increasing incidence of asthma at an average rate of 5 % per year in developed as well as developing countries is creating a consistently high demand of inhalers or MDIs (about 50 to 60 million patients are relying on MDIs).

### Definition

The word aerosol means: "Aero= air, Sol = solution". Aerosol is a "Pressurized package".

**"Aerosols are a suspension of small solid particles or droplets suspended in a gas or vapor."**

**"Aerosols are the products that depend on the power of a compressed or liquefied gas to expel the contents from the container."**

"Pharmaceutical aerosols are products that are packaged under pressure and contain therapeutically active ingredients that are released upon activation of an appropriate valve system. They are intended for topical application to the skin as well as local application into the nose (nasal aerosols), mouth (lingual aerosols), or lungs (inhalation aerosols). These products may be fitted with valves enabling either continuous or metered-dose delivery; hence, the terms "[DRUG] Metered Topical Aerosols," "[DRUG] Metered Nasal Aerosols," etc." [USP definition]

**Learning the definition**

**Active drug → dissolved, suspended or emulsified in propellant→** to release drug in the form of **mist, spray** (Figure 31.1**)** → to topical, nasal, oral, pulmonary and other body cavities **for local and systemic therapeutic** use

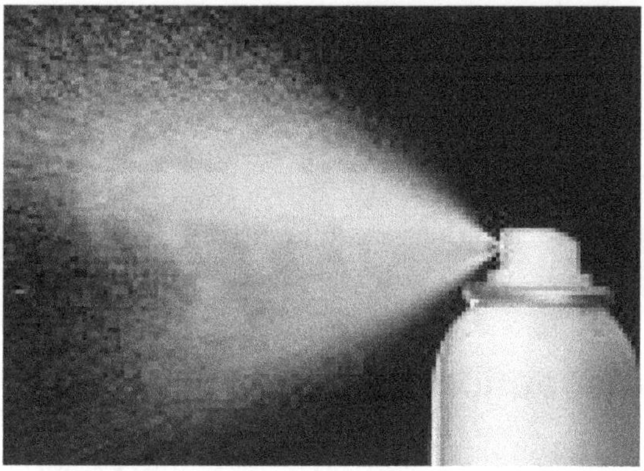

**Figure 31.1** Aerosol Spray.

**Advantages**

- **Easy administration:** The product is administered easily and quickly.
- **Portable:** Aerosols are portable and tamper-proof.
- **Minimum dose required:** Lower dose of drug can be used and hence
- **Minimize adverse and side effects** A dose can be removed without contamination of materials.
- **Direct delivery of drug to target area:** The medication can be delivered directly to the affected area
- **Better spreading due to spray/ mist type of delivery:** Drug is delivered in a desired form, such as spray, steam, quick breaking foam or stable foam, Application of medication in thin layer.
- **Quick onset of action:** Drug acts quickly due to direct delivery at affected area and that to in spray form.
- **Lower irritation**: Irritation produced by the mechanical application of topical medication is reduced or eliminated.
- **Dose to dose to maintenance of sterility:** When sterility is an important factor, it can be maintained while a dose is being dispensed.
- **Better protection for oxygen and or moisture sensitive drugs:** Stability is enhanced for these substances adversely affected by oxygen and or moisture
- **Avoid first pass metabolism:** Avoidance of degradation of the drug in the GIT and first pass effect

**Limitation**

- Not Cost effective (diclo spray v/s diclo tablet)
- Proper use needed to get the effect. (prone to incorrect use)

- Limited safety hazard
    - Flammable
    - Pressurized
    - Inadvertent inhalation
- Ancillary devices are required with an MDI (like holding chambers and spacers)

## Uses of Pharmaceutical Aerosols

Since decades, pharmaceutical aerosols have played an important role in treating respiratory disorderslike asthma and chronic obstructive pulmonary disease (COPD), and MDIs and DPIs have become an important part of that treatment. But the use of aerosol products are not limited to the pulmonary route, these can be administered by various routes of administration (ROA) for various therapeutic effects. These can be administered by topical, nasal, ocular, oral, rectal and vaginal routes also.

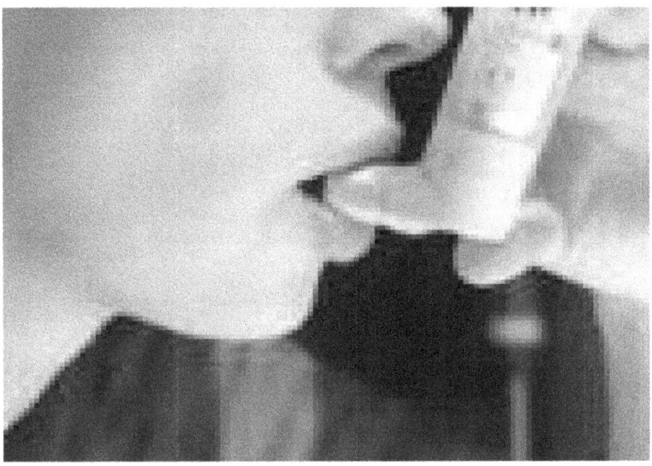

**Figure 31.2** Oral and Lingual Aerosols.

## Oral and Lingual Aerosols

As the name suggests, these are meant for oral delivery (Figure 31.2)

- Easy access to hard-to-reach sites
- Easy access to systemic circulation
- Avoid FPM

- Examples: Anti-anginals (e.g. Nitroglycerin) in emergency, Local anesthetics (e.g. Lidocaine) for dental use, Antacids (e.g. Aluminum and magnesium silicate), Antiseptics (e.g. Chloroseptic)

## Topical Aerosols

These aerosols are meant for delivering drug onto skin (Figure 31.3).

- Convenient as compared to application
- No need to touch skin
- Unused product is not contaminated
- Examples: Spray on bandages, Antifungal sprays (Miconazole), Antibacterials(e.g. Neomycin), Wound washing, Rubiferants (e.g. Methylsalicylate), Anti-inflammatory steroids (e.g. Dexamethasone), Local anesthetics (e.g. Benzocaine).

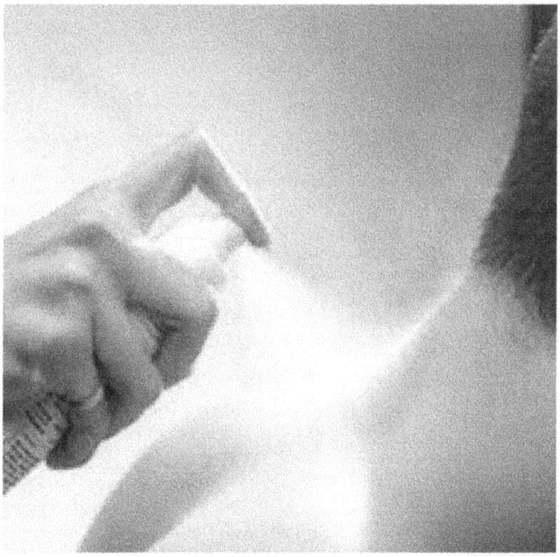

**Figure 31.3** Topical Aerosols.

## Vaginal Aerosols

These aerosols are intended to deliver drugs to vaginal cavity (**Figure 31.4**).

- Easy access
- Expands to fill available space
- Provide complete surface coverage
- Example: Contraceptive Foams (e.g. Nonoxyenol-9)

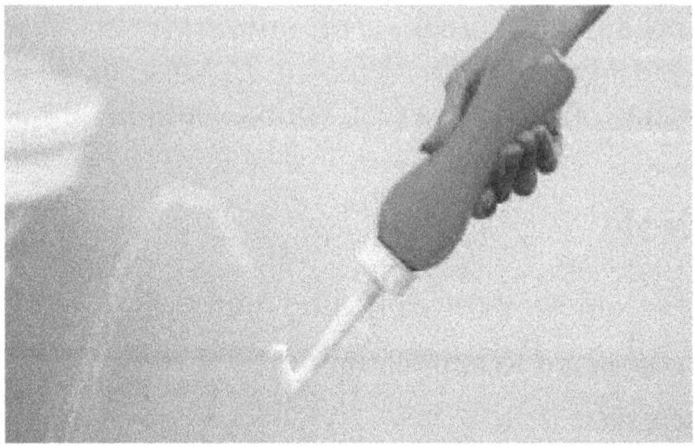

**Figure 31.4** Vaginal Aerosols.

## Rectal Aerosols

These aerosols are intended to deliver drugs to rectal cavity (**Figure 31.5**).

- Easy access
- Expands to fill available space
- Provide complete surface coverage
- Example: Anti-inflammatory steroids (e.g. Hydrocortisone), Local anesthetics (e.g. Pramoxine)

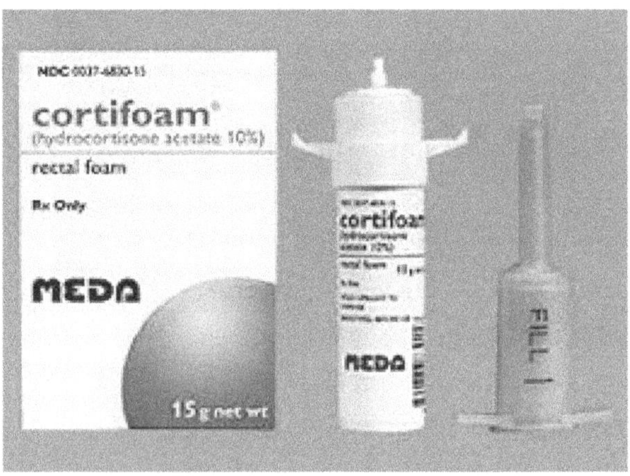


**Figure 31.5** Rectal Aerosols.

## Nasal Aerosols

These aerosols are intended to deliver drugs to nasal cavity (**Figure 31.6**).

- Easy access
- Minimal dripping
- Example: Decongestants (e.g. Phenylephrine), Antiallergics (e.g. Cromolyn sodium), Anti-inflammatory steroids (e.g. eclomethasone),

  Antismoking (Nicotine), Moisturizers (e.g. Normal saline), Systemic access of Antidiuretics (e.g. Desmopressin)

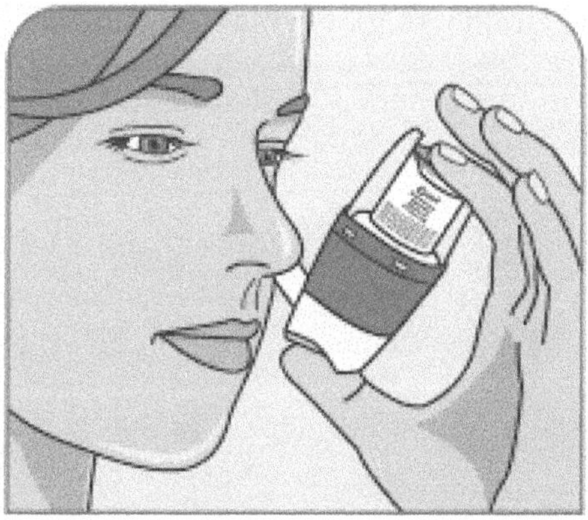

**Figure 31.6** Nasal Aerosols.

## Ocular Aerosols

These aerosols are intended to deliver drugs to ocular region (**Figure 31.7**)

- Easy access
- Minimal dripping
- Contact lens cleaning solutions (not applied directly to eye)

**Figure 31.7** Ocular Aerosols.

## Respiratory Aerosols

These aerosols are intended to deliver drugs to respiratory system (**Figure 31.8**).

- Local as well as systemic action is obtained
- E.g. Anti-inflammatory steroids (e.g. Beclomethasone), Antiallergics (e.g. Cromolyn sodium), Antivirals (e.g. Ribavirin), Bronchodilators (e.g. Albuterol), Migraine (e.g. Ergotamine tartrate), Smoking cessation (e.g. Nicotine)

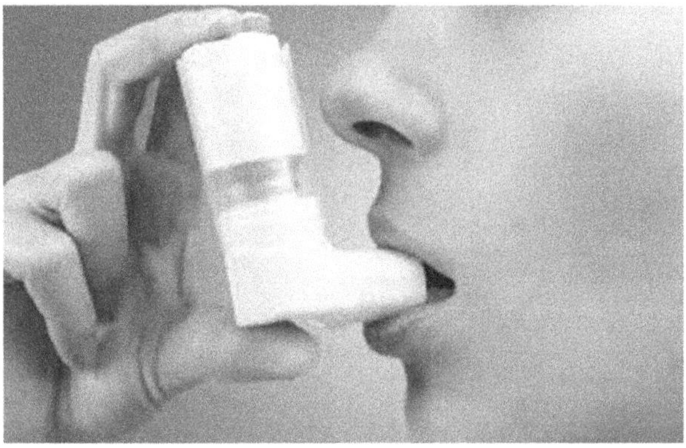

**Figure 31.8** Respiratory Aerosols.

## Take away Message

- Aerosols are pressurized package.
- Drug is dissolved suspended or emulsified in propellant and dispensed in the form of mist or spray for local or systemic action.
- These are used by various ROA like oral, rectal, vaginal, topical etc.
- Low dose, quick onset of action, high bioavailability, low adverse effect, avoiding FPM are the main advantages.

## Further Readings


- "Industrial Pharmacy-I" SWAYAM MOOC: www.swayam.gov.in
- Banker & Rhodes, Modern Pharmaceutics, CRC Press.
- Aulton ME (ED), Pharmaceutics: The science of Dosage form design, II edn, Churchill Livingstone, London, 2002.

- Semalty et al., Essentials of Pharmaceutical Technology, II Edn. Pharma Med press, Hyderabad, India

## References


- USP
- Semalty et al., Essentials of Pharmaceutical Technology, II Edn. Pharma Med press, Hyderabad, India, ISBN 9789386819994

# CHAPTER 32

# Pharmaceutical Aerosols II (Components of Aerosols)

**Dr Ajay Semalty**
Department of Pharmaceutical Sciences,
H.N.B Garhwal University (A Central University), Srinagar Garhwal-246174

**Learning Outcomes**

After learning this chapter, you will be able to

- Compare the properties of different propellants
- Understand the role of propellants in aerosols
- Understand container types

**Lesson Plan**

- Propellants: concept
- Classification
- Nomenclature
- Types
- Advantages / limitations
- Uses
- Container (material)

So far, we discussed the definition, advantages, disadvantages and types of aerosols. **Now let's move to components of aerosols**

## Components of Aerosols

An aerosol system has following major components.

- Propellant
- Container
- Valve and actuator
- Product concentrate

## Propellant

Propellant is the heart of an aerosol package. It is develops the pressure within the container to expel the product when the valve is opened. It helps in the atomization or form production of the product.

Propellants provide the driving force to expel product from its container.

"It is a dispersion medium as well as the driving force provider for dispensing/discharge of product from container."

You can recall the advertisement "GAS VALA DEO". Actually it is just talking about the propellants only deopspray. In common language it is termed gas.

### Types of Propellants

The propellants are of two types (**Figure 32.1**)

I. **Liquefied gas** e.g. Hydrocarbons (HCs), Chloroflurocarbon (CFCs), Hydrofluoroalkanes (HFA)

II. **Compressed Gas Propellants**

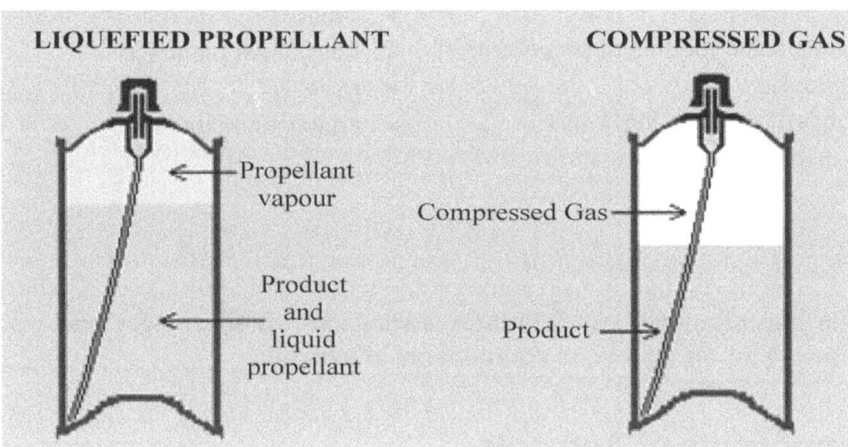


**Figure 32.1** Aerosols with different propellants.
*(Adapted from Semalty et al. Essentials of Pharmaceutical Technology, II edn, 2018, Pharma med Press, Hyderabad)*

I. **Liquefied gas:** These are materials that at room temperature and atmospheric pressure exist in the gaseous or vapor state and are capable of being liquefied at relatively low pressures or temperatures. Because the aerosol is under pressure the propellant exists mainly as a liquid, but it will also be in the head space as a vapour.

**Functioning:** When you open the valve → some propellant in vapor state is mixed with product for helping in spray formation and dispensed with the product.

Some of the liquid propellant immediately automatically converted in vapor state to compensate the vapor propellant mixed and discharged with the product concentrate. (**Figure 32.2**).

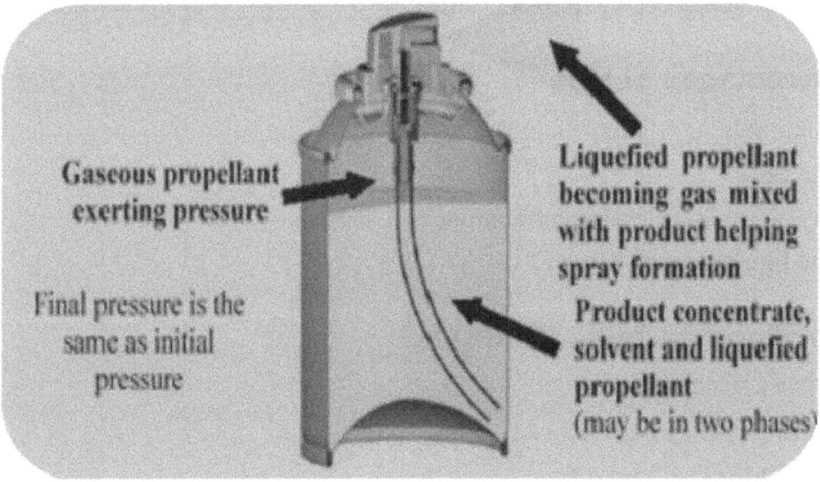


**Figure 32.2** Working of an aerosol system (with liquefied propellant).
*(Adapted from Semalty et al. Essentials of Pharmaceutical Technology, II edn, 2018, Pharma med Press, Hyderabad)*

By this way the headspace is always full of propellant vapor.

**Final pressure = initial pressure (throughout shelf life)**

## Types of LG propellants

- Hydrocarbons (HCs),
- Chloroflurocarbon (CFCs),
- Hydrofluoroalkanes (HFA)

## Hydrocarbons (HCs)

- **n-Butane,**
- **isobutane,**
- **propane**

## Advantages of HCs

- Cheap, cost effective
- Safe to ozone
- Negligible "greenhouse effect"
- Excellent solvents
- Expand well (Large expansion ratio)

## Disadvantages of HCs

- Flammable
- Aftertaste
- May be toxic following inhalation
- Low liquid density

## Chlorofluorocarbons (CFCs)

- CFC-11 ($CCl_3F$),
- CFC-12 ($CCl_2F_2$),
- CFC-114 ($C_2Cl_2F_4$)**

**What does these digits mean? These digits indicate their names. Let's see what is this nomenclature all about.**

# Nomenclature of CFCs

The **A**merican **S**ociety of **H**eating, **R**efrigerating, and **A**ir Conditioning **E**ngineers (**ASHRAE**) has created a standard for a Halocarbon Numbering System. In this system the CFCs and HFAs are designated with 3 digits followed by an alphabet if required.

- I digit = No. of Carbon atoms −1;
- II digit = No. of hydrogen atoms + 1;
- III digit = No. of Fluorine atoms;
- All remaining atoms are assumed to be chlorine atoms. An initial zero (indicating a one-carbon compound) is omitted.
- Most symmetric structure is designated by numbers only and as the asymmetry increases a, b, c, etc. follow the number.

**Example**

For example: 1,1,1,2,3,3,3-heptafluoropropane has:

three carbon atoms (3 – 1 = **2**),

one hydrogen atom (1 + 1 = **2**),

seven fluorine atoms (7 = **7**)

and no chlorine atoms therefore it is

named as **HFA 227**.

**CFC-114 for dichlorotetrafluoroethane;**

**CFC-12 (012) for dichlorodifluoromethane.**

### Advantages of CFCs

- Less toxic upon inhalation
- High chemical stability
- High purity
- CFC-11 is a good solvent

### Disadvantages of CFCs

- High cost
- Contribute to "greenhouse effect"
- Ozone depleting
- Being phase out by HFAs and
- banned by many countries except their use in some essential medicines- **bronchodilators, ergotamine tartrate, certain topical antibiotic sprays and contraceptive vaginal foams.**

## Ozone Depleting Effect of CFCs

CFCs Show detrimental effect on the Earth's ozone layer. Montreal Protocol on Substances That Deplete the Ozone Layer (January 1989) set a timetable for elimination of CFCs. Urgent measures introduced to protect the ozone layer resulted in a ban on the production and use of fully halogenated chlorofluorocarbons (CFCs) in the developed world with effect from January 1996. The only exemption was for "essential" uses. However, these "essential" CFCs are no longer deemed essential because there are now many alternatives/substitutes to CFC containing MDIs available.

*Germany has already banned CFC-MDIs containing drugs of the following classes:*

- *short-acting beta-sympathomimetic bronchodilators (salbutamol, terbutaline, fenoterol, bitolterol, and procaterol) as of January 2001,*
- *inhaled steroids (beclomethasone, dexamethasone, flunisolide, fluticasone, budesonide and triamcinolone) as of January 2003,*
- *and intends to ban CFC-MDIs containing anticholinergic bronchodilators comprising ipratropium bromide and oxitropium bromide.*

*Various other national transition strategies for the phase-out of CFCs in MDIs are published, among others in Australia, Europe, New Zealand, Japan, USA and Canada. The Canadian Transition Strategy is as follows:*

- *as of January 2003: CFC-MDIs containing salbutamol prohibited*
- *as of January 2004: CFC-MDIs containing corticosteroids forbidden*
- *as of January 2005: Prohibition of all MDIs containing CFCs (production and import).*

*Furthermore, Austria, Belgium, Denmark, Finland, France, Germany, The Netherlands, Portugal and the United Kingdom formally determined that most of the short-acting beta-agonist CFC-MDIs are no longer essential.*

*In Europe, this has already resulted in a more than 50 % reduction in the total CFC quantities used in MDIs; from 5,600 tonnes required in 1997 to approx. 2,500 tonnes in 2002.*

*In total, approx. 500 million MDIs are manufactured, corresponding to approx. 8,500 tonnes of propellant, traditionally consisting of CFCs. When substituted by HFAs, the global warming potential is reduced by more than 75 %. The total global warming contribution of HFA-MDIs is less than 0.5 % of the total greenhouse gas emissions.*

*HFAs are being used as alternatives and have less of an effect on the environment. CFCs are exempted for a very few class of aerosols- MDIs for oral/nasal steroidal drugs - bronchodilators, ergotamine tartrate, certain topical antibiotic sprays and contraceptive vaginal foams*

## Hydrofluoroalkanes (HFAs)

- 1,1,1,2,3,3,3-Hepta-fluoropropane (HFA-227)
- 1,1,1,2 – Tetra-fluoroethane (HFA-134a)

**Advantages**

- Less toxic on inhalation
- High chemical stability
- High purity
- Not ozone depleting

When **CFC are substituted by HFAs,** the **global warming** potential is **reduced by more than 75 %.** The total global warming contribution of HFA-MDIs is less than 0.5 % of the total greenhouse gas emissions.

**Disadvantages of HFAs**

- High cost
- Poor solvents
- Minor "greenhouse effect"

**Compressed Gas (CG)**

- $CO_2$, $N_2$, $N_2O$

**Advantages**

- Not costly
- only occupy the head space
- Less inhalation toxicity
- High chemical stability
- High purity
- No environmental hazard

**Disadvantages of CGs**

- Nonvolatile co-solvent are required to be used
- Expand less (Little expansion ratio)
- Produce coarse droplet sprays
- Use is limited to applications where type of spray is not critical e.g. dental creams, hair spray, germicide etc.

Upon valve opening the gas pushes the liquid and product is dispensed (**Figure 32.3**). Now the remaining amount of gas has more space to occupy in head space. So after use the pressure drops and goes on decreasing with the passage of time during use.

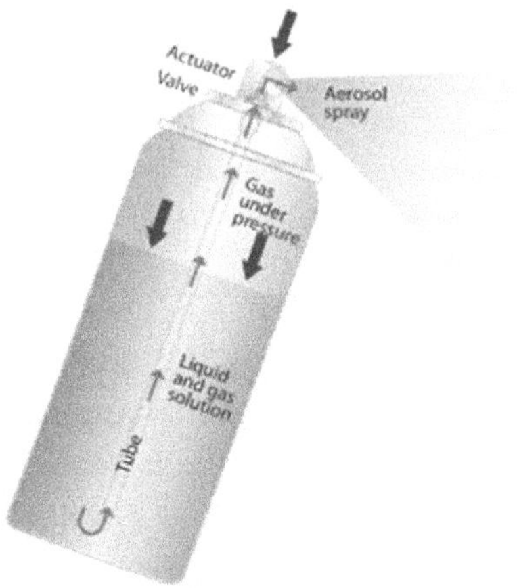


**Figure 32.3** Working of CG based aerosols.

## Container

Aerosol's container must withstand pressure as high as 140 to 180 psig (pounds per sq. inch gauge) at 130 $^0$F (**Table 32.1**). Containers may be made of followings:

A. Metals
1. Tinplated steel
2. Tin free steel
3. Aluminum
4. Stainless steel

B. Glass
1. Uncoated glass
2. Plastic coated glass

**Table 32.1** Maximum tolerable pressure by different aerosol containers.

| Container | Maximum pressure (psig) | Temperature $^0$F |
|---|---|---|
| Tinplated steel | 140 to 180 | 130 |
| Aluminum | Up to 180 | 130 |
| Stainless steel | Up to 180 | 130 |
| Plastic | Less than 25 | 70 |
| Uncoated glass | Less than 18 | 70 |
| Coated glass | Less than 25 | 70 |

(Adapted from Semalty et al. Essentials of Pharmaceutical Technology, II edn, 2018, Pharma med Press, Hyderabad)

## Tinplated Steel

- Light and inexpensive
- May be coated with organic coating for additional protection against corrosion. e.g. oleoresin, phenolic, vinyl or epoxy coating
- Coating also solves the compatibility issues.
- Used in topical pharmaceutical aerosols

## Aluminum

- Less reactive,
- Light weight,
- Seamless,
- Easy to fill and crimp and
- Shows greater resistance from corrosions
- Visually appealing
- Incompatible with some propellants and solvents so may be coated with organic coating
- Used in oral, topical and most MDIs

## Stainless Steel

- Extremely strong,
- Resistant to most materials
- No extra coating is required
- Used in smaller sizes only due to high cost and production problem
- Used for inhalation aerosols

## Glass

- High aesthetic value and compatibility
- Allow visibility of contents
- Use limited for products with lower pressure (upto 25 psig) and lower percentage (about only upto 15%) of propellant
- Plastic coated glass is used for avoiding shattering
- Used for some topical and MDI aerosols

## Plastic

- Cheap
- Durable
- Light weight
- Used in small size
- Can withstand lower pressure (less than25 psig at 70 °F)
- Incompatible with some solvents
- Used for nasal sprays, rectal sprays, vaginal sprays.

## Take Away Message

- Propellants are the heart / driving force of aerosols
- Liquefied gas and compressed gases are used as propellants
- CFCs and HFAs are liquefied gas propellants
- HFAs are preferred over CFCs due to environmental hazard; CGs are cheap but pressure is not maintained with use.
- Tin plated steel, Al, stainless steel, plastic and glass are used as container material.

## Further Readings

- "Industrial Pharmacy-I" SWAYAM MOOC: www.swayam.gov.in
- Banker & Rhodes, Modern Pharmaceutics, CRC Press.
- Aulton ME (ED), Pharmaceutics: The science of Dosage form design, II edn, Churchill Livingstone, London, 2002.
- Semalty et al., Essentials of Pharmaceutical Technology, II Edn. Pharma Med press, Hyderabad, India

## References


- USP
- Semalty et al., Essentials of Pharmaceutical Technology, II Edn. Pharma Med press, Hyderabad, India, ISBN 9789386819994.

CHAPTER 33

# Pharmaceutical Aerosols III (Components and Systems of Aerosols)

**Dr Ajay Semalty**
Department of Pharmaceutical Sciences,
H.N.B Garhwal University (A Central University)
Srinagar Garhwal-246174

### Learning outcomes

After learning this chapter, you will be able to understand

- Know about the construction of aerosol
- Understand the different systems of aerosol and
- Discuss manufacturing of aerosols.

### Lesson Plan

- Valve and actuators
- Aerosol systems
- Different type of systems
- Manufacturing of aerosols

## Components of Aerosols

An aerosol system has following major components.

- Propellant
- Container
- Valve and actuator
- Product concentrate

So far, we have discussed the definition, advantages, disadvantages, types of aerosols, propellant (Heart of an aerosol package) and container (different types Al, SS, plastic, glass). Now, let's move to valve and actuator, and product concentrate.

## Valve

It is the vital component of an aerosol package. It helps to deliver the drug in desired form. It determines the performance of a pressurized package. Major functions of valves are as followed: (RPG)

- Regulating the flow of product out of the container
- Providing discharge of desired amount (when needed) and preventing loss when not in use.
- Governing the characteristics of dispensed product.

*Remember the function with acronym RPG.*

## Types of Valves

- **Continuous spray valve:** These valves release the product as long as pressure is maintained on the actuator. These are employed in high speed production technique.
- **Metering valves:** A finite volume (25 -150 μL for inhalation aerosols, up to 5 ml for topical aerosols) of product is released when the actuator is pressed. No more product is released unless the actuator is returned to its rest position and repressed. Dispersing of potent medication at proper dispersion can be done by these valves.

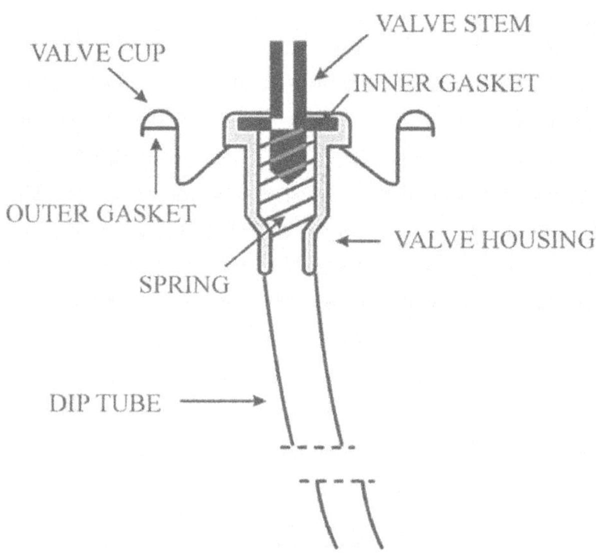


**Figure 33.1** Components of Valves.

(Adapted from Semalty et al. Essentials of Pharmaceutical Technology, II edn, 2018, Pharma med Press, Hyderabad)

## Components of Valves

Generally pharmaceutical aerosol valve comprises of following components (Figure 33.1).

## Valve Cup (Mounting Cup/ferulae)

It is used to attach the valve properly to the container. It is typically constructed from tinplated steel or aluminum.

## Outer Gasket

This is the seal between the valve cup and the aerosol can.

## Valve Housing (Valve body)

It is manufactured from nylon or delrin. It contains an opening at the point of the attachment of the dip tube (0.013 inch to 0.08 inch). Sometimes it may contain another opening called vapor tap. Vapor tap prevents clogging, helps in satisfactory dispensing, decreases the chilling effect (of propellant on skin) and flame extension. It contains the valve stem, spring and inner gasket.

### Valve Stem

It is the tap through which the product flows. It is made of nylon or delrin.

### Inner Gasket

It covers the hole in the valve stem. It is made of BUNA-N and neoprene rubber.

### Valve Spring

It holds the gasket in place and closes or opens the gasket. It is usually made of stainless steel.

### Dip Tube

It allows the liquid to enter the valve. It prevents propellants from escape without dispensing the contents. Its inner diameter is 0.120 inch to 0.125 inch, while it may be slightly large (upto 0.195 inch) for viscous products.

### Actuator

It provides rapid and convenient means for releasing the contents from a pressurized container. An actuator fits onto the valve stem (**Figure 33.2**). It ensures that aerosol product is delivered in the proper and desired form i.e. fine mist, wet spray or semisolid stream etc. Different types of actuators are available for different type of dispensing like Spray actuators, Foam actuators,

Solid steam actuators, Special actuators etc. Mechanical breakup actuators are used for systems with low percentage of propellant.

**Figure 33.2** Standard Actuator.

To summarize:

- Valve may me continuous / metering
- Valve cup, gasket, valve body, dip tube and actuator are the component s of valve body.
- Product concentrate is good mix of API with other ingredients

Now we will move to types of aerosol systems.

## Classification of Aerosol Systems

The aerosol systems can be classified on the basis of propellant or container and dosage form (**Figure 33.3**).

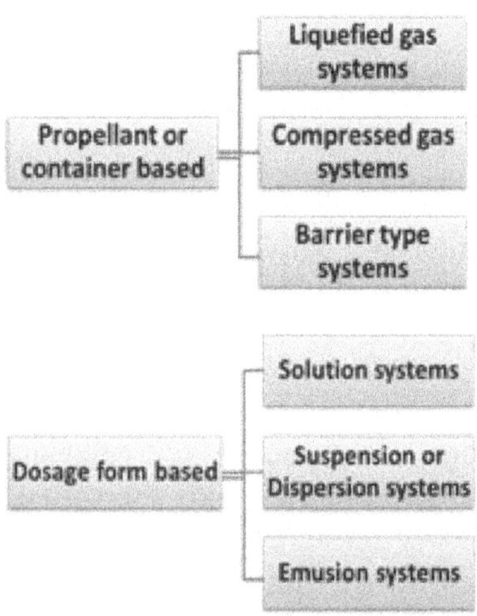


**Figure 33.3** Classification of Aerosol Systems.

## Liquefied Gas System

These systems employ liquefied gas propellants. The liquefied gas propellants generally have boiling point below 21 °C.

They generally exert a vapor pressure of 13.4 to 135 psia at 21 °C. In the system pressure on liquid phase push product concentrate and propellants up in dip tube and dispensed due to large expansion in atmospheric pressure.

Initially there is just a temporary fall in pressure, which is restored when pressure is released and sufficient molecules change from liquid to vapor state.

Further Liquefied gas systems may be classified in two and three phase systems (**Figure 33.4**).

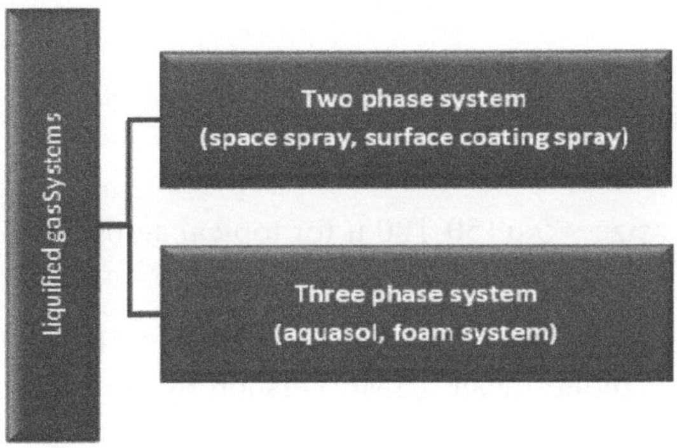


**Figure 33.4** Liquefied gas system.

## Two Phase System

### Solution System

Drug may be dissolved in the propellant system. It consists of a solution of active ingredients in pure propellant or a mixture of propellant and solvents.

It is easy to formulate, provided that the ingredients are soluble in the propellant. Smaller spray particle size can be achieved after complete propellant evaporation.

Chemical degradation may occur faster in solution systems. A general formula of solution system is as followed.

| **Ingredients** | **wt%** |
|---|---|
| Drug/active ingredient | 10-15 |
| Propellants 12/11 (50:50) to | 100 |

## Suspension/dispersion System

These systems can be used to deliver insoluble drugs. Higher doses can be delivered by suspension systems. Constant agitation during manufacturing and use is required for these systems.

But these systems may be associated with physical instability (due to agglomeration, caking, particle-size growth and valve clogging or closing).

A general formula of suspension system is as followed.

| **Ingredients** | **wt%** |
|---|---|
| Drug/active ingredient | 0.5 to 1 |
| Sorbiton trioleate (STO) | 0.5 |
| Propellants 12/114 (49.5:49.5) to | 100 |

**Improving** the stability of aerosol dispersions

- Lower the Moisture content (< 300 ppm)
- Use API's derivative
- Reduce particle size < 5 μ (50-100 μ for topical aerosols)
- Adjust density of propellants and /or suspenoid
- Use dispersing agent like surfactant with HLB < 10 *e.g.* Sorbiton trioleate (STO), Sorbiton mono-oleate (SMO), Isopropyl myristate (IPM), Minerol oil

Summarizing, so far

- The aerosols may be classified in different systems on the propellant/container based or dosage form based.
- Propellant/ container based are 3 systems: LG, CG and barrier type systems
- Dosage form based they may be solution suspension or emulsion type
- Liquefied gas systems may be 2 or 3 phase systems
- System stability must be focused for aerosol specially with suspension type systems.

Now let's move to 3 phase systems.

## Three Phase/water based System

It allows greater use of liquid components not miscible with the propellants. These include formation of three phases consisting of liquid propellant, vaporized propellant and aqueous solution of active ingredient.

As low percentage of propellants is used in these systems, special types of actuators (Mechanical breakup actuators) are needed.

A general formula of water-based systems or aquasol is as followed.

| **Ingredients** | **wt%** |
|---|---|
| Drug/active ingredient | 40-85 |
| Surfactant | 0.5-2 |
| Propellants to | 5-10 |

## Working of Aquasol

Vapor phase of propellants + Product → Mixing chamber in actuator through special ducts. Vaporized propellant enters moving at tremendous speed and product is forced to actuator by the pressure of propellants. So, the product and vaporized propellants get mixed and dispensed in spray form.

### Foam or Emulsion Systems

In these systems, propellants are emulsified. These are suitable for topical aerosols.

Propellants are used at 40-50 psig at 21 $^{0}$C with 4-7 % concentration.

Two types of emulsions can be formulated-o/w or w/o.

- If the propellant is in the internal phase → O/W emulsion → foam is emitted.
- If the product concentrate is dispersed throughout the propellant → W/O emulsion → the product is dispensed as wet stream

### Compressed Gas System

These are used to dispense semisolid, foam or spray discharge. An initial high pressure of 90-100 psig at 21 $^{0}$C is required for these systems (**Figure 33.5**).

## Barrier Type Systems

In these systems propellants are separated from the product with some physical barrier (**Figure 33.6**). The pressure outside the barrier pushes the contents from the container. On the basis of type of barrier these aerosol systems are classified as followed.

(i) **Piston type:** For semisolid dispensing, e.g. Ointment, cake decorating creams

**(ii) Plastic Bag type:** Provides stream, fine mist dispensing, e.g. Creams, ointment, gels.

**(iii) Can in Can type:** Nasal aerosols with aqueous solution of Insulin

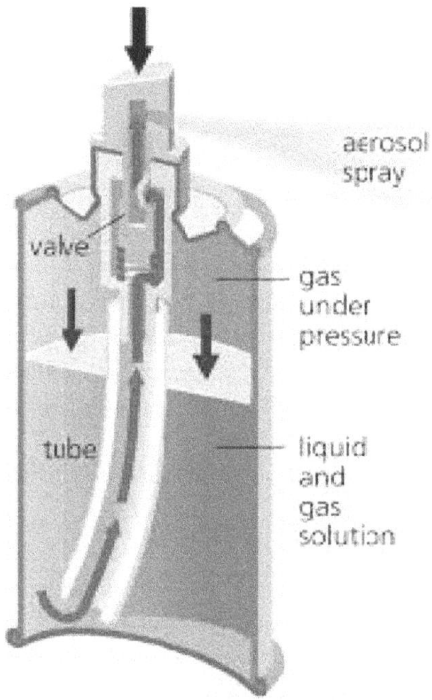


**Figure 33.5** Compressed gas aerosol: working.

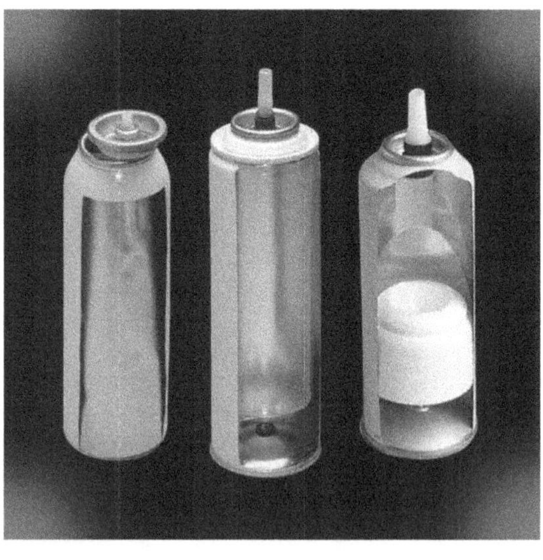

**Figure 33.6** Barrier type aerosols.

## Manufacturing of Aerosols

Aerosols are generally manufactured by following methods:

- Pressure filling
- Cold filling

## Pressure Filling (Figure 33.7)

- **Step 1:** Chilled product concentrate is added to an open container
- **Step 2:** Valve is crimped in place
- **Step 3:** Propellant is added under pressure through the valve
- **Step 4:** The filled pack is passed through the water path (for leak test)

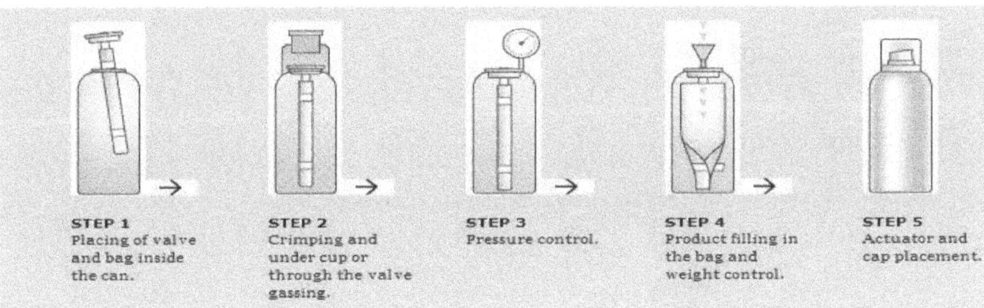


**Figure 33.7** Steps of pressure filling (Commercial manufacturing steps).

## Cold Filling

- **Step 1:** Product concentrate is cooled/freezed to -30 to -40 $^0$C
- **Step 2:** Cold concentrate is added to chilled container.
- **Step 3:** Propellant is added
- **Step 4:** Valve is crimped in place
- **Step 5:** The filled pack is passed through the water bath at 55 $^0$C (for leak test)

***Selection of Drug Particle Size with Reference to Pulmonary Delivery***

- *Administration of drugs by the pulmonary route is technically challenging because oral deposition can be high, and variations in inhalation technique can affect the quantity of drug delivered to the lungs.*
- *Therefore, there have been considerable efforts to provide more efficient and reproducible aerosol systems through improved drug delivery devices and through better formulations that disperse more readily during inhalation.*

- *The size of the suspended drug particles depends on the intended use of the product. Particle size plays an important role in lung deposition, along with particle velocity and settling time.*
- *As particle size increases above 3 μm, there is a shift in aerosol deposition from the periphery to the conducting airways. Oropharyngeal deposition also increases as particle sizes increase above 6 μm. Exhaled loss is high with very small particles of 1 μm or less. These data support the view that particle sizes of 1-5 μm are best for reaching the lung periphery, while 5-10 μm particles deposit preferentially in the conducting airways (Figure 33.8).*
- *Aerosol devices in clinical use produce heterodisperse (also termed polydisperse) particle sizes, meaning that there is a mix of sizes in the aerosol.*

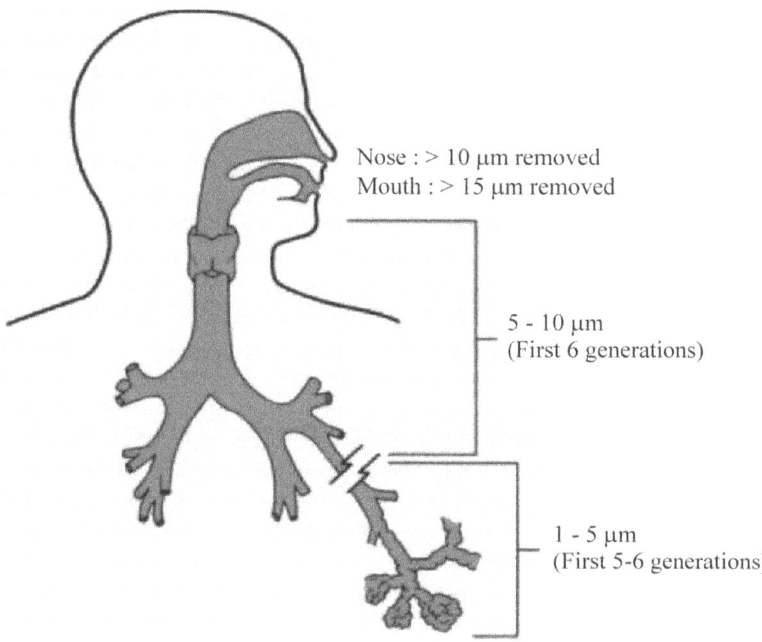


**Figure 33.8** A simplified view of the effect of aerosol particle size on the site of preferential deposition in the airways.(Adapted from Semalty et al. Essentials of Pharmaceutical Technology, II edn, 2018, Pharma med Press, Hyderabad).

- *This is contrasted with monodisperse aerosols, which consist of a single particle size. A measure that can be useful in describing a polydisperse aerosol is the mass median diameter (MMD), which is defined as the particle size (in μm) above and below which 50% of the mass of the particles is contained. This is the particle size that evenly divides the mass, or amount of the drug in the particle size distribution. This is usually given as the mass median aerodynamic diameter, or MMAD, due to the way sizes are measured. The higher the MMAD, the more particle sizes are of larger diameters and lesser is their respirable fraction.*

*So, for pulmonary delivery, the dry particles of drug in product concentrate of aerosol device must be prepared in respirable sizes. The production of respirable aerosol particles has traditionally been achieved by micronization of the drug. This involves the introduction of bulk particles on a gas stream under high pressure.*

*Particles impact on each other and are thereby ground into small particles, which ultimately pass through a cyclone separator and are collected in a vessel or a bag filter. These particles can be produced in size ranges less than 5 μm, which is suitable for lung deposition.*

*Nowadays spray drying is more popular for the production of more spherical particles. Spray drying is also more suitable method than jet milling for the production of thermolabile substances. The recently developed and more successful method for the production is the supercritical fluid technology. This technology involves controlled crystallization of drugs from dispersion in supercritical fluid, notably carbon dioxide.*

## Take Away Message

- Valve function: RPG
- The components of valve.
- The classification of aerosol systems: LG, CG and Barrier type
- LG: sub classified into 2 and 3 phase systems
- All aerosol systems need stability but suspensions type systems need utmost attention.
- Cold and pressure filling are two major methods of aerosol manufacturing.

## Further Readings


- "Industrial Pharmacy-I" SWAYAM MOOC: www.swayam.gov.in
- Banker & Rhodes, Modern Pharmaceutics, CRC Press.
- Aulton ME (ED), Pharmaceutics: The science of Dosage form design, II edn, Churchill Livingstone, London, 2002.

- Semalty et al., Essentials of Pharmaceutical Technology, II Edn. Pharma Med press, Hyderabad, India

## References


- Lachman L, Lieberman HA, Theory and Practice of Industrial Pharmacy, Varghese Publishing House, Bombay, India
- Semalty et al., Essentials of Pharmaceutical Technology, II Edn. Pharma Med press, Hyderabad, India, ISBN 9789386819994.

CHAPTER 34

# Pharmaceutical Aerosols IV (Inhalers and Evaluation of Aerosols)

**Dr Ajay Semalty**
Department of Pharmaceutical Sciences,
H.N.B Garhwal University (A Central University), Srinagar Garhwal-246174

**Learning Outcomes**

After learning this chapter, you will be able to

- Know about the most common type of aerosol inhalers
- Understand the evaluation of aerosol

**Lesson Plan**

- Type of aerosol inhalers
- Evaluation of Aerosol

## Types of Aerosol Inhalers

There are three common types of aerosol generators for inhaled drug delivery of drugs in treating pulmonary diseases.

- Metered dose inhalers (MDIs)
- Dry powder inhalers (DPIs)
- Small volume nebulizers (SVN)

### Metered Dose Inhalers (MDIs)

MDIs are one of the most polar inhalers with following properties (Figure 34.1).

- Canister, Metering valve /metering chamber & Expansion Chamber
- 25 μL to 100 μL of fixed volume range.
- The dose filled in metering chamber is delivered
- Inverted canister with the valve below it; this in turn assists gravitational refilling of valve
- These valves may differ in designs

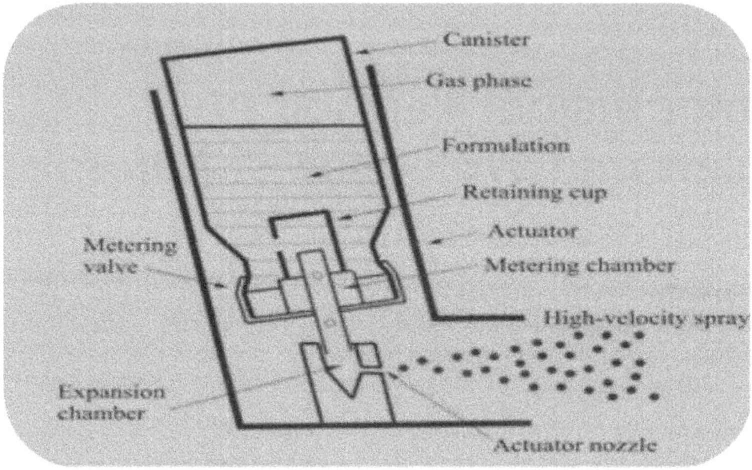


**Figure 34.1** Basic Components of MDIs(Adapted from Semalty et al. Essentials of Pharmaceutical Technology, II edn, 2018, Pharma med Press, Hyderabad).

**Metering valves** are the most critical component of MDIs. The metering valve crimped onto the container is the most critical component of the pMDI (pressurized metered-dose inhaler), and has a volume ranging from 25 μL to 100 μL. While there are many designs of metering valve, they all operate on the same basic principle. Before firing, a channel between the body of the container and the metering chamber is open, but as the pMDI is fired, this channel closes, and another channel connecting the metering chamber to the atmosphere opens. The pressurized formulation is expelled rapidly into the valve stem, which, together with the actuator seating, forms an expansion chamber in which the propellant begins to boil. The canister is used in the inverted position, with the valve below the container so that the valve will refill under gravity. Some valves are surrounded by a retaining cup that contains the next few doses of drug. Several other valve designs aimed at improving the precision of dosing have also been reported.

**Advantages of MDIs**

- Portable and compact
- Short treatment time
- Reproducible dose emitted

**Disadvantages of MDIs**

- Hand–breathing coordination is difficult for many patients
- Proper inhalation pattern (slow inspiration to total lung capacity) and breath-hold can be difficult

- Canister depletion is difficult to determine (no dose counter)
- High oropharyngeal impaction unless a holding chamber or spacer is used
- Failure to shake can alter drug dose
- Fixed drug concentrations
- Reaction to propellants or excipients have occurred in some patients
- Foreign body aspiration from debris-filled mouthpiece
- Limited range of drugs

## Small Volume Nebulizers (SVN)

"the devices which deliver solution and suspension in the aerosol form capable to be inhaled into Lower Respiratory Tract (LRT)"

Three types of SVN

- Pneumatic jet nebulizers
- Ultrasonic nebulizers
- Mesh nebulizers

## Pneumatic Jet Nebulizers

Pneumatic means liquid based, Jet: pressurized air flow. These are the oldest form of aerosol generator, and their basic design and performance have changed little in the past 30 years (Figure 34.2).

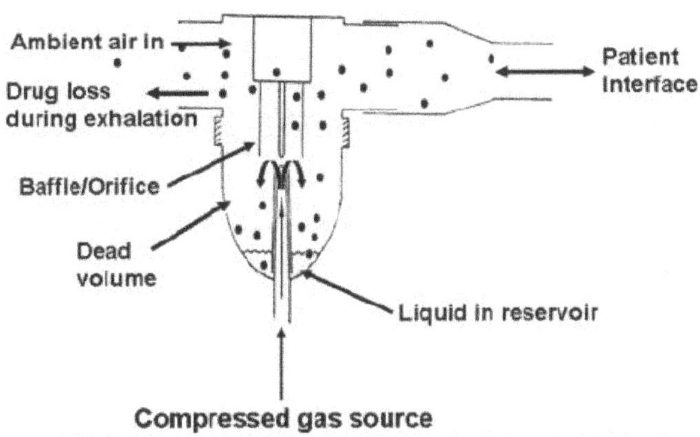


**Figure 34.2** SVN: Pneumatic Jet Nebulizer(Adapted from Semalty et al. Essentials of Pharmaceutical Technology, II edn, 2018, Pharma med Press, Hyderabad).

A pneumatic nebulizer delivers compressed gas through a jet, causing a region of negative pressure (Figure 34.3). The solution to be aerosolized is entrained into the gas stream and is sheared into a liquid film. This film is unstable and breaks into droplets due to surface tension forces. A baffle in the aerosol stream produces smaller particles.

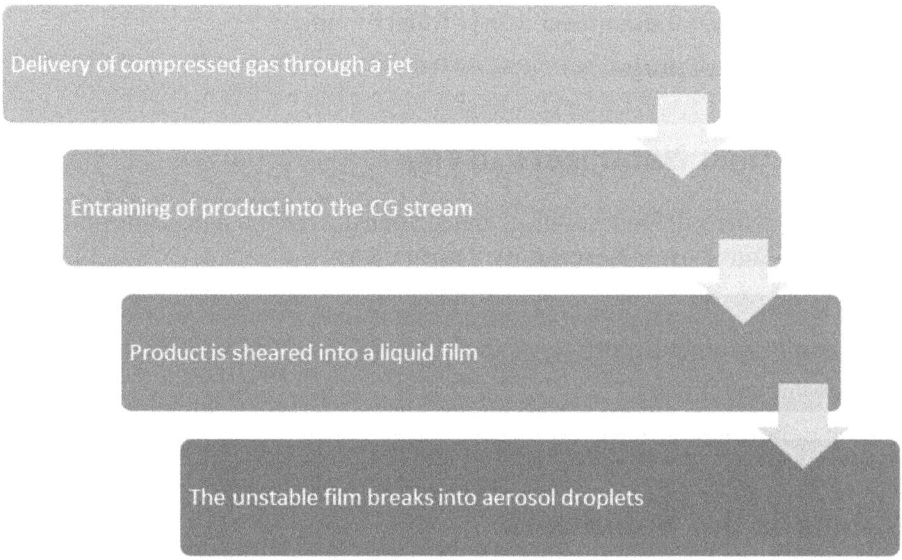


**Figure 34.3** Working of Pneumatic Jet Nebulizer.

## Ultrasonic Nebulizers

In ultrasonic nebulizers, electricity is used to generate ultrasonic waves and it convert a liquid into aerosols which can respired/inhaled.

The transducer vibrates at the frequency of the ultrasonic waves applied to it (piezoelectric effect). Ultrasonic waves are transmitted to the surface of the solution to create an aerosol (Figure 34.4).

Small volume ultrasonic nebulizers are commercially available for delivery of inhaled bronchodilators. A potential issue with the use of ultrasonic nebulizers is the possibility for drug inactivation by the ultrasonic waves, although this has not been shown to occur with common aerosol medications. Use of these devices has been hampered by their tendency for mechanical malfunction.

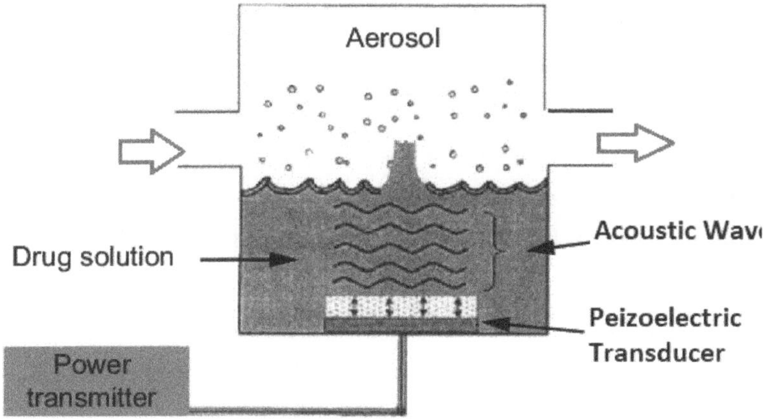


**Figure 34.4** Working of Ultrasonic Nebulizer.

## Mesh Nebulizers

It involves use of a mesh or plate with multiple apertures to produce a liquid aerosol. This operating principle uses an aperture plate attached to a piezoelectric material that vibrates at high frequency. The rapid vibration of the aperture plate creates a pumping action to produce the aerosol from a liquid solution (Figure 34.5).

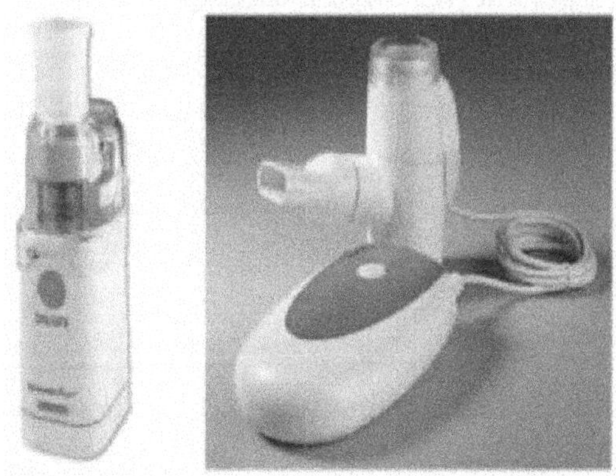

**Figure 34.5** Mesh Nebulizer.

Alternatively, the solution can be forced through the mesh to create the aerosol. These devices are able to generate aerosols with a high fine-particle fraction, which results in more efficient drug delivery compared to conventional nebulizers.

**Advantages of SVNs**

- Ability to aerosolize many drug solutions
- Ability to aerosolize drug mixtures (>1 drug), if drugs are compatible
- Normal breathing patterns can be used
- Useful in very young, very old, debilitated, or distressed patients
- An inspiratory pause (breath-hold) is not required for efficacy
- Drug concentrations can be modified

**Disadvantages of SVNs**

- Treatment times are lengthy for pneumatically-powered nebulizers
- Equipment required may be large and cumbersome
- Need for power source (electricity, battery, compressed gas)
- Variability in performance characteristics among different brands
- Possible contamination with inadequate cleaning Wet, cold spray with facemask delivery Potential for drug delivery into the eyes with facemask delivery

## Dry Powder Inhalers (DPIs)

DPIs are very common in anti-asthmatic drug delivery.

- Small portable, propellant free, breath-actuated inhalers (Figure 34.6).

**Figure 34.6** Common Dry Powder Inhaler (DPI).

- Post Montreal Protocol inhalers
- Inhalers developed for phase-out of ozone-destroying CFC propellants in MDIs.
- Various commercial respiratory sprays of insulin have also been approved by USFDA.
- E.g. EXUBERA®, AIRx® etc.

[Can you search some more such examples of Insulin or anyother protein delivery by inhaler/sprays with the link where it is mentioned?]

**Advantages of DPIs**

- Small and portable
- Built-in dose counter
- Propellant-free
- Breath-actuated
- Short preparation and administration time

**Disadvantages of DPIs**

- Dependence on patient's inspiratory flow
- Patients less aware of delivered dose
- Relatively high oropharyngeal impaction can occur
- Vulnerable to ambient humidity or exhaled humidity into mouthpiece
- Limited range of drugs

## Let's Summarize

- Most common inhalers : MDI, SVN and DPI
- MDI: Inverted Canister, Metering valve /metering chamber & Expansion Chamber
- SVN: Pneumatic, Ultrasonic and Mesh nebulizers
- DPI: Portable, Propellant free breath actuated inhalers.

Now let's move to evaluation of aerosols

## Evaluation of Aerosols

- Flammability and combustibility
- Physiochemical characteristics
- Performance
- Therapeutic activity

## Flammability and combustibility

It consist of two types of tests.

- Flame Projection
- Flash Point

## Flame Projection

In this test effect of an aerosol on the extension of an open flame after exposure of spray for 4 sec in flame is recorded.

## Flash Point

The test is done in Tag Open Cap Apparatus (Figure 34.7)

- Chilled Aerosol (–25° F) transferred to the test apparatus
- Slow increment of temperature is done
- Vapor ignition temperature is noted as flash point

**Figure 34.7** Tag Open Cap Apparatus.

## Physiochemical Characteristics

Physiochemical characteristics are evaluated as followed.

- Vapor pressure - Determined by pressure gauge.
- Density - Determined by hydrometer or a pycnometer.
- Moisture content - By Karl Fischer method
- Identification of propellants - By I.R spectrophotometry

## Performance Test

- Aerosol valve discharge rate/Delivery Rate
- Delivered-Dose uniformity
- Net contents/ Minimum fill
- Leakage
- Particle size distribution

## Aerosol Valve Discharge Rate/Delivery Rate (USP)

Select not fewer than four aerosol containers, shake, if the label includes this directive, remove the caps and covers, and actuate each valve for 2 to 3 seconds. Weigh each container accurately, and immerse in a constant-temperature bath until the internal pressure is equilibrated at a temperature of 25 as determined by constancy of internal pressure, as directed under the Pressure Test below. Remove the containers from the bath, remove excess moisture by blotting with a paper towel, shake, if the label includes this directive, actuate each valve for 5.0 seconds (accurately timed by use of a stopwatch), and weigh each container again. Return the containers to the constant-temperature bath, and repeat the foregoing procedure three times for each container. Calculate the average Delivery Rate, in g per second, for each container.

- *Delivered-Dose uniformity:*
    - To determine amount of medication actually received by the patient evaluation of dose uniformity is done.
    - The method involves accurate weighing of filled container followed by dispersing of several doses
    - Container can is reweighed
    - Difference in weight divided by No. of dose, gives the average dosage.

## Acceptance Criteria: Nasal Spray USP

"not more than 2 of the 20 doses are outside the range of 80% to 120% of label claim, and none are outside the range of 75% to 125% of label claim, while the mean for each of the beginning and end doses falls within the range of 85% to 115% of label claim. If 3–6 doses of the 20 doses collected are outside of 80% to 120% of the label claim, but none are outside of 75% to 125% of label claim, and the means for each of the beginning and end doses fall within 85% to 115% of label claim, select 20 additional containers for second-tier testing."

### II Tier testing

- For second-tier testing, the requirements are met if not more than 6 of the 60 doses collected are outside the range of 80% to 120% of label claim, none are outside the range of 75% to 125% of label claim, and the means for each of the beginning and end doses fall within the range of 85% to 115% of label claim."

## Delivered-Dose Uniformity for MDIs and DPIs

"Unless otherwise specified in the individual monograph, the requirements for dosage uniformity are met **if not less than 9 of the 10 doses are between 75% and 125%** of the specified target-delivered dose and **none is outside the range of 65% to 135%** of the specified target-delivered dose."

### General Sampling Procedure USP

- Use mechanical means of actuating to deliver doses for collection
- Actuation force, actuation speed, stroke length, rest periods like parameters must be controlled.
- The test must be performed on units that have been primed according to the patient-use instructions.
- For suspension products, the delivered dose should be delivered into scintillation vial.

### Net Content// Minimum fill

- Weight filled full container after removing labels and cleansing outer surface (n=10)
- Remove all the contents, heat them at 100 °C for 5 minutes then reweigh all the containers individually
- The difference in weight, will be the net fill weight

### Acceptance Criteria (USP)

"The requirements are met if the net weight of the contents of each of the 10 containers is not less than the labeled amount."

## Particle Size Distribution

- Particle size is generally evaluated by using Cascade Impactor
- In this apparatus, particles are carried in a stream of air through a series of consecutively smaller jet openings
- The heavier and larger diameter particles are impacted on a slide under the larger opening
- As the openings get smaller, the velocity of the stream increases and the next larger particles are deposited on the next slides.

## Therapeutic Activity

- By standard *in vivo* tests and pharmacological models
- For assessing inhalers, specially designed insufflators are used to deliver powders or solutions to test animals
- Gamma scintigraphic and single positron emission computer aided tomography imaging techniques are used
- For topical sprays normally applied on test animals.

## Take Away Message

- Inhalers may be MDI, SVN, and DPI.
- Aerosols may be evaluated for Flammability and combustibility, Physiochemical characteristics, Performance and Therapeutic activity.

## Further Readings

- "Industrial Pharmacy-I" SWAYAM MOOC: www.swayam.gov.in
- Banker & Rhodes, Modern Pharmaceutics, CRC Press.
- Aulton ME (ED), Pharmaceutics: The science of Dosage form design, II edn, Churchill Livingstone, London, 2002.
- Semalty et al., Essentials of Pharmaceutical Technology, II Edn. Pharma Med press, Hyderabad, India

## References


- USP
- Lachman L, Lieberman HA, Theory and Practice of Industrial Pharmacy, Varghese Publishing House, Bombay, India
- Semalty et al., Essentials of Pharmaceutical Technology, II Edn. Pharma Med press, Hyderabad, India, ISBN 9789386819994.

CHAPTER 35

# Cosmetics I (Introduction)

**Dr Mona Semalty**
Department of Pharmaceutical Sciences,
H.N.B Garhwal University (A Central University), Srinagar Garhwal-246174

**Learning Outcome**

- What are cosmetics
- What are different types of cosmetics
- Permeation through skin- different mechanism of skin permeation
- Skin care products
- Cold cream /vanishing cream

**Lesson Plan**

- Introduction to cosmetics
- Structure of skin and absorption through skin
- Classification of cosmetics
- Skin care products –creams

## Introduction

It means any articles intended to be rubbed, poured, sprinkled, or sprayed on or introduced in to or applied to any part of the human body, for cleaning, beautifying, promoting- attractiveness or altering the appearance & includes any articles intended for use as a component of cosmetics.

Cosmetic product" can be defined as "any substance or preparation intended to be put in contact with the different superficial parts of the human body (epidermis, head and body hair, nails, lips and external genital organs), or with the teeth and the mucous membrane of the mouth in order to exclusively or generally clean, perfume, modify their appearance and/or correct body odors, and/or protect or keep them in good condition“.

(Article 2 of the European regulation n°1223/2009 of November 30th 2009 concerning cosmetic products.)

## Classification of Cosmetics

1. Cosmetics as per its use-
   - SKIN- Creams, Powders, lotions

- NAIL- Nail polish
- TEETH-Dentifrices (Tooth paste)
- EYE- Eye creams, Eye lotion, Eye liner
- HAIR-Shampoo, Hair remover

2. Cosmetics as per their function.
   - CURATIVE - e.g. Antiperspirant.
   - PROTECTIVE- e.g. Face powder.
   - CORRECTIVE - e.g. Face powder.
   - DECORATIVE - e.g. Lipsticks,Nail polish.
3. Cosmetics as per their physical nature
   - AEROSOLS- Hair perfumes
   - CAKES - Makeup compact powder
   - EMULSION - Cold & Vanishing creams.
   - PASTE- Tooth paste.
   - POWDER -Face & Tooth powder.
   - SOLUTION- Aftershave & hand Lotion.
   - OILS - Hair oils.
   - STICKS- lipsticks
4. Other way of classifying cosmetics
   - Herbal Cosmetics –Herbal oils, creams, shampoo
   - Medicated Cosmetics-toothpaste for sensitive
   - General general purpose

## Structure of Skin

The skin of an average adult body covers a surface area of approximately 2 sq.m. and receives about one third of the blood circulating through the body. Human skin serves as a permeability barrier against the transdermal absorption of various chemical and biological agents.

The skin has a wide variety of functions:

- Protect the organism from water loss and
- Protects from mechanical, chemical, microbial, and physical influences

Skin consist of three layers (Figure 35.1)

- Epidermis

- Dermis
- Subcutaneous fat tissues (hypodermis)

The main route for the penetration of the drugs is generally through epidermal layer. Stratum corneum is the rate limiting barrier in passive percutaneous absorption of drug.

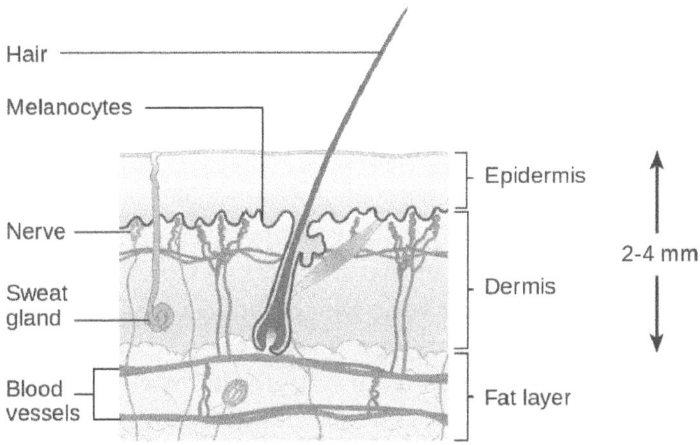


**Figure 35.1** Structure of Skin.

## Epidermis

The epidermis is the outermost layer of the skin 0.02 to 5 mm thickness Consist of several zones

- Basal layer (Stratum basale)
- Spinous layer (Stratum spinosum)
- Granular layer (Stratum granulosum)
- Cornified layer (Stratum corneum)

## Dermis

The thick sensitive layer of skin or connective tissue beneath the epidermis

**Collagen**

- Elastin
- Papillary Layer
- Reticular Layer

Dermis gives elasticity and tensile strength to epidermis of the skin. It offers a wide variety of functions including protection from mechanical injury, water retention, thermal regulation and sensation. Dermis with the help epidermal layer maintains the properties of both tissues. It also helps in repairing and remodeling of the skin after wound healing.

## Hypodermis

It is lowermost fatty layer of skin that develops from lipocytes as lobules. Hypodermis contains collagen, elastic fibers, large blood vessels, lymphatic vessels, hair follicle roots. It varies in thickness and acts as storehouse of energy. It helps to insulate body in low temperature environment. it is also considered as an endocrine organ because lipocytes produce leptin hormone that acts as messenger to regulate body weight through hypothalamus.

### Routes of Skin Penetration

Diffusional routes to penetrate intact skin are-

**The Trans-appendageal route**

- Hair follicles and sebaceous glands
- Sweat glands

**Transepidermal transport (molecules cross the intact horny layer).**

- The transcellular (or intracellular) route
- The intercellular pathways

The Trans-appendageal route is high permeability; they are of less importance because of their relatively small area 0.1% of the total skin. The skin behaves as a passive barrier to diffusing molecules. Penetrations of molecules through various regions of skin depend on the type and nature of components. The Trans-appendageal route is suitable for absorption of ions and large polar molecules. Hydrophilic drugs partition into the intracellular pathways, whereas lipophilic drugs traverse the stratum corneum via the intercellular route into the dermis via into blood stream.

Mechanisms of action by which materials enhance absorption through stratum corneum is either by enhancing drug release from the formulation to the skin and reduction of the resistance of the stratum corneum by altering it physicochemical properties.

This can be achieved by:

- Altering the hydration of the stratum corneum using occlusive formulations
- Transporting ionizable drug through carrier mechanism
- Directly influencing the stratum corneum(chemical/physical mean)

Chemicals interact with the keratin structure in the stratum corneum and open the tight protein structure, this leads to increase the diffusion coefficient D for substances which uses the transcellular route. Ex. Surfactants, Dimethylsulfoxide (DMSO) ,Urea and Ethanol. Chemical enhancer which inters into the structured lipids of the horny layer and disrupt the packing and makes the regular structure more fluid and increases the diffusion coefficient of drugs .Example -Azone, Oleic acid, isopropyl myristate, alcohol, acetone, polyethylene and propylene glycol.

## Skin Care Cosmetics

Skin care products are used to improve the appearance and health of skin. They are formulated for different types of skin and associated characteristics. Skin care products include creams, cleansers, facial masks, toners, moisturizers, sunscreen, tanning oils and lotions, skin lighteners, and anti-aging creams.

The skin care creams can be classified on the following basis:-

- According to emulsion type:
  - W/O creams -Cold cream
  - O/W creams -Vanishing cream.
- According to function: Cleansing, foundation, moisturizing etc.

## Cold Creams

Cold cream is water in oil type of emulsion. Cold cream has emollient action and prevents dehydration of skin. Cold cream is called cold cream because breaking up of emulsion on application to skin leads to evaporation of water giving cooling effect which is produced from slow evaporation of the water contained in the emulsion.

Cold cream was traditionally based on a mixture of natural waxes and vegetable oils (beeswax and olive oil) stabilized with borax. Earlier mineral oil was used as a base but it is replaced by the more unstable vegetable oils. Replacement of part of the mineral oil with up to 15% of petroleum jelly can be used to produce different textures and consistencies. Further substitution with fatty acid esters such as isopropyl myristate improves the thixotropic behaviour of the cream, thus improving its spreading properties.

## Purpose of Cold Cream

- To protect skin from dehydration
- Prevents the roughness and maintains smoothness due to its emollient property.
- Protects skin from rupture or crack formation.
- Oil phase of cream gives emolliency to the skin.
- Gives elegancy to the skin.

## Ideal characteristics of Cold Cream

- Should have optimum pH (4.6-6).
- Consistency should be optimum
- Should not be sticky
- Should be attractive in appearance
- Penetration through epidermis of skin should be desirable.
- Must be non-irritant and non-inflammatory.
- Should give cooling effects.

**Ingredients used for preparation of cold cream**

- Mineral oil ( liquid paraffin )
- White beeswax : Thickening agent and emulsifier (Base for the cream)
- Borax: Used as emulsifier and responsible for the whiteness of cold cream.
- Alcohol, glycerin, and lanolin
- Perfume: Provides Fragrance

## Special Ingredients

Alpha hydroxyl acids (Lactic Acid). These help in removing-

- Fine lines
- Irregular pigmentation
- Age spots

**Side Effects:** Mild irritation and sun sensitivity.

## Beta Hydroxy Acids (salicylic acid)

- Remove dead skin cells and improve texture.
- Helps with removing acne.

## Hydroquinone

- Used in lightening dark spots and age spots
- Hence are also called bleaching or lightening agents.

### Retinol

- Helps improve skin texture and tone
- Removes fine lines and wrinkles
- It is also one of the best anti-ageing mineral.

## Kojic Acid

Is a chelating agent produced by several species of fungi, especially Aspergillus oryzae. It slows the production of melanin (brown pigment) and works similarly to hydroquinone.

## Hyaluronic Acid

Hyaluronic acid is often touted for its ability to "reverse" or stop ageing. It is found naturally in young skin and gets destroyed by age. Products with hyaluronic acid are most often used for wrinkle treatment.

### Copper Peptide

Copper peptides promote the synthesis of hyaluronic acid. Studies also show that copper dependent enzymes benefit natural tissue building processes.

### L-Ascorbic Acid

It is one of the forms of vitamin-c. With age and sun exposure collagen synthesis in skin decreases leading to wrinkles. It is the only antioxidant proven to stimulate collagen synthesis minimizing lines, scars and wrinkles.

## Cold Cream

Type of Emulsion - Water in Oil

Beeswax acts as base for the cream. Borax is used as a preservative.

- White beeswax-20g

- Mineral oil-50g
- Water-28.8g
- Borax-0.7g
- Perfume-0.5g

### Procedure

- Heat the mineral oil and beeswax in a jacketed vessel at 75°C and maintain heat.
- In another container, dissolve borax and preservative in water and heat to 75°C (Aqueous phase).
- Slowly add this aqueous phase to the mineral oil-beeswax heated oily phase.
- Cool to 35°C and add perfume.

## Vanishing Cream

Vanishing cream is oil in water emulsions that contains large percentages of water and stearic acid or other oleaginous components. After application, the continuous phase evaporates, leaving behind a thin residue film of the stearic acid.

Ideal properties of vanishing cream

- High melting point
- Pure whiteness
- Very little odor and low iodine number
- Rubbed easily on the skin

## Major Ingredients

### Stearic Acid

- Major component of vanishing cream and it governs the consistency of the cream
- Soap formed in-situ by the reaction between a suitable alkali and stearic acid determines hardness of the cream.

### Humectants

It is added to prevent excessive drying out of cream

- Glycerol most favored followed by sorbitol and propylene glycol

## Alkali

Potassium hydroxide, sodium hydroxide, sodium carbonate, triethanolamine and borax are few examples of alkali used in vanishing cream. Potassium hydroxide is mostly used since makes a cream of fine texture without excessive harshness. Sodium or potassium hydroxide when used alone forms hard cream hence used always in combination. Borax used in combination with potassium hydroxide or triethanolamine to form white emulsion.

### Procedure

Dissolve the sodium hydroxide and potassium hydroxide in water, add glycerol and preservative and heat to 80°C.In another vessel, melt the stearic acid, cetyl alcohol and isopropyl myristate (oily phase) and heat to 75°C.Add the alkali solution to the melted oily phase with good agitation.

- The polyol (glycerol) prevents loss of moisture.
- Sodium stearate crystals give pearly shine.

When the mixture is cooled to about 45°C, add the perfume and continue slow mixing until cool. Cover and let it stand overnight. Remix briefly next day before pack.

## Further Readings


- "Industrial Pharmacy-I" SWAYAM MOOC: www.swayam.gov.in
- Semalty M, Lectures on Cosmetics: http://tiny.cc/SEMALTYCOSMETICS
- http://cnx.org/contents/14fb4ad7-39a1-4eee-ab6e-3ef2482e3e22@11.1
- https://link.springer.com/content/pdf/bfm%3A978-4-431-54061-8%2F1.pdf
- Schneider, Günther et al (2005). "Skin Cosmetics" in Ullmann's Encyclopedia of Industrial Chemistry, Wiley-VCH, Weinheim. doi:10.1002/14356007.a24_219


## References


- Shah R.N, Mithal B.M, A, Handbook of Cosmetic Page No.1.005; 10(3): 194-7.

- Thomssen, B. S. (1947). *Modern cosmetics* (3rd ed.). New York: Drug & Cosmetic Industry.
- COSMETICS : Formulation, manufacturing and Quality Control Fifth Ed., 2014 by P.P. Sharma
- Administration, Australian Government Department of Health. Therapeutic Goods (2017-01-11). "Literature review on the safety of titanium dioxide and zinc oxide nanoparticles in sunscreens". Therapeutic Goods Administration (TGA). Retrieved 2018-07-17.

CHAPTER 36

# Cosmetics II (Sunscreen Preparations and Dentifrices)

**Dr Mona Semalty**
Department of Pharmaceutical Sciences,
H.N.B Garhwal University (A Central University), Srinagar Garhwal-246174

### Learning Outcome

- What are the Requirements of sunscreen products?
- Different types of sunscreens agents
- SPF
- What are dental preparations?
- Requirements of dental products
- Formulation of dental products

### Lesson Plan

- Sunscreen products
- Ideal properties of sunscreen
- Types of sunscreen agents
- SPF how to calculate SPF Factor affecting SPF
- Dentifrices
- ideal properties/advantages and disadvantages
- Formulation of dentifrices
- Evaluation of the same

## Sunscreen Preparations

These preparations help to protect the skin from the harmful effects of UV rays (**Figure 36.1**). In cream, lotion and spray under various brand names. Applied to the face, neck and ears prior to going out in sun.

### Ideal Properties of Sunscreens

- Absorb or filter out UV rays in the region of 2900 to 3300 angstroms.
- Have good absorption and spreadability
- Be stable nontoxic and nonirritating
- Be free from any side effect.
- Have low water solubility

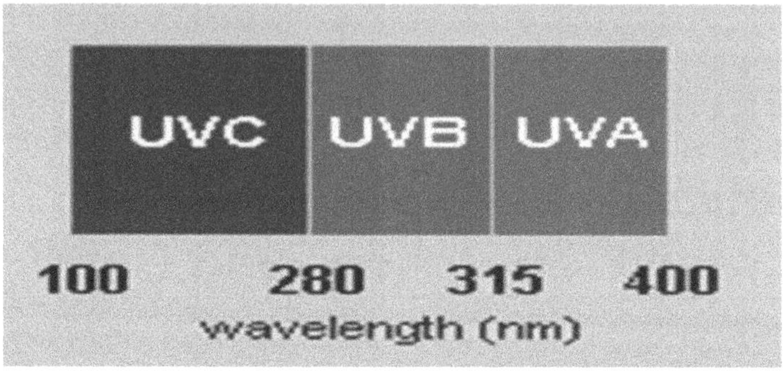


**Figure 36.1** Types of UV rays.

### Organic Sunscreen Agents

It reflect UV light absorption and blocks the penetration of UV radiations through the epidermise.g.Para-amino benzoic acid (PABA), PABA esters, benzophenones, salicylates, cinnamates, butyl-methoxy-dibenzoyl-methane, anisotriazine.

## Physical Sunscreen Agents

Most common photostable component of routine sun screen products. Protect the skin by reflecting and scattering UV rays. E .g.: Titanium dioxide (Ti02) and zinc oxide (ZnO).

Sun Protection Factor

(SPF) = MED of Photoprotected Skin /MED of Unprotected Skin

MED is minimum dose of radiation which produces erythema; Determined indoors using xenon lamps which approximate the spectral quality of UV radiation.

Ideal sunscreen should have SPF value of 15 atleast.

### Factors Affecting Effectiveness of SPFs

- Difference in skin types.
- Thickness of the applied sunscreen.
- Time of day.
- Altitude: each 1,000 ft increase adds 4% to the intensity of erythema producing UV radiation.

- Environment: snow/white surfaces reflect 70-90%, and when directly overhead water reflects nearly 100% of UVR.
- Vehicle: determines skin penetration of sunscreen.

### Evaluation of Sunscreen

- Photostability
- Water Resistance
- Other Evaluation parameters

## Dentifrices (Dental Products)

- Oral health care products which are used for Improving and maintaining oral hygiene.
- Dentifrices carry an inert and bioactive substance that helps in maintaining oral hygiene and provides cosmetic and therapeutic benefits.

### Classification of Dentifrices

- Regular cleansing dentifrices
- Medicated (therapeutic) dentifrices.

### Regular Dentifrices

- Used for cleaning and polishing the surfaces of teeth from for maintaining good oral hygiene.
- Help inhibit the formation of unpleasant odors and freshen the breath.
- Medicated dentifrices these are cleansing preparations for preventing tooth decay (cavities) and/ or other periodontal disease.
- Additional medicaments such as bactericidal, bacteriostatic, enzyme inhibiting and acid neutralizing agents.

## Anatomy of Teeth

The different parts of a tooth are shown in **Figure 36.2** and described hereunder:

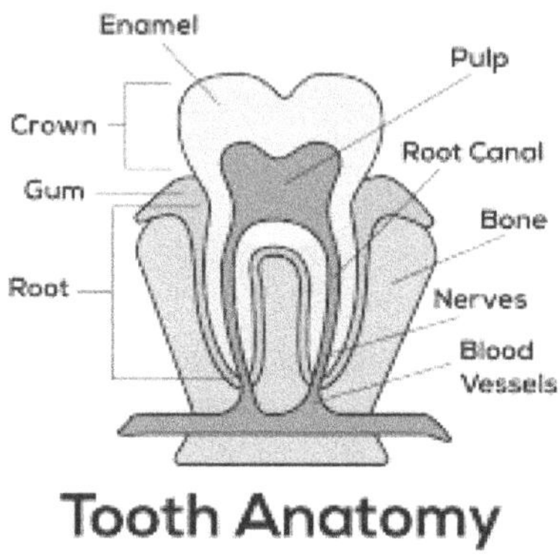


**Figure 36.2** Anatomy of tooth.

## Structures around the Tooth

- Periodontal ligament
- Oral Mucosa
- Gums
- Bone
- Nerves and blood supply

**Periodontal ligament:** Basically, these are fibers which lead the tooth to the jawbone and act as shock absorbers for the tooth which is subjected to heavy forces during chewing. Oral Mucosa: This is the term used to describe the moist tissue that lines the mouth. Gums: These are the soft tissues surrounds the teeth and bone. It gives protection to the bone and the roots of the teeth Bone. It provide a socket to surround and support the roots of the teeth. Nerves and blood supply and blood supply is necessary to maintain the vitality of the tooth. Each tooth and periodontal ligament have a nerve supply teeth are sensitive to a wide variety of stimuli.

## Toothpaste

Most popular and widely used preparations for cleansing the teeth and possess largest market share amongst all dentifrices. Though they are more expensive than tooth powders.

## Properties of Toothpaste

- Attractive consistency.
- Better coverage of dental set up.

- Easy to take measured quantity on the tooth brush.
- No spillage and wastage.

**Advantages**

Delivers active ingredients such as fluoride or xylitol to help prevent tooth and gum disease.

Recent advances in toothpaste enable high efficacy of oral health delivery. Special toothpaste for kids with fluoride and relatively low abrasion value Desensitizing toothpaste. Whitening toothpaste

'Easy to use, available in collapsible tubes. Combination of various contents available as to combat different oral healthcare needs at once.

Fluoridated toothpaste can cause fluorosis if swallowed consistently. Triclosan, an active ingredient in many types of toothpaste can combine with chlorine in tap water to form chloroform which is a human carcinogen. According to some scientists it can leave unborn babies brain damaged. Although in several studies whitening toothpaste show the ability to improve tooth color they have side effects. The most significant one is enamel and dentin abrasion which in turn leads to increased tooth sensitivity.

**The ideal Characteristics of Toothpaste**

- It should be non-toxic and non-irritant to teeth, gums and buccal mucosa.
- Very fine particle size and should be free from grittiness.
- Must clean the dental surface properly without any scratches.
- It should be easily squeezed out to spread on the brush without sinking into it.
- The consistency should be uniform
- It should not dry quickly.
- It should not interact with the container parts.

## Formulation of Toothpaste

The raw materials used for manufacture of toothpaste can be classified as

**I Basic ingredients**

- Abrasives
- Detergents
- Humectants
- Binding agents

- Sweetening Agents
- Flavors
- Preservatives

**II Special ingredients**

- Coloring agents
- Bleaching agents
- Lubricants
- Therapeutic ingredients

## Abrasives

They also help in removing some stains from the teeth. Usually, the amount of abrasive(s) is about half of total weight of a toothpaste. Commonly used abrasives are calcium carbonate, tricalcium phosphate, dicalcium phosphate, aluminium sulphate, magnesium trisilicate etc. Transparent toothpastes, commonly called gel toothpastes, are prepared by mixing certain abrasives.

## Detergents (1-3 %)

Cleansing action of the detergents (surfactants) is due to their lowering of interfacial tension and production of foam thus helping in wetting and dispersion of powdered materials in the paste. Detergent helps in penetration tooth paste into the fine cracks and other places thus assisting in removal of food particles and debris. By their emulsification capability they help in removal of mucus.

Synthetic detergents are widely used surfactants in toothpastes. Sodium lauryl sulfate is one of the most commonly used detergents. Others are magnesium lauryl sulfate, sodium lauryl sarcosinate, diethyl sodium lauryl sarcosinate. Detergents may lower the abrasive effect of toothpastes.

## Humectants (20% to 35%)

Retain moisture and prevent drying out of the toothpaste and thus impart plasticity to the product. They prevent loss of water, and subsequent hardening of the paste, when it is exposed to air. Less amount of humectant is used in substances with lower specific gravity. Commonly used humectants in toothpaste are glycerin, sorbitol and propylene glycol. Of these, glycerin is most widely used. It also imparts some sweetness.

## Binding Agents

Binding agents are used in toothpaste to control viscosity and maintain creamy consistency. They also prevent separation of toothpaste. Hydrocolloids are used for this purpose usually in concentration of 1-2%. Earlier starch, liquid glucose and simple syrup were used; now they are replaced by mucilages of karaya gum, tragacanth and gum arabic.

## Sweetening Agents (0.05-2%)

These agents are used to improve the taste of the preparation in the mouth. Saccharine sodium is the most commonly used sweetener. The exact amount is determined by the quantity and sweetness of other ingredients present like glycerin.

## Flavors

Flavoring agents are essentially used in toothpaste for fragrance and good feel after its use .Flavors are blending of volatile oils which produce a pleasant and refreshing smell in the mouth after use. Peppermint oil, spearmint oil clove oil cassia oil, cinnamon oil, menthol etc

## Preservatives

Preservatives are essentially added in toothpaste to prevent microbial growth due to presence of gum and water. Sweetening agents like glycerin and flavors may add to antimicrobial action of the preservatives. Commonly used preservatives in toothpaste are methyl para hydroxybenzoate (0.15%) and propyl para hydroxybenzoate (0.02%).

Specialized ingredients used in toothpaste

**Anti-cavity Agents-Prevents formation of cavity**

- Sodium Monofluorophosphate ($Na_2PO_3F$)
- Sodium Fluoride (NaF)
- Organo (amine) Fluorides
- Stannous Fluoride ($SnF_2$)

## Anti-tartar Toothpastes

Dental plaque leads to tartar built-up (it is yellow or brown colored deposit when plaque hardens on your teeth.

- Tetra sodium pyrophosphate (TSPP)
- Tetra potassium pyrophosphate (TKPP)
- Disodium dihydrogen pyrophosphate

Clinical studies have shown that, starting from a clean mouth, toothpastes containing 3.3% pyrophosphate ion can inhibit the growth of tartar by approximately 30 % after three months of regular use.

## Example of a Toothpaste Preparation

### Ingredients %w/w

- Calcium carbonate 56.0
- Sodium lauryl sulfate 1.0
- Gum Tragacanth 1.5
- Glycerin 22.0
- Saccharine sodium 0.1
- Water 19.4
- Flavor q.s.
- Preservative q.s.

### Procedures for preparation of toothpastes

Toothpastes can be made in stainless steel mixer or planetary mixer or any other mixer used for used for making semisolid preparations.

- Mix the gum with a suitable quantity of humectant without any water.
- Other colloids like methyl cellulose may be dispersed with cold water. Ethyl cellulose should be mixed in warm water.
- Pass the other powder ingredients through a suitable sieve and add gradually to the above binder mixture with continuous stirring.
- Then add the above mixture to the aqueous medium.
- Finally add the flavor and detergent and stir further to obtain the final product

## Evaluation of dental care products

### Abrasiveness (Visual Observation)

Abrasiveness can be tested by rubbing the toothpastes or toothpowders on extracted.

Dental set and then observing the abrasive function visually or mechanically.

### Particle Size

Determined by microscopically or by sieving. The particle size should be ideal in order to provide good abrasiveness without any gritty feel and to minimize damage to the gums.

### Volatile Matter and Moisture

A predetermined quantity of the product is taken in a dish and is dried till a constant weight is obtained. Change in weight will indicate the percentage of moisture and volatile matter.

### Limit Test for Heavy Metals

The dental products are also tested for the content of arsenic and lead as these are very toxic metals and can harm the user if found in excess quantity.

### Consistency

The viscosity of the paste and rheology of the powders should be optimum to ensure smooth flow of product from the container.

### Cleansing Action

This can be assessed by brushing the teeth for 2 weeks with the toothpaste/powder and then examining the appearance of the teeth before and after use by comparing the photographs.

### pH of the Product

A 10% dispersion of the product is made in water and pH is determined. It should be optimum so as not to damage the teeth and the gums.

## Foaming Property

This test is essential for evaluation of foam producing dentifrices. A fixed amount of the product is mixed in sufficient quantity of water and stirred vigorously. The foam generated is then observed for its nature, density, stability and washability.

## Further Readings

- "Industrial Pharmacy-I" SWAYAM MOOC: www.swayam.gov.in
- Semalty M, Lectures on Cosmetics: http://tiny.cc/SEMALTYCOSMETICS
- https://books.google.co.in/books?isbn=1118764706
- https://www.wiley.com/en-us/Introduction+to+Cosmetic+Formulation+and+Technology-p-9781118764893
- https://www.medicalnewstoday.com/articles/306838.php
- https://en.wikipedia.org/wiki/Toothpaste

## References


- http://www.chymist.com/Sunscreens.pdf
- brainstrom.org/a-general-overview-on-dentifricess
- https://cosmeticsinfo.org/products/toothpastes
- https://www.sciencedirect.com/science/article/pii/B9780444826541500259
- http://priede.bf.lu.lv/grozs/AuguFiziologijas/Augu_resursu_biologija/gramatas/Perfumes%20Cosmetics%20Soaps.pdf

CHAPTER 37

# Cosmetics III (Shampoo, Hair Dye and Lipstick)

**Dr Mona Semalty**
Department of Pharmaceutical Sciences,
H.N.B Garhwal University (A Central University), Srinagar Garhwal-246174

### Learning Outcome

- Formulation and evaluation of shampoo/ hair dye
- Introduction to lipstick
- Formulation , methods of preparation and evaluation of lipstick

### Lesson Plan

- Introduction to shampoos, ideal requirements, raw material and evaluation of shampoo
- Introduction to lipstick
- Ideal properties of lipstick
- Raw material and formulation of lipstick and evaluation of the same

## Shampoo

Shampoo is a cosmetic preparation, basically used to provide cleansing actin to hairs. It includes removal of dust oil, sebum and any other debris and prevent their redeposition. Modern shampoos are expected to be much more than just providing cleansing action. They are expected to not dry out the hair and to produce lather in hard and soft water when applied to oily hair. Different types of shampoo are available for man aging different type of hair and scalp conditions.

### Requirements of Shampoo

- It should effectively and completely remove dust or soil, excessive sebum or other fatty substances and loose corneal cells from the hair.
- It should produce a good amount of foam to satisfy the psychological requirements of the user.
- It should be easily removed on rinsing with water.

- It should leave the hair non -dry, soft, lustrous with good manageability and minimum fly away.
- It should impart a pleasant fragrance to the hair.
- It should not cause any side -effects / irritation to skin or eye.
- It should not make the hand rough and chapped.

## Classification of Shampoos

- Normal Shampoo
- Herbal Shampoo
- Anti-Dandruff Shampoo

## Raw Materials used in the Preparation of Shampoo

**Cleansing agents**: The cleaning action of shampoo to the hair is due to the detergent. A detergent molecule in a shampoo works as a surfactant, meaning it lowers the surface tension between the water and the sebum. So surfactants are used for this purpose. Different types of surfactants like anionic cationic and non-ionic surfactants are used based on their efficiency and compatibility with other ingredients used.

## Thickening Agents

Shampoos need an optimum viscosity necessary for easy application into the hair. So, the correct blend of different viscosity building agents is required so that the shampoo is not too thin and not too thick. If it is too thin it will be drained out easily during application to the hair and if it is too thick it will be difficult to apply it on hairs. Cellulose derivatives and Polymers of acrylic acid and vinyl pyrrolidone have been employed to enhance the viscosity of shampoos.

## Aesthetic Additives

These include additives which enhance the appearance, color, and smell of the mixture. These additives are used to improve the hair condition so that the customer can get a good feel of the shampoo itself. Some additives can also control the acidity of the shampoo by obtaining a goal pH level, typically around a value of 4. Examples of such additives include polyquaterniums, silicone additives, proteins and amino acids, ceramides, panthenol, glutamic acid derivatives.

## Conditioning Agents

Conditioning agents are used to provide the strength to hairs (Mechanical and chemical both).Combing and brushing damages the hairs due to its mechanical stress or due to chemical treatments such as permanent hair waving and colouring. Examples of conditioning agents includes fatty substances such as vegetable oils, wax, lecithin and lanolin derivatives, protein hydrolysates (collagen, silk, animal proteins), quaternary ammonium compounds, silicones and dimethiconecolpolyols. These agents greatly improve combing and antistatic properties when used in low concentrations (0.1-0.5%).

## Preservatives

Preservatives are added to shampoos to protect them from bacterial contamination and any kind of decomposition.

- Organic acids and their derivatives, e.g. parahydroxybenzoic acid ester, salicylic and sorbic acid
- Parbens: Methylparaben
- Formaldehyde releasers, e.g., 1,3-Dimethylol-5,5-dimethylhydantoin.

## Pearlizers and Opacifiers

These agents are used to give the shampoo a creamy appearance or we can say less transparent consistency. Pearlizers give the solution a more luxurious, rich appearance. Otherwise it would be dull in appearance watery, grayish and maybe a little cloudy. The most common pearlizing agent in shampoos is Glycol Stearate, also known as Glycol Monostearate or Ethylene Glycol Monostearate (EGMS). Chemically, Glycol Stearate is the ester of ethylene glycol and stearic acid.

## Evaluation of Shampoo

Physical appearance and visual inspection involves:

- Clarity
- Foam producing capability
- Fluidity.

**Determination of pH:** pH is an important parameter while formulating shampoo. The pH is determined by making 10% shampoo solution in distilled water and then measuring pH using pH meter at room temperature (25°C). The acceptable limit for pH is between 4-9.

## Rheological Evaluations

Viscosity is important while formulating shampoo. Too high and too low viscosity is not desired as it creates difficulty during use of shampoo. The viscosity of the shampoos can be determined using Brookfield Viscometer.

## Dirt Dispersion

Dispersion of dirt is determined by adding two drops of shampoo in a large test tube that is filled previously with 10 ml of distilled water. To this test tube, 1 drop of Indian ink is added and shaken for ten times. The content of ink is recorded as heavy, moderate, light or nil in the form produced.

## Foaming Ability and Foam Stability

Foaming ability of the shampoo can be determined by the cylinder shake method. In this method 50 ml of the 2% shampoo solution is placed into a 250 ml graduated cylinder. The cylinder is then covered with hand and shaken for 10 times. Immediately after shaking the volume of foam at 1 minute intervals for 4 minutes is recorded.

## Eye Irritation Test

For eye irritation test, albino rats are preferred. About 1% of the shampoo solutions are instilled drop wise into the eyes of six albino rabbits. Further, the eyes are observed for any irritation/or damage and recorded at definite intervals over a gap of 4 seconds.

## Detergency and Cleaning Action

Cleansing power is evaluated by the method of Barnet and Powers. 5gm sample of soiled human hair is placed at 35°c in water containing 1 gm. of shampoo. The flask is shaken 50 times in one minute for 4 minutes. Then washed once again with sufficient amount of water, then after filtration the hairs are dried and weighed. The amount of soil is removed under this condition is calculated.

## Foam and Foam Stability

Cylinder shake method was used for determining foaming ability. 50 ml of the 1% shampoo solution was put into a 250 ml graduated cylinder and covered the cylinder with hand and shaken for 10 times. The total volumes of the foam contents after 1 minute shaking were recorded. The foam volume was calculated only immediately after shaking the volume of foam at 1-minute intervals for 4 minutes were recorded.

### Packaging of Shampoos

Ideal requirements for packaging:

- The packaging must be able to protect the product from environmental conditions.
- The packaging material must not be reactive with the product.
- The packaging should not impart to the product odour.
- The packaging material must be nontoxic

Packaging of shampoo is one of the important determinants of its market appeal, besides its quality. The shampoo package should contain necessary information such as name of the product, brand, composition, usage instruction and warnings. Also, the container should be made such that to allow the product to come out but not to go in so that any contamination is avoided.

## Sachets

Sachets are small pouches which are very flexible; require very less storage space and they are easy to carry along. Now a day's sachets are used for almost all shampoos. This is very convenient for users to try new products. This helps them to save their money and due to their flexible packaging, these are easy to carry specially during journey.

Bottles: As per Indian Standards, shampoo shall be packed in a glass or plastic container with proper sealing. The bottles must be light in weight, convenient to use, tamper proof and reusable.

## Lipsticks

Lipstick is a cosmetic product containing pigments, oils, waxes, and emollients that apply color, texture, and protection to the lips. Its name suggests it is (stick) of material, within a tube type container (usually around 10mm in diameter and 50mm in length). The containers and the packing may differ from product to product and to attract the customers.

*"Lipsticks are cosmetic products used to impart color and shine to the lips and also used to protect lips from cracking/ drying due to exposure of dust and different weather conditions."*

## Ideal Properties

- It should be nontoxic & nonirritant to the lips.
- It should impart uniform color to the area of application.
- It should provide smooth appearance to the lips
- It should have stability towards environmental conditions.
- It should completely free from grittiness
- The handling of container should smooth and simple
- Melting point that is high enough to ensure that it does not soften during the warmer summer months;
- A pleasant taste and lasting color that will remain on the lips for a considerable period of time.

**Raw materials used in lipstick** Waxes

- Oils
- Pigments and dyes
- Alcohol and fragrance
- Preservatives and antioxidants

## Wax

Wax provides the structure to the solid lipstick. Lipsticks may be made from several waxes such as beeswax, ozokerite and candelilla wax. Ozokerite Wax is a white, crystalline, odorless and tasteless solid made-up of blends of paraffin and microcrystalline waxes .Ozokerite wax is a hard wax with a relatively high melt point can be used to provide structure and strength to lipstick. This property encourages its use in lipstick and lip care products to establish its structure and its strength.

**Oil:** It is the addition of oil that gives lipstick its shine and translucent effect. Different types of oils, like castor oil, vegetable oil, lanolin and mineral oil are used in lipsticks.

**Pigments and Dyes**: These are used in lipsticks to impart the desired color or shade to the lipstick. The dyes used in a lipstick include bismuth oxychloride, manganese violet, titanium dioxide, D&C Red No. 6, D&C Red No. 21.

## Alcohol and Fragrances

Alcohol is used as a solvent for the wax and oils used in making lipsticks. Fragrance is used for imparting a pleasant scent to the lipstick and to mask the smell of other ingredients.

### Preservatives and Antioxidants

These are added to the lipstick to increase its shelf life and to prevent it from becoming stale or rancid.

**Preservatives**: Methyl paraben, propyl paraben, Antioxidants: Gallic acid, propylgalate, BHA, BHT are few examples of antioxidants.

**Manufacturing process of lipsticks**

- Color Grinding
- Melting & Mixing
- Molding
- Flaming
- Packaging

## Color Grinding

Pigments and dyes are available in amorphous form.so we have to convert into powder form.

Equipment used for grinding are-

1. Roller mill 2. Colloidal mill

### Mixing and Melting

First the raw materials like solvents, oils and waxy material are melted in separate stainless-steel container. The solvents and oils are mixed with color pigments.

Then the mixture is passed through roller mill grinding the pigments to avoid grainy feel in lipsticks. After the pigment mass is grounded and mixed it is added to hot wax until uniform color and consistency is obtained.

### Molding

- Once the lipstick mass is mixed and free of air, it is ready to be poured in tubes.

- The melted mass is dispensed into a mold, which consists of bottom portion of metal and a shaping tube.
- Lipstick is poured upside down so that bottom of tube is at top of mold. Any excess material is scrapped out.
- The lipstick is cooled and separated from mold and bottom of tube is sealed.
- The lipstick is passed through flaming test to seal the pinholes and to give finish to the product.

### Labelling and Packaging

The lipstick is retracted, and tube is capped. The lipstick is ready for labeling and packaging.

## Evaluation of Finished Products

**Color control:** Colorimetric equipment is used to control the colors. This equipment gives a numerical reading of the shades. When mixed so that it can be matched with the previous batch.

### Determination of Melting Point

Standard melting point apparatus is used.

**Softening point:** Ideal lipstick should be resistant to varying temp so that it can be used in all-weather conditions it is done by ring and ball method.

**Microbial testing:** Microbial testing is done by plating a known mass of sample on two selected culture media suitable for growth of bacteria. Sample is incubated for specified time and observed for any growth of bacteria (Results should be within the specified limits as per the compendial requirements).

### Breaking Load Test

The protruded lipstick is subjected to a number of weights hanging from it; the weight at which lipstick breaks is its breaking load.

**Rancidity** is decomposition of fat/oil and other lipids by hydrolysis of oxidation and it may lead to development of bad odor and taste. The lipstick may be sticky or there may be change in color of the product. It is tested by determining the peroxide numbers.

## Hair Dye

Hair dye or hair color is a cosmetic product applied to hair either to cover gray/white hairs or for special purposes . Hair colors are also used specially by new generation to do fashion.

Properties of hair dye

- It should impart the same color which it indicates on its label.
- It should not be toxic to the skin or hair and should not impart the natural gloss and texture of the hair.
- It must color the hairs only and not the skin.
- The color that it imparts to the hair must be stable to air, light, water and shampoo.
- It should be easy to apply.
- It should not be allergic and a dermatitis sensitizer.
- It should impart color to the hair in a short contact time.

Hair dye or hair coloring involves the use of Chemicals that are capable of removing, replacing or covering up pigments naturally found inside the hair shaft. Use of these Chemicals can result in a range of adverse effects including temporary skin irritation or allergy, hair breakage, skin discoloration etc.

### Types of Hair color

Classifications of hair color-

- Temporary
- Semi-Permanent
- Permanent
- Lighteners and bleaches

## Temporary Color

These types of hair colors used to color the hair for temporarily. The colorants which are used don't penetrate into the hair or surroundings. Temporary color can be easily rinsed off after one shampooing. Temporarily hair coloring some time used to apply finely ground metals by means of a "Puffer Spray". Such metals, which include brasses, bronzes and aluminum, both untreated and anodized in various colors, it provides metallic effect when applied to hair, mainly used for highlighting.

- Powders, setting lotions, crayons are used for temporary color.
- Hair spray is used to prevent the powder 'brushing-off' easily.

The various types of products used for temporary coloring of hair include rinses, lotions, aerosols, crayons, etc.

- In rinses aqueous or hydro alcoholic solutions of simple dye stuffs are used.
- In lotions dyes in solution with a transparent polymer, such as 3% polyvinyl pyrrolidone in water or aqueous alcohol.
- Crayons are used either directly rubbed on to the wet hair or applied with the help of hairbrush.

**Semi-Permanent Colorants**

- Most of them are basic dye stuffs, whose cationic character gives them a natural affinity for the hair.
- Metallized dye stuffs in combination with nitro derivatives of aromatic diamines or aminophenol.
- Shampoo is the most commonly used base.
- Performance of colorants can be enhanced by the inclusion of solvents.
- Semi-permanent dyes contain mainly either Nirtophenylene diamines either Nitroaminophenes or either Aminoanthraquinones.

## Permanent Hair Color

These are most popular hair dye products. The dyes are formed during the dyeing process and are not present as such in the solution before application. It consists of two parts

(i) Dye intermediate

(ii) Oxidizing agent

Dye intermediates are blends of primary intermediates and coupling agents or modifier, in a suitable base. During the dying of hair, the intermediate solutions and the oxidizing solutions are mixed and applied to the hair. The primary intermediates are gradually oxidized and then undergo coupling reaction with modifiers.

## Permanent Hair color

Permanent dye systems are able to dye hair a lighter shade than the original. Peroxide and ammonia, present in excess to control oxidation of intermediates and simultaneously bleach hair. These dyes are capable of confusing the difference in color between individual hairs and they can cause some hair damage.

### Evaluation Parameter of Hair Dye

**Consistency:** The consistency of hair dye preparation should be optimum as if it is too viscous application will become difficult and if it is less viscous it will drain off easily from the surface of application. So, the consistency should be optimum.

**Spreadabillity:** Hair dye should be easily spreadable so it can easily be applied evenly.

**Color Uniformity:** The color of hair dye and hair color should be uniform. Color shade should remain same and it should give desired color after application.

**pH:** pH should be neutral. It is determined by pH meter.

### Allergy Test

Apply a small quantity of unmixed colorant product sufficient to cover an area of 1-2cm$^2$ behind the ear, using a cotton bud, (e.g. the size of a small coin). Reapply two or three times allowing it to dry between each application. Carefully reseal the colorant container and keep it for the application 48 hours later. Leave for 48 hours without washing, covering or touching.

If during this period you notice any abnormal reactions, such as itching, redness or swelling in or the test area, do not apply the product.

## Further Readings

- "Industrial Pharmacy-I" SWAYAM MOOC: www.swayam.gov.in
- Semalty M, Lectures on Cosmetics: http://tiny.cc/SEMALTYCOSMETICS
- https://books.google.co.in/books?isbn=1118764706

- https://www.wiley.com/en-us/Introduction+to+Cosmetic+Formulation+and+Technology-p-9781118764893
- http://www.madehow.com/Volume-1/Lipstick.html

## References


- Mitchell, Claudia, and Jacqueline Reid-Walsh. Girl Culture: An Encycloped Beauty: The New Basics. New York, NY: Workman Publishing, 2001. ISBN 978-0-7611-0186-4 (0761101861).
- Forman-Brunell, Miriam. Girlhood in America: An Encyclopedia. Santa Barbara, California: ABC-CLIO, 2001. ISBN 1-57607-206-1.
- Mansour, David. From Abba to Zoom: A Pop Culture Encyclopedia of the Late 20th Century. Kansas City, Missouri: AndrewsMcMeel Publishing, 2005. ISBN 978-0-7407-5118-9
- https://www.springer.com/gp/book/9784431540601
- https://www.sciencedirect.com/topics/chemistry/shampoo

CHAPTER 38

# Packaging Materials Science I Materials

**Dr Ajay Semalty**
Department of Pharmaceutical Sciences,
H.N.B Garhwal University (A Central University), Srinagar Garhwal-246174

### Learning outcomes

After learning this chapter, you will be able to understand

- Role, importance and requirements of Pharmaceutical packaging
- Basic properties of different packaging materials

### Lesson Plan

We will be covering this module under the heads

- Purpose and requirements of Pharmaceutical packaging
- Types and properties of materials for packaging
- Containers
- Closures

## Introduction

What is the topmost factor you consider for buying a product (for a consumer product or anything)? What do you see? The topmost feature.... Yes, It's the Package, the very first impression. First impression is the last impression. And that first impression is given by packing or packaging of the product. It indicates the quality of the product. And it ensures those three key words: "STABILITY, SAFETY, EFFICACY"

To ensure these three factors packaging is the utmost important factor.

What is Packaging?

*"Packaging is the science, art and technology of enclosing or protecting products for distribution, storage, sale, and use."*

Pharmaceutical packaging means the combination of components necessary to

- Contain,
- Preserve,
- Protect
- Deliver a safe, efficacious drug product,
- Such that at any time point before expiration date of the drug product, a safe & efficacious dosage form is available.

It means during the entire shelf life the package should be able to protect the integrity and maintain quality of the product. And that is the ultimate aim of packaging.

## Role of Packaging (IPIPC)

I have an acronym for the role of packaging (IPIPC). We always enchant IP, Indian Pharmacopoeia. So, we can learn like this.

- Identification (green strip)
- Protection
  - light
  - moisture
  - air/reactive gases
  - microbes
  - physical damage
  - adulteration
- Information
- Presentation
- Convenience

### Identification

Like you always identify, even the layman identify the painkiller tablets: Oh this is the green strip. This is identification. The package gives the identification to the product.

## Protection

Protection from what? Packaging provides protection against light, moisture, air/reactive gases, microbes, physical, damage and adulteration.

## Information

It provides Information. When you see a package. You see what is written there, what is the name of the product, and ancillary information uses, doses, manufacturing date and so many features are there. Even in the FMCG consumer goods you will find the information like calories if it is a food product, and what are the contents like that. The information is provided by the package.

## Presentation

It provides a way of presentation. Have you imagined a perfume spray in aplastic bottle like Vaseline bottle, No! It is always in an attractive glass package. Because the presentation does matter.

## Convenience

Convenience is also an important factor. For patient, have you seen a box in which ten or twenty tablets, for ten tablets always a strip is convenient rather than a box/ plastic box. So, convenience is also a matter of fact. You can carry a strip you cannot carry them lose. It provides convenience to the patients, to the pharmacist to the doctor with respect to dispensing and use.

# Types of Packaging Systems

**Primary package system:** Made up of those package components & subcomponents that come into direct contact with the product, or those that may have a direct effect on the product shelf life. E.g. ampoules, vials, strip blister pack etc.

You take the tablet directly from the strip. The tablet is in direct contact with that strip or the packaging. So, it is a primary packaging.

**Secondary or tertiary package system:** You might have seen a strip containing ten tablets and these three strips inside a paper box. Or you might have seen a syrup bottle in a paper box. It is secondary packaging. And what is tertiary packaging. These paper boxes are enclosed in carton that is a tertiary package system.

So, primary, secondary and tertiary are three major packaging system.

## Pharmaceutical Packaging: Requirements

(i) Protect the preparation from environmental conditions/ damage or breakage.

(ii) Non-reactive with the product and so does not alter the identity of the product

(iii) Does not impart taste or odors to the product

(iv) Nontoxic

(v) FDA approved

(vi) Meet tamper-resistance requirements, wherever applicable.

**(vii)** Adaptable to commonly employed high-speed **packaging equipment. It should be in good tune with the equipment.**

## Pharmaceutical Packaging: Criteria for the Selection

How you will select a package or packaging material depend on the following factors.

- Stability
- Compatibility with the contents
- Strength of container and the degree of protection required (very consumer goods which were coming in glass bottles are now available in plastic bottles e.g. many hair oil bottles etc.)
- Moistureproofness
- Resistance to corrosion by Acids or Alkalis
- Resistance to grease
- Protection against salt
- Resistance to microorganisms, insects and rodents
- Resistance to differences in temperature. A packaging system must be able to withstand in the changes in temperature. Because the changes in temperature may change the physical and chemical stability of the chemical.
- Protection against light, fire and pilferage
- Odor retention and transmission: Its own odor must be retained.
- Aesthetic value: It must have a good aesthetic value. And it is also a plus point like other consumer goods. We can say that it hold true for pharmaceutical products.

- Cost (very important factor) have you seen salt in protein like attractive pack? No, because it will just add the cost. Just see the benefit to risk ratio with respect to cost when you are deciding the package system.
- Machine suitability of packaging and the filling method
- Convenience of the packaging for the physician, pharmacist and finally the patient (size, weight, method of opening/re-closing, legibility of printing)

## Possible Interactions b/w Packaging Materials and Product

- Chemical leaching from components of the packaging materials to the product. This leaching may alter the chemical composition.
- The release of visible and/or sub visible particles from container to the product. That may cause instability.
- The absorption or adsorption of pharmaceutical components by the packaging materials may also lead to some problems. And the interaction may be triggered.
- Chemical reactions between product & the packaging materials
- The degradation of packaging components in contact with products may lead to interaction and degradation of the product.

## Presentation & Information

- Packaging is essential source of information on medicinal product.
- Information provided may include (D&C Act 1940 & rules 1945)
    - Identification no. for dispensing records.
    - Name, strength & quantity
    - Storage instructions.
    - Direction for use.
    - Name and address of dispensers/mfg.

## Pharmaceutical Containers

"A container for a pharmapoeial article is intended to contain a drug substance or drug product with which it is, or may be in direct contact. The closure is a part of the container." IP

It should be easy to use, protection and shelf life are the key points with respect to choosing the container for pharmaceutical dosage forms.

## Types of Container (IP)

Indian Pharmacopoeia classifies the container in certain types which are defined here. Please learn these definitions verbatim.

"**Airtight container:** A container that is impermeable to solids, liquids and gases under ordinary conditions of handling, storage and transport. If the container is intended to be opened on more than once, it must be so designed that it remains airtight after re-closure." (**Figure 38.1**)

**Figure 38.1** Airtight container.

"***Hermetically Sealed container*:** A container that is impervious to air or any other gas under normal conditions of handling, shipment, storage and distribution, e.g. sealed glass ampoule, gas cylinder etc." (**Figure 38.2**)

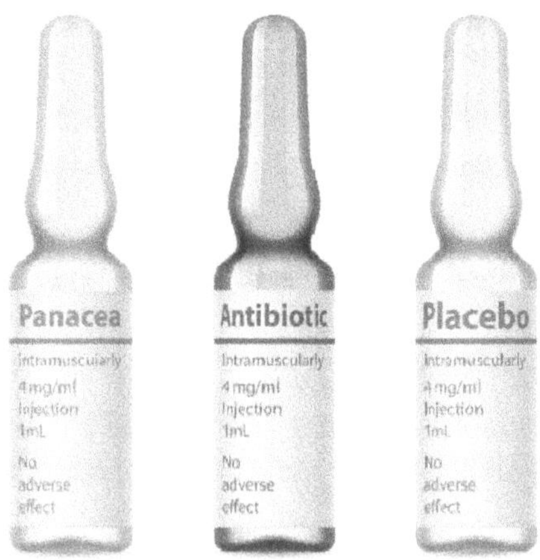


**Figure 38.2** Hermetically Sealed container.

"**Light-resistant container**: A container that protects the contents from the effects of actinic light (UV) by virtue of the specific properties of the material of which it is made." **(Figure 38.3)**.

(Alternatively, a clear and colourless or a translucent container may be made light-resistant by means of an opaque (light-resistant) covering and/or stored in a dark place; in such cases, the label on the container should bear a statement that the opaque covering or storage in dark place is needed until the contents have been used up.)

**Figure 38.3** Light-resistant container.

**Multidose container:** A container that holds a quantity of the preparation suitable for two or more doses.

**Sealed container:** A container closed by fusion of the material of the container.

**Single-dose container:** A container that holds a quantity of the preparation intended for total or partial use as a single administration.

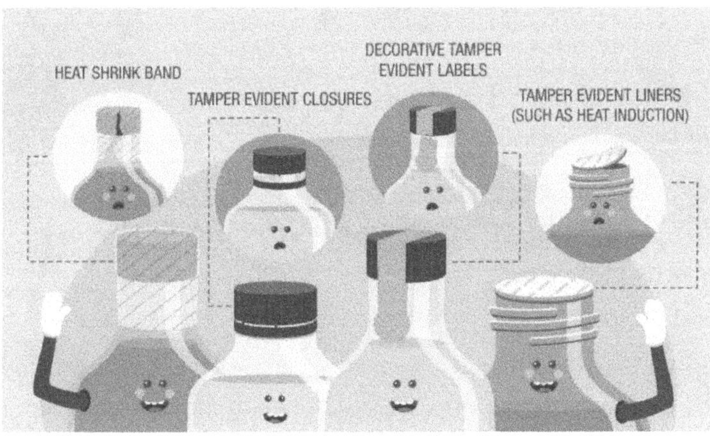


**Figure 38.4** Tamper-evident containers.

**Tamper-evident container:** A container fitted with a device or mechanism that reveals irreversibly whether the container has been opened (**Figure 38.4**).

- **Tightly-closed container.** A tightly-closed container protects the contents from contamination by extraneous liquids, solids or vapours, from loss or deterioration of the article from effervescence, deliquescence or evaporation under normal conditions of handling, shipment, storage and distribution. A tightly-closed container must be capable of being tightly reclosed after use.
- ***Well-closed container.*** A well-closed container protects the contents from extraneous solids and liquids and from loss of the article under normal conditions of handling, shipment, storage and distribution.

## Packaging Materials & Closures

- Glass
- Plastic
- Metals
- Paper and Board
- Rubber
- Cotton
- Adhesives and Inks
- Closures

# Glass Containers

### Advantages

- Superior protective qualities
- Economical
- Readily available in a wide variety of sizes & shapes
- Essentially chemically inert, impermeable, strong and rigid
- Has regularity clearance
- Does not deteriorate with age
- Provides an excellent barrier against every element except light with a proper closure system. Colored glass, especially amber, can give protection against light

**Disadvantages:**

- Fragility
- Heavy Weight

## Glass Containers: Composition of Glass

Glass is mainly made up ofSand – pure silica, Soda-ash – sodium carbonate, Limestone – calcium carbonate, Cullet – broken glass that is mixed with the batch & acts as a fusion agent for the entire mixture (**Figure 38.5**).

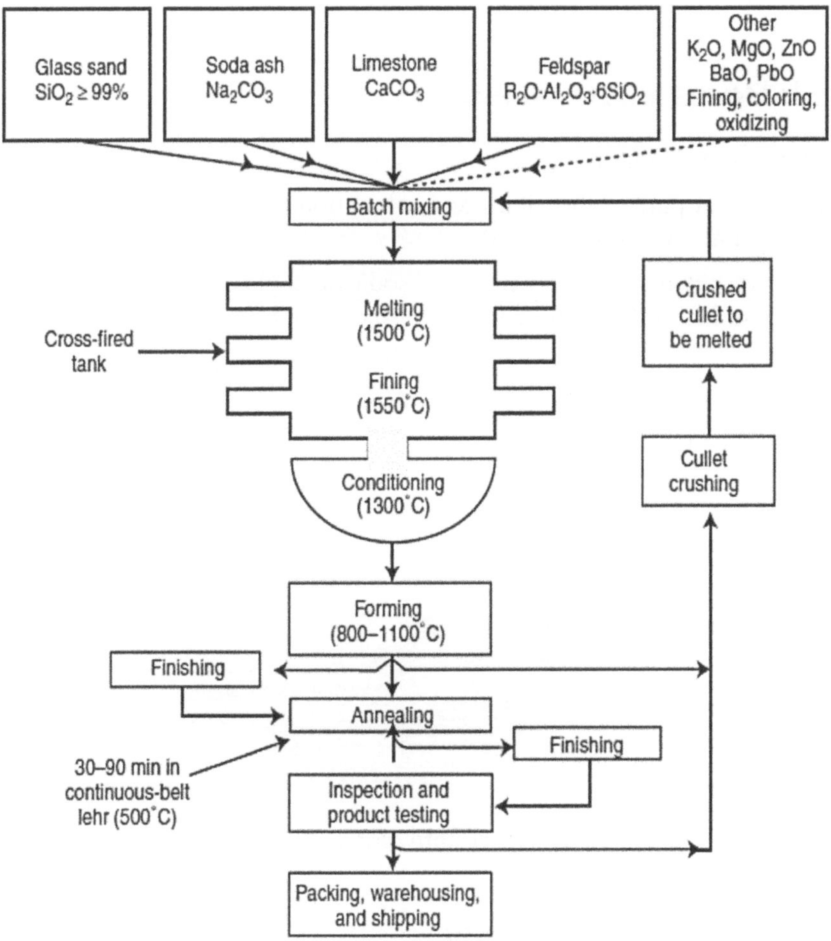


**Figure 38.5** Composition of glass.

The most common cations found in pharmaceutical glassware are silicone, aluminium, boron, sodium, potassium, calcium, magnesium, zinc & barium. The only anion of consequence is oxygen.

## Types of Glass

- Type I – Borosilicate Glass
- Type II – Treated Soda-Lime Glass
- Type III – Regular Soda-Lime Glass
- Type NP – General Purpose Soda-Lime Glass

## Type I: Borosilicate Glass

- Highly resistant glass
- A substantial part of the alkali & earth cations is replaced by boron and/or aluminum & zinc (Figure 38.6).
- It is more chemically inert than the soda-lime glass (which contains either none or an insignificant amount of these cations).
- It is used to contain strong acids and alkalies as well as all types of solvents.
- The addition of approximately 6% boron to form type I glass reduces the leaching action.

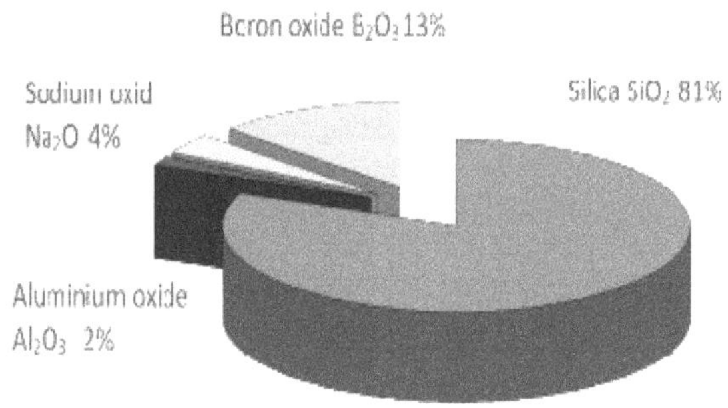


**Figure 38.6** Composition of borosilicate glass.

## Type II: Treated Soda-Lime Glass

When glassware is stored for several months, especially in a damp atmosphere or with extreme temperature variations, the wetting of the surface by condensed moisture (condensation) results in salts being dissolved out of the glass. This is called "blooming" or "weathering" & it gives the appearance of fine crystals on the glass.

Type II containers are made of commercial soda-lime glass that has been de-alkalized or treated to remove surface alkali.

The de-alkalizing process is known as "sulfur treatment" and virtually prevents "weathering" of empty bottles.

Some manufactures expose the glass to an atmosphere containing water vapor & acidic gases. This results in a reaction between gases & surface alkali, which makes it resistant to attack by water. The alkali removed from the glass appears on the surface as a sulfate bloom, which is removed when the containers are washed before filling. Thus, sulfur treatment neutralizes the alkaline oxides on the surface & thus rendering the glass more chemically resistant.

## Type III – Regular Soda-Lime Glass

- Containers are untreated & made up of commercial soda-lime glass of average or better-than-average chemical resistance.

## Type NP – General Purpose Soda-Lime Glass

- Containers made up of soda-lime glass are supplied for non-parenteral products, those intended for oral or topical use.

Use of different types of glass as packaging materials of different formulations has been summarized in **Table 38.1**.

**Table 38.1** Package type and type of formulation for suitable glass type

| Package type | Type of formulation can be packed | Minimum quality of glass that can be used |
|---|---|---|
| Ampoule | Aqueous Injectables Of Any pH | Type I |
| | Aqueous Injectables Of pH Less Than 7 | Type II |
| | Non-Aqueous Injectables | Type III |
| Vial | Aqueous Injectables Of Any pH | Type I |
| | Aqueous Injectables Of pH Less Than 7 | Type II |
| | Non-Aqueous Injectables | Type III |
| | Dry Powders For Parenteral Use (Need To Be Reconstituted Before Use) | Type IV |

**Table 38.1** ***Contd...***

| Package type | Type of formulation can be packed | Minimum quality of glass that can be used |
|---|---|---|
| Bottles and Jars | Tablets, Capsules, Oral Solids & Other Solids For Reconstitution | Type IV |
| | Oral Liquids (Solutions, Suspensions, Emulsions) | Type IV |
| | Nasal & Ear Drops | Type IV |
| | Certain Types of External Semisolids (Rubefacients, Local Irritants) | Type IV |
| | Blood & Related Products | Type I |
| Dropper | Auxiliary Packaging Device with certain kind of products | Type IV |
| Aerosol container | Aerosol product (solution, suspension, emulsion or semisolid type) | Type I |

## Plastic Containers

**Advantages:**

- Ease of manufacturing
- Available in various types of quality
- Freedom of design to which they lend themselves
- Extremely resistant to breakage

## Plastic Interactions / Limitations of Plastic Materials

- Permeation
- Leaching
- Sorption
- Chemical modification
- Alteration on the properties of plastics or product

Choice of different types of plastic as container has been summarized in Table 38.2.

**Table 38.2** Choice of plastic as container.

| Pro-perty | Polyethylene | | Poly Prop-ylene | PVC | Poly Styrene | Acrylic Multi-Polymer | Nitrile Polymer |
|---|---|---|---|---|---|---|---|
| | Low Density | High Density | | | | | |
| **Cost** | **Low** | **Low** | **Low** | **Mod** | **Low** | **Mod** | **High** |
| Typical Uses | Cosmetics<br>Personal Products<br>Foods | Deterge-nts<br>Blea-ches<br>Milk<br>Foods<br>Indus-trial<br>Clean-sing<br>Powders<br>Drugs<br>Cosme-tics | Drugs<br>Cosm-etics<br>Syrups<br>Juices | Sham-poos<br>Bath Oils<br>Deter-gent<br>Whisky<br>Wine<br>Floor<br>Waxes<br>Vinegar<br>Salad Oil | Dry<br>Drugs<br>Petroleum Jellies | Foods<br>Drugs<br>Cosm-etics | Foods<br>Drugs<br>Cosmetics<br>Chemicals<br>Aerosols<br>Carbo-nated<br>Beverages |

## Metal Containers

- Aluminum & stainless steel are the metals of choice for both primary & secondary pharmaceutical packaging.
- Form excellent tamper-evident containers.
- Metals are strong, impermeable to gases & shatterproof, so they are ideal packaging material for pressurized containers.

Choice of metal container for dosage forms has been summarized in Table 38.3.

**Table 38.3** Choice of metal container for dosage forms.

| Package type | Formulation | Remarks |
|---|---|---|
| Strip, blister | Tablets, capsules | Polymer coated aluminum with various thickness are available to improve the sealability of the pack and stability of the product. |
| Collapsible tubes | Ointments, creams, gels & other semisolids | The tubes with internal protective coating of polymers with spike & without spike are available. |
| Cans | Aerosols, inhalers, sprays etc. | Pressure resistant and internal polymer coated aluminum containers are available. |

## Films, Foils & Laminates

- **Regenerated cellulose film based on viscose** (chemical used for manufacturing of rayon) & laminating two or more types of films, cellulose coatings, foil and paper play different roles such as supportive, barrier, heat seal & decorative.
- In the newer technology "Co-Extrusion", a number of plastic plies are extruded in combination to produce cheaper laminations.

## Closures

- Depending upon the type of container, closures may have different shapes & sizes.
- Special design of stopper may also be required for some pharmaceutical production processes such as lyophilization.
- Closures, which form a part of the primary packaging system, are very important & should be therefore carefully selected. They form essential component of the container & an integral part of the drug preparation.

## Closures: Requirements

- Resistant & compatible with the product & the product/air space.
- If closure is re-closable, it should be readily openable & effectively resealed.
- Capable of high-speed application for automatic production by high speed machines without loss of seal efficiency.
- Decorative & of a shape which blends in with the main container.
- Offers such additional functions: aid-pouring, metering, administration, child resistance, tamper evidence, etc.
- Prevents exchange with the outside atmosphere to a permissible level
- **Screw caps** – In metal or plastic, preheated or rolled on with or without a wadding system (i.e. wadless). Wad is a mass of soft material used to stop hole (**Error! Reference source not found.**).
- Wadless thermoplastic caps using a crab's claw seal or a skirted bore seal are very popular.
- **Plug in** – A friction push in fit
- **Push over** – A flanged or raised ring portion is pressed over a bead or lip.

## Functions of Closures

- Hermetic seal: Permits no exchange between the contents & the outside of the pack, e.g. a fused glass ampoule.
- Effective microbiological seal e.g. rubber cork & metal overseal.
- Effective seal, acceptable to the product.

## Take Away Message

- To ensure safety stability and efficacy packaging plays vital role.
- Packaging materials must be inert, nontoxic/ nonreactive to products and compatible with packaging machines.
- Learn the verbatim definitions of Containers: air tight, hermetically sealed, well closed etc.
- Glass, plastic, metals, paper, board, closures are used
- Selection of material: according to properties of product and material

## Further Readings


- "Industrial Pharmacy-I" SWAYAM MOOC: www.swayam.gov.in
- USP/ IP
- Banker GS, Rhodes CT, Modern Pharmaceutics, CRC Press.
- Aulton ME (ED), Pharmaceutics: The science of Dosage form design, II edn, Churchill Livingstone, London, 2002.
- Qiu Y, Chang Y and Zhang GZ (Exe. Eds), Developing solid oral dosage forms: Pharmaceutical theory and practice, Elsevier, 2009.
- Dean. Evans, Hall, Pharmaceutical Packaging technology, Taylor &Francis, London.


## References


- USP/ IP
- Ansel's Pharmaceutical Dosage Forms and Drug Delivery Systems. Philadelphia: Lipincott Williams and Wilkins.
- Augsburger LL, Hoag SW (Eds), Pharmaceutical Dosage Forms: Tablets, Volume 1, III Edn, Informa healthcare, 2008
- https://www.wikihow.com/Open-a-Child-Proof-Pill-Container

- Augsburger LL, Hoag SW (Eds), Pharmaceutical Dosage Forms: Tablets, Volume 1, III Edn, Informa healthcare, 2008
- https://www.wikihow.com/Open-a-Child-Proof-Pill-Container

# CHAPTER 39

# Packaging Materials Science II Official Requirements & Stability Aspects

**Dr Ajay Semalty**
Department of Pharmaceutical Sciences,
H.N.B Garhwal University (A Central University), Srinagar Garhwal-246174

In the earlier chapters, we discussed about the packaging material science. What is packaging, what is the requirements of packaging materials, what are the types of packaging materials and we discussed all types of packaging materials their properties and some essential requirements or selection criteria for the packaging materials. Now, we will be dealing with the official requirements and stability aspects of packaging materials science in this module.

### Learning outcomes

After learning this chapter, you will be able to understand

- Legal and official aspects of pharmaceutical packaging
- Stability aspects of pharmaceutical packaging

### Lesson Plan

- Legal requirements of Pharmaceutical packaging
- Official guidelines for pharmaceutical packaging
- Stability aspects

## Packaging Material Science

We discussed that to ensure safety stability and efficacy packaging plays a vital role. Packaging materials must be inert, nontoxic/ nonreactive to products and compatible with packaging machines. We studied various types of containers like air tight, hermetically sealed, well closed etc.

As the material of packaging glass, plastic, metals, paper, board, closures are used. The packaging materials are selected on the basis of properties of product and material.

## Legal Requirements: Pharmaceutical Packaging

Now, dear learners, let us see, what are the legal requirements.

The regulator sees the pack as having the following characteristics. Regulator means the regulatory body, it may be FDA, it may be CDSCO. So, different country and different regulatory agencies in general have the same concept with respect to these factors:

- Containing the product
    - Protection of the product
    - Protection of the consumer
    - Dosage control
- Carrying the label
    - Legal control of the product
    - Informing the recipient
- Contaminating the environment
    - Packaging waste
    - Ozone depletion
- Protecting the consumer
    - Child-resistant closures
    - Tamper-evidence.

The packaging technologist had been saying for years that packaging development cannot be separated from product development. You cannot separate the packaging development and product development. It had been insisted that it was not possible to separate the pack and product. Why then has the attitude of industry and the regulators changed? Why they have been rendered different.

There are several factors, as below

(a) Increasing sophistication of the pack

(b) Increasing sophistication of the product

(c) Incorporating a device into the pack

(d) Cost of development

These are the four major factors which have separated the packaging development from product development.

Now moving to the first head.

**(a) Increasing sophistication of the pack**

- Using glass over plastic packaging is the best example
- Glass is preferable because of its inert nature
- Plastics tend to interact with product and destabilizes the formulation
- So regulatory authorities are very cautious about the selection of the right packaging material

**(b) Increasing sophistication of the product:** To develop a new drug is very much time taking and costly process. So industry has shifted its focus of research to the improvement of existing formulation. Rather than investing in the new drug development (though it being invested) but their focus has shifted from new drug development to the improvement of the existing formulation (**Figure 39.1**). So, changing in the packaging or innovative packaging is the most reliable method to improve the stability of product. And by this way they can have the market gain.

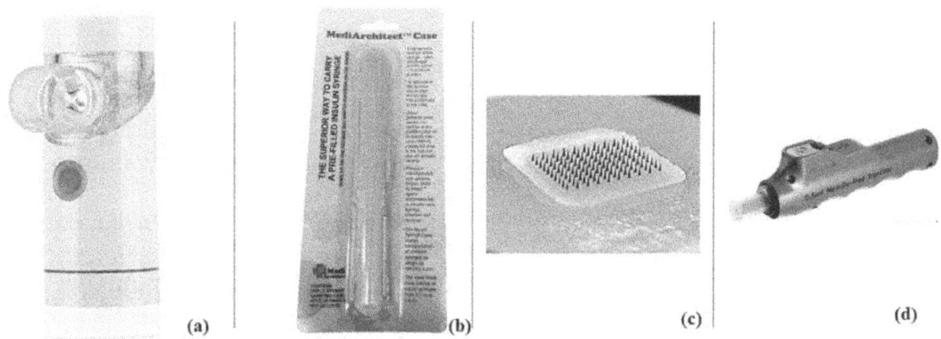


**Figure 39.1** Device into the Pack (a) Nebulizer with metered dosing (b) Prefilled insulin syringe (c) Microneedles (d) Painless needles.

**(c) Incorporating a device into the pack:** What is a device into the pack? Aerosol. Aerosol is itself a device into the pack. Rather it's a package as well as the product.

- Metering the dose using advanced containers. We are using the metering the doses with the advances containers in so many ways (you might have seen).

- Nebulizers and insulin syringes are the best examples in this category.
- Painless needles and dry vaccine delivery systems are also underdevelopment.

(d) **Cost of development:**The cost of developing a safer and advanced packaging technique is much cheaper than the development of a new advanced chemical entity.

It is with respect to the benefit to risk ratio as you see. There is less risk when you go for the advancement of packaging rather than going for a new drug delivery or searching or researching/ developing the new chemical entity (**Figure 39.2**).

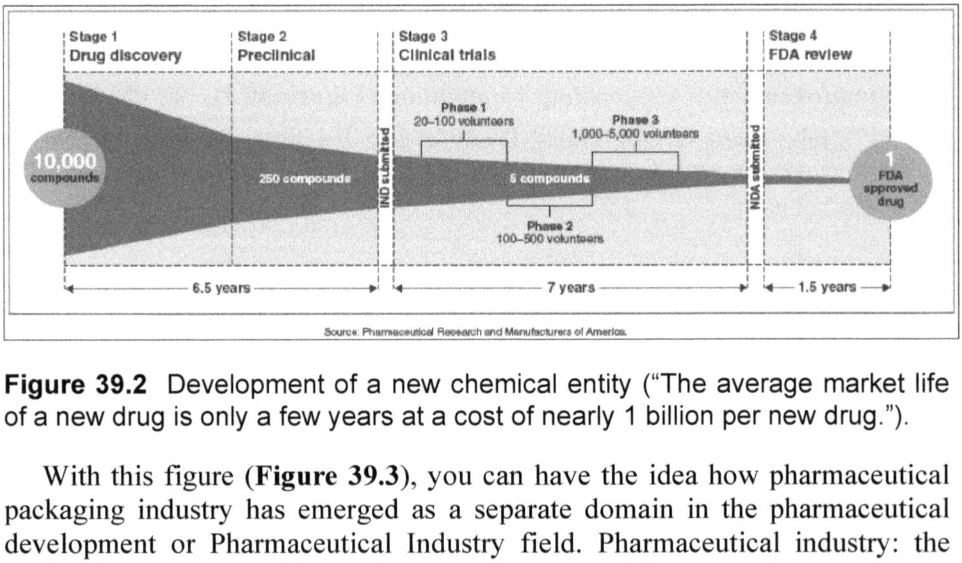


**Figure 39.2** Development of a new chemical entity ("The average market life of a new drug is only a few years at a cost of nearly 1 billion per new drug.").

With this figure (**Figure 39.3**), you can have the idea how pharmaceutical packaging industry has emerged as a separate domain in the pharmaceutical development or Pharmaceutical Industry field. Pharmaceutical industry: the production industry and the packaging industry are different, and the packaging industry has a huge potential as evidenced by the graph.

## Other requirements of Pharmaceutical Packaging

The functions of packaging should be protective. The selection of a packaging material should be compatible to formulation. The filling and assembling of package should be easy. The sterilization should be possible for each and every material of packaging ideally. The product should be stable in storage as well as the shelf life of the product.

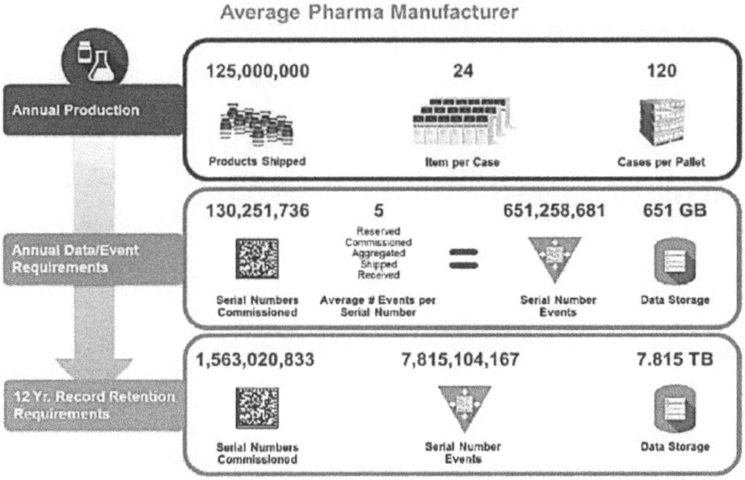


**Figure 39.3** Potential of Pharmaceutical Packaging Industry.
(Source: Pharmaceutical Packaging Trends eBook, https://info.pharmamanufacturing.com/packaging_trends_ebook_stt_pkg_str)

## Special Types of Closure

### Tamper-evident Closures

- To prevent tragic accidents and especially malicious tampering some special types of closure are developed.
- Manufacturers try to create safe packaging.
- Governments continue to update regulations for developing these kinds of closures.
- The closures must be sealed in such a manner that the contents cannot be used without destroying the seal.

So, the seal and closure system must be in tamper evident mode. Let us learn the verbatim definition of tamper evident closure.

### Tamper Evident Closure

"Having an indicator or barrier to entry which, if breached or missing, can reasonably be expected to provide visible evidence to consumers that tampering has occurred." - USFDA

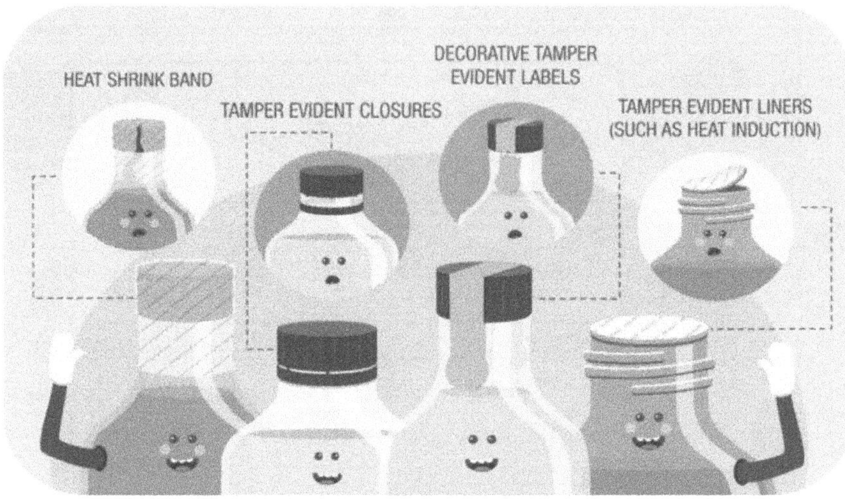


**Figure 39.4** Tamperproof closures: Tampering indicators (Adapted from https://www.wikihow.com/Open-a-Child-Proof-Pill-Container).

There are 11 technologies capable of satisfying the definition of tamper-evident packaging (**Figure 39.4**).

- Film wrappers
- Blister packs
- Bubble packs
- Heat-shrunk bands or wrappers
- Paper foil or plastic packs
- Bottles with inner mouth seals
- Tape seals
- Breakable cap-ring systems
- Sealed tubes or plastic blind end
- Heat-sealed tubes
- Sealed cartons
- Aerosol containers and all metal and composite cans

## Child-resistant Closures

These are the closures which are difficult for drug packaging to be opened by young children while allowing adults the easy access (**Figure 39.5**). These are designed to minimize accidents involving the drug intoxication of children.

There are the three most common reclosable child-resistant types of closure are

- The "press–turn"
- The "squeeze–turn"
- A combination lock

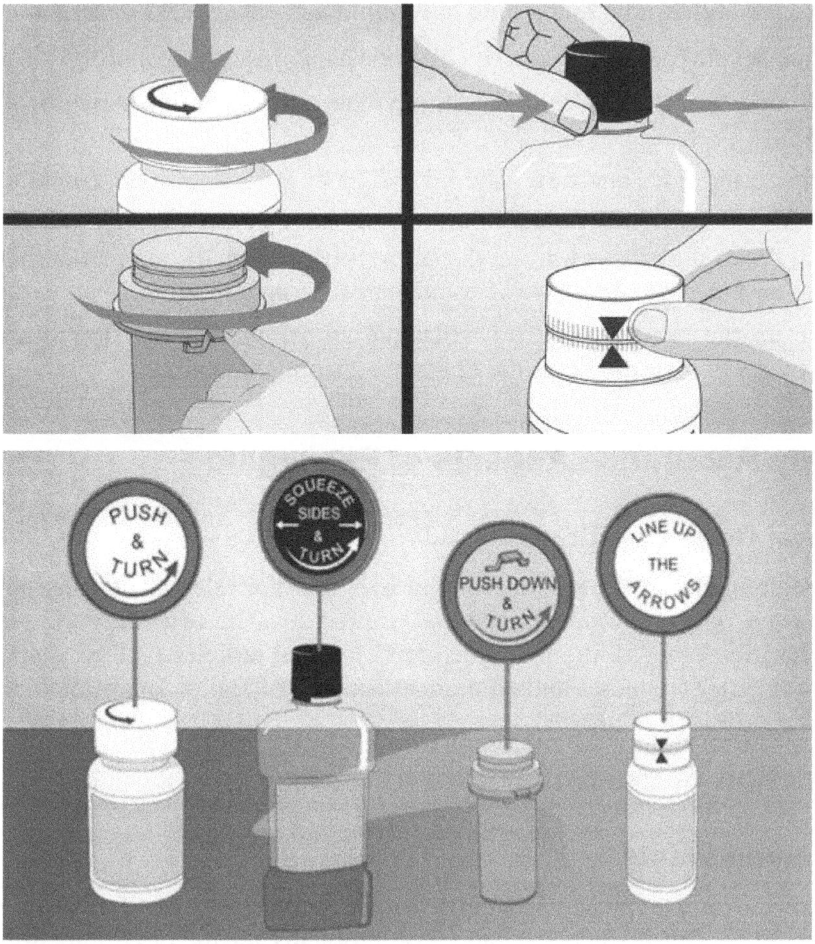


**Figure 39.5** Child resistant closures.
(Adapted from https://www.wikihow.com/Open-a-Child-Proof-Pill-Container)

The European Committee of standardization defines the Child resistant Packing as followed.

"Which makes it difficult for young children to gain access to the contents, but which is not too difficult for adults to use properly in accordance with the requirement of this European Standard - The European Committee for Standardization

The child resistance package closure requires two hands to open the closure unlike other types of closures. A child psychology says that a child cannot perform two parallel motions. If you give a bottle having a lid which is to be opened by pressing and turning both at the same time. An adult can press with the pressure and turn both at a time but a child can either press or turn at a time.

There are several possible types of child resistant closures, including:

- Push and turn down - the lid will have an arrow pointing down or a label that says Push.
- Squeeze the sides and turn - the lid will have grooves around the lid to help you squeeze and turn it easily.
- Push down the tab and turn - the lid will have a small, raised tab that says Push on it and possibly arrows to indicate a turning motion.
- Line up the arrows - the lid will have an arrow pointing downward and another arrow on the lip of the container pointing upward.

## Quality Assurance Aspects of Packaging

### General Considerations

The requirements of the national authorities and the relevant legislation must be followed. The requirements must be worked out with respect to the product, the production process, the manufacturers' internal policies (safety, marketing, etc.), packaging processes and equipment need of validation/qualification.

## Protection of the Environment

### Packaging Waste

Packaging waste represents a very small percentage of industrial waste (**Figure 39.6**). But its disposal can cause problems for the environment. There are two categories of this waste.

- Uncontaminated waste (assimilated to domestic waste: paper, cardboard, glass, plastic)
- Contaminated waste (paper, cardboard, glass, plastic), e.g. Waste that has been in contact with blood, blood-derived products, radioactive products or cytotoxic products

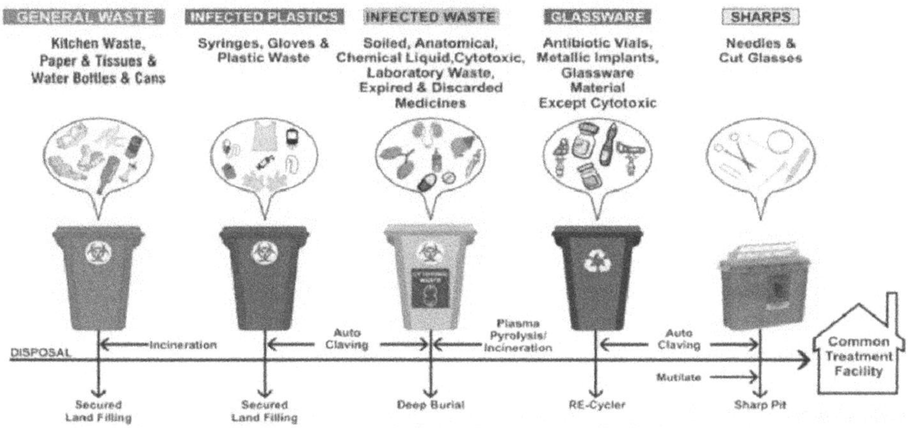


**Figure 39.6** Pharmaceutical waste management.
(Source: http://www.continentalhospitals.com/bio-medical-waste-management/)

These kinds of hospital born contaminated waste must be dealt properly and carefully. The following table shows how we deal with the different materials with respect to the disposal of packaging material either we recycle, landfill or incinerate it (**Table 39.1**). We can see that the glass can be recycled very easily while the plastic cannot. As far as the landfill is concerned plastics must not be disposed beneath the land. By this way we can classify and deal with the various materials of packaging waste.

**Table 39.1** Method of uncontaminated packaging disposal.

| Material | Recycling | Landfill | Incineration |
|---|---|---|---|
| Paper, cardboard | +++ | ++ | ++ |
| Plastics | ++ | + | +++ |
| Glass | +++ | ++ | NA |
| Rubber | + | ++ | +++ |
| Metal | +++ | + | NA |

+++: High recommended; ++: recommended; +: acceptance; NA: not applicable

## Waste Policies

- **Reducing packaging:** Efforts should be made to reduce the volume and weight of packaging materials, and to eliminate packaging which is not essential for the protection of the contents of medicinal products

- **Salvaging and recycling packaging:** The use of environmental friendly packaging needs to be considered, i.e. recyclable or degradable packaging. However, materials that have been in contact with toxic or highly potent drugs require special consideration.

## Stability Aspect of Packaging

The purpose of stability testing can be listed as followed (**Figure 39.7**).

**Figure 39.7** Packaging material providing stability against environmental conditions.

- To provide evidence on how the quality of a packaging material varies with time under the influence of a variety of environmental conditions such as temperature, humidity and light.
- To establish a shelf-life for the pharmaceutical packaging
- To determine the storage conditions
- The in-use stability should be conducted on the dosage form packaged in the container closure system proposed for marketing
- Ultimate proof of suitability of the container closure system and the packaging processes established by full shelf-life stability studies
- Stability testing of pharmaceutical products is a complex set of procedures involving considerable cost, time consumption and scientific expertise

The most important steps during the developmental stages include pharmaceutical analysis and stability studies that are required to determine and assure:

- Identity
- Potency
- Purity

of ingredients, as well as those of the formulated products

**Stability testing** is termed as a complex process because of involvement of a variety of factors, influencing the stability of a pharmaceutical product. These factors include:

- Stability of the active ingredient(s)
- Interaction between active ingredients and excipients,
- Manufacturing process
- Type of dosage form
- Container/closure system used for packaging
- Light, heat and moisture conditions encountered during shipment, storage and handling

**Stability testing** is a routine procedure performed on drug substances and products and is employed at various stages of the product development.In early stages, accelerated stability testing (at relatively high temperatures and/or humidity) is used in order to determine the type of degradation products which may be found after long-term storage.

The stability testing under less rigorous conditions i.e. those recommended for long-term shelf storage, at slightly elevated temperatures is used to determine a product's shelf life and expiration dates (**Figure 39.8**). Stability testing aim to provide reasonable assurance that the products will remain at an acceptable level of fitness/quality throughout the period during which they are in market place available for supply to the patients and will be fit for their consumption until the patient uses the last unit of the product.

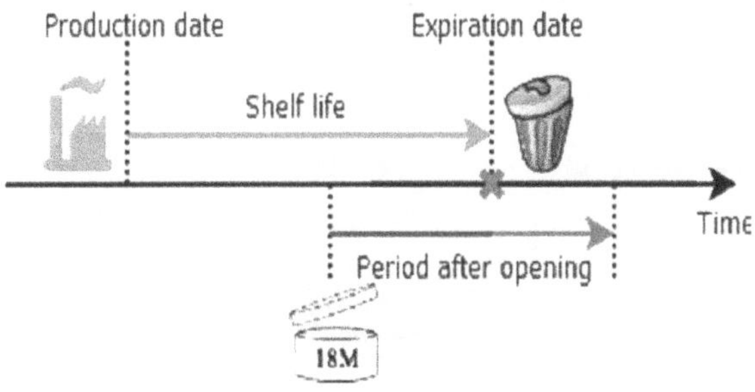


**Figure 39.8** Aim of the stability testing: ensuring quality till shelf life.

## Stability Test Protocols

The protocol for stability testing is a pre-requisite for starting stability testing and is necessarily a written document that describes the key components of a regulated and well-controlled stability study. In addition, the protocol can depend on whether the drug is new or is already in the market.

It also holds true for packaging materials.

The protocols mean a set of well-defined steps which are recommended by regulatory body. In this way the stability study are mentioned in ICH guidelines. What is ICH? International Council for Harmonization of Technical Requirements for Pharmaceuticals for Human Use (ICH) formerly known as International Conference on Harmonization. It is an organization in which several countries have joined there hand together to have the uniform guidelines on various aspects of quality control test and all the guidelines. So that the harmonization must be there with respect to production, storage, stability and all other aspects (the guidelines are uniform). Because now drug industry, every industry is global. We are producing here marketing in the US or exporting in US. So, we will have to abide by the rules of the state and US or any other country wherever you want. So, it is better to have a harmonized guideline for a set of test. That's why ICH works on that and ICH guidelines on stability testing is there. It is freely available on net and you can go through these guidelines for your further study.

Because the testing condition is based on inherent stability of the compound, the type of dosage form and the proposed container-closure system, the protocol depends on the type of drug substance or the product. The protocol should also reflect the regions where the product is proposed to be marketed.

## Compression Strength Testing

Packages behave differently when exposed to compressive forces (Figure 39.9). It uses testing capabilities to apply compressive forces to packages and products. It provides a comprehensive report with data on the strength of a package

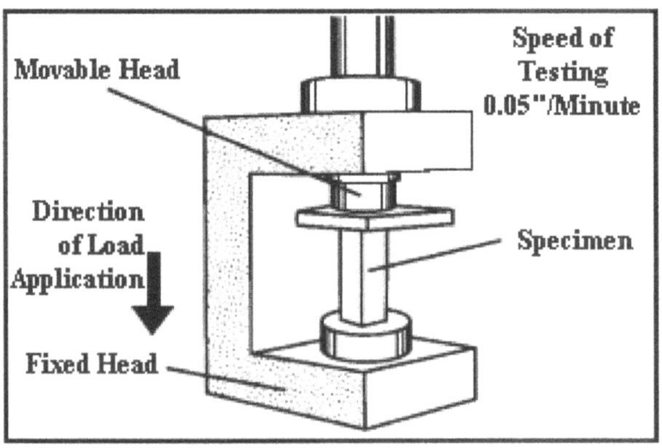


**Figure 39.9** Compression Strength Testing.
(Source: http://www.matweb.com/reference/compressivestrength.aspx)

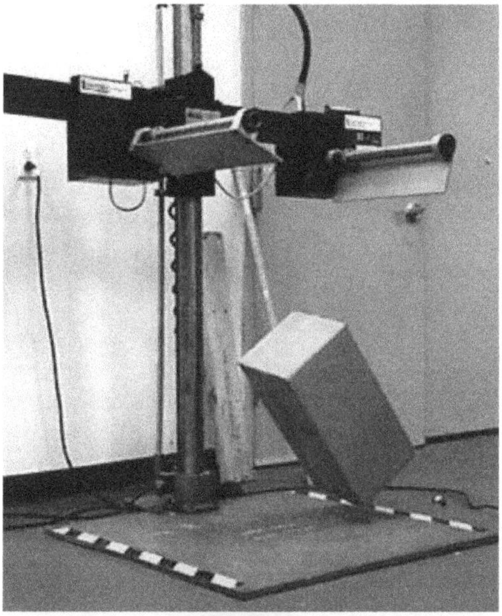

**Figure 39.10** Distribution Simulation Testing.
(Source: http://www.cryopak.co.uk).

## Distribution Simulation Testing

Packages experience many different forces during the shipping and distribution process. It is the product manufacturer's responsibility to evaluate and document the ability of the package to withstand the distribution and storage environments (**Figure 39.10**).

## Package Strength Testing

Package strength testing is conducted to measure and ensure that the components of the package will not separate when specific forces are applied.

The testing of flexible components such as pouches, seal peel or burst testing are methods used to prove the packages strength (**Figure 39.11**).

## Package Integrity Testing

It uses established tests to test the integrity of a pharmaceutical package. Such tests include dye leak, visual inspection, vacuum leak and bubble leak testing to inspect the package's integrity capabilities (**Figure 39.12**).

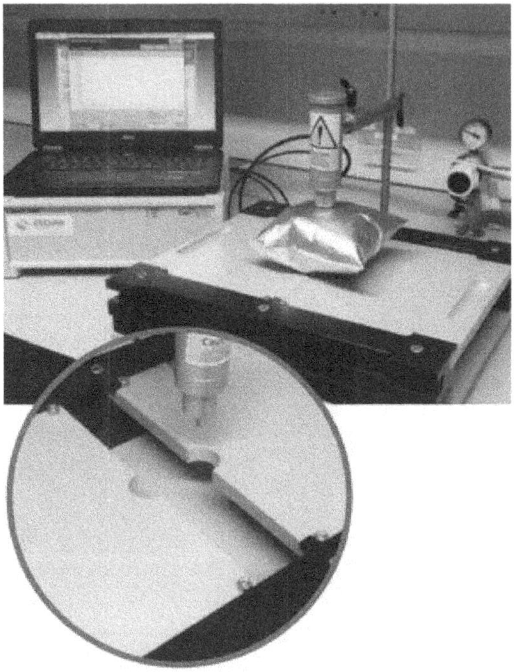

**Figure 39.11** Package Strength Testing "The burst strength of a flexible pack is determined by pressurizing the package until it bursts. The position and type (seal or material) of failure is recorded in addition to the burst pressure value. Alternatively the resistance to creep failure at a specified hold pressure can be determined." (Source: https://www.smitherspira.com/services/primary-pack-testing/burst-strength).

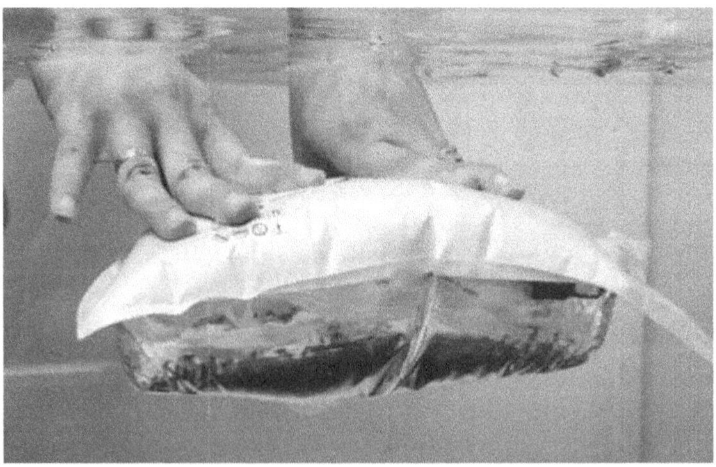

**Figure 39.12** Package Integrity Testing (Source: http://www.cryopak.co.uk).

## Take Away Message

- Packaging innovation and development is one of the best alternate strategy as compared to development of new chemical entity which is very expensive and time consuming.
- Legal and regulatory aspect of package must be followed as per the country's requirement for drug, package, closure, tamper proofing etc.
- Waste management policies should be environment friendly.
- Stability testing of packaging material must ensure the quality of the product and the package throughout its shelf life. The testing protocols must be in good tune with the product, package, region, handling environment and all other aspects. For further study, refer ICH guidelines.

## Summary

Packaging industry is the integral part of product industry. It has got its own capability. But, it has to follow the rules/recommendation and guidelines of the regulatory bodies. There are certain set of legal bindings which must be followed by the pharmaceutical packaging systems. There are the protocols with respect to the uses, its user friendliness, protection, protection to the environment, protection to the consumers, easy access and other properties which make the packaging system use effective and safe. The stability aspects are governed by some regulatory protocols. These protocols must be followed for ensuring the stability of the package system. We must learn these as per the different regulatory bodies. However, you must have a gross idea that what are the certain protocols which you must learn. For your further studies you can learn ICH guidelines. What is ICH guidelines: International Conference on Harmonizaton. Refer the guidelines which is freely available on net.

## Further Readings

- "Industrial Pharmacy-I" SWAYAM MOOC: www.swayam.gov.in
- Semalty et al., Essentials of Pharmaceutical Technology, II Edn. Pharma Med press, Hyderabad, India, ISBN 9789386819994
- USP/ IP
- Banker GS, Rhodes CT, Modern Pharmaceutics, CRC Press.
- Aulton ME (ED), Pharmaceutics: The science of Dosage form design, II edn, Churchill Livingstone, London, 2002.

- Dean. Evans, Hall, Pharmaceutical Packaging technology, Taylor & Francis, London.
- Biopharmaceutical Research Development: The process behind new medicines, http://phrma-docs.phrma.org/sites/default/files/pdf/rd_brochure_022307.pdf


## References


- USP/ IP
- Ansel's Pharmaceutical Dosage Forms and Drug Delivery Systems. Philadelphia: Lipincott Williams and Wilkins.
- Augsburger LL, Hoag SW (Eds), Pharmaceutical Dosage Forms: Tablets, Volume 1, III Edn, Informa healthcare, 2008
- https://www.wikihow.com/Open-a-Child-Proof-Pill-Container
- Pharmaceutical Packaging Trends eBook, https://info.pharmamanufacturing.com/packaging_trends_ebook_stt_pkg_str
- http://www.continentalhospitals.com/bio-medical-waste-management/
- http://www.matweb.com/reference/compressivestrength.aspx
- http://www.cryopak.co.uk/cold-chain-services/packaging-distribution-simulation-integrity-testing/
- https://www.smitherspira.com/services/primary-pack-testing/burst-strength

CHAPTER 40

# Packaging Materials Science III QC Tests of Packaging Materials

**Dr Ajay Semalty**
Department of Pharmaceutical Sciences,
H.N.B Garhwal University (A Central University), Srinagar Garhwal-246174

**Learning outcomes**

After learning this chapter, you will be able to understand

- The standard methods of ascertaining quality of packaging material and containers

**Lesson Plan**

QC tests for packaging materials

- Glass
- Plastic
- Metal
- Closures

## QC Test for Glass

The QC tests for glass are as followed (as per Pharmacopeias)

- Hydrolytic Resistance
- Powdered glass test.
- Water attack test.
- Arsenic limit test.
- Light transmission test

## Hydrolytic Resistance (IP)

The test is done to determine whether the alkali leached form the surface of a container is within the specified limits or not. The amount of acid that is necessary to neutralize the released alkali from the surface is estimated in this test. The leaching of alkali is accelerated using elevated temperature for a specified time. Methyl red (acid-base titration) is used as end point indicator.

To conduct the test specified number of containers and specific volume of test solution is used (**Table 40.1**).

**Table 40.1** Choosing container numbers/ volume.

| Capacity of container(mL) | No. of container used | Volume of test solution to be used for titration (ml) |
|---|---|---|
| upto 3 | 20 | 25 |
| 5 or less | 10 | 50 |
| 6 - 30 | 5 | 50 |
| More than 30 | 3 | 100 |

There are two kind of test are official Test 1 & test 2. Test is summarized in Figure 40.1. Test 1 is called Surface glass test. Test results are interpreted with the help of Table **40.2**. Volume of 0.01M HCl per 100 mL of test solution is noted and it should be within the prescribed limit for particular capacity of container of different types of glass.

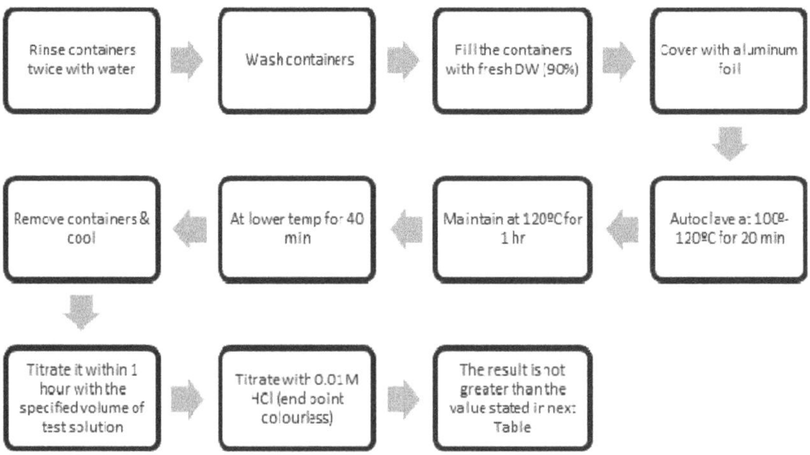


**Figure 40.1** Test 1 -Surface glass test.

## Test 2

- Rinse container twice with water and with 4% volume solution of HF
- Allow to stand for 10 min
- Empty the container
- Rinse 5 times with water
- Carry out test similar to test 1

**Table 40.2** Prescribed limits for hydrolytic resistance test.

| Capacity of container [corresponding to 90 per cent average overflow volume (ml)] | Volume of 0.01 M hydrochloric acid per 100 ml of test solution | |
|---|---|---|
| | Type I or II glass (ml) | Type III glass (ml) |
| Not more than 1 | 2.0 | 20.0 |
| More than 1 but more than 2 | 1.8 | 17.6 |
| More than 2 nut not more than 5 | 1.3 | 13.2 |
| More than 5 nut not more than 10 | 1.0 | 10.2 |
| More than 10 nut not more than 20 | 0.60 | 6.1 |
| More than 20 nut not more than 50 | 0.60 | 6.1 |
| More than 50 nut not more than 100 | 0.50 | 4.8 |
| More than 100 nut not more than 200 | 0.40 | 3.8 |
| More than 200 nut not more than 500 | 0.30 | 2.9 |
| More than 500 | 0.20 | 2.2 |

## Powdered Glass Test USP (PGT)

The PGT is performed to estimate the amount of alkali leached from the powdered glass at the elevated temperatures. Leaching is assessed by acid base titration with 0.02 N sulphuric acid using methyl red as an indicator.

- Step 1: Preparation of glass specimen:
- Step 2: Washing the specimen:

**Step 1:** Preparation of glass specimen:

Few containers are rinsed thoroughly with purified water and dried with stream of clean air. Grind the containers in a mortar to a fine powder and pass through sieve no.20 and 50.

**Step 2:** Washing the specimen:

10gm of the above specimen is taken into 250 ml conical flask and wash it with 30 ml acetone. Repeat the washing, decant the acetone and dried after which it is used within 48hr.

**Procedure (Brief)**

- 10gm sample is added with 50ml of high purity water in a 250mL flask.

- Place it in an autoclave at $121^0C \pm 2^0C$ for 30min.Cool it under running water.
- Decant the solution into another flask, wash again with 15ml high purity water and again decant.
- Titrate immediately with 0.02N sulphuric acid using methyl red as an indicator and record the volume.

The detailed procedure of PGT is shown in **Figure 40.2**.

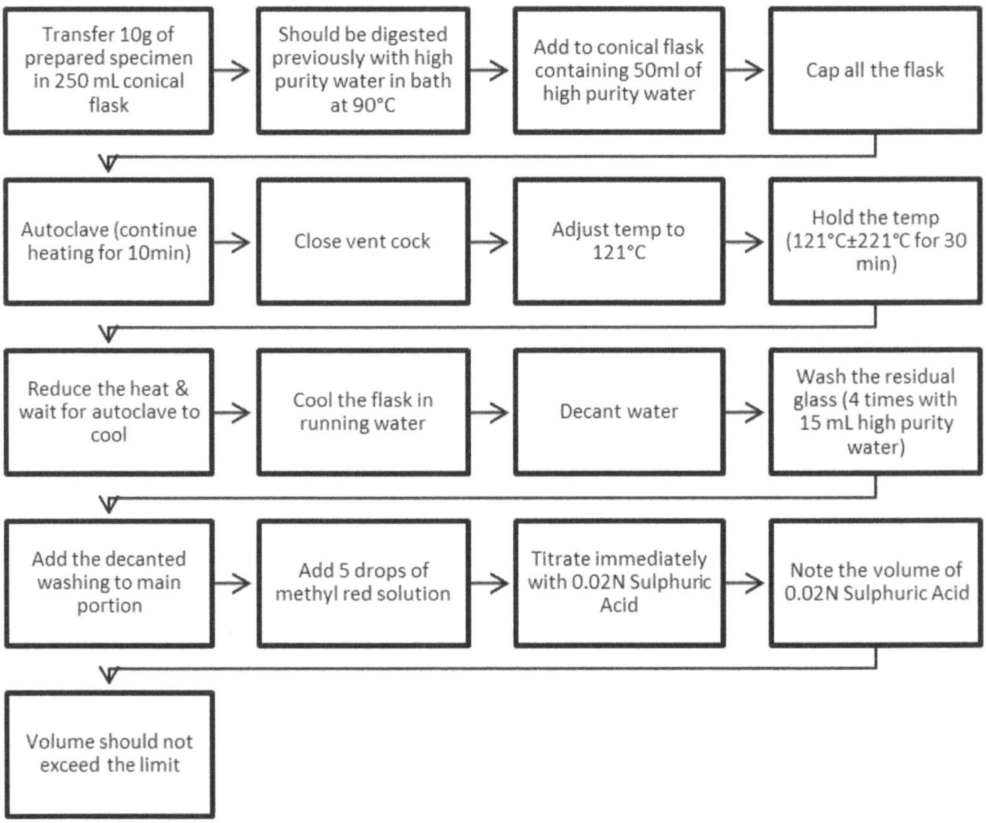


**Figure 40.2** Detail Procedure Powdered Glass Test (PGT) USP.

The acceptance criteria or the limit of Volume of 0.02N sulphuric acid (mL) is mentioned in Table 40.3

.

**Table 40.3** USP acceptance criteria PGT.

| Type of Container | Volume of 0.02N sulphuric acid (mL) |
|---|---|
| Type I | 1.0 |
| Type II | 8.5 |
| Type III | 15.0 |

## Water Attack Test (USP)

The test is done only for treated soda lime glass containers under the controlled humidity conditions which neutralize the surface alkali and glass become chemically more resistant.

**Principle:** To detect the leached alkali from the surface of the container.

## Brief Procedure (WAT)

- Rinse thoroughly with high purity water.
- Fill each container to 90% of its overflow capacity with water.
- Autoclaved at $121^0$C for 60min then it is cooled and the liquid is decanted which is titrated with 0.02N sulphuric acid using methyl red as an indicator.
- The volume of sulfuric acid consumed is the measure of the amount of alkaline oxides present in the glass containers.

## Detail Procedure (WAT)

- Rinse 3 or more containers with high purity water,
- Fill each container to 90% of its overflow capacity,
- Cap all the flasks, autoclave for 60 min,
- Empty the contents & cool the contents in 250ml conical flask to a volume of 100 ml,
- Add five drops of methyl red solution,
- Titrate with 0.02N Sulphuric Acid,
- Record the volume consumed,
- Volume should not exceed limits mentioned by USP (Table 40.4)

**Table 40.4** USP acceptance criteria WAT.

| Type of CONTAINER | Volume of 0.02N sulphuric acid (mL) |
|---|---|
| Type II (100 mL or below) | 0.7 |
| Type II (About 100 mL) | 0.2 |

## Arsenic limit test

- Inner & outer surfaces are washed 5 times with freshly prepared distilled water;
- Prepare 50 ml using adequate number of test solution;
- Pipette out 10 ml of test solution from combined content of ampoule into flask;
- Add 10mL of $HNO_3$;
- Evaporate the dryness on water bath;
- Add the residue in an oven at 130°C for 30 min;
- Cool, add to hydrazine molybdate reagent to dissolve;
- Heat under reflux on water bath for 20 min;
- Cool to room temperature;
- Determine the absorbance of reducing solution at 840nm using hydrazine molybdate reagent as a blank.

## Light Transmission Test

Maximum % light transmission at any wavelength between 290-450nm.

Information provided to patient may include:

- Identification no. for dispensing records.
- Name, strength & quantity.
- Storage instructions.
- Direction for use.
- Name and address of dispensers.

## Thermal Shock Test

- Place the samples in upright position in a tray. Immerse the tray into a hot water for a given time and transfers to cold water bath, temp of both are closely controlled.
- Examine cracks or breaks before and after the test. The amount of thermal shock a bottle can withstand depends on its size and design. Small bottles withstand a temp differential of 60 to 80 $^0$C and large bottle 30 to 40 $^0$C.
- A typical test uses 45 $^0$C temperature difference between hot and cold water.

## Leakage Test

- Fill 10 containers with water, fit with intended closures and keep them inverted at room temperature for 24 hr.
- The test is said to be passed if there is no signs of leakage from any container.

## Internal Bursting Pressure Test

- Instrument used is American glass research increment pressure tester
- The test bottle is filled with water and placed inside the test chamber.
- A scaling head is applied, and the internal pressure automatically raised by a series of increments each of which is held for a set of time.
- The bottle can be checked to a preselected pressure level and the test continues until the container finally bursts.

## QC test for Plastic Containers

A. Noninjectable preparations

- Collapsibility test
- Clarity of aqueous extract
- Non-volatile residue

B. Injectable preparations

- Collapsibility test
- Leakage (as in glass test)
- Clarity and colour of solution
- Acidity or alkalinity
- Reducing substances
- Light absorption
- Water vapor permeability
- Transparency

## Collapsibility Test

Applicable to containers which are to be squeezed in order to remove contents. Yield: 90%of its contents at required rate of flow at ambient temp.

## Clarity of Aqueous Extract

Select unlabelled portion from a suitable containers. Cut these portions into strips. Wash it with extraneous matter by shaking with two separate portions of distilled water. Transfer to flask – previously washed with chromic acid. Rinse with distilled water add 250 ml DW. Cover the flask autoclave at 121 $^{0}\dot{C}$, 30 min It should be colourless and free from turbidity.

### Clarity and Colour of Solution

- Solution S is clear and is colorless.

## Solution S

- Fill a container to its nominal capacity with water and close it, if possible using the usual means of closure; otherwise close using a sheet of pure aluminium. Heat in an autoclave so that a temperature of 121 ± 2° is reached within 20 to 30 minutes and maintain at this temperature for 30 minutes.
- If heating at 121° leads to deterioration of the container, heat at 100° for 2 hours. (*Use solution S within 4 hours of preparation*)

### Blank

Prepare a blank by heating water in a borosilicate glass flask closed by a sheet of pure aluminum at the temperature and for the time used for the preparation of solution S.

### Non-volatile Residue

- Evaporate 100 ml of the extract obtained in the test for Clarity of aqueous extract to dryness and dry to constant weight at 105 °C.
- The residue weighs not more than 12.5 mg.

### Acidity or alkalinity

- To a volume of solution S corresponding to 4 per cent of the nominal capacity of the container add 0.1 ml of phenolphthalein solution.

- The solution is colorless. Add 0.4 ml of 0.01M sodium hydroxide.
- The solution is pink.
- Add 0.8 ml of 0.01M hydrochloric acid and 0.1 ml of methyl red solution.
- The solution is orange-red or red.

## Reducing Substances

- To 20.0 ml of solution S add 1 ml of dilute sulphuric acid and 20.0 ml of 0.002 M potassium permanganate.
- Boil for 3 minutes. Cool immediately.
- Add 1 g of potassium iodide and titrate immediately with 0.01M sodium thiosulphate, using 0.25 ml of starch solution as indicator.
- Carry out a titration using 20.0 ml of the blank prepared as described under Solution S. The difference between the titration volumes is not more than 1.5 ml.

## Light Absorption

- The light absorption in the range 230 nm to 360 nm of solution S using a blank prepared as described under Solution S is not more than 0.20.

## Water Vapor Permeability

- Fill 5 containers with nominal volume of water and heat seal the bottles with aluminium foil.
- Weigh accurately each container and allow to stand for 14 days at humidity-60 ± 5% temp. 20 °Ċ and 25 °Ċ.
- Reweigh the containers.
- Loss in wt. in each container is NMT 0.2%.

## Transparency Test

- ***Standard suspension preparation***: 1gm hydrazine sulphate in 100ml water and set aside for 6hr.
- Take 25 ml of this solution and add 25 ml of 10 %w/v hexamine and stand for 24 hr.
- ***Test solution preparation:*** Sample is prepared by 16fold dilution of the standard suspension.

- Fill 5 containers cloudiness detectable when compared to water filled containers.
- Absorbance is measured at 640 nm and the range is within 0.37 and 0.43.

## Quality Control of Closures

- **Sterility**
- **Fragmentation**
- **Self sealability**
- **pH of aqueous extract**
- **Light absorption test**
- **Reducing substances**
- **Residue on evaporation**

## QC: Closure

***Preparation of Sample (SOL.-A):*** Wash closures in 0.2%w/v of anionic surface active agents for 5min. Rinse 5 times with distilled water and add 200ml water and is subjected to autoclave at 119 to 123:C for 20 to 30min covering with aluminum foil. Cool and separate solution from closure (soln-A).

- Step 1→ Wash closure in 0.2% w/v of anionic surfactant for 5 min
- Step 2→ Rinse 5 times with distilled water and add 200ml
- Step3 → Further subjected to autoclave and covering with aluminum foil
- Step 4 → Allow to cool and separate solution from closure

1. **Sterility Test:** When treated closures are subjected to sterilization test at 64-66 °C and a pressure of about 0.7 KPa for 24 hr. Sterility test is performed through culture media.
2. **Fragmentation test**
   - Take 12 clean vials and place closures containing 4 ml of water
   - Allow to stand for 16 hrs.
   - Use hypodermic needle to inject 1 m1 of water into the vial & remove 1 ml of air
   - Pass the water present in vial through a filter with pore size of 0.5 μm
   - Carry this operation for 4 times with new needle each time.
   - No. of fragments of closure retain should be as per the limits.

**Limit:**

No. of fragments – Not More than 10 (in case of butyl rubber)

No. of fragments – Not More than 15

3. **Self-sealability:** The test is Applicable to closures intended to be used with water.
4. pH of aqueous extract
   - Take 20 ml of sample solution.
   - Add 0.1 ml of bromothymol blue.
   - Add 0.01 M of NaOH till color change from Blue to Yellow.
   - Volume required is measured.

**Limits:**

- Vol. of NaOH — NMT 0.3 ml
- Vol. of HCl—NMT 0.8 mL

## Light Absorption Test

The test must be done within 4hrs of preparing solution A. It is filtered through 0.5 μ filter and Its absorbance is measured at 220 to 360 nm.Blank is done without closures and absorbance is NMT 2.0.

### Reducing Substances

- 20 mL of solution A is added with 1ml of 1M $H_2SO_4$ and 20ml of 0.002 M $KMnO_4$ and boil for 3 min
- Cool and add 1gm of potassium iodide which is titrated with sodium thio-sulphate using starch as an indicator.
- Blank titration is done and the difference between titration volumes is NMT 0.7ml.

### Residue on Evaporation

50 mL of solution A is evaporated to dryness at 105 ° C. Weigh the residue. Limit: NMT 4mg.

### Penetrability

- To measure the force required to make a hypodermic needle penetrate easily through closure.

- measured by using piercing machine.
- The piercing force must not exceed a stated value, the hypodermic needle can get damage as a result of undesirable hardness of closure.

## QC Test for Metallic Container

### Step 1

Take 50 empty tubes filled with ointment base, sealed & kept overnight

### Step 2

A metal bacteriological filter assembly fitted with filter paper & heated to melting range of ointment base

### Step 3

Base from all tubes squeezed at certain rate & passed through filter under vacuum. Then wash with $CHCl_3$ and observed for particles.

**Acceptance criteria**

| | |
|---|---|
| Particles 1 mm and above | 50 |
| Particles 0.5 mm to 1 mm | 10 |
| Particles 0.2 mm to 0.5 mm | 02 |
| Particles less than 0.2mm | Nil |
| Total score | 62 |

The acceptance limit is as shown in **Table 40.5.**

**Table 40.5** Acceptance Limit for particulate matter in metallic tubes.

| Total Score | Test result/ remark |
|---|---|
| < 100 | Lot of tube passes test |
| > 150 | Lot of tubes fails |
| 100 – 150 | test is repeated again with 50 more tubes |

## Quality Control of Strip and Blisters

- 3/4th of water is poured in desiccator
- Strip and Blister are placed inside desiccators
- Apply vacuum
- Strips & blisters are taken out

- Wipe the water present at surface
- The content is removed
- Presence of moisture is checked
- If content is not wet, no leakage is there
- It indicates perfect sealing

## Take Away Message

- To ensure safety, stability and efficacy packaging QC tests are performed.
- HRT, PGT, WAT, transparency glass test
- For plastic, collapsible tubes, metallic tin, rubber closures

## Further Readings

- "Industrial Pharmacy-I" SWAYAM MOOC: www.swayam.gov.in
- Semalty et al., Essentials of Pharmaceutical Technology, II Edn. Pharma Med press, Hyderabad, India, ISBN 9789386819994
- USP/ IP
- Banker GS, Rhodes CT, Modern Pharmaceutics, CRC Press.
- Aulton ME (ED), Pharmaceutics: The science of Dosage form design, II edn, Churchill Livingstone, London, 2002.
- Dean. Evans, Hall, Pharmaceutical Packaging technology, Taylor & Francis, London.

## References

- USP/ IP
- Ansel's Pharmaceutical Dosage Forms and Drug Delivery Systems. Philadelphia: Lipincott Williams and Wilkins.
- Augsburger LL, Hoag SW (Eds), Pharmaceutical Dosage Forms: Tablets, Volume 1, III Edn, Informa healthcare, 2008

www.ingramcontent.com/pod-product-compliance
Ingram Content Group UK Ltd.
Pitfield, Milton Keynes, MK11 3LW, UK
UKHW020226290926
15470UKWH00001B/396

9 789391 910815